*The world's largest collection of illustrated travel guides*

# Kenya

Edited by Mohamed Amin, James Eames
and Deborah Appleton
Editorial Director: Brian Bell

**APA** PUBLICATIONS L

Part of the Langenscheidt Publishing Group

*Höfer*

**I**nsight Guide: Kenya, which has been fully updated for this edition, was Apa Publications' first venture into Africa. Having published prize-winning, commercially successful guide books on Asia, Europe and America, the team was determined to produce a world-class guide to Kenya, which would combine the photographic excellence and journalistic skills for which the series was renowned.

Long popular with African specialists, Kenya has only recently been discovered by a wider travel constituency. It is a multi-faceted country of extraordinary wildlife, fascinating cultural mix and a modern society with one of Africa's most stable governments. All this is revealed in the book's initial chapters, which provide a full historical summary and cultural background. The Places section which follows explores, with detailed maps, the country's many towns and villages, beaches, mountains, lakes, parks and reserves.

**Mohamed Amin**, a native of Kenya, and **John Eames**, an award-winning cameraman who had lived in Kenya for over 20 years, assembled a highly qualified team to produce the text and images that comprise this book. Together with **Ian Parker**, who was recruited for much of the research, writing and revision editing, Eames contributed about a third of the final manuscript. (Tragically, Mohamed Amin, a publisher in his own right, was to die in an aircraft hijacking in 1996.)

A later edition was supervised by project editor **Deborah Appleton**. Appleton has written numerous travel articles on Kenya and worked as a consultant for the United Nations Environment Programme (UNEP) in Nairobi.

This edition was revised by **Dr Matthias Brenziger**, a professor of African Studies, with additional help from **Sarah Griffiths**, a social anthropologist and frequent visitor to the region and Kenyan resident, **Sonya Laurence Green** updated the Travel Tips section.

**Edward Rodwell**, manager and editor of the *Mombasa Times*, gave a description of the 2,000-year history of the Kenya coast, He is the author of a dozen books, the most notable of which is a light, whimsical series called *Coast Causerie*.

**Dr Daniel Stiles** wrote the chapters on Kenya's prehistory from the possible origin of the human species at Koobi Fora to the early immigration of races and tribes as the basis of the present "cosmopolitan" population of the country. With a doctorate in anthropology from the University of California, Berkeley, Stiles first became interested in archaeology after reading Richard Leakey's account of the unearthing of ancestral man at Lake Turkana. A visit there on a dig in 1971 was followed by periodic research and excavation for prehistoric cultures in other parts of Africa, Europe and Asia. Later, he established an undergraduate curriculum for archaeology at Nairobi University.

**A**stute political commentator **Chege Mbitiru** contributed the chapter on the complex development of local African political aspirations from their first stirrings in the 1920s to *Uhuru* ("freedom") from colonial rule in 1963. Mbitiru, managing editor of the popular *Sunday Nation*, is a graduate in science journalism at Ohio Univeristy.

**Alastair Matheson** covered the story from British settler resistance to African takeover and post-Independence politics. One of the most respected journalists and authors in Kenya,

*Rodwell*

*Stiles*

*Mbitiru*

*Matheson*

*Appleton*

*Round-Turner*

*Fitzgerald*

he is formerly a Director of Information for the UN Environment Programme.

**David Round-Turner** wrote the chapter on Kenya's economic development. A man of great industry and talent who cites his life's achievement as "never having suffered from boredom", he has been variously occupied over his 30-odd years in Kenya as a Government Officer and safari operator. He was sports correspondent for the BBC and local media and wrote "A Medley on Sports".

The authority on the old Northern Frontier District – the Samburu-Turkana scrub desert – is **Mary Anne Fitzgerald**. She gained her expertise from "pottering around with Samburu friends" on donkeys, on walkabouts, or in running a mobile clinic in the remote Ndoto Mountains. Fitzgerald has been an accredited correspondent of numerous newspapers and magazines, including the *Washington Post*, London's *Sunday Times*, the *Economist* and the *International Herald Tribune*.

The lively account on freshwater fishing came from the pen of **Peter Usher**, a long-time member of the Kenya Fly-Fishers' Club and a local authority on the sport. Usher is a scientist with UNEP who spends much of his spare time hauling out the fish from Kenya's mountain trout streams and freshwater lakes.

**Jean Hartley** wrote the chapter on Kenya's marine national parks and reserves. Hartley is a founder member of the Impala Sub-Aqua Clubs in Nairobi, a qualified instructor with the British Sub-Aqua Club, a courier-guide for visiting divers, and an expert marine-life photojournalist.

The original feature on food came from **Kathy Eldon**, a tourism consultant, freelance journalist and author of the local good-eating bible on where

to eat in Nairobi, the coast and the rest of Kenya.

**Joan Egan** mastered the task of collecting hard, factual information for the original Travel Tips, a section which has been continually updated. That Kenya offers riches to the visitor will never be in dispute; assembling a body of practical information of use to the traveller in search of those riches was guaranteed to tax anybody's ingenuity.

**Karl Ammann**, a long-time Kenya resident and an award-winning photographer, has travelled throughout Africa in search of his sometimes elusive but always fascinating wildlife subjects. He is a familiar figure to Apa, having been the principal photographer of *Insight Guide: East African Wildlife* and the author of *Maasai Mara*, Apa Publications' *Insight Topics* series of photobooks. His work in these books and his other photobooks, *Cheetah* and *The Hunters and the Hunted*, are fine examples of his patient, sensitive and rewarding style.

*Ammann*

Other photographers who contributed to this book include **Wendy Stone**, who has worked as a roving freelance photographer since 1985 for such organisations as the Rockefeller Foundation, the Ford Foundation and the *Washington Times*. She has also been involved in keeping the companion *Insight Guide: East Africa Wildlife* up to date. **Nickey Martin** and **Christopher Dracke** are photographers based in Sweden. Martin also contributed to *Insight Guide: East African Wildlife*. Special thanks go to **Sonya Belcher** of the Tamarind Group for the photographs from their restaurants. Additional images came from Mohamed Amin and his close associate for many years, **Duncan Willetts**.

# CONTENTS

# CONTENTS

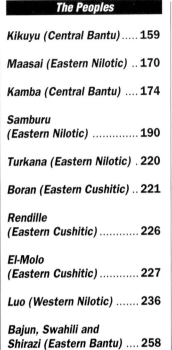

# TRAVEL TIPS

# SAND AND SAFARIS

The thousands of visitors who arrive in East Africa each year come for a variety of reasons, from mountaineering to scuba diving, from watching the Safari Rally to basking on fine sandy beaches. But what undoubtedly has many of them hooked is an image of beautiful, untamed landscapes that contain a potent mix of old-world charm and rugged individualism, a modern society on the edge of great adventures in the wild.

The country's image has been romanticised in books and in many memorable films. In 1953, Gregory Peck smouldered over Susan Hayward in *The Snows of Kilimanjaro* (you can still stay at the Amboseli Lodge built specially for the film set and see it through their eyes). Dennis Finch-Hatton's Gypsy Moth plane dramatically circled the Ngong Hills. And the colourful and sometimes scandalous colonial hay days were given a full airing with Karen Blixen's *Out of Africa* (1985) and James Fox's *White Mischief* (1987).

These images conjure pictures of nights under the African stars, their configurations upside down for northern hemisphere visitors; a flaring camp fire and sounds from the dark beyond; a moonrise chorus of crickets, frogs, nightjars, a racket of hyrax and the low grunt of a predator, probably a leopard. The hunter-guide tells the stories. And all the time there is attentive service from the bearers and retainers, dressed like the extras on the mess set of *Gordon of Khartoum*. They deliver shaken martinis, with ice, and dinner of roast haunch of impala from an ammunition box oven.

The old-style, custom-made safari is still on offer, but it is just one of umpteen options for travel and recreation in the country. Whichever way a visitor journeys, whatever the tour permutation, the land itself offers an endlessly unfolding drama that never disappoints.

Since the 1970s, package tours and burgeoning air routes have made Kenya a new and exciting destination, and a safari which was once a privilege of the rich has become an important part of everyone's holiday. Kenya, the great leisure destination, unfailingly manages to match anticipation and fulfil its promise. Modern communications and organisation ensure that today's adventurers are both safe and comfortable, but the old romance persists and a photo-safari remains an unforgettable experience.

**Preceding pages:** Batian and Nelion peaks top Mount Kenya; the Mara River winds its way past a tented camp; flamingos on a rainy day in the Rift Valley; Kenya coastal scene. **Left**, bejewelled Maasai maiden.

Kenya is a country of dramatic extremes and contrasts. Desert and alpine snows; forests, both lowland and montane; acacia woodlands and open plains; vast freshwater lakes and the superb littoral and beaches pounded by the Indian Ocean. Overall, it can be seen as almost the entire African continent in microcosm.

In terms of plain geography, Kenya is bounded to the north by Ethiopia whose highland bastions are the site of an ancient civilization, partly Christian. To the east and northeast is Somalia – a hot, arid lowland of semi-desert. The nomads and camels spill over into modern Kenya; but the fall of the dictator Said Barre in 1991 brought in a flood of refugees to Kenya.

Most of the country's eastern border – 300 miles (480 km) of it – is warm, unruffled and translucent ocean. Along the parallel strip of beach and tropical hinterland, the environment has all the attributes – and more – of a South Seas island.

To the south of Kenya is Tanzania, the border a division between political and economic ideologies – but more importantly between people of the same tribal origins. These are the *Digo* on the coast, the *Maasai* and the *Kuria* in the west, where the frontier ends at the inland sea of Lake Victoria. On the western flank is Uganda, scene of terrible civil war in 1994, which shocked the world for its ferocity.

Geophysically, Kenya divides into a number of distinct zones, by far the largest of which is the low-lying arid land in the north and northeast. This comprises about two-thirds of the country, most of it lies at an altitude of up to 3,000 feet (910 metres). It is hot and dry, with sparse ground-water and it is populated almost entirely by nomad pastoralists who are forever chasing the odd shower of rain and the short-lived green flush that follows it. Although this is the largest sector of the country, it inevitably supports few people, and they subsist almost exclusively on their stock of cattle, camels, sheep and goats.

**Left**, African fables narrated through native woodcarving.

A peninsula which juts south out of the arid north along the Somali border cuts off Kenya's coastal plain from the rest of the hinterland. This is well-watered in two monsoon seasons off the Indian Ocean and the land is lush, but cultivated only in patches with coconut groves, sugar and other agriculture. The gentle warm climate induces a pervasive attitude of "mañana" – *kesho* in Swahili – which encourages a far more relaxed pace of life than found elsewhere in the country.

The third and by far the most productive sector of Kenya is the southwestern quarter of high tableland, much of it above 5,000 feet (1,520 metres).

**Once higher than Everest:** This raised, volcanic block is split from north to south by the Great Rift Valley, leaving a third of the land area in the east; two-thirds in the west. Of the two parts, the east is the more dramatic since it is dominated by the mass of Mount Kenya, a giant extinct volcano once higher than Everest. Its rim has long since fallen away, leaving the eroded plugs as twin, snow-covered peaks above 17,000 feet (5,200 metres).

Close by, in a north-south traverse of this eastern Rift area, is the Aberdares or *Nyandarua* range. The mountains do not match the lofty grandeur of Mount Kenya, but are nonetheless impressive with the blunted peaks of Satima and Kinangop at well over 12,000 feet (3,600 metres).

The whole mass confronts the easterly winds of the Indian Ocean and drains them of the moisture they have carried – fairly meanly – across the dry lands separating the highlands from the coast. This rainfall, landing on fertile volcanic soil, has been mulched over the centuries by cycles of dense forest, making the eastern highlands among the world's richest agricultural lands. Nairobi, Kenya's capital, stands at the southern approaches to the Aberdares, its location influenced strongly by the region's natural wealth.

On the other flank of the Rift in the west, the ridges and peaks of the Mau Range are generally highest along the wall of the valley. It's almost as though they were scuffed upwards when the earth's crust faulted and fell in along the line of the crack.

The wall of the range rises above 10,000 feet (3,000 metres) into an "Afro-Alpine" zone, with the land falling away gently all the way to Lake Victoria. The highest point west of the Rift is another isolated and extinct volcano, Mount Elgon, whose western flank is bisected by the Kenya-Uganda border. At above 14,000 feet (4,200 metres), Elgon's peak is not high enough for a permanent white cap although there is brief snow cover from time to time.

As with the eastern highlands, the western sector is fertile and well-watered with most of the rainfall derived not from the ocean but

immigrants include the Oromo-speaking tribes from the north of the continent who arrived in the 16th century and east Cushitic Somalis in the 19th century.

Today, the different origins of Kenya's people are still apparent in a varied collection of languages, dress, customs and physical features. In spite of this, there are still distinctive tribes today, which may appear to be Bantu or Nilotic or Cushitic, though intermarriage between the various tribes and Christian and Muslim missionary work have blurred the cultural boundaries.

Linguistic traces of the first indigenous people, from 6,000 years ago, are all but undetectable. The last remnants occur

from Lake Victoria. This body of water is so vast that it creates local weather systems.

**Immigrants and Inhabitants:** The earliest inhabitants of east Africa were probably hunter-gatherers. Linguistically, they are related to the Khoisan hunters of southern Africa. Roughly 4,000–5,000 years ago, a wave of migrants from what is now Ethiopia settled in the region. These south Cushitic herders brought with them not only their own cattle but also skills in cereal growing. Two thousand years later, Bantus, mainly from southern Zaire, settled in east Africa. Waves of Nilotic pasturalists also headed southeast from the Nile in modern Sudan. More recent

among the *Dahalo*, a tiny hunting tribe that lives near the Tana delta on the coast. Although the language they speak is unlikely to be close to the original, it retains a few of the ancient, tongue and teeth-sucking "clicks" that characterise the old Bushman language.

While the people of inland Kenya evolved in their various ways, the coast was settled by mariners and colonists from other continents. After the rise of Islam, Arabs and Persians were sailing into the embryo ports of what was then called the "Land of Zinj" ("black") and some of them stayed. They intermarried with the locals and the Arab and African mix gave rise to the Swahili people, who retained a predominantly Islamic culture. Eventually a chain of city-states formed along the coast line – from north to south: Lamu, Mambrui, Malindi, Takaungu, Mtwapa, Mombasa and Vanga.

They lived – some of them thrived – on exports gleaned from the hinterland, such as ivory, rhino horn and gum arabic. But it was not until the 19th century, with the rocketing demand for ivory which had resulted from the West's industrial revolution, that the coast men turned their attention to the "dark interior".

**Forays into the Hinterland:** The first trading caravans organised by coastal traders – Arabic and Swahili – did not reach the highlands

and right of exploitation in the area to a private company, the Imperial British East Africa Company (IBEA). From 1887, the company men began moving inland along the coastal caravan routes, and they were received no less hospitably than were the Swahilis and Arabs.

They found the interior a feuding, warring Balkans of tribal territories, but dominated by the wide-ranging armies of the *Maasai*. On the coast was a group of very closely related tribes, the *Mijikenda*, and at the eastern periphery of the central highlands were the *Kamba* – redoubtable hunters and ivory traders. And on the slopes of the Aberdares, were the *Kikuyu*, a Bantu-speaking agricul-

of what is now Kenya until around the 1840s. Soon after, though, they fought, bartered and otherwise cajoled their way into the country as far west as Lake Victoria. Their methods and manners did not exactly make them popular with the indigenous tribes, which became increasingly hostile over the next four or five decades.

By then, Europe's eyes were on Africa and in the mid-1880s, the continent was divided into European "spheres of interest". Kenya went to Britain which initially gave authority

tural people and their cousins, the *Embu* and *Meru*.

Farther west, across the Rift were other Bantu-speaking cultivators, the *Gusii* and *Luyha*. Around Lake Victoria were the Nilotic *Luo*. On the higher western highland slopes were the *Kalenjin* people of much earlier Nilotic origin. And the Maasai spread themselves across the open grasslands of southern Kenya and northern Tanzania like a sea of red-robes, dominating all the other tribal lands. Everyone, including the caravan traders, paid "tribute" for permission to cross Maasailand.

The IBEA did some exploring, but found

**Left**, cheetahs in Nairobi National Park. **Above**, Mombasa train trip.

nowhere near enough resources to rule and develop the country. So, in 1895 the British Government took over responsibilities for the territories that were to become Kenya and Uganda.

Believing that rapid communications were the key to efficient administration and economic development, the British decided to build a railway from Mombasa on the coast to Lake Victoria. It was started in 1896 and completed five years later, at a cost of more than £5 million, which was an extraordinarily expensive undertaking for that time. To recoup the capital, the line needed to carry freight. As the tribes of inland Kenya were then not involved in cash economies or crops, the decision was taken to bring in white settlers to farm or ranch the land along the line.

**Sequestration and alienation:** A steady influx of Europeans – mainly Britons – therefore began to settle, and eventually they built up a modern agricultural economy in the Kenyan highlands without peer in the tropics. But this sequestration of mainly Kikuyu land led to alienation and bitter feelings between whites and Africans which erupted in the *Mau Mau* rebellion.

Even so, from then until 1963, when Britain relinquished control, the presence of a large white community in Kenya led to a more diverse and competitive economy than in most other African countries under colonial rule. Its positive aspects included giving the African people greater exposure to modern agricultural methods, to which they were quick to adapt, joining the national cash economy in the process.

The country's remarkable economic growth was also attributable, in part, to a large community of traders, artisans and professional people from what are now India and Pakistan. The skills, industry and capital investments of this "Asian" community contributed much to Kenya's prosperity, and still do.

Agriculture remains the base of the national economy. Kenya is the world's third largest tea producer, the biggest pyrethrum producer, and a major exporter of coffee and pineapples, as well as a diverse range of other agricultural and horticultural products.

Tourism ranks as Kenya's largest foreign exchange earner, through a monumental expansion from 10,000 visitors in 1963 to almost 750,000 today. In recent years, the traditional wildlife-based aspects of Kenyan tourism have been exceeded by the attraction for sun-starved Europeans of the uncrowded white beaches.

To some extent, all this makes up for the fact that the country has no oil – as yet – nor any substantial mineral resources. A brief gold rush occurred in western Kenya in the 1930s, but deposits were soon mined out. The only other minerals with any economic potential are fluorspar, soda and gemstones.

Constitutionally, Kenya has been a republic under an executive president since 1969. In 1991, after 10 years of a one-party state, the President, Daniel arap Moi, bowed to increasing national and international pressure and agreed to the introduction of a multi-party system. In the elections of December 1992, Moi and the KANU (Kenya African National Union) profited from the fragmentation of the opposition and won a decisive victory (*see The Modern Republic, page 77*).

There have been two long-serving presidents since 1964. The first, Jomo Kenyatta, will probably be rated by history as among the most outstanding politicians of the 20th century. Tough and shrewd, he remained in office until he died, having led Kenya well along the road to a liberal, capitalist system. This has not been substantially changed by his successor, the present incumbent, Daniel Toroitich arap Moi. Kenya has remained relatively stable, in sharp contrast to many other African countries which have been on the point of political and economic collapse.

Its most intractable problem is an exceptionally high rate of population increase, over 4 percent a year, and the escalating land hunger that goes with it. These trends will inevitably become sources of increasing social and political tension.

However, whatever the problems, Kenya is a perennial attraction to visitors, many of them returning time and again, since one trip can never be enough to take in even the main, broad facets of the safari and the beach holiday. It is a land of so many physical planes and layers of personality that visitors who came and stayed a lifetime are still discovering the country.

**Right**, an incongruous colonial legacy – a hunt meet in Nairobi forest.

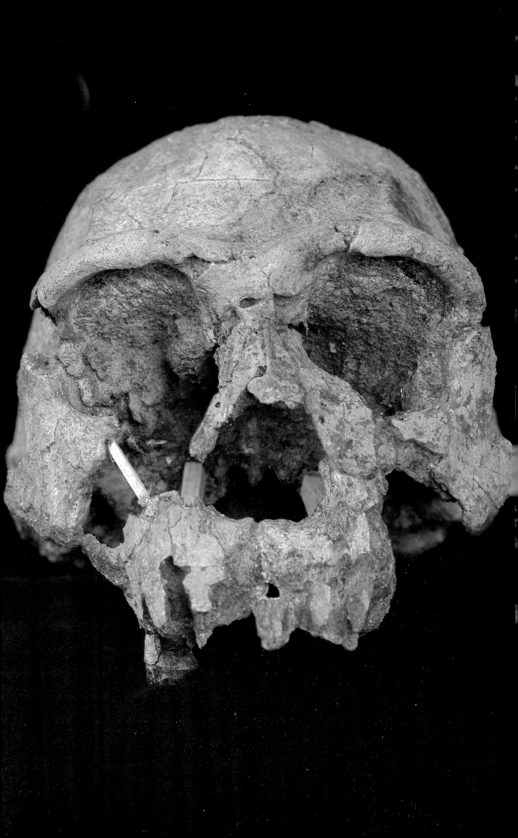

At the beginning of the Miocene epoch, some 25 million years ago, Kenya was an extensive plateau gently sloping towards the Indian Ocean in the east. A vast forest covered most of the land in which lived various species of human apes called *dryopithecine*. One of them, perhaps not yet known to science, was the human ancestor.

This primordial world was shattered and changed beyond recognition when, for reasons not yet fully understood, the crust of the Kenyan plateau began to rise up in a dome. The molten rock deep below erupted through the surface to form huge volcanoes, since worn down to the present stumps of Mounts Kilimanjaro, Kenya and Elgon. As the dome continued to swell, it cracked from north to south. In the west, the land sagged into a great depression, filling with water and creating the inland sea of Lake Victoria.

The crack in the crust widened, and in spasms of violent earthquakes over millions of years, joined with other fissures to form the immense sunken Rift Valley which runs from Jordan to Mozambique. In Kenya, streams flowed from the high ground on both sides of the fault into its rugged trough, laying down a series of lakes which expanded and contracted, depending on the intensity of the rainfall.

The formation of the giant volcanic mountains and the Rift had a profound effect on the vegetation and wildlife in prehistoric Kenya. The highlands created rain shadows on their leeward sides, resulting in a gradual die-out of the forests, particularly in the lower and hotter sections of the valley floor. The new ecological zone was savanna.

**Evolution of the Ape Man:** Much later, one of the ape species on the fringe of the forest moved into the open grassland, adapting and learning to exploit the area's resources. With time, these apes evolved into a creature – man – which would change the surrounding environment far more than any other animal.

The progenitor ape-men lived in the Rift Valley on the shores of the lakes and by the

streams which fed them. Ancient campsites, together with remains of animal meals and stone tools, were covered and preserved by silts or sands from the rising lake water or by ash from erupting volcanoes. Overall, the East African Rift Valley and its environs amount to a repository of the history of human evolution over 8 million years.

Little was known of this until an energetic, forceful and perhaps eccentric Kenyan by the name of Louis Leakey dug out the Rift's treasure trove of fossils in 1926. As a student and later a researcher for Cambridge University, he led several archaeological expeditions in Kenya and from these amassed tons of stone artifacts and numerous hominid (human) and ape fossils ranging over 25 million years.

Leakey married Mary, whom he met at Cambridge, and in 1935 started a joint career which was to shape much of our understanding of human evolution in East Africa. Their most important work was carried out at Olduvai Gorge in Tanzania between the 1950s and 1970s. From banded sediments in this deep fissure in the Serengeti plain, they attempted to trace man's biological and cultural development from about 1.8 million to 20,000 years ago. They established the theory, first prompted by finds in South Africa, that two different forms of man lived side by side during the early Pleistocene. One was small and tagged gracile (or "thin"), known today as *Australopithecus africanus*, while the other was larger and heavier, called *Australopithecus robustus*.

**The surviving breed:** Louis Leakey was convinced that they had found a third hominid type, more closely related to the Homo genus. They pieced him together from bits of fossils and called him *Homo habilis* ("handy man") because they believed he made the crude stone tools found in the lower deposits of the gorge. The implication was that the Leakeys' "handy man" had survived, whereas the *Australopithecus* had died out, leaving no descendants.

Throughout the 1960s and '70s, scientists all over the world debated the interpretation of the finds. Some insisted there was only one species of early man, and that the *robust*

**Preceding pages:** volcanic hills near Lake Turkana. **Left**, fossil skull ER 3733 found on the shores of Lake Turkana.

and *gracile* forms represented the male and female of the same species. Others agreed on two hominid types or supported the Leakey count of three.

Then the Leakeys' second son, Richard, got into the argument. In 1968, he established a base-camp on a sandy pit on the eastern shore of Turkana (Lake Rudolf) at a place called Koobi Fora. For the next 15 years, this arid, wind-blasted land would yield the most impressive collection of Plio-Pleistocene hominid and animal fossils the world has ever seen. Ironically, the finds did nothing to clear the confusion.

In 1972, one of the most dazzling fossil finds of the century was made by Bernard

however, was that it had been found in deposits thought to date back 2.9 million years. The Leakeys were elated: "1470" appeared to prove that humanity descended not from the little *Australopithecus* ape-man, as scientists thought, but from the contemporary third species Louis Leakey had proposed. He died that year, content that he had been right.

**The "Homo" jigsaw:** For a while, the Leakey theory was accepted reluctantly by most former doubters. Bur after a series of tests, it was finally agreed that "1470" man was closer to 2.2 million years old. It is suggested, therefore, that he could have been an early split from *Australopithecus*, although the argument is still open. In 1976, another

Ng'eneo, a member of Richard's team from the National Museums of Kenya. He came across some scraps of bone protruding from sandy deposits in the side of a steep gully. These were later identified as part of a hominid's skull. The gully slope was carefully scraped for more sediments; the fragments extracted and reconstructed revealed a skull that stunned the academic world. It was never named, merely dubbed for posterity by its catalogue number "1470".

The high forehead and relatively large cranial capacity of the skull put it squarely within the *Homo* genus, although the upper jaw is curiously primitive. Most significant,

skull was unearthed. It belonged to *Homo erectus*, a descendant of "handy man" and an undisputed ancestor of *Homo sapiens* – modern man. This was dated to 1.6 million years, when *A. robustus* was alive and well, and *H. erectus* was also clearly not a female of the species.

In the late 1970s, several other important finds were made in Hadar in Ethiopia's "Afar Triangle", and by Mary Leakey at Laetoli in Tanzania. Her hominid finds were at least 3½ million years old, but most scientists agree that these and other very early material can be assigned to one species now named *Australopithecus afarensis*.

Current theories for the complex evolution of man can be summarised as follows:

*A. africanus* evolved from *A. afarensis* around 2.4 million years ago. Between 200,000 and 600,000 years afterwards, *A. africanus* split into two branch lines, *A. robustus* and *Homo habilis*, which developed separately by adapting to different foods and lifestyles.

*A. robustus* concentrated on plant foods, developing huge rear teeth and powerful jaws to crush and grind fibrous matter. *Homo habilis* became a meat-eater, scavenging for kills and practising opportunistic hunting. He also made tools to help him hunt, hence developing the creature's capacity to think.

Fossil remains show that organised human behaviour had begun about 2 million years ago, when *Homo* lived in cooperative communities as an ancestral human society. Archaeologists classified the associated ancient cultures into "industries" based on the shape and technical features of artifacts found in a particular area.

**Man's first industries:** The first of these is called *Olodowan,* named after Olduvai Gorge. Tools were flaked cobbles and stone chips, made by *Homo habilis.* A more sophisticated "industry", called *Acheulian,* then developed and was named after St. Acheuls in France, where typical artifacts were first discovered. Hand axes and cleavers have since been found all over Africa, In East Africa, the first appearance of these tools coincides with the evolution of *Homo erectus.* A number of *Acheulian* sites may still be visited in Kenya at Olorgesailie near Magadi and Kariandusi near Nakuru.

*Acheulian* industry refined over the years. The crude hand axe made from a piece of lava 1½ million years ago at Koobi Fora has the same design idea as the slim, fine-honed axe made from a flake of stone 200,000 years ago at Kariandusi. While the *Acheulian* craft changed, *Homo erectus* went through anatomical and behavioural modifications. Almost all of these evolutionary changes, however, took place above the neck. (The basic human upright stance and locomotion on two feet during the *Australopithecine* stage, and increase in size was the main change below the neck over the next few million years, though with refinements.)

**Left, the Leakeys inspecting a dig.**

In 1984, Richard Leakey discovered the almost complete skeleton of a 12-year-old *Homo erectus* boy on the west side of Lake Turkana. Apart from his head, with its jutting brow ridges, low forehead and protruding jaw his presence today may go unnoticed.

By 300,000 years ago, the first *Homo sapiens* were beginning to evolve from *Homo erectus,* but there is such variation in the fossil record and uncertainty about dating that no clear picture yet exists. The fossil and archaeological record of these *Homo sapiens* is very sparse in Kenya, though some material has been found near Lake Baringo. *Homo sapiens* roamed East Africa at least 100,000 years ago as evidenced by three skulls found in the Omo River area of southern Ethiopia. By then man was a proficient hunter of antelope, gazelle and other wildlife of the savannas of East Africa.

Fully modern man, in the anatomical sense, emerged only around 40,000 years ago during the Middle Stone Age period, when most stone tools were made from flakes. By 20,000 years ago, he was learning to make small delicate objects from stone often hafted to wood or bone to make instruments used in daily life. The Stone Age technology carried on until the arrival of East Africa's first food producers, who were Cushitic pastoralists migrating from Ethiopia, and Bantu farmers from the Congo Basin equatorial forests.

The spectacular finds made, and that continue to be made in East Africa have shifted the world's attention away from Europe and Asia, and placed the cradle of mankind in the Rift Valley and surrounding acacia plains, in places that can still be seen today much as they existed in the past.

**Conservation battle:** Richard Leakey turned his attention to wildlife and was appointed by Moi in 1989 as head of the Kenya Wildlife Service (KWS). He successfully turned around Kenya's wildlife industry in a blaze of publicity that attracted foreign donors and tourists. However, amid accusations on both sides, Leakey resigned in June 1994, unable to work any longer under Moi's restrictions on conservation. The international reputation of Kenya's anthropologist turned conservationist as a protector of wildlife is so great that many saw his resignation as damaging to the tourist industry and a threat to the support of foreign donors.

The Indian Ocean, tumbling over the reefs and shores of Kenya is awash with history. At the centre of this coast, the industrial port of Mombasa is a museum of memories which date from the earliest days of marine navigation.

According to the 17th-century poet John Milton, writing his great work *Paradise Lost*, the seaport and the leisure centre of Malindi, to the north of Mombasa, were there soon after the Creation around 4026 BC. This was when the angel Michael was ing this filial branch of the Hamites and Canaanites, for which reason they were beaten in battle by Joshua and had to leave Palestine for the barren wastes of North Africa. Later, they were joined by the related tribes of Shem and started a long migration south and east through the Horn to the coastal hinterland of Kenya.

Solomon and Sheba were meanwhile active in the area, with the queen's domain extending from the Red Sea down to Mozambique, according to the Ethiopian *Book of*

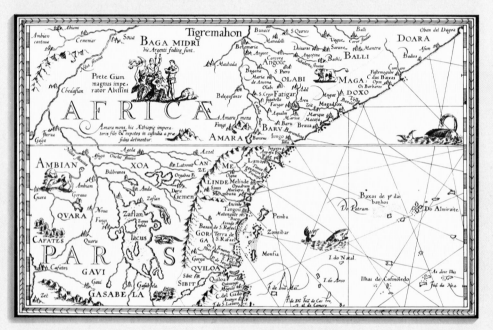

apparently providing a vision of the world to Adam:

*Nor could his eyes not ken*
*The empire of Negus to the utmost port.*
*Ercooco and the less Maritime Kings;*
*Mombasa and Quiloa and Melind;*
*And Sofala, thought Ophir to the realm*
*Of Congo and Angola, further south.*

**Old Testament Connection:** Noah, the owner of a vineyard and a notable imbiber of the wine, is Kenya's other Old Testament connection. It seems that the old man, "in his cups" one day, exposed himself to his family and started a row involving his son Ham and his grandson Canaan. Noah ended up cursing

*the Glory of Kings*. Solomon's navy was bringing up gold from the port-city of Ophir, mentioned by Milton, but now as mysteriously lost as Atlantis. (According to recent research, it may have been well south in the area of Mozambique.) The king's fleets were also collecting ivory, apes and peacocks from ports on the way back, which presumably included Mombasa.

About the same time as the Hamites and Shemites were moving in from the interior, the Egyptians were also exploring the coastal strip. A record of an expedition is depicted in the temple of Deir el Bahri at Thebes on the Nile, with one tablet showing a scene remarkably like that of Old Mombasa harbour. Ships are shown loading frankincense and myrrh, and there are orange trees in tubs and monkeys playing in the rigging.

Another expedition was dispatched in 600 BC by Nacho, the last of the pharaohs. They explored harbours in the "Land of *Punt*" which, according to Egyptologist Professor Petrie, is pronounced "Pwane", the name still applied to the Kenya coast by Arab navigators. If the Egyptian narratives in hieroglyphics and murals are insubstantial, the next mention of the Kenya coast is included in a Greek manuscript, *Periplus of the Erythraean Sea*, the plain log of a ship's captain who sailed out of Egypt in the middle

tortoise shell. In this place are sewn boats and canoes hollowed from single logs.

"The people of Muza held [the land] under his authority and send thither many large ships using Arab captains and agents who know the whole coast and understand the language and marry with the natives there…"

**Early trading centres:** So it would appear that even before Christ, the coast, particularly Mombasa and Malindi, were thriving centres of trade. It was then, one may assume, that the Swahili language was established as a hybrid of Arabic and the local vernacular. It also adopted the Arabic script.

In Egypt, the Greek traders prospered under the settled rule of the Roman Empire.

of the 1st century AD. The manuscript shows there was a solid commercial connection between Arabia, India and Mombasa. Even the imports and exports are mentioned: "There are imported into these places undressed cloth, robes from Aden, double-fringed linen mantles, articles of flint, glass and brass used for ornament and in cut pieces used as coin, sheets of soft copper, iron, olive oil, adzes, swords, girdles and honey from the reed called sacchari (sugar).

"There is exported ivory, rhinoceros horn,

**Left**, a 16th-century map of East Africa and Indian Ocean. **Above**, the coast in the 19th century.

Among the merchants venturing along the East African coast was one Diogenes who landed at Rhaptum (Pangani) and claimed to have travelled inland to the vicinity of "two great lakes and the snowy range of mountains from which the Nile draws its two sources". He said it took him 25 days, which would have been an amazingly swift safari. In any event, it was to Claudius Ptolemaeus (Ptolemy) that credit should go for noting the true source of the Nile, which was not officially "discovered" for another 17 centuries.

Ptolemy remained the authority on the geography of Africa until the Middle Ages. Not only did he pinpoint lakes and mountains, but spoke of the coast between the Juba River and Port Durnford, a stretch including the whole of the present Kenyan coastline. He termed this coast "Parvum Litus"; Lamu he called "Serapion"; Malindi, "Essina"; and Mombasa "Tonika". The earliest version of Ptolemy's map is dated AD 130.

**Trade and Prosperity:** Strangely enough, there are few records of Greek and Arab trading with the east coast. Arab Christians continued to settle and trade in and around places like Mombasa and Malindi. But it wasn't until the emergence of Prophet Mohamed that the trickle turned into a flood of immigrants fleeing southwards from Islamic political and religious dissension of the time.

of France through the Mediterranean, Red Sea and beyond to the borders of China and India. This was built, in effect, on the invention of the lateen sail, which was something of a revolution in the history of the sea since it meant vessels could sail into the wind and across it.

As it happened, the east coast of Africa was never part of the Arab Empire proper. But substantial benefits occurred from the trade. Technology, new goods, concepts and business practices brought the coastal towns in line with the cultures the trade connection had to offer. These were moderately peaceful days, for five or six centuries, until the advent of the Portuguese. Towns were ambi-

It was also then that the east coast cities began their Golden Age. The Arabs occupied Mogadiscio, Mombasa, Malindi, Lamu and seaports farther south. In the process, mud and coral rag houses and stores made way for buildings of architectural merit; agriculture flourished and the people were well-dressed. The Arab historian, Mahsaudi, who visited the east coast in the 9th century recorded in his *Meadows of Gold and Mines of Precious Stones* that Mombasa and Malindi were rich in gold and ivory.

After that, the Hegira Arabs began to trade with an empire which, in the 8th and 9th centuries, spread from the southern borders

tious places; the business of the ports brought stability and much contentment. Narrow streets, called *kitoto*, were crowded with slaves bearing parcels of freight to chanting oarsmen who ferried commodities to and from the large sailing vessels riding in the harbours.

Towards the end of the 15th century, the ordered East was assailed by Western exploration. King John of Portugal and his son, Prince "Henry the Navigator" inspired the extraordinary record of exploration and conquering energy manifested by Portugal up to the year 1700 or so. For the Kenyan coast, the year of the Portuguese was 1498. This was after Vasco da Gama had received orders from Prince Henry to round the Cape and find the sea route to India.

His small fleet reached Mozambique where it found the principal inhabitants to be Arabs. According to the record, "a few merchant dhows lay in the harbour, laden with rings and a quantity of pearls, jewels and rubies". The Arabs, possessive over their position in the area, were not pleased to see the Europeans. Dissension broke out and the Portuguese left in a hurry, vowing to return and teach the Arabs a lesson.

As they sailed, a small dhow set off to warn fellow Arabs farther north of what might be in store for them. Thus, when the Portuguese fleet arrived at Mombasa, a sea-borne guerilla attack was launched to cut the anchor ropes. To avoid a confrontation, da Gama retreated a second time to Malindi where, finally, he found a friendly Sultan.

It was altogether a pleasant visit, according to the record: "Malindi houses are lofty and whitewashed and have many windows. On the land side are palm groves and all around it, maize and vegetables are being cultivated. For nine days we had fetes, sham fights and musical performances." At the end of it, the Portuguese ships were loaded with fruit, vegetables and meat; the Sultan produced a pilot who knew the route to "Calicut" (Calcutta), and the voyage to India was accomplished.

**Long Portuguese Association:** The "friendly association" of the Portuguese and Malindi lasted for almost 200 years, but other ports on the coastline suffered reprisals for the impolite way they had received the first Europeans. Mombasa was sacked in 1500 by Cabral, in 1505 by Almeida and in 1528 by Nuña da Cunha.

In their chronicles, they wrote a description of the port: "Mombasa is a very fair place with lofty stone and mortar houses well aligned in streets; the wood is well-fitted with excellent joinery work. The men and women go very bravely attired with many fine garments of silk and gold in abundance. This is a place of great traffic and has a good harbour in which are moored crafts of many kinds."

**Left**, the triangular sail – Arabia's bequest to East Africa. **Right**, Lamu door with delicately carved calligraphy.

In 1593, the Portuguese started their construction of Fort Jesus overlooking Mombasa harbour. At first it was little more than a walled compound, but soon developed into the fortress that can be seen today. With this massive stronghold, they felt safe. Victualled, gunned and shotted, and defended with regular soldiers, they thought they would have a solid edge on the belligerent Arabs and local tribes. And for a while they were right.

The Arabs fought desperately on land and by sea to regain control, but were unsuccessful even with the support of Ali Bey, a Turk. They also had unlikely allies in the *Wa-Simba*, a warlike tribe which had suffered at

the hands of the Portuguese in Mozambique. These *WaSimba* ("lions" in Kiswa-hili) trekked northwards to Mombasa destroying everything in sight. Unfortunately they made no impression on the garrison at Mombasa, and so carried on to Malindi where they suffered a second defeat. They then withdrew and were not heard of again.

The Portuguese gradually spread along the coastline, demanding the payment of levies. Every part of the coast suffered under the harsh regime and there was severe retribution for the slightest offence. But as the administration entrenched itself, the Christian apostolic missions had almost no impact in the conversion of the Muslim Arabs and "pagan" Africans.

**A losing battle:** The Portuguese were in fact in a losing situation. All their supplies to Mombasa, except food, had to be imported from Goa in India. When their soldiers sickened and died from malaria and other scourges, the ships bringing in relief and reinforcements had to fight their way into the port. Finally, in 1696, the Arabs and allies began a siege of Fort Jesus that was to break Portuguese dominance forever.

This started on March 15, when an Arab fleet began to bombard Mombasa. Some 50 Portuguese, together with 2,500 local people, took to the fort and stayed there for nine

until, with the help of a passing Welsh captain and crew, the Arabs were finally able to scale the fortress walls. Only 11 men and two women remained alive; all of them were immediately run through with swords.

The siege of Fort Jesus which had lasted for 33 months was over. And, in 1720 – bloody and bowed – the Portuguese left the Kenya coast for good. From Paté to Vanga, the Arabs would again be masters until the coming of the British and Germans towards the end of the 19th century.

Although the Imam of Oman was then ruler of the coast, he was ineffectual. He appointed governors from the Nahaban family in Paté, the Mazruis in Mombasa and the

months, living on short rations which were smuggled in at night. Their spirits were almost broken when, on Christmas Day, four Portuguese warships sailed into harbour. The elation was short-lived, however; the Arabs guns were turned on the incoming ships, which pulled out and sailed away.

A month later bubonic plague broke out in the fort, and only a few stuck it out – the commandant, two children, a few local men and 50 women. A month later the commandant died. In September 1697, the fort was re-manned with 150 Portuguese and 300 Indian troops, arriving from Mozambique. The siege continued for another 15 months

El-Hathis in Zanzibar. The governors quarrelled among themselves and the people of the coast suffered. Trade dwindled; the wealth of the coast disappeared. It was not until the early 19th century when a new ruler in Oman came to East Africa that the coast recovered, politically and economically.

This was Seyyid Said who, in 1822, sent an army to quell Paté, Pemba and Mombasa, then occupied by the Mazruis. With this began the story of British intervention in the area since the Mazrui chief, Suleiman bin Ali, invoked the protection of England.

The following year, two British survey ships, *HMS Leven* and *HMS Barracouta*, were on a mission to survey the east coast of Africa. When the *Barracouta* arrived at Mombasa, Captain Vidal was begged by the local Mazrui Arabs to raise the Union Jack over the fort and place the island and its surrounding territory in the hands of His Britannic Majesty, the King of England. The request was refused. Captain Owen of the *Leven* had other ideas. On arrival at Mombasa, he agreed to establish a "Protectorate". Thus, on February 7, 1824, the British flag was hoisted over the fort.

Provisional arrangements were made, including the abolition of the slave trade. Lieutenant J.J. Reitz of the *Leven* was appointed Commandant, with an administrative staff of

basa politicians and merchants. To them the Union Jack was nothing more than symbolic protection against Oman's forces.

After three years, London's response to Captain Owen's action was received. It was repudiated and the British Protectorate over Mombasa was removed. This opened the way for Seyyid Said of Oman to restore his sovereignty, which he did in 1828. He brought in a fleet, placed a Baluchi garrison in the Fort and, in Zanzibar, began to lay out the clove plantations which have since brought considerable wealth to the island. In 1832, Seyyid transferred his court from Oman to Zanzibar and a period of prosperity followed. Within a few years the east Afri-

one interpreter, four seamen, a corporal of marines and three privates. Captain Owen's decision to assume authority was transmitted to India and London to await ratification. Among Reitz's orders was an instruction to travel and provide descriptions of the coastline. So in May 1824 he visited Pangani, but contracted malaria and died. He was succeeded by Lieutenant Emery, a stern officer who made his presence felt, but was almost driven mad by the prevarication of the Mom-

**Left**, yoked slave on the long 19th-century march from the interior to the coast. **Above**, 19th-century ivory caravan fords a river.

can coast, from Cape Guardafui to Cape Delgado, was an acknowledged dominion of the Sultan and his dreams of an African empire began to materialise.

**Slave trails open:** From this time, the coast was opened up for trade. German, British and American merchants established themselves and slave trails were run up through the hinterland to the great lake.

There was little thought of partition on the mainland during Seyyid's lifetime, but when he died in 1856, France, Italy and Germany began to show interest in East African colonisation. King Leopold of the Belgians had an eye upon Malindi as a potential start of a railway to the Congo, and three Egyptian warships sailed down to the coast under McKillop Pasha in the hope of securing a foothold at Mombasa, Malindi or Lamu. The warships were replenished by the new Sultan of Zanzibar, Seyyid Majid, on the condition that the fleet returned to Egypt.

When Majid died in 1870, his brother Seyyid Bharghash took over, and it was during his reign that the partition of East Africa took place. It began with the arrival of European explorers and missionaries, followed soon after by the vanguard officers of imperial interests.

**The British East African Association:** In 1886, Britain and Germany agreed to the extent of as "British East Africa". The Sultan in Zanzibar was paid an "honorarium" of £17,000 a year for British protection of his 10-mile strip of coastline.

A Scotsman, Sir William Mackinnon, the former chairman of the company, brought the first scheduled steamship line to the East African ports and built a road from Mombasa up-country to Kibwezi. Trade from the coast to the hinterland was then started up and brought about the building of the Uganda Railway and the end of the slave trade.

Construction of the railway out of Mombasa began in 1896 and reached Nairobi three years later in May 1899. On December 2, 1901, an engine finally steamed into Port

the Zanzibar dominion. The Sultan would retain the coastline to a depth of 10 miles, but as a British Protectorate. It was to stay this way right up to the Independence of Kenya in 1963, when Sultan Seyyid Khalifa ceded the territory to the new Kenyan Government.

In 1887, an administrative and trading concession was granted to a "British East Africa Association", which covered all coast from Vanga to Kipini. A year later, the company was incorporated under a Royal Charter but by July 1895 was virtually bankrupt. So for £200,000, the British Government acquired the company's assets and took over what is now the territory of Kenya

Florence (Kisumu) on Lake Victoria. Commerce then moved from Zanzibar to Mombasa with its railway terminus and ports. Steamships had replaced sailing vessels from Europe, although dhows remained for the Arabian and Indian trade.

Malindi, which had lost all of its former glory, became a centre of plantation activity which sadly died in the early stages when the bottom fell out of the rubber and copra markets. European and Asian companies set up agencies in Lamu.

Although the railway had brought prosperity to Mombasa, the resident companies soon acknowledged that their future lay in

Nairobi. As they moved up the line, so did the planters' association, the commercial associations and in the end the Government. Old Mombasa harbour was left to the sailing vessels and plans were made to build deep water berths at Kilindini harbour.

Electricity came in 1908; a motorcar appeared and Mr Jeevanjee imported a motor launch. In 1902 there was a daily newspaper at Mombasa and a steam laundry. Barclays Bank stood in Treasury Square soon to be joined by the Standard Bank. The official currency was the Indian rupee.

**The world wars and their effects:** Shipping lines employed local agencies and importing agencies began to handle almost the entire

slump hit Kenya as hard as anywhere else. There was little trade. Coffee was sold at the rock-bottom price of £32 a ton; sisal was as low as £11 a ton.

Wages were negligible, but those companies which were able to keep going began to pick up substantially in the 1930s, with World War II in the offing. From 1937, the country's economy improved and then boomed, so much so that the past 50 years is rated the best half-century of any in the history of the Kenyan coast.

**Modern Mombasa and Malindi:** Those who knew the country in the 1930s would find themselves in another world if they returned today. Mombasa and Malindi have ex-

Uganda trade. Produce had begun to flow outwards and the railway was being used more and more for freight and passengers.

World War I then boosted Mombasa's economy, with troops and material from overseas moving through the port. A new ferry was established from the island to Likoni on the south coast.

After the war, the impetus of business lasted for a few years, but then the world

**Far left**, Sultan Ahmed Fumoluti Al-Nabahani of Witu. **Left**, Witu postage stamp – Kenya's first. **Above**, Sultan Seyyid Bharghash who began the partition of East Africa.

panded beyond imagination, with the seaport of Mombasa now the largest on the northeast coast of the continent. Light and heavy industry is abundant. Tourist amenities have developed from a group of palm frond huts at Bamburi, to the ribbon development of international hotels all along the coast which cater for hundreds of thousands of tourists from all over the world.

The old Wilson Airways runway at Bamburi has given way to a vast Moi International airport at Changamwe. Roads, all of which were laid with murram dirt, are now among the best in black Africa, reaching to the borders of the republic and beyond.

Meanwhile, historical developments, quite apart from those of the coast, were also taking place back in the interior.

William Ewart Gladstone, Britain's prime minister in 1881, said that if the Germans wanted to colonise East Africa, then "God speed them!" They tried the following year when a Dr Gustav Fischer led a well-armed expeditionary force and reached as far as Lake Naivasha at the territorial border of the *il-Purrko* section of the Maasai. The tribe ambushed the army in a gorge called "Hell's Gate" and Fischer lost the fight around a tall obelisk of basalt rock which still carries his name: Fischer's Tower.

The way was then open for a young nature student from Scotland to take on the Maasai with a quarter of the German strength and fire-power, and fulfil the prophecy of Mbatyan, the Maasai's greatest medicine man. The old man had foreseen the imminent arrival of three plagues from the north which, by 1890, would virtually annihilate his people and leave the survivors standing to witness Kenya's great leap forward into the era of European civilization. The horsemen of the Maasai Apocalypse were smallpox, rinderpest and the white man, beginning with the British-born Joseph Thomson, then aged 29.

**Thomson and his tattered army:** Thomson rode in on a donkey at the head of a tattered enterprise by the Royal Geographical Society in March 1883. Born the working-class son of a stonemason in Dumfriesshire, Scotland, he talked his way into a job as second assistant field naturalist on an expedition to the Central African lakes in 1875. Five years later, he was the only experienced Africa hand willing to approach the Maasai with anything short of an artillery regiment.

He eventually took 143 men, only a dozen of whom could fire a rifle. His second-in-command was an illiterate Maltese sailor named James Martin; the rest he described as "the very off-scourings of the Zanzibar water-

front". Inevitably, they mutinied a few miles out on the road to Taveta, the first Arab staging post to Lake Tanganyika. Ringleaders were normally shot or hanged, but Thomson tried his Scottish brogue and the men responded, not to what he was saying – they understood not a word of it – but to the warm inflections in his voice. The fine-tuned African antenna had picked up the fact that the young man, the *kijana*, might be a lunatic in the head but was "good in the heart".

They were persuaded to go on, but only as far as Kibonoto, north of Kilimanjaro, where they caught sight of an advance guard of the Maasai *moran* (warriors) who had routed the Fischer expedition. It made no difference what Thomson said; they prepared to take off at dawn for Mombasa and beyond. But the young Scot was fascinated. His reaction to the sight of "the savages so long the subject of my waking dreams" was: "Oh what splendid fellows!" He then led a peace party of the *moran* warriors into the camp where they delivered "a mostly friendly and encouraging greeting, and with great cheerfulness, relieved us of the care of nearly 10 loads of goods".

Thomson told the story in a long book, although his speech immediately after the experience to an assembly of the Geographical Society in London was perhaps more graphic. "As the day wore on, matters became more ominous," he said. "The warriors grew boisterous and rude. One of them tried to stab me because I pushed him away, and we had to remain under arms from morn till night. On the morning of the third day, our worst fears were realised. We had been deluded and entrapped and we knew they were about to take their revenge on our small party for their failure to annihilate Fischer."

So, "with bitter disappointment, much chagrin, and the gravest doubts about the manifest cowards" of his crew, Thomson decided to return to the coast. They jogged all the way back to Mombasa, covering the 240 miles (390 km) in six days. Thomson refitted at the port, engaged a few more men and quoted Dickens at the unread Mr Martin. "Something will turn up in Taveta," he said – and he was right. He was able to back onto

**Preceding pages: lion mane and ostrich head-dresses adorn Maasai warriors in full regalia. Left, woodcut engraving of Joseph Thomson at the start of his 1883 trek.**

an Arab caravan and made a second, more confident move on Maasailand.

**Encounter with the Maasai:** He separated from the Arabs at Kilimanjaro and went north, on a direct bearing to Lake Victoria towards Amboseli, and it was there his "miseries started in earnest" in an encounter with the Matapato division of the Maasai. Thomson and his men were compelled to live wretchedly among the "most unscrupulous and arrogant savages in Africa". In spite of full defensive precautions, including surrounding himself with two thick thorn fences, Thomson was harassed daily by the *moran* who merely strolled past the armed guards and walked into camp. "They would

from the true negroes and the Galla and Somali. They are the most magnificently modelled savages I have ever seen or read of. Beautifully proportioned, they are characterised by the smooth and rounded outline of the Apollo-type, rarely showing the knotted and brawny muscles of the true athlete."

He was not seriously threatened until he deviated out of the Rift Valley towards *Ol-Doinyo Keri*, "the striped mountain" which was what the Maasai called Mount Kenya. The atmosphere there so reminded Thomson of home that he renamed the *Satima* range the "Aberdares". But nostalgia soon vanished with the arrival of a battalion of *moran* to subject him to the most severe and sus-

frequently push me aside and swagger into the tent, bestowing their odiferous, greasy, clay-clad persons on my bed or wherever it suited their ideas of comfort. I would have to say how delighted I was to see them and give them string after string of beads in the hope of hastening their departure."

Like many who were to follow him, Thomson was in two minds about the Maasai. They were monstrous, but on the other hand "a more remarkable and unique race does not exist on the continent of Africa. Indeed I might safely say in the two hemispheres. In their physique, manners, customs and religious beliefs they are quite distinct

tained provocation he had yet endured. He kept moving, but took a month on the journey which should have taken 10 days. He would not have survived if it hadn't been for the reputation he gained among the Maasai as "a great *Laibon*" or "Wizard of the North". Tricks that got him out of trouble included frothing at the mouth with the help of Eno Fruit Salts and the removal of two false teeth.

Thomson reached Lake Victoria in December 1883, and redrew the map of eastern Africa, putting in more water surfaces than were there previously. He toured Mount Elgon in the northwest and found the great caves in the mountain which Sir Rider Haggard would later use as a main set in his novel *She*. Thomson completed his survey and was ready to start back to the coast on New Year's Eve, but decided he would first treat himself to a traditional Scottish Hogmanay. In the absence of grouse or haggis on the Elgon moors, he opted for a buffalo steak and duly shot a large bull. He then discovered why hunters were later to rate the buffalo the most dangerous sport in the bush.

The "dead" animal got up, drove a horn into his thigh and tossed him several feet in the air. He landed on his head and laid there in a state of stunned euphoria, calmly waiting to be "pounded to jelly". Someone fired a shot as the bull advanced. Thomson opened

dysentery and was again put on a litter and carried the rest of the way to Mombasa, arriving in May 1884. The story was told later, with some irony, that his life had been saved by soup made from rotten meat supplied by his macabre friends, the Maasai.

**The first African safaris:** Thomson, a genuinely modest man, was a hero back in England. His adventure in the wilds of Africa fired the Victorian imagination and started the safari business. From then on, there were almost back-to-back tours to Kenya for gentlemen and politicians who were to carve East Africa into British and German spheres of influence. But prior to that, there were two other major path-finding missions into un-

his eyes and "with glad surprise, I found the beast's tail presented to my delighted contemplation." The buffalo was then dispatched with a fusillade from the bearers.

The explorer was borne away down through the Rift valleys to Naivasha. He convalesced at the lakeside for a while and recovered enough to go off on a side trip to map the country north of Lake Baringo. But he then went down with a near fatal attack of

**Far left**, Count Samuel Teleki von Szek. **Left**, 19th-century colonials among the tribes. Kenya. **Above**, the Maasai seer, the *laibon* Lenana, at Ngong with Sir Arthur Hardinge in 1898.

charted areas to the east of Thomson's route.

An Anglican bishop, James Hannington, went out in 1885 to start a diocese in Uganda. On the way he found a lake Thomson had missed just below Baringo, later called "Hannington" (and today "Bogoria"). He then went on to the Nile where he was killed, thus putting the bishop's Catholic mission to an end before it started.

The following year, preparations were made for a safari through the Kikuyu heartland and on to Lake Turkana which at that time was still called *Embasso Narok*, the "black lake", as known to the Maasai. The leader of this 700-strong expedition was a rich Austro-Hungarian count named Samuel Teleki von Szek. He took a diligent biographer with him, Lt. Ludwig von Höhnel, so that every step of the epic journey would be recorded for posterity.

Von Höhnel was also quartermaster for the trip and his inventory list was a volume in itself. It included 24,000 yards of *amerikani* calico; 115 loads of iron, copper and brass wire; and a ton of fashionable glass beads from Paris and the House of Filonardi in Italy. Teleki's "natives", mainly the Kikuyu as it turned out, were never so elegant.

The aristocratic count led his caravan of tinkers up from the coast in January 1887. They went across the dry Taru Desert to Kilimanjaro. By April, they were camped on the Ngong Hills in the Kikuyu region, within range of the Kikuyu's poisoned arrows. Nothing happened until Teleki moved up to the forest edge, fired a couple of shots to attract attention and thereafter received a few tattered Ndorobo hunters sent out as trade consuls.

**Honorary chief:** They were returned alive with samples of the count's haberdashery after which hordes of the tribal women appeared with goats, chickens and a vast array of horticulture. Finally the men arrived in full battle-dress, looking much like the Maasai – robed, red-painted and their hair in long ringlets set solid in mud and animal fat. In the trade-off, the Kikuyu received mirrors, cowries and cavalry swords and Teleki received a cape of colobus monkey skins as the mark of an honorary chief.

His position was only slightly inferior to the chief of what was probably the Waiyaki clan, which still command great respect in Kenya. The Waiyaki chief then protected Teleki's march up and down the ridges of Kikuyuland, harassed only occasionally by archers on the hills. They were deterred by a demonstration of the return fire-power of the white man's "spears", which could puncture a buffalo hide shield at a hundred yards. Once out of Waiyaki's protection, they had several scraps with more aggressive Kikuyu.

As for the country, up from the Ngong Hills through the Aberdares to Mount Kenya, the Austrian count found it green and pleasant. This was the land, or part of it, which the first British colonists later call "the White Highlands". It was observed to "grow nearly all the cereals and crops native to East Africa and it is, in fact, the granary of a very extended district". Listed among the main produce were millet, maize, potatoes, beans, yams, sugar-cane, bananas and tobacco.

Once out of the area, the caravan split for a while. Höhnel went to trade ivory and map the northern Laikipia shoulder of Mount Kenya and followed the Uaso Nyiro, the "brown river", into Samburu country in the north. Teleki climbed the mountain, taking his "perishing barefoot companions" up to 13,600 feet (4,100 metres) and then going on alone up the "Teleki Valley" to the ice-field at Point Lenana and the jagged peaks of Nelion and Batian, all three named after Maasai *laibon* (medicine men). From there on, the safari continued to a spur of the Marmanet range from where the view must be much the same today except that the Kalenjin goats have eaten the yellow-green slopes and the eroded top soil has made Lake Baringo into one large mud-bath for hippo.

The landscape from there to Lake Turkana is unchanged from the volcanic wasteland von Höhnel saw as "recently flung from some monstrous forge". The southern edge of the lake is an impassable jagged rubble of lava debris before the ridge which opens up a view of one of the most primitive and starkly beautiful fusions of all the elements on earth. The jade lake stretches away to the north; a barren island lies in the foreground; to the west is a chain of mist-blue mountains in Turkanaland; and in the east rises Mount Kulal which two or three times a day is sanded smooth by gales of 80 mph (130 kph).

Teleki's men made their way across a vast field of sharp-pleated lava and leapt into the clear water which turned out to be full of soda and drinkable only in a fizz of tartaric acid. The Austrian named the lake "Rudolf" after the crown prince who later shot himself and his mistress at Mayerling.

A couple of Americans, Donaldson Smith and William Chandler, surveyed the Tana River and the featureless *Commiphora* bush of the northeast. After that, the main structures of the land and people of Kenya were known to the outside world. It remained for the British to plough, build and reorganise in the colonial process they started in 1888.

**Right**, John Hanning Speke, one of many notable explorers who opened up East Africa, at the source of the Nile on the shores of Lake Victoria.

# THE RED BARON AND THE WHITE SETTLERS

The natives were restless in 1895 when the British Crown took over. Detachments of the British Army in India were brought over to deal initially with the Mazrui family which had organised attacks on Mombasa and Malindi in a unilateral declaration of independence for the coastal strip.

It then took four expeditions against sections of the Kamba tribe to persuade them to accept the British administration. Further up-country, more troops were garrisoned at Fort Smith close to the Maasai manyatta on the Nairobi River to control an opportunist territorial expansion of the Kikuyu out of the highland forests. Around Lake Victoria, the Nandi and other tribes started a guerrilla resistance in 1895 which was to last more than 10 years until the Nandi *laibon* and chief strategist was shot dead at peace talks with the ruthless but effective Captain Richard Meinertzhagen. Much debate went on about the incident; but it seems Meinertzhagen was justified since the old man had set up a murderous ambush anyway.

Only the Maasai came into the Protectorate of their own accord. At that time they were having difficulty dealing with predatory raids of the Kikuyu and Kamba since the prophesied plagues of rinderpest and smallpox had virtually wiped them out. According to Bishop Tucker of the Anglican diocese around Nairobi, they were down to 25,000, with total extinction imminent from starvation after the loss of almost all their stock.

**The warrior people:** In the north, a revival was started with food-aid cattle from the Protectorate and a couple of seasons of good rain. The Maasai *moran* picked themselves up and replenished the tribe with cattle and women collected in reprisal raids against the Kikuyu and their Meru and Embu cousins on the eastern shoulder of Mount Kenya.

By the end of 1895, the British rated the Maasai "a menace and a force to be reckoned with" after they massacred half a caravan of 1,100 men in the Kedong section of the Rift

**Left**, ancient and modern: the 1983 Provincial Commissioner's office towers above its 1913 predecessor in Nairobi.

Valley above Nairobi. It started with some of the caravan's crew paying too much attention to the *moran's* girlfriends and ended with merciless and bloody butchery all the way up the valley to Mount Margaret where the scene of the final bloodletting would be marked, 80 years later, by a satellite communications centre.

A passing trader, Andrew Dick, decided to exact retribution on behalf of the Crown. He attacked the sentries guarding the cattle, made off with a large herd, and was halfway up the eastern escarpment before the main body of the *moran* caught up with him. Trader Dick was thus added to the casualty list which also included 452 Kikuyu and 98 Swahili dead. At the official Court of Inquiry, the Maasai were found to have been unreasonably provoked. They were "acquitted", but charged compensation for the massacre in the amount of the cattle taken by the deceased Mr Dick.

**The "iron rhinoceros":** The following year, the British started to build the Uganda Railway from Mombasa to the lake. The ultimate injustice of the white man – as foreseen by the dying *laibon* – became symbolised by his hissing, clanking "iron rhinoceros".

The original purpose of the railroad was strategic, to get a permanent line of communication into Uganda ahead of the Germans coming up from the south. A vocal opposition group in the British Parliament called it a monumental waste of time and money, "a lunatic line to nowhere". But the scheme went ahead in 1896, with the import of 32,000 coolie labourers from Gujarat and the Punjab in India, and the first plate-laying along Mackinnon's Road to the bridge over the Tsavo River.

It was there that several elderly male lions made a feast of the workforce, eating 28 of the Indians and an uncounted number of Africans. Farther up the line, at Kima, one European sleeping in a tent beside his wife and two small children was also dragged out and eaten. Somehow, the animals avoided every trap and after a while one was confident enough to board the train and drag off its victims. The terror lasted 10 months until the man-eaters were ambushed and shot; thereafter, 8,000 sq. miles (20,720 sq. km) of the dry bush country on both sides of the track were left as wildlife reserves and later as the twin Tsavo East and West National Parks.

The line was then driven ahead along the divide between Maasai and hostile Kamba territory until a temporary halt was called at mile peg 317 at the Nairobi River. The ground was higher and healthier a few miles further on, but not so flat and the city of Nairobi was founded as a tented stores depot on a dank, evil-smelling swamp, infested with frogs and larger wildlife wandering in from the Athi Plains.

The Maasai stayed aloof from it all, but the Kikuyu came in to market their cereal crops,

Elmenteita and Nakuru, up the gentler wall of the Mau Range to an English country landscape around Njoro, and on down a fractured but steady gradient to the sub-tropical shores of Lake Victoria. The last spike was driven in at Port Florence (later Kisumu) on December 19, 1901, just over five years after construction started. The single-track railroad covered 581 miles (935 km) and cost the British taxpayer £9,500 a mile, a phenomenal amount in those days.

**Rail returns:** Commissioner Sir Charles Eliot decided that the only way to return the investment was through European settlement along the line, wherever the land could be farmed or ranched. Thomson's Scottish-

vegetables and livestock. The first coffee was planted by Catholic fathers at St Austin's mission on the outskirts of the township and tea was started on the wooded uplands of Limuru close to the 2,000-foot (610-metre) precipitous drop into the Rift Valley. This was the worst of the natural obstacles in the way of the line which was negotiated first by a funicular system of cables and winches, with loaded cars going down and rigged to haul up an empty train on a parallel track. Later a zigzag slant was cut out on the face of the scarp.

From there on it was fairly easy going across the Rift floor to lakes Naivasha,

looking Aberdares, with their cool climate and fertile valleys, offered the best prospect for arable development and several of the first farmer-settlers were the rootless middle sons of the minor British aristocracy. In a sense, these "White Highlands" became the officers' mess of colonial Africa, with the Asians barred from owning land in the area and the Kikuyu either retained as labour or asked to remove themselves to a patchwork reserve on the range's lower eastern slopes.

The Rift itself and the western highlands of the Mau were occupied off and on by the Maasai whom Sir Charles both admired and disdained. He liked their manly appearance, but, because of their top dressing of red ochre and rancid mutton fat, preferred "to interview them out of doors and at a distance".

In a dispatch to London he rated the Maasai the most advanced and worthwhile of the local natives. He recommended that the *moran* armies be broken up and the tribe dispersed into the highlands as farm labour and perhaps later as tenant farmers of the new landed gentry. But he was overruled by a British Parliament which had acquired a liberal "Native Affairs" lobby. The tribe would stay intact and merely move out of the way of the white settlement.

Thereafter, Sir Charles resigned over a "nursery rhyme" policy which had 10,000

tion for the tribe – called "Maasaiitis". At first the *moran* did nothing but look on sardonically as the cranky, red-haired gnome of a man lost a fortune trying high-grade Australian sheep on land they never grazed. It was mineral deficient and the sheep died.

Delamere then ploughed in English clover, restocked with sheep and watched the clover fail; the local African bees were unable to pollinate it. The next move was to import English bees and it worked. But with no winter to keep the crop down in a dormant period, and no frost to kill off the pests, the clover grew into a giant green jungle and the sheep died of foot rot. Further up the valley

Maasai marching up the hill to Laikipia on Mount Kenya and down again to an expanded reserve fanning out from Nairobi to the Tanganyika (presently Tanzania) border.

A few stayed in the Rift on a 100,000-acre (40,500-hectare) ranch one settler had acquired between Nakuru and Njoro. Lord Delamere, from stately Vale Royal in Cheshire, had a touch of what was to become a common roseate rash of European admira-

in Molo District, flocks of hybrid local and imported stock did well and still do.

**A Maasai soul-mate:** The baron then tried cattle, mixing good beef stock looted from the Vale Royal estate with the hump-backed, long-horned Boran cattle of the northern tribes. The progeny were resistant to most of the local viruses, but not to a new East Coast fever from German East Africa which wiped him out once again. After that, the "mad" Englishman was immediately a soul-mate of the Maasai.

They took over Delamere's stock management and, reinforced by imported veterinary science, built up the cattle on sections of the ranch they knew could support the herds. Lord Delamere was greatly obliged and from then on supported the Maasai in land battles with the British administration led by their own advocate, *Ole Legalishu*.

With ranching back on track, Delamere took on more rich and benign-looking acres of the Rift Valley and all the violent African blights and pest infestations they produced. In an expensive process of trial and error he demonstrated how his fellow settlers might ruin themselves over a range of agricultural enterprise, including coffee, flax, and sisal for hemp ropes.

The next venture was wheat, ploughed over a vast acreage by oxen brought up from South Africa. The wheat grew thick on Delamere's rolling downs as a favoured breakfast cereal for every wild plains animal in the Rift Valley. What the game left was then destroyed by several species of wheat rust. Delamere beat the disease with a full-scale research laboratory which eventually produced the national rust-resistant strain. He beat the game by shooting everything in sight which ran him into further trouble with what was, by then, the established bureaucratic enemy in Nairobi.

**Wild parties in town:** Delamere was marked down as a "damned scalliwag", but was never worse than when he led his subordinate settlers into town for a party after months of isolation on the farms. They might arrive with a cavalry charge down Victoria Street, shooting out the glass oil lamps as they rode by, and then going on to some rude assault or other on a polite society which was set up with all the genteel rituals from ladies' garden parties to gentlemen's clubs. Evening entertainment was diverse, bawdy if possible, but always drunken, with the small red Baron seen frequently hurtling down the bar counter of the new Norfolk Hotel.

But Delamere was also serious and effective in leading the settlers' political opposition against government policy which, after Eliot, tended towards support for the rights of the dispossessed Africans. As minister at the Colonial Office, Winston Churchill supported the policy of the Protectorate Government but was apparently softened by Delamere at a pig-sticking party at Elmenteita. The courage and ferocity of the African warthog and the rough terrain over which it rode, he said "would well deserve the serious and appreciative attention of the most accomplished members of the Meerut Tent Club fraternity of pig-stickers in India".

Churchill added a significant postscript on the 4 million Africans who then inhabited the Protectorate. "Just and honourable discipline, careful education, sympathetic comprehension are all that are needed to bring a very large proportion of the tribes of East Africa to a far higher social level than that at which they now stand. *And it is, after all, their Africa.*"

With that disruptive parting shot, he was seen off on the train to Uganda. Delamere and his disciples then set about consolidating the White Highlands and by 1912 had the

Protectorate paying its way on the basis of a mixed agricultural economy.

**Good hunting grounds:** The support sector of tourism was started a year after Churchill by the hunting and shooting President Theodore Roosevelt, his son Kermit and a large party of scientists. They shot indiscriminately for sport, but also selectively for the Smithsonian Institute. They also inspired a successful advertising campaign by the Uganda Railway, promoting "The Highlands of East Africa as a Winter Home for Aristocrats". A poster showed the full range of game species lined up to attack the train, with the caption proclaiming: "Uganda Railway Cars Pass through the Greatest Natural Game reserve in the World. Sportsmen in search of Big Game make it a Hobby. Students of Natural History revel in this field of Nature's Own Making."

A hiatus followed – the wildly romantic, but largely irrelevant theatre of the 1914–18 war opened in East Africa. Two-thirds of an estimated 3,000 settlers left their wives to manage the farms while they rode after the Germans in irregular cavalry units. Delamere himself took off into the Maasai reserve with a party of *moran* scouts who were not greatly effective. They soon became bored, returned to the ranch and thereafter the Maasai resisted strenuous attempts to conscript them into the regular army.

At first the war was a series of minor but highly cinematic episodes. The German commander, Paul von Lettow-Vorbeck, was far and away the star performer, first defeating the British embarrassingly at Tanga and then leading a hit-and-run campaign against the railroad supply line from behind the hills of Taita and central Maasailand. Out in the ocean, the battle-cruiser *Koenigsberg* was disrupting the sea-lanes to India until it was forced to hide in the Rufiji River delta. It was eventually found by a Boer elephant hunter in native disguise, after which two intrepid pilots threw bombs at it from the cockpits of flimsy planes. The ship was later disabled by armed shallow-draught launches, but its captain managed to dismantle one of the big guns and wheel it off to Vorbeck's artillery.

On the other side of the continent, the Royal Navy brought off a similar feat of heavy transportation by hand-carrying the parts of two gun-boats up the Congo Basin to Lake Tanganyika. The British also successfully attacked at Lake Victoria, with the galloping settler brigades engaged in the capture of the German post at Bukoba.

Finally, Jan Smuts from South Africa started Vorbeck on a fighting retreat around Central Africa which achieved the German general's objective of occupying a large force of the British Army for the duration of the war. He was leading 155 Germans and 3,000 Africans into Portuguese Angola in November 1918, when he received the white flag of the armistice – to the sustained applause of the British.

**The outcome of the war:** Vorbeck was thus undefeated, but his country lost Tanganyika in the Treaty of Versailles. Britain was assigned to govern the larger part of it under a League of Nations mandate and began thinking of an economic federation of the three East African territories.

The second significant political consequence of the war was thus the British Government's decision to offer estates in the highlands to veterans of the European campaign in what was called the "Soldier Settlement Scheme". Farms were given away to

winners of a lottery or sold at nominal cost on long-term credit. By 1920, the white population was around 9,000 when the country was designated the "Colony of Kenya" with the coastal strip detached for a few years on a courtesy lease from the Sultan of Zanzibar.

For Delamere settlers, all this advanced their objective of a permanent white man's Kenya – but they were soon disillusioned. A government White Paper in 1923 revived and reinforced the old "indefensible" policy of Africa for the Africans. In what was seen as a Bill of Rights for the black Kenyans, the key paragraph stated that "Primarily, Kenya is an African country. H.M. Government

**Left, settler-tamed zebra and owner. Right, forgotten graves of British officers in Nairobi, including that of Lt. Alfred Harrison who was killed by a lioness in 1898.**

think it necessary definitely to record their considered opinion that the interests of the African native must be paramount, and that if and when those interests and the interests of the immigrant races should conflict, then the former should prevail."

From then on a succession of colonial governors were obliged to apply the paper policy, with or without personal conviction, against the cantankerous and abusive opposition of Delamere and his "Kenya Cowboys" on a national Legislative Council. A takeover attempt by the settlers was always a possibility, but there were never enough of them for any open rebellion or for the political fight which was probably lost when the

urban community groups as channels for government protection of the tribal interests. But the fundamental issue was land, and the early associations of the Kikuyu in Nairobi were revivalist meetings for the return of the "alienated" highlands.

About this time, a remarkable former herd-boy called Johnstone Kamau took a job reading water meters for the Municipal Council. He later changed his name to Jomo Kenyatta as he increased his involvement in the political organization of the Kikuyu in what was to become a long and eventually traumatic struggle with the settlers.

If the urban Kikuyu were the main political constituents of the Crown in Kenya, the

administration's power base at Nairobi began a rapid expansion from the mid-1920s.

**The tribes move to town:** The Africans streamed in to build up the one-street frontier town with sprawling settlements along the Nairobi River and around the railroad. On the surface it was a major social revolution of mostly the adaptable Kikuyu – the great quantum leap from the African bush to the European town with its complex lifestyle and cash economy. But the main life-lines were unbroken; senior wives were left on the ridges to work the patch of land, or "shamba" which retained its mystic, almost religious significance. A few young Kikuyu formed

Asians were the natural clients of a burgeoning Civil Service bureaucracy. They were prolific, as Winston Churchill had forecast, working all hours in closed mutually supportive communities to establish a near monopoly in the broad sector of trade, light industry and semi-professional service.

Some of them collected enough capital to put up much of the local development finance in partnership with the government. They also provided credit between harvests to the settlers who were not always appreciative of this economic bridge between two socially distant communities. The response ranged from bemused acceptance of the changing relationship between the Indian and the Raj to offensive hostility toward the Aryans, labelled "the Jews of East Africa".

**English county set:** The third, upper level of Nairobi society was an alliance of officers of government and of the British Army commanding African infantry battalions. Some of them were socially acceptable to the settlers, but not all were ready to join what they saw as a pretentious, eccentric and slightly ridiculous tropical transplant of the English "county set". One of them was the Earl of Lytton who much preferred the solitude of a command up at Baragoi, in the desert of Samburu country, and the occasional company of the respected Captain Baron von

The Muthaiga Country Club was the settlers' political headquarters in Nairobi, and also the venue for the hunt balls, the occasional elegantly wild party and other revels said to include a half-clandestine wife-swapping in an extension of what was also said to be the gay, permissive scene upcountry in the Wanjohi or "Happy Valley" of the highlands. The moment of serious drama in all this was the unsolved shooting of the noted ladies' man, Lord "Joss" Erroll, a close friend of the lady who was to become the wife of Delamere's son and heir.

Another more significant casualty of the period was the first Baroness Blixen whose hunter husband, Bror, went off with another

NAIROBI TO LONDON IN **6** DAYS ● TO CAPE TOWN IN **3** DAYS BY AIR!

Do you realise how swift, luxurious, and inexpensive is travel by Imperial Airways? You save time and money on journeys in Africa and from Africa to Europe or to India and the Far East. You reach Cairo from Nairobi in three days and Johannesburg in two days!

And all in the greatest comfort! The air liners are as quiet as Pullman cars and are equipped with armchair seats, luggage accommoda-

tion, and lavatories. You sleep on land each night, and this accommodation, as well as all meals and even tips, is included in the fare.

The comfort and lack of fatigue make air travel especially suitable for women, children, and elderly people. It is also the perfect transport for mail and freight; it means less time in transit, less packing, less insurance, and the swift and safe arrival of perishable goods.

**NAIROBI** TO CAIRO £72 **IN 3 DAYS!**
TO CAPE TOWN £51

Imperial Airways' fares are very little higher than those charged by surface transport companies, and some of them are lower, and the shortness of the journey saves the heavy incidental expenses. There are NO "extras" so that you can travel from end to end of Africa with only a few shillings in your pocket and suffer no inconvenience.

20% REDUCTION
RETURN TICKETS: A reduction equivalent to 20% (twenty per

cent.) of the single fare for the homeward journey is allowed on return tickets taken in advance. There are also special reductions for British Government Officials and officers of H.M. Forces.

Bookings and information from the principal travel agents or from Imperial Airways Ltd., Nairobi Aerodrome, Nairobi. Telegrams: Flying, Nairobi.

# IMPERIAL AIRWAYS
THE GREATEST AIR SERVICE IN THE WORLD.

Otter who led a long campaign against the wild and dissident Turkana tribe.

The new wave of immigrants to Nairobi were also automatically in the upper social bracket. All of them were entrepreneurs of some sort – commercial speculators, professionals, skilled artisans and remittance men. Most of them were allied to the administration since only a few could "make the grade" to the settler establishment.

**Left**, Delamere Avenue (now Kenyatta Avenue) in the 1940s. **Above**, air travel to Nairobi was pioneered by Imperial Airways, the forerunner of British Airways.

woman and left her to go bankrupt on a suburban Nairobi coffee farm under the Ngong Hills. Her memoir, *Out of Africa* – remarkable for its stylish insight on the country and people – was also eloquent on the since exaggerated and romanticised highlife of Kenya in the 1920s and 1930s. She entertained Edward, Prince of Wales, and she had her own romantic interlude with a raffish member of the club, the Hon. Denys Finch-Hatton. But the overall impression was that of the slightly desperate gaiety of an Anglo-African "Cherry Orchard" before the peasant revolution – the arrival of the Kikuyu woodsmen who would chop it down.

One day in early March 1922, a crowd of Africans gathered outside the Central Police Station where the main campus of the University of Nairobi stands today. A few settlers stood watching outside the nearby Norfolk Hotel. It was generally calm, as one European noted, except for the squalling of Nairobi's prostitutes.

Inside the police station, under arrest, was Harry Thuku, leader of the "Young Kikuyu Association". There are conflicting reports about what happened. One, widely circulated, was that a woman lifted her skirt and derisively told the men to give the women their trousers. "Our leader is there," she cried, "Why don't you go and get him?"

It was then that shots rang out from the police station and, according to some reports, from the direction of the Norfolk Hotel. Officially, 21 people died but the Africans claimed over 100 were killed.

Thuku was eventually detained in Kismaiyu, a small town on the northern Kenya coast. But the episode outside the police station marked the beginning of a sustained fight for political, economic and social rights for Kenya's African Society. Even from that early date, they were out to take over from the British and run the country themselves. This was to be *Uhuru* – Kiswahili for "Freedom" – and it was to be a long struggle that would also acquire racial overtones.

When the crowd gathered outside the Central Police Station on that fateful day in 1922, European settlement in Kenya had been established for 20 years. Through the 1902 Land Acquisition Order in Council, "White Settlers" from as far afield as Britain, Canada, Australia and South Africa had acquired the most fertile land in Kenya.

Led by their undisputed leader, Lord Delamere, they had also become politically dominant in a Legislative Council created after the country ceased to be a Protectorate and was placed under the jurisdiction of the Colonial Office in London.

The settlers successfully pressured the colonial government in Nairobi to allocate more and more land to European settlement and also to pass laws that forced Africans to seek employment from settlers. These laws were ruthlessly enforced through an elaborate system of chiefs and headmen established by the government in the early 1900s.

The land they coveted and acquired had an air of England about it – temperate in the highlands and scenically not far removed from the rolling downs of Wiltshire. But all on a much larger scale, with immense space

in landscapes and skies which gave some of the settlers a sense of grandeur. To this rich land without winter or a dormant season, the immigrants brought with them all the trappings of European civilization – heirloom furniture, china, gilt-framed ancestral portraits, and whatever they could loot from family estate back home.

**Soapbox Rallies:** In *The Politics of Independent Kenya*, Cherry Gertzel wrote that "Government policies on land, labour and distribution of services favoured the European minority at the expense of the African majority."

It was also noted in the local newspaper in

**Left**, late Chief Njiri with Royal portrait in the 1950s. **Right**, painting of Mzee Jomo Kenyatta's arrest on October 20, 1952.

1922: "Out at Pangani village (close to Nairobi), the Natives are very busy these days holding meetings of the mass kind. Every Sunday, thousands of *Njoroges* and *Kamaus* may be seen listening raptly to others of their kind holding forth on presumably the question of the hour... And it is fairly apparent that these meetings have a savour of politics about them and that the Natives are discussing matters connected with registration, taxation and so on."

These meetings were attended by up to 5,000 people and were multi-tribal in character. For this reason, Kiswahili was used as the language of address. The main complaints were over the forced labour practices

build up the institutions they needed to make their presence felt and gain greater consideration of their interests."

This started, essentially, in 1924 when a Kikuyu Central Association (KCA) was formed with Kenyatta as its secretary. The KCA worked closely with the Kavirondo Taxpayers Welfare Association, a grouping of the tribal Luo, the second largest tribe from around Lake Victoria.

In a memorandum, the KCA complained against the government's policy of dividing the tribes and asked for the establishment of a Central Native Council. Likewise, the Kavirondo Association also called for a national political organisation for Africans.

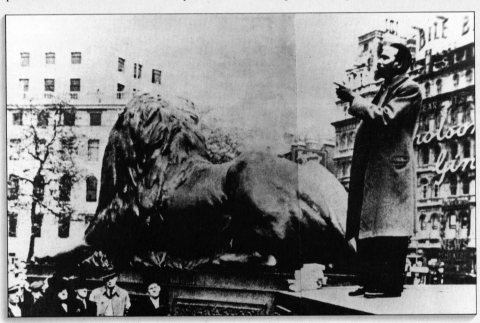

and the imposition of a "hut tax", which most people couldn't afford. Among the many Africans who attended these rallies of discontent was the young Kikuyu Johnstone Kamau. Born before the British settlement, he grew up as an orphan and was educated by missionaries. As Jomo Kenyatta, his name would be indelibly marked on Kenya.

At first, the Colonial Government was not fully aware of the extent to which the Africans were prepared to fight. As one historian noted: "For the next two decades the Europeans from their position of strength would increase their influence to the utmost, while the Africans in their weakness struggle to

Instead, they were fobbed off with "Local Native Councils" made up of chiefs and appointed members and charged with giving "the younger and more educated Natives a definite avenue along which to develop".

The boundaries of assigned "Native Reserves" were published, but it was clear to everyone – not excluding the government – that more land was about to be taken later for white settlement. By 1928, 10,200 sq. miles (26,420 sq. km) of the colony's best arable land was being ploughed, mostly for cash crops by the European immigrants. This exclusive white preserve was shaped like a fist, thrust into the heart of the country gripping the most fertile soil. It was narrow at Sultan Hamud, south of Nairobi, but expanded in the rain-fed lee of the Aberdares Range and Mount Kenya. The White Highlands then took in the western folds of the Western Rift, the Mau Range, extending to Mount Elgon and the Uganda border.

**Social conflicts:** In 1929, there was another complicated social controversy over female circumcision. The church expelled anyone who supported the practice, and many a Kikuyu regarded this as another interference with fundamental tradition. The affair led to the formation of independent schools and church movements, and these splinter developments were to become useful to Kenyatta,

to present the Africans' case. He reported back, but then went off again in 1931 for what would be a 15-year odyssey in the western world, including some time in Stalin's Soviet Union. Three years later, the Africans were better organised than they had ever been to confront the colonial government. They were also articulate and forceful in presenting their views to the "Carter Commission", a commission of inquiry on the disposition of land in Kenya. The basic decision of the Commission, however, went against them; all African claims to the "White Highlands" were disallowed. As a result, the "social" organisations proliferated. In addition to the KCA, the Luo re-

the KCA and other Kikuyu-based political organisations as it was in the independent schools that the Kikuyu sense of identity and African nationalism were inculcated.

Harry Thuku was let out of jail in 1930 on the condition that he would cooperate with the government. When he agreed, it isolated him somewhat as a "stooge". Many of his supporters joined the KCA.

Meanwhile, Kenyatta had gone to London

**Left,** Jomo Kenyatta crusades for liberation at Trafalgar Square, London, 1938. **Above,** British soldier guards Mau Mau freedom fighters after mass arrests in Nairobi.

formed into the North Kavirondo Central Association; the Taita Hills Association represented the Taita people west of Mombasa; and the Ukamba Members Association, the numerous Kamba tribe southeast of Nairobi. Opposition to the colonial government became more effective.

In late May 1940, 23 leaders of these associations were detained under newly promulgated "defence regulations". They were held on suspicion of consulting with the Italian Consulate in Nairobi, a potential enemy of the king. A copy of Adolf Hitler's *Mein Kampf* at the KCA headquarters compounded the felony.

Many Kenya Africans then fought for the king in North Africa, the Middle East, Ethiopia and Burma (Myanmar). Once the war was over, these worldly wise veterans became an additional political force, aware that the mighty Europeans were vulnerable like anyone else. They could also handle arms, of course, and many resumed "active service" in the *Mau Mau* rebellion a few years later.

**The Kenya African Union:** Although the KCA and other associations were banned in 1940, a more potent political organization came into being. This followed the appointment of Eliud Mathu – a product of Balliol College, Oxford – as the first African member of the Legislative Council. Recognising the need

a chance of uniting the Africa challenge to the colonialists.

With Kenyatta at the helm and using the Kikuyu independent schools and churches machinery, KAU grew in strength in Nairobi, Central Province and among Africans working in the "White Highlands". They also stepped up confrontation with the government, which included a KAU-supported strike at the docks at Mombasa. This was ruthlessly suppressed. And at Uplands, a few miles north of Nairobi, police shot several strikers at a bacon factory. In the same year, 1947, police fired at a number of demonstrators against intimidation of a Kikuyu chief.

At this time, Kikuyu oathing ceremonies

to have a base, Mathu formed the Kenya African Study Union with its constitution written by Indian lawyers. The venerable Thuku joined the new organization and when, in 1946, it changed its name to the Kenya African Union (KAU), Thuku became its first chairman. He was ousted a few months later and replaced with another venerable Kikuyu *mzee*, James Gichuru.

Although KAU had an inter-tribal outlook, its leadership was dominated by former KCA Kikuyu members. It was not surprising, therefore, that when Kenyatta returned from Britain in 1946, Gichuru stepped down in favour of his mentor – the only man who had

started on a large scale. These secret oaths of loyalty to political objectives – notably land issues – were fed by strict enforcement of regulations against Africans squatting in the highlands. While the authorities, including African chiefs, viewed the oathing as a threat to law and order, the missionaries and their Christian African followers saw the ceremonies as anti-Christian. This caused a deep social rift, so that when the *Mau Mau* war started, prime targets were the Christian Kikuyu. Many were killed.

At the same time, two religious groups clearly manifesting African nationalism came into being. One, led by Elijah Masinde, was called *Dini ya Msambwa*. It was mostly active in western Kenya and some parts of Kalenjin country, bordering the "White Highlands" around the Uasin Gishu Plateau near the Uganda border. Violently anti-European, *Dini ya Msambwa* led to disturbances and a European officer was killed. In the Central Province, *Dini ya Yesu Kristo* was also active.

KAU remained the main spearhead of African political expression and when the Colonial Secretary, James Griffiths, visited Kenya in 1951, the Union presented him with a memorandum. More aid for African education, higher posts for Africans in the Civil Service and trade unions, prohibition of racial discrimination by law, and another eight representative members (in addition to the then existing five appointed members) in the Legislative Council, were among the requests made in the memorandum. It was a foregone conclusion that none of KAU's demands would be met. The oathings continued, some of them binding the participants to kill Europeans and their collaborators.

As political fervour increased, songs to Christian melodies chanted out grievances, although they were regarded as blasphemy by the body of churchgoers. At the same time, supportive oathing spread among tribes like the Maasai, the Luo, the Luhya and to a certain extent, the Kamba and the Kipsigis. There was then a wave of destruction of settlers' property, and murders of chiefs and other Africans loyal to the government. The *Mau Mau* rebellion had begun.

**State of emergency:** Not everyone was involved or sympathetic. Most people were looking for a peaceful way to political, economic and social equality. Early in 1952, the Kenya Citizens Association was formed as suggested by the son of a Kikuyu senior chief, Mbiyu Koinange. The association wanted peaceful change but it was too late. On October 21, 1952, Governor Sir Evelyn Baring declared a "state of emergency". Kenyatta and 82 other nationalists were arrested and detained. Military reinforcements were flown into Kenya and war was declared on the *Mau Mau*.

Before the month was over, Kenyatta and

five of his colleagues were charged with managing this "unlawful organization". And, despite a spirited defence by a team of international lawyers, Kenyatta was convicted and sentenced to serve seven years in jail. Walter Odede, a Luo, took over leadership of KAU, but the party was banned soon afterwards and the new leaders detained. By then, accordingly to the colonial government, at least 59 leading Africans had been murdered. The reprisal – the arrest of the KAU leaders – only made the matters worse. It was followed by an outpouring of Kikuyu from the "White Highlands" and many urban areas into the forest enclaves of the *Mau Mau* around the Aberdares and Mount Kenya.

The government resorted to drastic measures to deal with the rebellion. With the Malaya experience in mind, they collected and herded rural communities together, cramming the people into "protected villages" surrounded with barbed wire and trenches spiked with sharpened bamboo. Anyone found outside during a strict night curfew was shot. To augment the police and the army, the government recruited 20,000 Kikuyu "Home Guards", a move that, together with Christian opposition to the *Mau Mau*, expanded the rebellion to civil war.

During 1953 and 1954, a number of pitched battles at company and platoon lev-

**Left**, As Jomo Kenyatta is freed, his supporters celebrate. **Above**, Kenyatta celebrates Kenya African National Union's election triumph.

els took place between *Mau Mau* fighters and government troops. After these, the rebels were more or less on the run. The Colonial Secretary, Oliver Lyttelton, then turned up in Kenya, after which a document known as the "Lyttelton Constitution" was produced. This created a multi-racial Council of Ministers, which infuriated the settlers and split them down the middle. Some, led by Sir Michael Bluncell, went along with the Council. The rest stayed aloof, espousing apartheid-type policies. They formed a Federal Independence Party, led by an ex-airman, Group-Captain L.R. Briggs.

In June 1955, the government announced that Africans could form political parties at

nated after independence; Ronald Ngala, who died in a road accident; and Oginga Odinga, an important political figure.

Six months before Kenyatta's jail term ended, the "LEGCO" Africans started a clamour for his release. The government gave way to agitation and lifted the "state of emergency" in 1960, although not without resistance at first. By then, the count of casualties was 13,577 killed and 3,595 wounded. Of the dead, little more than 100 were Europeans. It also became clear that a settler-dominated government could no longer be sure of maintaining law and order in Kenya. This, together with the continued agitation of the African elected members,

district levels – except in the *Mau Mau* heartland of Central Province – "to encourage a simple and orderly development of African political life". A majority of the settlers were far from accepting Africans as partners in the government, while a majority of Africans no longer cared what the Europeans thought. The following year saw yet another Constitution which gave the Africans eight seats in the Legislative Council – this time elected by all constituents of the country's eight provinces.

These first full representatives of the Kenyan majority included Daniel Toroitich arap Moi, later President, Tom Mboya, assassi-

led to the British Government to convene the 1960 "Lancaster House Conference" on the future of the colony.

**Independence achieved:** Advising the Africans was a future US Supreme Court Justice, Thurgood Marshall, but as usual, they failed to get what they wanted. Even so, the principle of majority rule and ultimate independence for Kenya as an African – and not a white man's – country was endorsed.

At the inaugural meeting in Kiambu, a 15-minute drive from Nairobi, the party's name was changed for no apparent reason to the Kenya African National Union (KANU). But there was almost instant division. The coast's man, Ronald Ngala, joined other leaders from tribes like the Luhya, the Kalenjin and the Maasai. And, at a meeting in Ngong – another 15-minute drive from Nairobi in Maasai country – the Kenya African Democratic Union (KADU) was formed with Ngala as its president.

Apart from their mutual insistence on *Uhuru* and Kenyatta's release, the two parties had nothing in common. KANU wanted a unitary form of government with firm control from Nairobi. KADU wanted a federal type of government to safeguard the rights of the minorities; it also had support from a considerable number of the settlers.

Finally, Kenyatta was released on August

take over as president of the party. The next step was to get into the Legislative Council. One of the members stepped down in his favour, and Kenyatta duly took his seat. He was cheered by his countrymen, but hardly by the settlers who were distinctly jittery over their prospects if Kenyatta eventually took over the government.

**Final agreement:** Kenyatta led KANU's delegation to another round of talks at Lancaster House in London on November 6. Haggling, threats and compromise went on for two years until the Colonial Office finally got KADU and KANU to agree on a date for the end of colonial rule – December 12, 1963.

It rained the night before, but the crowds

15, 1961, and returned to Nairobi to find two hostile groups of African nationalists in the Legislative Council. This was all exacerbated by the fact that KADU – the minority party after elections that year – had been asked to form the government. For a while Kenyatta toyed with the idea of forming his own political party. But, because of his long association with the people and ideas that dominated KANU, he eventually agreed to

**Left**, Prime Minister Kenyatta talks to settlers in Nakuru, 1963. **Above**, Mzee Jomo Kenyatta welcomes returning freedom fighters for Independence celebrations.

were impervious to it as they gathered in their thousands towards midnight at a makeshift "Independence Square". This was barely 3 miles (5 km) from the site of the 1922 shooting. Men and women all over the country had their eyes glued to their watches and their ears tuned to their radio sets. Then it happened – midnight and "freedom" – the embattled, long-delayed *Uhuru*.

Just a few minutes before, the lights at the square had dimmed. And when they were turned on again, the Union Jack was nowhere to be seen. From the flagstaff flew the black, red and green ensign of the new Republic of Kenya.

As the flag of independent Kenya was being raised for the first time on December 12, 1963, there was a momentary hitch as the rope snagged. The visiting Duke of Edinburgh, never at a loss for a quip, said to President Jomo Kenyatta: "Do you want to change your mind? There's still time!"

The story may be apocryphal, but it matches the spirit of joviality and happiness with which Kenya entered its new era as a free nation, after a bitter and bloody struggle during which relations with the colonial

have severely strained not only Kenya's economy but have held back necessary development plans, the basic unity of its people have remained solid. Kenyans had a fleeting glimpse of the grimmer side of the coin for just a few hours on August 1, 1982, when law and order broke down briefly during a foiled coup attempt. Anarchy roamed the streets of Nairobi, as looters descended on the shopping centres and goods were carried off by hordes of plunderers who seized the opportunity to share in the world of the "haves".

power were strained to the limit. In the years since that historic moment, Kenya has fared better than most of the 50 or so independent African nations on a continent plagued above all by climatic hardships and natural disasters, as well as by civil strife and numerous military coups and insurrections. Even so the country has not escaped the severe economic battering which has been suffered by most African nations as the ever-increasing costs of imports are not matched by a corresponding rise in the prices paid for Kenya's agricultural exports, which are still the main source of foreign exchange.

Despite these external problems which

Events beyond Kenya's borders also made their impact felt in Kenya. Hardly had independence been granted when all of East Africa was set aflame by revolutions and coups, and rumours of Communist subversion ran rife. President Jomo Kenyatta and the ruling party, the Kenya African National Union (KANU), were committed to a policy of strict non-alignment, and hoped to exist with both Capitalism and Communism.

**Troops deployed:** Within a month of Kenya becoming a self-governing state within the Commonwealth, a bloody revolution not only ousted the Sultan of Zanzibar but led to a pogrom on Arabs by the non-Arab (mostly

African) majority. The dust had hardly settled when the army mutinied in neighbouring Tanzania. President Julius Nyerere was forced into hiding and had to call in British troops to overpower the mutineers.

**The Communism scare**: Mutinies also broke out in Uganda, and then in Kenya, About 5,000 British troops were stationed in East Africa and some were deployed to quell all three mutinies. While Communists may have been involved on Zanzibar, the mainland troubles showed no such external influences; trade unions were seen as the main instigators. Nevertheless it was a chastening experience for all three East African governments, and several leaders in Kenya became

jittery about the "Red menace", especially at the time when the Chinese and Soviets were trying to expand their influence in Africa. Luo leader Oginga Odinga offered himself as the principal scapegoat, with such sayings as "Communism is like food for me". (By then, he had become the first Vice-President of the new Kenya republic).

It was not long before the Communist

**Preceding pages**: Jomo Kenyatta takes oath as President. **Left**, President Jomo Kenyatta with former President Julius Nyerere of Tanzania and President Kenneth Kaunda of Zambia. **Above**, President Daniel arap Moi.

threat seemed even more apparent when Chinese Premier Chou En-lai arrived for an African tour, during which he noted that "the revolutionary prospects are excellent throughout the African continent". Before long this had been paraphrased into "Africa is ripe for revolution against oppressive regimes". Soon the Communist influence was carefully weighed by East Africans against the more subtle influences of the Western powers. In Kenya, the two media-identified protagonists were Odinga (or "Double-O" as he was called) for the East, and Tom Mboya for the West.

The Soviet-sponsored Lumumba Institute, which had been opened with a flourish in Nairobi after independence, was soon closed down by the government. The institute's supporters, including Odinga and his friends, claimed it was "a centre for rehabilitating the colonial mentality", whereas its opponents regarded it as a "Marxist brainwashing institution".

At this time, Kenya was dragged into the bloody civil war in the Congo (now Zaire) between the Tshombe Government in Kinshasa and the leftish "Simba" rebels operating around Stanleyville (now Kisangani). Kenyatta had been charged with heading a mediation commission appointed to solve the dispute between the rival factions, but at a crucial juncture in the delicate negotiations, US aircraft dropped Belgian paratroops on Stanleyville in a bid to rescue the many hostage held by the Simbas.

Meanwhile Kenya had become a *de facto* one-party state, with the voluntary dissolution of the opposition KADU (Kenya African Democratic Party) in November 1964 and the two-chamber Legislature becoming the single chamber National Assembly. It seemed tribal rivalries had been put aside in favour of a "coalition" type government.

Due to allegations that Odinga was plotting to overthrow the Government, he was eased out of the top KANU hierarchy by 1966. Infuriated, he resigned as Vice-President of Kenya and later formed his own rival party with many of his supporters. He named it the Kenya People's Union (KPU), and once more the country had an opposition party. Odinga was replace as Vice-President by Joseph Anthony Zuzarte Murumbi.

A so-called "little general election" in the following year tested the newly-formed KPU at the polls. Nine Members were returned to Parliament. Since the rival voting symbols were the KANU cockerel (*jogoo*) and the KPU bull (*dume*), this was also labelled the "cock and bull election". Odinga meanwhile faced further accusations of subversion, including giving Chinese money to former freedom fighters, a charge he vehemently denied.

Tom Mboya, who had become Minister for Economic Affairs, also faced critical allegations; he was accused of being "a tool of the imperialists". Ironically it was Mboya who had been directing Kenya's policy of non-alignment from the time the country had achieved independence. When a "Sessional Paper" was issued in 1965, Mboya gave

yatta might have ideas about succeeding the *Mzee*. It was not long before an amendment was made to the Constitution raising the age limit for a Kenyan President from 35 to 40 which effectively ruled out young Mboya from the presidential stakes. Changes and proposed changes to this Constitution were to become crucial to the country's security in the years to come.

Within three months of Daniel arap Moi's appointment as Vice-President of Kenya on January 1976 (filling the gap left by Murumbi's resignation) several other important changes were made to the Constitution, including the election of a President by the electorate instead of an electoral college, and

practical examples of non-aligned "African Socialism" in these words: "It would enable us to co-operate, when desirable for Kenya's welfare, with Russia, China or other Eastern countries without looking over our shoulders to see what the British are saying or thinking about us, and even without bothering whether someone calls us Communists…" Mboya also stated that Kenya should have the freedom to cooperate with the West without being called Capitalist.

But by this time others were sniping at the up-and-coming Mboya, including some influential Kikuyu who feared the young and ambitious Luo confidante of President Ken-

a provision to enable a Vice-President to succeed automatically – but for 90 days only – on the death of a President.

After a relatively peaceful interval, tragedy again struck Kenya in July 1969, with the gunning down of Tom Mboya who died before reaching hospital. A young Kikuyu of the KANU party was duly charged and convicted of the killing. He was executed within only four months of the assassination.

The murder of one of Africa's most promising young statesmen soon aroused tribal tension and violence spilled out in the capital, with a near-riot during the memorial service. The body had to be moved to a distant grave on Rusinga Island in Lake Victoria to avoid any problems with over-emotional mourners. There was renewed violence this time in Kisumu – in the Luo heartland and base of Oginga Odinga – when President Kenyatta paid the town a visit some months later. Eleven bystanders in a crowd were killed when his bodyguard opened fire on what they regarded as a hostile demonstration. Odinga was promptly blamed for the trouble and was immediately detained along with most of his leading supporters. The KPU party was banned from further operations.

**"Operation Doomsday":** Even with Odinga and his opposition politicians out of the way, peace did not return to Kenya immediately and 1971 saw the country's first sedition trial, arising out of a coup attempt which failed. The plot, code-named "Operation Doomsday", was to have overthrown the Kenyatta Government on the Easter weekend when Nairobi was preoccupied with the Safari Motor Rally. It was nipped in the bud by President Nyerere of Tanzania informing Kenyatta that the plotters had been to see him for arms and money.

In 1973 Kenya celebrated both its 10th year of independence and a decade of Jomo Kenyatta's rule. Achievements noted were a doubling of the national income, free education up to the first four grades, school attendance up by 150 percent, a tripling of tea production and a 50 percent rise in coffee. The first oil price hike, however, had contributed towards a 20 percent inflation rate.

In the 1974 elections, however, 88 MPs lost their seats and the casualties included 4 Ministers. At the start of 1975, the new Parliament showed it was still composed of individuals who were not afraid to speak out when they saw things they did not like. Among the most vociferous of the back-benchers was J.M. Kariuki, a Kikuyu and former *Mau Mau* fighter who had built up a large following through his public appearances and lack of tribal prejudice. He had been an Assistant Minister until he lost his post in the recent Cabinet changes – a sure sign of the Establishment's displeasure. One of the remarks they disliked – and he repeated it often – was: "Kenya has become a nation of 10 millionaires and 10 million

beggars." Much of his criticisms were directed openly at the extended "family" of President Kenyatta which he accused of amassing great wealth through land purchases and trading in gemstones.

In March 1975, the disfigured body of Kariuki was identified in the Nairobi mortuary by his wife Terry following concerns over his sudden disappearance some weeks previously. His corpse had been found lying on the slopes of the Ngong Hills, 20 miles from Nairobi, by a Maasai herdsman and brought to the mortuary where it was labelled simply "unidentified African male".

Kariuki's killing was even more of a mystery than that of Mboya. He was a Kikuyu, although clearly not an Establishment man; he was an "outsider", considered dangerous because of his talk of "freed things", including land for the landless and other such topics no longer publicly discussed. A Parliamentary Select Committee laid the blame on the government's doorstep. In its report of June 3, 1975, the Committee concluded that: "Although a very large number of witnesses were located and interviewed, its inability to take a more conclusive report before Parliament is largely due to the refusal of the heads of police to render any assistance even by disclosing the names of witnesses who might have been of value to the Committee and subsequently the Committee can only conclude that the police investigators do not wish the Committee to make any progress towards the bringing to justice of Mr Kariuji's murderers." Up to this day, no further light has been shed on Kariuki's death.

**The making of a new president:** By 1977 the subject of who would succeed Jomo Kenyatta had ceased to be academic, in view of the President's rapidly failing health. His deteriorating condition caused the cancellation of the KANU party elections in spite of the fact that none had been held for 11 years. He died in Mombasa on August 22, 1978, while on "working holiday" at the coast. Vice-President Moi temporarily took over the running of the country, at the same time making arrangements for the obligatory presidential elections within 90 days.

The election was held within 50 days of the President's death and it became a formality when a groundswell of public support for Moi was clearly apparent. There was no opposition despite rumours of a prominent

Kikuyu contesting the post. Mwai Kibaki, Minister for Finance and Planning, was elected unopposed as Vice-President.

No major changes were made in the Cabinet, but there was a major shake-up in the security services and Immigration Department. The new President announced a stern crackdown on corruption, smuggling and nepotism, but promised that political detention would only be "a last resort".

Concluding that eventful year were the KANU national committee elections, when almost all candidates on a mysterious "approved list" were elected. These incoming senior party officials were appointed on a regional basis.

identifying the plotters as the inner circle of a Kikuyu social organisation. As there was no attempt to ban the publication, it was assumed to have official sanction.

According to Njonjo, a group of 200 trained assassins concealed in the paramilitary General Service Unit (GSU), as a "Stock Theft Unit", were to have sprung into action the moment Kenyatta drew his last breath. Moi, Kibaki and Njonjo were to have been summoned to the death-bed and were to have been gunned down by the "assassination squad" hidden nearby, and the dead President's body then riddled with bullets. The shocked public would have been told that the trio had been caught in the act of

**Assassination sensation:** As Attorney-General supervising the constitutional transition from Kenyatta to Moi, Charles Njonjo was in the limelight. He caused a sensation when he blandly revealed in Parliament that in spite of the seemingly smooth hand-over, things might have been very different if certain unnamed plotters had not been foiled in their bid to carry out an assassination plot in which not only Vice-President Moi would have been killed, but also Mwai Kibaki and Njonjo himself. Despite no corroboration for his story, two years later a book called T*he Kenyatta Successio* was published garnishing the facts with more gory details, and

"murdering" the President and afterwards killed in the shoot-out. The plotters would then have presented themselves as the true heirs of the martyred leader.

Subsequent inquiries revealed there was a group within a "Stock Theft Unit" which had undergone intensive parachute and commando training around Nakuru. The plot went wrong because Kenyatta died in Mombasa instead of in Nakuru, as the plotters had expected and planned for.

More credence was lent to the extraordinary story when a senior police officer later fled to Europe. Subsequently, Njonjo alleged that this officer had been one of the ringleaders and charged that politicians, who had been against the Vice-President, automatically succeeding Kenyatta, were also involved in the plot.

Just over a year later, after an Interpol search, the defecting police officer returned home to "face the music" from self-imposed exile in Switzerland. On arrival in Nairobi, he was immediately driven off in a police car. On January 24, 1980, Charles Njonjo revealed that the officer had received a presidential pardon and stated that the entire "Ngoroko affair" was closed. ("Ngoroko" had been a nickname given to the Stock Theft Unit, and was a play on the Turkana word for cattle rustler.)

Like many other odd occurrences in Kenya during the 1970s, nothing more was heard about the bizarre plot and those involved were allowed to go free – in the case of the policeman, to settle down as a farmer not far from the late President's property at Rongai, west of Nakuru.

**In Kenyatta's footsteps:** Meanwhile "Chapter Two", as the new Moi era was known to some Kenyans, or *Nyayo* ("footsteps") to others, was by now well under way and the old rallying cry of *harambee* ("all pull together") was heard less frequently. The reference to "footsteps" was taken to mean that Moi was closely following the former President's policies.

President Moi made it known in the middle of 1980 that all tribal societies would be disbanded immediately. The Kikuyu society's chairman, Njenga Karume, tried to prevaricate saying it would destroy the tribe's cultural heritage. But the ban was enforced in order "to stamp out the negative aspects of tribalism", even to the extent of changing household names such as Luo Union, Gema, and Kenya's soccer teams Gor Mahia and Abaluhya FC – which became AFC Leopards.

Much speculation followed the voluntary retirement of Njonjo from his post of Attorney-General, which he held since Independence. He denied suggestions he was seeking the post of Vice-President, or had ambition to become President. After securing his seat in the National Assembly in an unopposed by-election, he was made Minister for Home

and Constitutional Affairs. (His old political adversary, Oginga Odinga, who had been on the verge of making a political come-back, fell from grace after he called the late President Kenyatta a "land-grabber".)

By mid-1981, President Moi had been elected Chairman of the Organisation of African Unity (OAU) at its Nairobi summit and he was obliged to hold this onerous "Mr Africa" post for two years (1981–2) in addition to handling serious problems at home. Of these, the most serious were a food shortage resulting from a long drought following the export of strategic maize reserves.

After what the Government saw as a dangerous Leftist tendency developing at the

university and other higher education institutions, it clamped down on demonstrations and closed the university several times. The mounting tension between the Government and the university continued into 1982 and was heightened when doctors went on strike. Unrest then developed among the nation's many teachers. On August 1, 1982, it was announced on the official Voice of Kenya radio that the armed forces had deposed Moi's Government and a People's Redemption Council had been set up. Later that Sunday morning, loyal elements of the Kenya Army retook the radio station which had been seized during the previous night by

**Left**, verdant highlands and rich soil. **Above**, tea plucking in the highlands.

rebels of the Air Force. The loyal soldiers dislodged mutineers from vital installations in the capital and quelled another mutiny at the Nanyuki air base.

Before order could be restored in Nairobi, however, there was widespread looting in the shopping areas and some university students demonstrated in support of the rebels.

**Plotters executed:** Two self-confessed ringleaders of the abortive coup were later court-martialled. Together with 10 other airmen, they were sentenced to death for treason. Another 900 or so airmen received prison sentences for taking part in the mutiny and the entire Kenya Air Force was replaced by a new unit called the "82 Air Force".

No inquiry was held as to the causes of the coup attempt or to ascertain if highly placed people had been involved, but sweeping changes were made in the security services and many top officers were dismissed.

Less than a year later, President Moi startled the citizens with his announcement that a "traitor" within his Government was being secretly groomed by unnamed foreign powers to take over the Presidency. Speculation and innuendos in Parliament pointed towards the Minister for Constitutional Affairs, Mr Njonjo. Later Njonjo was suspended from the Cabinet, followed by voluntary resignation of his seat in Parliament only hours before expulsion from KANU.

Civilians suspected to have been involved in the abortive coup were thrown into detention, including former MP George Anyona (also earlier accused of planning to form an opposition political party with Oginga Odinga) and a prominent Nairobi human rights lawyer, Dr John Khaminwa. Anyona and Khaminwa were detained without trial in June 1982 before Parliament passed a constitutional amendment which made Kenya a one party state and prohibiting the formation of other political parties in the future. Oginga and Anyona were expelled from KANU in the same year following a crackdown on "dissidents".

A year ahead of schedule, general elections were held in September 1983 by President Moi, "to give the country time to clean up its house". A judicial commission was later set up to inquire into allegations against Njonjo, the Government emphasising it was not a criminal trial, but a tribunal. On December 12, 1984, Njonjo was found guilty of most charges, including corruption, involvement in the illegal import of firearms, and an attempt to topple the Government of the Seychelles. Njonjo was given a presidential pardon, but the 64-year-old former Minister could not rejoin the ruling party and was to repay the funds that he had misappropriated.

Coming at the end of Kenya's first 21 years of independence, the Njonjo enquiry was one of the most sensational disclosures of disturbing events which plagued this time of Kenya's history. In 1985 Party elections from grassroots to national levels were held in order to rid the party and the government of "disloyal", "anti-Nyayo" and "undesirable" elements. President Moi then embarked on a wide-ranging re-organisation of the party, turning it into his own power base.

Between 1985 and 1989 KANU became the supreme organ of the land, intolerant of criticism and reverting to a system of warnings, suspensions, party expulsions and name-calling. Critical lawyers, clergymen and others earned such labels as "tribalists", "unpatriotic" and "in the pay of foreign masters". In addition to party disciplinary measures, a number of leaders including non-party members were picked up by police for questioning. Some were released, others detained. KANU also expelled some 45 people from the party and others were suspended for varying periods over the next decade.

In 1988, amid strong protest from lawyers, the clergy and other interested parties, the Kenya Constitution was amended to remove the security of tenure of judges of the High Court and the Court of Appeal and members of the Public Service.

Introduction of new rules where KANU members nominated candidates for Parliamentary and civic seats by queuing behind chosen candidates was passed amid strong protests. Critics argued that the system enabled party candidates to become MPs without being elected by secret ballot, and was both illegal and anti-constitutional, taking away the rights of the majority of voters.

The growing dissatisfaction with the financial and political mismanagement of the country under a party that did not allow any political opposition came to a head in 1990. The unexplained murder in February of the Minister for Foreign Affairs, Dr Robert Ouko, was followed a few months later by the death of an outspoken government critic, the Rev. Alexander Muge, in an accident. There were strong rumours of government involvement in both deaths.

Meanwhile, following the political turmoil in the Soviet Union and Eastern Europe, Kenya was pressured by Western donor countries to set up multi-party elections. Pro-democracy demonstrations in July and subsequent government crackdowns by its paramilitary security forces resulted in 20 deaths and led to the detentions without trial of Mr Raila Odinga (son of Oginga Odinga) and two former cabinet ministers, Mr Kenneth Matiba and Mr Charles Rubia. Later in the year the razing of shanty villages around Nairobi by the City Commission raised political temperatures.

**Multi-party elections:** KANU's answer to the widespread discontent was to set up a 19-man committee under the chairmanship of the Vice-President, Professor George Saitoti, to tour the country gathering the people's views. Recommendations included the immediate reintroduction of the multi-party system, the limitation of the presidential term of office to two terms of five years, the return of the secret ballot and the return of the security of tenure and the independence of the judiciary. Further pressure was exerted by the International Monetary Fund (IMF) in November 1991 when it suspended aid to encourage reform. Moi, however, replied to this by printing KSh 9 billion (US$250 million). His political campaigns seemed subsequently better funded, but the printing was not supported by reserves and caused economic chaos, with inflation increasing. Kenya is still suffering from the consequences of this act, and also from the resultant increase in crime levels.

In December 1992, the first multi-party elections for 25 years were held with three branches of the Forum for the Restoration of Democracy (FORD) in opposition. Using several blatant tactics to ensure success, KANU and Moi were re-elected, with FORD-Asili's Kenneth Matiba as Vice-President. Oginga Odinga, who was the candidate for FORD-Kenya, died in 1994 at the age of 82, having seen Moi in 1993 throw the IMF out of the country, effectively and controversially suspending foreign aid. However, the IMF was subsequently reinstated, releasing US$40 million in aid.

Kenya has long been surrounded by conflict: wars in Ethiopia, Sudan and Somalia, and bitter civil wars in Uganda and Rwanda. But, regardless of Kenya's turbulent politics since independence, the country has remained – in the eyes of the East Africans at least – a haven of peace.

**Left**, a truly multi-racial Kenya.

# A MODEL FOR AFRICA

The ever-present prophets of gloom predicted decline and decay in the years following Independence in 1963, but they were confounded when the new Government ushered in a period of sustained stability which, although far from trouble-free, brought far-reaching changes in Kenya's major industries and economic structure.

Changes were implemented most rapidly in agriculture. Before 1963, the large-scale farms in the "White Highlands" were in the hands of some 4,000 settler farmers and produced most of the grains, dairy and meat which fed a steadily increasing population. Then, as now, it was land which presented the thorniest political problems. Settlers who had carved their farms from persistent bush or empty plains, surviving drought, locusts, animal and plant disease, viewed the advance to independence with alarm and dismay. Handing over their hard-won land to appease political and social demands of either a colonial or an independent government was unthinkable. There was talk of a "scorched earth" policy, of abandonment. Production slumped.

**Systematic land transfers**: The turning point – and arguably the most significant pre-independence watershed – was a meeting in 1963, called by the Kenya National Farmers Union (KNFU) at Nakuru. Lord Delamere, son of one of the earliest and most influential settler pioneers, was chairman and sensibly invited Jomo Kenyatta, Kenya's first prime minister, to address the farmers.

Kenyatta used the occasion to proclaim his liberal policies and commitment to an orderly and fair redistribution and transfer of land. "Willing buyer, willing seller" was to be the criterion. This statement of the new government's respect for the sanctity of title restored confidence and a mammoth programme of land purchase started, funded largely by Britain.

Thousands of acres were involved in a new agricultural revolution. First to be bought out were the mixed farms which were split

into smallholdings for the purpose of settling African families. Within five years of Independence, more than 45,000 families had been settled and more than 2 million acres (800,000 hectares) were transferred to Africans, mainly in cooperative societies formed specially for the purpose.

The success produced more funds to extend the scheme to the larger farms. The big coffee and tea plantations remained intact, as shareholdings were often held overseas. But shares gradually passed into local hands and few of the large plantations today are owned entirely by outside interests.

Coffee and tea had long been vital export commodities and the new government encouraged development. Programmes to stimulate smallholder growing were introduced, and quickly a substantial proportion of total coffee and tea production came from cooperatives, producing high-quality tea and coffee crops. Kenya is now the world's third largest tea producer, after India and Sri Lanka.

Coffee has been Kenya's largest foreign exchange earner since the 1930s but, since the drop in global prices in 1990, it has fallen behind tourism and tea.

Concurrent with the acquisition of farms for settlement, many farms were purchased as units and left intact. The buyers in some instances were local companies, but mainly the farms were bought by individual Africans. Vast cattle ranches in the arid north were little sought after, however. The extensive style of livestock ranching held little attraction for new farmers in the early years. Many ranches remain under their longstanding settler ownership, while a few others have been bought by ultra-rich Continental Europeans and Middle East oil barons. Cattle and sheep production, despite vulnerability to drought, has risen, and a significant livestock surplus is exported to new markets in the Middle East and within Africa.

Kenya's favourable and diverse climate has allowed the horticultural industry to produce a wide variety of high-quality crops such as French beans, tomatoes, grapes, mangoes, bananas, pineapples, avocados, oranges and flowers which are exported to the expanding markets in Europe, Japan and elsewhere. The horticultural sector earns around 15 percent of Kenya's total agricultural income – over Kshs 2 billion in foreign exchange. Improved methods, involvement of the small farmers and increased air cargo space will further expand markets in North America, the Middle East, and emerging democracies in Eastern Europe and the former Soviet Union.

**Coffee boom:** In the mid-1970s an unprecedented high price for coffee brought a boom in a steady but unspectacular property market, and commercial constructions increased, as did sales and transfers. Many borrowers were also able to pay off loans and to dispense with the professional management demanded by the lenders.

But, as coffee prices subsided to more realistic levels, the property market declined and then stagnated, and many borrowers found that their revenue expectations had been over-optimistic. Subsequent business failures sparked a new boom for accountancy firms specialising in receivership.

This period coincided with the world recession and for Kenya a severe foreign exchange fall-back. Effective, though unpopular, measures were taken to stem the flow of imports generated by the coffee boom. Interest rates rose and curbs were imposed on spending. The aid donors rescheduled debt repayments. As a result, foreign reserves, which had fallen to a near-crisis level, rose again. As the recession was world-wide, tourism earnings dropped sharply and underlined an over-reliance on agricultural exports and fluctuations in world prices.

The uncertainty in agriculture was shared by the urban industrial community. Currency controls were introduced early, made necessary by the flight of capital immediately before and after Independence. But Jomo Kenyatta's liberal policies slowly restored business confidence, and investment from abroad gathered momentum. Concern over the repatriation of capital and dividends was allayed by the "Certificate of Approved Enterprise". This guaranteed foreign industrialists that, under the approval system, repatriation of capital and royalties was assured. Factories burgeoned and industrial areas expanded as a result.

The German Government was enlisted to form the Kenya Industrial Estates, which provide factories and production space for smaller businesses, together with financial advice and technical assistance. This plugged an import gap by industries producing a range of domestic items from tissue paper to zip fasteners, largely from local materials. There was a need to revise the Government's financial requirements and development goal in the 1990–91 financial year. The economy was coming under severe strain from the Gulf War, the soaring oil prices, the country's decreasing income from its principal export commodities such as coffee and tea, falling tourism earnings, and rising import costs.

In 1990 the World Bank organised meetings with donor countries in Paris. Kenya received pledges for aid of about US$1 billion over the following two years to offset the soaring current balance of payments deficit and the increasing burden of servicing external debts (which in March 1991 stood at around US$1 million). Some $8 billion pledged by multilateral and bilateral donors was also available to Kenya through the World Bank Special Programme for Assistance for Sub-Saharan Africa, and aid to Kenya was increased from $200 million to $300 million in 1991, with emphasis on export promotion, government divestiture of state corporations (parastatals), price decontrol, the development of the informal "jua kali" sector, education, health and population control.

Kenya launched a major export drive through relaxation of import tariffs and duties; export compensation and simplification of investment regulations; promotion of manufacturing under bond; re-organisation and strengthening of investment and export promotion bodies; and establishment of export promotion zones (epzs), to make Kenya a producer and exporter of processed goods rather than of primary products.

However, changes in the world political climate and the end of the Cold War caused Kenya to come under increasing pressure from foreign donors threatening to withhold foreign aid unless it held multi-party elections (*see previous chapter*). To comply, President Moi staged the elections, won, and then threw the IMF out of Kenya in 1993. Moi afterward reversed this bold expulsion, and donors released US$40 million.

**Automobiles and the "*Wa-benzi*"**: Limited motor vehicle production, through importing kits for local assembly, had been in existence for some time prior to the post coffee-boom recession. Restrictions on the import of saloon cars, however, gave added impetus to the assembly plant in Mombasa, operated by Associated Vehicle Assemblers (AVA) which builds pick-ups and panel vans for the local market. By the mid-1980s all these new vehicles were being assembled by AVA. The US giants General Motors and Firestone Tyres have also set up in Nairobi.

Registration of new vehicles in general declined steeply after the imposition of restrictions on imports. However, there is no apparent reduction of sleek Mercedes Benz cars, long the accepted symbol of position in

origin, and claims by Somalia to the area had lain dormant during the colonial era. Border claims are an endemic source of friction in Africa, the consequence of the arbitrary frontiers drawn by the colonial powers.

In Kenya, the guerrilla fighting dragged on and loss of life seemed interminable. Eventually the dispute was resolved at a meeting in Arusha, Tanzania, through the diplomacy and negotiation of Kenyatta himself. The possibility of oil lying beneath the vast desert wastes may have added impetus to the Somali claims for an otherwise empty and problematic area. However, although large reserves have apparently been discovered in Sudan, the quantities are not exploitable.

Kenyan society, where the monied elite are known as the *"Wa-benzi"*.

**Border wars**: Economic growth was slowed in the years immediately following Independence due to the border dispute with neighbouring Somalia, which led to a *shifta* (Somali rebels) war. Men of the Armed Forces and equipment were deployed for many months in the arid North Eastern Province. The cost was one which Kenya could ill afford. The Kenya-Somalia border cuts across an area inhabited by people of Somali

**Above**, a batch of freshly baked bread leaves Nairobi bakery.

Western aid, and the accompanying diplomacy, gave Kenya the foundation of an international community. The white population had always been European, predominantly British, but as the settler farmers were bought out and left, the social framework changed. Britain funded a large education programme, sending several hundred school teachers to Kenya, making a large contribution to the Harambee secondary schools. This, together with the Swedish-funded Kenya Science Teachers College and the Canadian-sponsored Kenya Technical Teachers College, has made Kenya self-reliant in qualified teachers.

**The communal Harambee principle:** The

Harambee ("all pull together") system may not be unique to Kenya, but was it endorsed by Jomo Kenyatta and is very successful in providing a source of capital and revenue for rural projects starved of funds.

The principle involves the public collection of funds from within the community, including urban-based relatives, at meetings presided over by a prominent personality. Since Kenyatta's days, the system has been extended to raise funds to build cattle dips, dams, and to provide water supplies, higher education establishments and other amenities. However, following growing abuses of the system, a 1990 report by the Vice-President, Professor George Saitoti, concluded

that, although the Harambee movement had played a pivotal role in Kenya's development, its function as a strategy for future development needed to be critically and urgently re-examined.

The argument was that Harambee undermines the importance of the function of planning, assessment and budgeting, and places undue pressure on political leaders, encouraging corruption because civil servants have to raise the Harambee money to meet their bosses' targets. Stricter auditing was to be instituted at all levels. Following the report, the President banned civil servants from presiding at Harambee meetings, then suspended the Harambee meetings completely. However, the Harambee Principle has since been reinstated and is functioning strongly.

Experts in a range of technologies were dispatched to Kenya by donor governments and by corporations which had decided to invest. The flow of capital and commercial activity required the back-up financial services of banks, insurance companies and finance houses – and growth in this sector also has been phenomenal.

At the time of Independence, there were four international banks operating in Kenya. Twenty years later, 12 banking institutions were licensed under the Banking Act, all incorporated in Kenya. Similar growth can also be found in non-bank financial institutions, and finance houses which provide long- and short-term credit. In 1963, there were only two, but by 1984 there were 43. A number of finance houses have since collapsed, necessitating tough controls on the licensing of new firms and stricter supervision of existing ones by the Central Bank.

**UN headquarters in Nairobi**: In the early 1970s, the United Nations established a UN headquarters in Africa, and Nairobi was chosen to house a new UN Environment Programme (UNEP). This decision was significant in that Geneva and Vienna, at that time, were the only cities outside New York in which UN headquarters were located.

UNEP moved into the newly completed Kenyatta Conference Centre, but was later transferred to a specially designed $30 million complex at Gigiri, which is some 10 miles (16 km) from the city centre and now houses United Nations Centre for Human Settlements (Habitat) and a number of UN agencies and programmes. UN activity has created a cosmopolitan community of 3,000 people requiring housing and possessing significant purchasing power.

**Medical contributions**: Out in the country, animal disease has for years preoccupied the minds and bank balances of stock farmers. East Coast fever, *trypanosomiasis* (sleeping sickness), red-water, *anaplasmosis* and the spectre of the terrible rinderpest which wiped out whole herds of cattle and decimated the buffalo populations in the 19th century, have commanded the attention of researchers for more than 50 years. Excellent work has been done by the Government Veterinary Laboratories at Kabete, and the establishment of a thriving livestock industry owes much to that organisation.

Nairobi has become an international centre for coordinating further research into killer diseases. The International Laboratory for Research on Animal Diseases (ILRAD), the International Centre of Insect Physiology and Ecology (ICIPE), and the International Livestock Centre for Africa (ILCA) which conducts the livestock productivity and "trypano-tolerance" programmes, all work to solve the problems of the loss or debilitation of valuable livestock.

**The Asian tradition**: The record of achievements in post-independence Kenya would be incomplete without recognition of the role of the Asian population. The word "population" is used rather than "community", since it comprises a spectrum of religions, cultures and castes found elsewhere only on the continent of Asia.

In the early years of Independence, Asians were affected by the "Africanisation" process, the rapid advancement of Kenyan African nationals. Those who remain – about 80,000 – are those who have acquired Kenyan citizenship and are well-established in business, or who possess British citizenship and have invested heavily in industry, transport and in financial services. They fill many vital roles in the economy and their contribution to industry and commerce is immense. Through their involvement in the welfare sector, Asians are also a mainstay of many charity institutions and programmes. Kenya's culture and economy are all the richer for the Asian presence, and there are many vital areas where Asian capital, expertise and hard work make a contribution immeasurable in terms of output.

**Modern-day tourism**: Few industries have blossomed as spectacularly as tourism. The introduction of package tours and the beach holiday have transformed the industry, which is now a major earner of foreign exchange. East Africa had long been a tourist destination only for the wealthy, Teddy Roosevelt having set the trend with a major safari in 1909. From then on, Kenya became known as the land for "safari", a Kiswahili word meaning journey. Tourists came essentially for big game hunting, and a few for

animal photography. Professional hunting at one time was an honourable profession, but fell into disrepute in the early 1970s. Abuses of the system, erosion of the ethics and just plain greed led to the cessation of hunting by government decree in May 1977.

The first game park lodge was built at Kilaguni in Tsavo West National Park in 1962, followed by Keekorok in the Maasai Mara National Reserve. Since then, a surge in construction has seen comfortable, well-equipped lodges built in almost every game park and reserve, supported by tented camps. The majority were built with private capital, though with the occasional co-investment of government. It is this capitalist enterprise,

with a modicum of state control, which has become the pattern of Kenya's economy since 1963 – and has arguably made it more successful than other African economies.

**The one million target**: Few people foresaw the explosion in tourist development after 1969. In that year, 275,000 visitors came to Kenya and tourist revenue was US$2 million. By 1984, nearly 400,000 visitors were recorded, with receipts from tourism provisionally put at around $15 million, the figures being adjusted for inflation over those years. In the mid-1980s, with long-haul tour operators bringing in wide-bodied aircraft, the targets were raised to 1 million. The

**Left**, Kenya Airways, the national flag carrier. **Above**, a day at the Nairobi race course.

introduction of luxury cruise ships to tourist destinations on the East African coast and the Indian Ocean islands greatly increased Kenya's share of the world tourist trade, and by the early 1990s some 14 luxury cruise ships a year were docking at Mombasa.

The stable environment, the profusion of wildlife and a friendly population all made Kenya an attractive destination, but the flow of tourists has faltered significantly five times since Independence: first, after the worldwide fuel crises resulting from the Arab-Israeli war of 1973; second, following the attempted coup d'état in August 1982 by the Kenyan Air Force; third, after the murder of a British tourist, Julie Ward, in the Maasai

greater than can be accommodated. There are good ecological reasons, however, for not expanding capacity to meet the demand. Animals may have become accustomed to a proliferation of vehicles which intrude daily, and they may ignore camera-laden tourists, many of whom show scant respect towards the animals they photograph; but there is evidence that prolonged exposure to such intrusions produces stress which affects the animals' breeding habits and behaviour.

Nowhere has the expansion of facilities for tourists been more evident than along the coast. The white beaches, unpolluted warm waters of the Indian Ocean, constant sunshine and relaxed freedoms have proved to

Mara Game Reserve in 1989; fourth, because of the possibility of instability due to the elections in 1992 and the currency crisis; and fifth, by reports that Somali refugees had been moving south. Nevertheless, tourism has continued to be a lucrative industry, Recent press reports of increased crime, particularly in the cities, is a further hindrance to the country.

**Beach holidays and safari tours**: Targets for visitors have also been affected by another factor. Although beach holidays have to some extent supplanted the game park safari tour in popularity, the number of people wishing to visit the major wildlife areas is

be irresistible to Europeans, with some towns being completely taken over at certain periods of the year.

There was a time when the coast was simply a haven for jaded Nairobi businessmen and up-country farmers. Hotels were few and far between, but today they abound on every beach, handling a two-weekly turnover of holidaymakers throughout the season. The investment has been colossal, and again much of the capital financing the hotel building programme was generated locally, with the rest originating abroad. The coffee boom yielded yet more cash to finance construction.

Some years ago, a few days at the coast would be tacked on to the end of a wildlife safari. Today the situation is reversed – a beach holiday may encompass a few days in a game park. The coast offers a wide range of holiday activities, and tourism has brought it an undreamed-of prosperity.

**A young nation, a growing population:** The liberal social and economic policies introduced by Jomo Kenyatta and pursued by his successor, Daniel arap Moi, have encouraged a steady expansion of the economy whilst satisfying many of the more urgent political problems which faced the newly independent state. There have been fewer setbacks than might reasonably have been

expected and there is no indication that the pattern may change.

The end of the Cold War has had some far-reaching consequences for developing countries; for one thing, they can no longer play off one superpower against the other for economic gain. In Africa, criticisms of government corruption and mismanagement have become more vocal. The World Bank and the International Monetary Fund argue that such corruption and mismanagement

**Left**, graduation day at Nairobi University. **Above**, Kenya's youths give a rousing salute to 28 years of independence.

are the main obstacles to increasing economic prosperity. In this regard, Kenya's economy has not been given a clean bill of health. By the mid-1990s inflation was running at over 30 percent and Moi's government was coming under increasing attack. The economy stands vulnerable to one major threat which lurks in the background, but one which is in the forefront of the minds of economic planners – that of a rapidly increasing population that has virtually doubled since Independence and may redouble by the turn of the century. A growing population may mean a growing labour pool, but it also means that the provision of goods and services must rise faster than the birth rate.

The great majority of the population is under 20 years old. Kenya has not escaped urban drift and consequent overemployment in unskilled sectors. Skilled workers are always in demand and the training programmes which have produced many skilled people to replace expatriates cannot satisfy the demand. On the other hand, there is underemployment in the rural areas and, if Kenya is to retain the ability to be self-sufficient in food, a reliable as well as an adequate workforce is essential to maintain the massive contribution which agriculture makes to the country's economy.

Positive efforts are being made to promote family planning, supported by government. It is vital that these succeed and that the explosive population growth, which is approaching 4 percent, is curbed. If it is not, industry and agriculture may be hard pressed to maintain present levels of supply and output, let alone expand. The Government's strong commitment to the provision of public services such as food and nutrition, education, health services, water and housing has greatly improved the country's standard of living. Infant mortality is declining and life expectancy has increased from 35 years in 1948 to the current 56 years.

With a population of 26 million and with one of the world's highest population growth rates, the Kenyan Government, through the National Council for Population and Development and with the help of voluntary organisations, is trying to educate its people on the need for family planning. The objective is to reduce the population growth rate to the desired level of around 3 percent by the year 2000. But it's a race against time.

Culturally, linguistically and geographically, Kenya is one of the most diverse countries in Africa. You can walk down the main street Nairobi and in 10 minutes you will pass people representing almost every major language stock in Africa and every other continent in the world – and they could all be Kenyan citizens.

To reconstruct the history of its various people is not easy, but the research of many scholars in the fields of archaeology, historical linguistics, oral traditions, Arabic and colonial records has resulted at least in a general idea of how the people arrived in Kenya.

Language is the most common factor in classifying different groups of people, partly because of the close correlation between language and culture, and also because a language can be described accurately and compared with others. This comparison has become a useful tool in reconstructing the history of non-literate peoples and is based on the principle that the more similar two languages are, the more closely the people are related historically.

Linguists have attempted to estimate the dates of language divergence, which usually occur at times of geographical separation. Migration patterns have been reconstructed and word borrowings from other languages have been used as evidence of contact between groups. Archaeology and oral tradition have also both helped in unravelling the intricate weave of Kenya's history.

There are no written sources in east Africa and so the work of linguists and archaeologists has a special importance. In the 1960s linguists devised a method of measuring not just the extent of the relationship between languages, but also the intervals between any changes in the language. Using their findings, the dates of population movements from north and south can be established, as well as the routes that were taken and the contacts that were made between the tribal

groups. About 30 different African tribes now live in Kenya, each with their own language.

The American linguist, J. Greenberg, has found four language groups in Africa and three of them are to be found in Kenya. Bantu, a language belonging to the Niger-Congo language group, is spoken by 65 percent of the Kenyan population, while Nilotic – a member of the Nilo-Saharan group of languages – is spoken by about 30 percent of the population. Cushitic, the only

Afro-Asiatic language, is spoken by only 3 percent of Kenyans. Khoisan is the fourth language group but it is no longer spoken in Kenya.

**The first immigrants:** There has been a long series of migrations which lasted until the 19th century. This was the ancestral influx of ethnic groups found in Kenya today.

The first immigrant wave was from Ethiopia – tall, lean nomadic peoples speaking Cushitic languages. They moved south from Lake Turkana, beginning sometime around 2000 BC. In addition to living off livestock, they possibly cultivated sorghum and made stone tools and vessels including bowls from

**Preceding pages:** traditional Luo warrior with hippo teeth horns and cowrie shell necklace. **Left,** Giriama flute player. **Right,** veiled Islamic women in Lamu with their *bui-bui* cloaks.

lava and pumice. Later, when rainfall began to decrease and the lake levels fell, these Southern Cushites restarted their migration in search of better grazing. They encountered little resistance from the indigenous people, whoever they were, and moved leisurely southwards all the way into central Tanzania.

Another group of pastoralists followed the trail of the Southern Cushites approximately 3,000 years ago. These were a group called the Yaaku, a tribe of Eastern Cushites, who occupied a large part of central Kenya for several centuries. Today they are represented by a small and little-known group called the Mukogodo who live near the forest

their territories and eventually occupied much of the rich highland area in western Kenya. Later this Kalenjin group developed into the present Kipsigis, Nandi, Marakwet, Tugen and other tribes. They were originally pastoralists, but also cultivated sorghum and finger millet.

A distinctive custom was the extraction of their lower incisor teeth, which is explained by current practitioners as necessary for the feeding of milk and medicines to victims of lockjaw. The Kalenjin also took up the practice of male and female circumcision from the Southern Cushites. The Kalenjin still live today mainly in the western highlands around Kitale, Kericho, Eldoret, the Uasin

of Mukogodo, northwest of Mount Kenya.

Over the next millennium, between 500 BC and AD 500, the roots of almost all of the present-day Kenyans spread in from all parts of the continent. A tide of Cushitic, Nilotic and Bantu groups arrived as inquisitive tourists and then stayed on, attracted by good farming and grazing land, and abundant water flowing from the forest-clad highlands around Mount Kenya.

**The Kalenjin group:** The ancestors of the present Kalenjin group, for instance, arrived from the area of the Nile Valley between 2,000 to 2,500 years ago. They began pushing the Southern Cushites and Yaaku out of

Gishu plateau and the Cherangani Hills. A related tribal group, the pastoral Pokot, occupy the drier lowlands north of Lake Baringo.

One other splinter group of Kalenjin-speaking people are the Okiek who, until very recently, were scattered in the mountain forest of central and western Kenya. These people, called the Dorobo by the Maasai, live by hunting and pot-making, and the gathering of wild plant foods and honey. Their origins are not known, but most likely, the Okiek are the product of interbreeding between the first Kalenjin immigrants and the ancient hunters. With a population of close to 2 million, the Kalenjin are the fourth largest group in Kenya today. Farming has largely replaced pastoralism as the mainstay of their economy, and much of Kenya's tea is produced in Kalenjin country.

**The Bantu:** About the time these Southern Nilotes were entering Kenya from the northwest, different groups of Bantu peoples were streaming in from the west and south. The movements of these iron-making farmers are still not known with any certainty, but their expansion, which began 2,000 years ago in southeastern Nigeria, was explosive. Today, Bantu speakers occupy a great deal of central, southern and eastern Africa.

In Kenya, they were influenced by the Mount Kenya, with the Kamba down in the southeast occupying hilly, drier country. Together, these highland Bantu produce most of Kenya's food and export cash crops, notably coffee and tea.

Another group of "lacustrine" Bantu, as the name implies, lives near a lake – in this case, Lake Victoria. These tribes, such as the numerous Luyha (about 2½ million), the Gusii (about 1 million) and the Kuria (100,000), have been influenced greatly by the Kalenjin and other Nilotic people from a long history of close contact and interaction, though not always a friendly one. They live to the east of the lake around the towns of Kisii, Bungoma and Kakamega and are fa-

Southern Cushites and Southern Nilotes and, in turn, influenced them. After complicated migrations, mixings and splittings, the Bantu only ended up at their present locations in the 19th century – and movements into new lands are still going on.

The main cluster is in central Kenya, comprising the Kikuyu (about 3½ million); the Kamba (about 2 million); the Meru (about 1 million); and many other sub-groups. They all live on rich farmland in the vicinity of

**Left**, schoolchildren in celebration dance. **Above**, school choir Independence anniversary serenade.

mous, or notorious, for their high birth rate.

There is no doubt that some Bantu groups were on the coast when early Arab traders arrived in the 8th century. These Arabs, together with Persian traders, came in dhows in search of ivory, slaves and skins and some settled in African villages close to the beach. They built in stone, using coral and lime, and introduced Islamic architecture and culture, eventually developing sizable townships such as Shanga, Gedi and Takwa. By the 14th century, a new civilization and language called Swahili were fully developed. Some think the name comes from the Arabic word sahel meaning "coast".

**The Swahili language:** The Swahili language, which is essentially Bantu, with an infusion of Arabic, Asian and European words, has become the *lingua franca* for about 60 million people in eastern Africa. But at the same time, Swahili culture has in effect faced away from the African hinterland towards the sea and countries of the East which gave the people their sense of identity, their religion and markets. Until Kenya's independence in 1963, the coastal strip was nominally under the authority of the Sultan of Zanzibar.

Another set of coastal Bantu, distinct from the Swahili mix, are the Mijikenda, made up of nine related tribes (Giriama, Kauma,

Boran-Galla drive south, but they held out; their descendants still occupy a long swath of land inland from the coast from the Tana River well down into Tanzania. No one knows for sure whether Shungwaya really existed, but it is mentioned frequently in the local oral traditions, in particular those of the Bajun sub-group of the Swahili.

Back in the dry north of Kenya, an Eastern Cushitic language group had developed from the original immigration into the area 2,000 years before. These were the *Sam* people, the name for some reason derived from their word for "nose". They were pastoralists and ranged out to occupy most of Kenya east of Lake Turkana, reaching to the

Chonyi, Jibana, Kambe, Ribe, Rabai, Duruma and Digo). They claim they originated from Shungwaya, which is thought to have been in southern Somalia on or near the coast. It was said to have been a kingdom, with a capital city of stone buildings, where people lived peacefully until the coming of the Galla marauders from the north.

These Oromo-speaking tribesmen had originally moved into southern Somalia in the 16th century, driving the previous occupants before them. They then continued as far south as the hinterland of Mombasa and are today they are known as the Orma people.

The Mijikenda were casualties of this

Lamu hinterland and then north into Somalia. Over time, these Sam have diversified into numerous sub-groups, such as the Rendille nomads and the Aweer or Boni hunter-gatherers of Lamu District. About 500,000 of their kin, the Somali, occupy most of northeastern Kenya, with another 4 million living in the neighbouring Republic of Somalia.

**The myth of the Hamites:** To outsiders, perhaps the best known of the peoples of East Africa are the Maasai. Like the Kalenjin, the ancestors of these proud cattle people came in from the Nile Valley. On arrival, they interacted with Eastern Cushites in the Lake

Turkana region, and it may have been from these people that the Maasai acquired many of their cultural and social traditions, including possibly the class system as well as injunctions against eating most wild game, fowl and fish.

Although there is little Eastern Cushitic influence on the Maasai or Maa language, the tendency among writers is to refer to both the Maasai and the "off-shoot" Samburu as "Nilo-Hamites", reflecting a recognition of Cushitic influence on them. An emerging recognition of Cushitic imprint on the peoples of Kenya, however, is somewhat embarrassing to African historians who have spent much time and effort trying to dispose of the

"Hamitic myth". This dates from the early part of this century, most explicitly propounded by C.G. Seligman who wrote: "The incoming Hamites were pastoral Caucasians, arriving wave after wave, better armed as well as quicker-witted than the dark agricultural Negroes."

The implication was that the "superior" Hamites introduced just about everything of value into Africa, bestowing the Caucasian civilisation on the backward locals.

**Far left**, Bok woman with pitcher. **Left**, Nubian elder in Nairobi. **Above**, Loita Hills Maasai woman bedecked with tribal jewellery.

With its racist connotations, the "Hamitic" tag is therefore usually replaced by the term "Cushitic". The Cushites did not, in fact, come from Caucasia as has always been asserted, but from the Ethiopian uplands, from where many east Africans originated. According to the most recent classification, they are not strictly "Nilo-Hamites" but South Nilotic (for example the Kalenjin) or East Nilotic (the Maasai and Turkana). The "pure" Nilotic tribes, like the Luo, are now called West Nilotic.

Like the Cushites before them, the Maasai maintained a southward migration and by the 14th century had occupied much of the Rift Valley and the adjacent highlands, extending into Tanzania. They became a large and powerful people, greatly feared for their predatory raids for women and cattle by their armies of young male warriors (*moran*). This lasted until the arrival of the British in Kenya, when Maasai power was largely broken and the tribe was moved off the rich highland areas to make way for colonial settlement.

Today they live in the southern part of Kenya and number about 250,000. Their cousins, the Samburu (75,000), are in the desert north and a third Maa speaking group, in a small sub-tribe called the Njemps, lives on the southern shore of Lake Baringo.

**Group affinity:** There is clearly some affinity or acculturation between the Maasai groups and the peoples previously referred to as "Hamites" – the Galla, or more correctly, the Oromo. Of these, there are about 30,000 Gabbra, a tribe of hardy camel nomads who roam the arid northern lands around the Chalbi Desert (over an area the size of Switzerland). About 75,000 of their cousins, the Boran, live to their east, ranging with their livestock well north into their original Ethiopian homeland and also south down as far as Isiolo.

The Oromo-speaking tribes, numbering about the same as the Gabbra, live along the Tana River in arid bush country and can often be seen driving herds close to the coast either to market or in search of pasture. The Sakuye are a small group of mainly camel-herding people who live to the east of Mount Marsabit. Some say that their name derives from the mountain, which in Oromo is called Saku. All these people have complicated cyclic generation-set systems which strictly control their social and economic life, although to some extent these are now breaking down with the intrusions of modern life.

**The Turkana:** At the time the Boran were destroying Shungwaya, the Turkana, a warlike cattle-herding people, began an invasion in the Maasai's Embasso Narok ("black lake") area, later "Rudolf" and now named after the Turkana people. They began pushing the Pokot, Rendille and Samburu out of the land west of the lake and by the mid-19th Century were rampaging around the southern and eastern shores, until they were finally subdued by *Pax Britannica* in the early part of the 20th century. Following droughts in the 1960s and 1970s, the Turkana have

resumed their expansive wandering and can be found both east of the lake and in Samburu country, mingling with the Eastern Nilotic relatives.

Finally, the remaining major tribal group in Kenya is the Nilotic Luo, numbering about 2.2 million and forming the third largest group after the Kikuyu and Luhya. Originally from the Bahr-al-Ghazal region of southern Sudan now occupied by the related Dinka and Nuer, the Luo began to move into western Kenya through Uganda in the early 16th century. Small groups pushed into western Kenya between 1520 and 1750, displacing or absorbing the resident Bantu

speakers. They then spread south around Lake Victoria to occupy and proliferate in their present Nyanza homelands.

In addition to this complex, indigenous African make-up of Kenya, there are a number of immigrant communities.

Some 40,000 Kenyans claim to be Arab, most of them are descendants of the early coastal traders but infused with African culture over generations. Many families still maintain contacts with Oman, the Yemen and Saudi Arabia.

Not so well-known or documented are the early arrival and settlement of the coast by people from India and Pakistan. Immigrants from Gujarat and Kutch in southwest India probably began settling in the coastal Afro-Arab trading towns as early as the 10th to 12th centuries, although there is no evidence that they mixed with the local population as the Arabs did. The Indian influence on Swahili culture is most evident in the architecture and artifacts.

**Asian arrivals:** Most of Kenya's present-day Asian community arrived in the 19th century as workmen on the British railroad or as small-scale businessmen. They number about 80,000 today and they are mostly settled in the larger towns and cities which bear the exotic stamp of their culture in mosques, temples, bazaars and suburbs of squat, pastel-coloured villas. The Asians have also prospered in all sectors of the country's economy.

There are also some 40,000 inhabitants of European descent, most of whom arrived in the late 19th or early 20th century from Britain, South Africa, Italy, Greece and elsewhere to establish farms in the rich highland areas. An additional community of about 40,000 European and American expatriates now live in Kenya, many of them employed on short-term contracts in commerce, the diplomatic corps, the United Nations and many other institutions.

The peoples of Kenya strive for harmony despite their tremendous diversity. But, although each group adds to the richness of the country's culture, difficult economic conditions cause pressures which can all too easily magnify the frictions that inevitably exist.

Left, an Okiek bride. Right, a beaded and braided member of the Samburu tribe. Note his traditional ivory earplugs.

Africa can be divided into a number of distinct zoological and botanical regions. In the north, along the Mediterranean and separated from the rest of the continent by the vast sterile expanse of the Sahara, the flora and fauna are predominantly European in character. Below this, the essential nature of Africa starts in an arid swath of desert and semi-desert: the Sahel extends from Cape Verde in the west to Cape Gardafui in the east, and is broken in two by the Nile and the Ethiopian highlands. The western and larger part is still the Sahara; the east is the "Horn of Africa". The Guinea Savanna, a band of deciduous woodland, separates both Sahara and Sahel from the tropical rain forests of West Africa and the Zaire (Congo) Basin.

In the same latitudes, on the eastern side of the continent are the East African highlands with their vast plains and folded ranges. Farther south, another band of deciduous woodland spans Africa almost from coast to coast; below that is the Kalahari Desert, the South African highveld grasslands; and eventually the Mediterranean-like tip of the Cape of Good Hope.

Each stratum of the continent has its distinctive fauna and flora and a shared range of species; but none of these zoological zones has stayed constant. With changes in the world's climate they have waxed and waned to an enormous degree. It is suggested, for instance, that no more than 20,000 years ago thick mountain forests may have extended from the Ethiopian highlands to the Cape of Good Hope in an uninterrupted belt. By the same argument of fluctuating climate, the arid zones were once far larger than now.

This background of mobility has characterised the nature of Kenya and determined its great faunal and floral richness. The country is a repository of species from all the zones. It contains representative sectors of the east coast forests, highland plains, savannas, montane forests and alpine areas, as well as remnants of lowland West African forest;

**Preceding pages: elephants bathed in warm evening light, Tsavo West; happiness is a wet wallow. Left, mother and cubs survey the Mara plains. Above, rhino grazes by a giant cactus.**

Kenya may be regarded as the complete zoological and botanical garden of Africa.

**Lion almost everywhere**: In this, the mammal predators, particularly the cats – lion, leopard and cheetah – are still relatively plentiful and have been driven out only where the land is intensively farmed. A special relationship seems to exist between man and lion, with these great tawny cats held almost in awe. They are often featured in heraldic devices all over the world, even in countries where they don't exist, an indica-

tion of just how deeply impressed they are in man's psyche, traditions and mythologies.

In Kenya, lions are found in all habitats from near desert to alpine – except closed forest and densely populated areas. They tend to prey on herbivores, upward from small gazelle to young elephants. Cattle are within the range of preferred prey, so there is little love lost between lion and rural man, especially since man himself figures in the diet from time to time. For this reason, as human populations increase, the lions are on their way out, perhaps ultimately with only the national parks and reserves to ensure the survival of the species in Kenya.

**Leopard, the survivor:** Understandably, the leopard is seen as the most wildly beautiful of all the big cats. Whereas lions symbolise regality among other attributes, the much smaller leopard has an image of unbridled ferocity. The species is the most catholic of cats, seen in much of Asia as well as in Africa. In Kenya, every habitat is home to the leopard, from forest through the declension of landscapes to desert.

The key to their astonishing success is the wide range of prey and carrion they eat. Leopards can – and do – kill animals up to medium-sized antelopes, but they are also able to live off minor prey such as rats and mice, which explains why leopards still hold

providing a memorable after-dinner story for a family of tourists by trying to break into their room. The following night, it called at one of the lodges, seized a waiter by the head and dragged him off. He was rescued later by his companion.

Leopards were heavily poached until recently when an international treaty banned all commerce in their fur. The trade ban has since helped the species recover, especially in areas where its population was reduced severely by the poaching activity.

**Cheetah, the fastest mammal:** Cheetahs, the fastest quadrupeds, are also found widely in Kenya, although they stay out of forest and all areas of dense vegetation, including the

out in areas of dense human settlement, long after other big mammals have been displaced. Regardless of how abundant leopards may be, they are not commonly seen. They are solitary and nocturnal, around only when tourists are asleep except where they have become "habituated" to people and vehicles in one or two habitats. They are seen sometimes in baited trees at forest lodges.

Like lions, however, they occasionally turn man-eater and their presence among people is never fully accepted. They are normally shot, but in one recent incident a man-eater was caught and released in Tsavo West National Park. It spent the first night

taller grasslands. Cheetahs are gazelle-hunting specialists, and their distribution is roughly related to the open dry range of the antelopes. They are particularly prone to competition from lions, leopards, hyenas and even smaller predators in the parks, so their long-term survival may be confined to the vast arid lands outside the protected areas. But contrary to such predictions, the species is holding its own and is still widespread in Kenya's range-lands.

The most specialized of the big African cats, they hunt by day using a technique which is only successful in relatively open unbroken terrain. Instead of using the stealth and brutal force of lions and leopards, cheetahs chase their victims for up to 600 yards (500 metres) before tripping them, seizing them by the throat and suffocating them. The flat-out sprint usually leaves the prey with no reserves to put up a fight.

**The elephant in conflict with man**: The elephant creates more environmental change than any other animal, with the exception of man. These giant herbivores may dig for water in dry country and make it available to other species; opening up bush and thickets, they provide passage for lesser beasts; and, in the extreme extension of their influence, they can turn dense woodland into open grassland, thereby replacing one complete

crease. In parallel, the most severe decline of elephants was recorded in the same period, and the trend is continuing. In 1925, 90 percent of Kenya's land area was elephant range. This fell to 71 percent in 1950 and to 23 percent in 1975. Today, it's less that 20 percent. As with the lion, perhaps more so, the future of this magnificent animal lies in the national parks where people cannot live.

**The threatened rhino**: Another great mammal fallen on hard times is the black rhino, the emblem of the Kenyan national parks. Unable to live among people, it has also lost ground throughout the century. More than half its 1925 territory was gone by 1950 and now its total range must be below 10 percent

set of plants and animals with another. It is scarcely surprising that such an efficient agent for change is often in head-on conflict with man. Elephants can co-exist with nomadic humans, but they can never co-exist in organised ranching, agriculture or forestry. Thus human increase and expansion can only come about at the expense of the elephant – a fact that has been evident throughout the 20th century. Between 1970 and 1980, Africa's human population rose by about 79 million in its most dramatic in-

of Kenya's land surface. The rhinos have valuable horns, a fact that accelerates the process of their disappearance. Money made from rhino horn – around $364 per pound ($800 per kilo) – is irresistible to the poor in rural Africa. The high price stems from the use of rhino horn in the Far East to reduce fever, and not as an aphrodisiac as maintained in Western mythology.

Again, the future of the species depends on an effective national park management. But perhaps the prognosis is already evident: 10 years ago, visitors to Kenya could be certain of seeing rhinos in the parks; today they would be lucky to do so.

**Left**, rutting impala vie for supremacy. **Above**, giraffes, which are common in the parks,

**Antelopes in abundance**: Unique in Kenya is the tiny *Adder's duiker*, of the antelope family, which lives in the Sokoke-Arabuko forest at the coast. It's a one-foot high (30-cm) cinnamon-coloured creature of deep shade, with curious white dappled brown stockings. Though relatively common in its habitat, the animal is unlikely to be seen unless the visitor has adequate time and boundless patience to sit, watch and wait.

A large species of rare antelope is *Hunter's hartebeest*, a long-faced, lugubrious looking animal with a red pelage, thought to be similar in appearance to the progenitor of the diverse hartebeest family. It's a relic species, probably numbering between

populations of both species in the natural forests high on the mountains. The *yellow-backed* is a creature of deep gloom and is seldom seen. Its stronghold in Kenya is the southwest Mau Forest Reserve, where travelling around is difficult. *Bongo* on the other hand, occur in both the Mount Kenya and the Aberdares national parks and, with a little luck, may be seen under floodlights at the water holes on both Mount Kenya and the Aberdares. *Roan* and *sable antelopes* occur in a few small pockets as hangovers from a time when the southern African deciduous woodlands spread well to the north. The *sable* can be seen in Shimba Hills National Reserve, close to Mombasa.

30,000 and 40,000, and does not occur naturally in any of the protected areas. A few were placed in Tsavo East National Park and apparently a small population has developed. But anyone wanting to find them should look in their natural habitat north of the Tana River towards the Somalia border.

Four other antelopes – *bongo, yellow-backed duiker, roan* and *sable* – are also relics of an age when their habitats were better established in Kenya. Both the *bongo* and the *duiker* are survivors from the time when western lowland forests covered large parts of the country. The retreat of this habitat, a few millennia ago, left behind isolated

Other herbivores – wildebeest, eland, oryx, hartebeest, gerenuk, Grant's and Thomson's gazelle, impala, buffalo, warthog, giraffe and zebra – are common in the national parks and are widely distributed elsewhere in the country. Topi and giant forest hog are more restricted in range. Hundreds of species of small carnivores, insectivores, rodents and bats may be seen all over the country but these, and an even larger host of reptiles, amphibians and insects, are largely invisible to the traveller unless specifically sought out.

**Creatures of the air**: This is not so with the birds, which are everywhere on view in

Kenya, and often strikingly so. More than 1,100 species are resident in the East African region, most of them in Kenya. The list is augmented during the European winter by several hundred migrant species.

Each part of Kenya has its distinctive bird fauna, although the majority of species are common throughout the country. Of these, some are closely associated with man. They include the *African kite*, a long-winged bird of prey; the *marabou stork*, a huge, long-legged bird that stands more than three feet (1 metre) in height and has a wingspan of nine feet (2.7 metres); and the *pied crow*, a typical crow with a large white bib. All three are scavengers which profit from man and large numbers of them roam in and around human settlements, looking for scraps

Some birds, like the *Sudan dioch* or *quelea*, are pests and they create much economic havoc. These small, brown, seed-eating birds associate with millions of their brethren, migrating in thick clouds along the rain belt as it moves seasonally across East Africa. They are partial to wheat and millet, and a single visitation of quelea has stripped many a farmer of his crop. Huge amounts of money are spent in trying to annihilate the species; a special section of the Ministry of Agriculture is devoted to the purpose.

Another pest of a lesser order is the *Indian house crow*. This bird, similar to the European jackdaw, was introduced from India to Mombasa and has spread up and down the coast. Wherever it has settled – always close to human settlements – it has all but annihilated the indigenous birds. There seems little hope of containing its proliferation, so the bird presents a major conservation problem.

Fortunately, the vast majority of birds live, if not quietly, then peacefully with man in the habitats he creates. Sunbirds, for instance, whose males are usually arrayed in rich metallic greens, blues, bronzes and reds, are attracted to the flowers of suburban gardens.

Starlings also specialize in iridescent blues. Representing them at many tourist lodges in the parks is the *superb starling* – a handsome species in shining blue topcoat and chestnut waistcoat. Still the pride of place among the starlings goes to the *golden-breasted* variety. This species of the arid

zones is bluey violet above, a lustrous yellow-gold below, and without doubt, a contender for the most beautiful bird in Africa.

Another bird, also of surpassing beauty, is *Narina's trogon*, from the deep shade of the forests. A shiny bottle green above and a delicate powder-puff pink below, it is a relative of the legendary quetzal of Central America whose name was given to Guatemala's currency. Sitting quietly among forest boles, these trogons are often overlooked. Yet by imitating their call – an alto "hoom-hoom" at regular intervals – they can be brought right up to the caller.

Yet another forest bird, which has taken to Nairobi's suburbia, is *Hartlaub's turaco*. A

pigeon-sized bird with a rather long, floppy tail, it is green and blue above and green below – a body colouring enough to make it a handsome species, but when it takes off, it surpasses itself with a spectacular crimson flash of flight feathers.

Among the air fauna is a multitude of weaver bird species, so named for the rough nests they weave. Most are gregarious; many adult males sport bright yellow colouring, which is sometimes seen in both sexes. One species, the *spot-backed* or village weaver, seems to deliberately seek out human habitation and establish its noisy, colourful nesting colonies in trees surrounded by huts.

One could walk, of course, like just about everyone else in Kenya. The nomads up north – the Samburu, the Turkana and so on – think nothing of a 25-mile (40-km) hike in a single day. In the past, joggers with a message in a cleft stick would cover up to 70 miles (110 km).

**Luxury camel safaris:** None of this is particularly recommended to visitors, but one exception, however, is to walk along with a camel train, a fully rigged safari operated by ex-hunters or ranchers on the fringe of the northern deserts around such places as Rumuruti.

These are marvellous expeditions, the best of them with a great retinue of staff, liveried in the red loincloths of the Samburu who carry spears in their hands. There may be a dozen camels, carrying everything from the morning coffee to the evening bath; plus the ex-white hunter, who knows the Latin name for every blade of grass, and a *cordon bleu* chef in the background organising the bush luncheon and a three-course campfire dinner in the evening.

A normal day begins with an early rise, around dawn, after a pot of tea has been served. There is no need for bed-making or tent-tidying, and all the chores are taken care of by the retinue. Those who wish can take a warm shower before sitting down to a full English breakfast served under an umbrella acacia, as chattering weaver birds alight on the table for bits of toast. Down below in the wide sandy *luggas* of Samburu country, the camels are getting up – rear ends first – making the most excruciating bleats and grunts of protest. Gradually they're loaded up, two or three of them saddled.

The camels carry a fly-camp, a canvas "Hilton" complete with such basic necessities as cans of Naivasha asparagus and red wine. The white wine will probably have gone ahead in the fridges which are transported in the main camp's trucks heading 15 or 20 miles (24–32 km) up river, ready for the trekkers to arrive the following day.

**Preceding pages:** going on a camel safari. <u>Left</u>, turn-of-the-century drawing satirises "The Great White Hunter". <u>Above</u>, hunting plains game.

Apart from the fridge, you won't want much during the trek. A running buffet is maintained through the day, with bottled beer or soda kept cool in canvas bags, stuffed with wet straw, swinging in the wind from the camel's loads.

Most people walk, plodding along the hard sand in the middle of the dry river beds or on the flat banks, where bright green grass is cropped short into lawns by Samburu goats and cattle. Alternatively, the camels can be ridden. First comes a back-arching balletic

movement as the animal gets up, followed by a sensuous backwards and forwards movements – almost a glide along. It's easy even for novices.

The trek normally stops around lunchtime. And afterwards, almost certainly, is a couple of hours' siesta, afternoon tea, and then maybe an expedition off the river course into the bush. It could be that the hunter has spotted kudu tracks, or signs of some other wildlife, possibly elephant. In that event it's like an old-fashioned hunt: two or three hours with the spoor, the African trackers leading and the gun-bearers following.

It could lead up to the animals, in which

case the climactic shot has to be with a camera, as unlicensed hunting is, of course, strictly banned. But the travellers may get to taste a haunch of impala, which is best when marinated for a week in wine and herbs, then stewed. It makes a delicious main course at dinner.

Whatever the food, the evening meal is always an event in the bush. Any operator who is any way sensitive to the needs of the visitors, particularly those on safari for the first time and more used to modern comforts, will try to make it something of an event. Visitors may be enjoying themselves thoroughly, perfectly at ease with wild Africa during the day, but as night falls and the

which are in fact ideal for independent safari purpose – high clearance, reliable air-cooled engines (if they're Volkswagens) with elevated, all-round vision for game spotting. They're good for almost all itineraries, except the rough and gullied eastern side of Lake Turkana. Even so, many locals use their own camper-buses and usually make it without trouble. One exceptional all-in safari is the "Turkana Bus", an enterprise of a greatly experienced local "bush-whacker", Dick Hedges. This takes all comers, but mostly youths, on an inexpensive ride up to Lake Turkana, with camp accommodation and food included.

**Rentals:** Cross-country vehicles are all

unfamiliar sounds come through the darkness some reassurance of civilisation is required to stop anxieties setting in.

**Package and independent safaris:** The most popular tourist transport is the ubiquitous **mini-bus** – the seven- or nine-seaters all tour operators use for rattling around the country on various permutations of the main safari circuits. Passengers can book for all-in tour packages, which include accommodation, meals, transport and so on. In addition, some firms run regular or even scheduled mini-bus safaris – like the United Touring Company's "Safaritrail" programme.

It's also possible to hire the mini-buses,

available for hire, at least in Nairobi, but they're expensive. Usually the rentals are sedans or small station wagons from scores of car hire firms, ranging from the multinationals like Avis and Hertz down to streetcorner garages. At the coast, the open and airy Minimoke is a popular hire.

Most first-time visitors to Kenya prefer to be "packaged", with a local and experienced driver-guide squiring them round unfamiliar country, although the straight run to Mombasa or the main safari routes are not too problematic even for drivers new to the country. Maps are adequate and the circuit roads reasonable, except perhaps in the bush, where someone is almost bound to help. But it's advisable, before driving off, to seek local advice about road conditions and any predictable hazards. The Automobile Association of Kenya (AA) is usually helpful.

Also, before camping out in the bush, take advice from locals or perhaps one of the tour firms which offer this more adventurous safari option. It's safe in established sites in the national parks and reserves since most of them provide water, cooking fuel and other basic facilities. It's also all right elsewhere in the country, where the chief menace is the friendly curiosity of children if the tents are parked anywhere near a village. Occasionally – very occasionally – there are reports of

cannot be duplicated by commercial firms.

The private guide will cost around $250 per person per day for a party of six, or around $1,000 a day for a single client. He will provide a comfortable cruising vehicle (more than one if necessary), backed up with a seven-ton truck which carries the staff and camping equipment. Each client or couple will have an insect-proof sleeping tent, a bath or shower tent, and the camp will have a large dining tent. Refrigerators are part of the equipment and cold drinks and ice are always available. The chefs turn out exquisite meals in the roughest of surroundings. (Put them in well-appointed kitchens and they would be utterly lost).

attacks on camps. But again, many locals have been camping out in the wilds for years without incident, except the positive and memorable that make after-dinner stories.

**Luxury safaris:** Some large firms provide deluxe safaris, and the best of the old safari style is still provided by ex-hunters who operate as family concerns. The success of a safari was and is determined by the personal relationship and rapport built up between client and guide, and this is something that

**Left**, these photo fiends have two willing subjects. **Above**, chasing giraffes, but only to shoot pictures.

Usually the lorry and camp staff will have preceded the clients to the appointed destination, so that it's all ready for them – cold drinks, hot baths, whatever – when they arrive after a long, dusty drive. Later, congenial company and a nightcap around the embers of the campfire combine to make the safari one of the most satisfying of all travel experiences.

**Individual itineraries:** Before any safari, the guide will have mapped out a rough itinerary to suit the client's needs. Applying his local knowledge he will try to ensure that, as far as possible, the client will be kept off the beaten tracks and regular circuits. Even in the parks and reserves, he will try to keep the tour private. Knowing the country well, he will often be able to take the visitor to rewarding places on private land or elsewhere – far from the formal sanctuaries. And he will be using his own campsites.

**Other transports:** Hitchhiking is not recommended, although plenty of youngsters do it, especially between Mombasa and Nairobi. Long-haul Kenyan drivers tend to be generous with lifts, unworried by the prospect of muggings and the like, which are rare, or at least rarely reported. Similarly, hikers are unlikely to be robbed or physically harmed.

It's not difficult to get around on regular transport, starting at the budget end of the

anything from short, squat buses to a moving chassis and superstructure with seats. There is only one common denominator for this extraordinarily motley collection of vehicles – they're always crammed to the gills. Eight-seaters carry 20; the *manamba* (conductor) swings from the rear door, and – as in the Nigerian cartoons – bodies fly off round every bend.

Where they're going is an enigma for the uninitiated but wherever it is, almost always, it's too fast. Most drivers suffer a total amnesia of the rules of the road – notably the speed limit – and operate with the guidance system of a suicidal bat. Sometimes the scenario is amusing but, too often, it's tragic. The hide-

options: the **country buses**. Cheap and cheerful, these can be an experience in themselves, with squawking chickens, maybe a goat on the roof-rack, and at least a houseful of possessions piled up to staggering heights. For some expatriates who have been in the country for years, the cranking, diesel-belching rural bus system is unthinkable, but the organised, methodical and persistent visitor may be happy with public transport. There are severable useful and usable routes, such as the one from Malindi up to Lamu – straightforward, but long, hot, crowded and bumpy depending on the state of the roads.

Then there are the **matatus**. These are

ous pile-ups of these matatus are legion. As may be gathered, they're not exactly recommended to visitors.

But the **train** is recommended. The overnight from Nairobi, at maybe 12 mph (20 km/h) for much of the way, is as sedate as in the old days of steam. Pre-book a first- or second-class *couchette*, since the journey from the capital is over-night, from 6 or 7pm arriving at the coast about 8am the following morning. The return trip has a similar timetable. A reasonable meal in the dining car relieves the possible tedium of gazing out of the window at Africa if it is a moonless night.

Kenya Railways operates 1,645 miles

(2,650 km) of line, mostly up-country – in much the same leisurely, well-serviced style as the coast trip – to Kisumu and Malaba on the Uganda border. The route is down and across the Rift Valley, then up the western scarp to the highest railhead in the Commonwealth, at around 9,000 feet (2,750 metres), near Timboroa. Then it's a fairly gentle run down to Lake Victoria.

A recent innovation there is the reopening of a **lake steamer** service – luxury in first-class – which connects the Kisumu terminus with Mwanza, one of the Tanzanian ports. From there, it's possible to board the old German-Tanganyika rail line to Dar es Salaam or Arusha for the Sergengeti, Ngoron-

The hub of the network is the national Wilson Airport in the southern suburbs of Nairobi. In the early 1970s, before the bite of world recession, this was the busiest in Africa, averaging 15,000 movements a month. Since most of these were during daylight hours, the momentum of take-off and landings built up to one every one and a half minutes. It has slackened a little now, but the flow of traffic is still frenetic, from hardly more than toy aircraft to executive Lear jets.

At least half a dozen companies charter chauffeured planes out of Wilson, some with branch operations in Mombasa and some running scheduled departures for places like Lamu. Visiting pilots might also be able to

goro and the rest of the Tanzanian "milk run" circuit of national parks.

**Light aircraft** provide another obviously up-market option for travelling around Kenya. Landing grounds are littered about the country. They're in all the main parks and reserves, normally close to the lodges or luxury tented camps which send small fleets of ground transport to meet the tourist air delivery. There are also strips close to townships, hamlets, ranches and large farms.

**Left**, a safari camping scene from the 1930s.
**Above**, camping on the "Ostrich Hill", otherwise known as Mount Kenya.

hire aircraft from the "Aero Club" in Nairobi, provided of course all the licensing meets local requirements. A further limited air option is with Kenya Airways' internal services to and from Nairobi, Mombasa, Malindi and Kisumu.

Any visitor to Kenya, however, can be sure that whatever mode of transport, and whatever their budget, the thrill of the first sight of wildlife will be a moment to remember. No matter how many television programmes on African wildlife you watch or how many zoos you visit, the enormity and freedom of these majestic animals in their own habitat is an overwhelming experience.

# A MEDLEY OF SPORTS

With fine and usually predictable weather, Kenya affords endless opportunities for the player, spectator and even the critic of sports. The country's enthusiasm for varied sporting activity is indicated by the existence of more than 40 different associations and management bodies which control a diversity of sports and pastimes, ranging from athletics to windsurfing.

**Athletic golds:** The athletes of Kenya, traditionally the source of Africa's finest middle-distance runners, won 17 Olympic track medals in the 20 years between 1964 (in Tokyo) and 1984 (in Los Angeles). That this record was achieved in only four Olympic appearances in that period says much about the calibre of Kenyan runners. (Kenya did not compete at the 1976 and 1980 Olympiads due to political boycotts being imposed). The 1988 Olympics in Seoul and the 1992 Olympics in Barcelona, however, brought Kenyan athletes their share of medals in the long-distance track events.

Kipchoge Keino, convincing winner of two Olympic golds – the 1500-metre and the 3000-metre steeplechase – was the runner who put Kenya firmly on the world's athletics map. His relaxed style and devastating finish won him a host of admirers and emulators on the tracks of Europe and America. No top-class athletics meet was complete without Keino, a running legend abroad as much as at home.

Keino's mantle fell upon Henry Rono, who in the 1970s held no less than four world athletics records. Rono was at his peak for the Montreal (1976) and Moscow (1980) Games, and will go down in history as the finest world record holder who *never* competed in the Olympics. Among his records was the 3000-metre steeplechase, a gruelling event at which Kenyans excel. The Olympic gold medals for this event at Mexico (1968), Munich (1972) and Los Angeles (1984), all went to Kenya.

In the World Cross Country Championships Kenya has always excelled and the

men's team succeeded in winning the event in 1994 for the ninth successive year.

Athletics does not receive the spectator support and following at home it deserves, and Kenya's athletes are often better known abroad. Many are snapped up by overseas universities and awarded sports scholarships with the result that much of their running is on foreign soil. But with the new stadium within the Nairobi City boundary and a massive new sports complex a short distance from the city, there is a revival of local athletics interest and activity. Kenya's first composition or "tartan" track has been in action since 1984. During the season, from May to October, there are frequent meets which afford an opportunity to see near world-class athletes in action.

**Home soccer**: While Kenya's athletes make sports headlines abroad, it is Association Football, or soccer, which commands the attention within Kenya. While never reaching the fervent support which accompanies the game in South America or Europe, soccer is played by thousands on any level ground with anything that reasonably represents a ball. Thousands of supporters cram the stadiums for the weekend league and cup matches, although – as elsewhere – over-exuberance from the crowds occasionally requires police intervention.

The Kenyan national team – the Harambee Stars – proved themselves in international competition within Africa by winning the East and Central Africa Challenge Cup three years in succession. The two top clubs, Gor Mahia and AFC Leopards, have each won inter-Africa cup competitions and are regarded with respect beyond the continent. Gor Mahia won the Nelson Mandela Cup in the Africa Cup Winners Tournament, and although no major trophies have been won in recent years, Kenya is a popular tour destination for European clubs, and local amateur teams acquit themselves with distinction against visiting professionals.

**Scenic golf:** It is unlikely that a visitor to Kenya will wish either to compete in an athletics meet or to play soccer, but golf is another matter. The world's largest participant sport claims a band of devotees who

**Preceding pages: basketball, a fast-growing sport in Kenya. Left, Kipchoge Keino returns home to his son with an Olympic Gold.**

will travel the globe in search of a new golfing experience. The golfer who extends his search to Kenya will find some superb scenic courses to choose from – at sea level all the way up to a course which boasts the highest tee in the Commonwealth, at over 7,800 feet (2,380 metres).

New arrivals in Nairobi, driving in from the airport, are often startled to see a golf course nestling within a nine-iron lob of the Parliament Buildings in the city centre. This is the Railway Course – once the Kenya Uganda Railway Course – and is the junior of three within the city limits. Royal Nairobi was built in 1906 and claims seniority. The retention of the "Royal" title is not the

tional expectations, there are no doubts that improvement in this area is a major feature of development planning.

New athletics stadiums will mean improved performance and more frequent participation in Kenya by international athletes, which will do much to foster interest among the young. On a social level, which embraces the vast majority of sports played, facilities are good and the standards high. The club is the focus of much sport; in Nairobi alone, there are more than 20 clubs which cater for one or more sporting activity.

The highlight of Kenya's golfing year is the Kenya Open Golf Championship in March. Played over the Muthaiga course, the

anomaly it may at first seem in an independent republic. The title was bestowed on the Nairobi Golf Club in 1935 by King George V and it is agreed universally, not only among the golfing community, that such an honour should not be discarded lightly. Muthaiga Golf Club boasts a championship course and, like Royal Nairobi, is within a 10-minute taxi ride of Nairobi's central hotels.

So, in general, sport is an important part of the Kenyan way of life in all areas of the country. Newspapers devote no less than two full pages to report and comment on local and overseas sporting events. Although facilities for some sports are below interna-

Kenya Open is part of the African Safari Circuit staged by the European Professional Golfers Association (PGA). The circuit embraces the Open Championships of Nigeria, Ivory Coast, Kenya and Zambia. Although the Kenya Open prize money does not match the large sums of money at stake in other parts of the world, the total purse of some $80,000 has been enough to persuade some eminent professionals to make the trip. In the past, players of the calibre and stature of Billy Casper, Doug Sanders, Seve Ballesteros, Tony Jacklin, Nick Faldo and Sandy Lyle have lent lustre to the field, together with a host of younger hopefuls, lesser known perhaps, but many of whom have gone on to higher and better things.

Visitors are welcome at all Kenya golf clubs. Green fees are moderate and caddies are always available. At the more popular and crowded courses, there are restrictions on visitors at weekends, but it's usually possible to play with members at those times. A round of golf on a Kenyan course can have diversions beyond the vagaries of directing the ball in the right direction. Exotic and sometimes noisy birdlife is profuse, and a number of clubs have local rules which may appear strange to those who play the game in more ordered climes. The course at Kisumu, on the shores of Lake Victoria, for example,

ings. Throughout the year, apart from a short break in August, horse racing is held every Sunday and on most public holidays at the Ngong Road Racecourse. The picturesque course is well patronised on racing days, and the standard of racing is high. Good quality breeding stock has been imported over many years and there is a flourishing bloodstock industry, with horses exported to other African countries. There is a tendency for horses to grow rather more "leggy" than their northern counterparts, but there is remarkable quality to be seen throughout the 300 or so horses in training.

Racing is run professionally, with stipendiary stewards and a qualified handicap-

has a local rule which always intrigues a visitor: "If a ball comes to rest in dangerous proximity to a hippopotamus or crocodile, another ball may be dropped at a safe distance, but no nearer the hole, without penalty." This rule, it must be said, is no joke – it has been invoked.

**The sport of kings:** The climate and open spaces provide limitless scope for a range of equestrian activities, the envy of those who perforce dwell in more constricted surround-

per and Kenya racing has rid itself of the slightly unsavoury reputation held some years ago. Run right-handed, the entire course is visible from the stands. With an eight-race card, the entrance fee also gives access to the stands and clubhouse. Catering and other facilities are splendid, and with both tote and bookmakers on hand to take care of the gambling urge, there can be few more enjoyable ways of spending a Sunday afternoon.

During the British winter, several professional jockeys enjoy a working holiday by riding in Nairobi. The legendary Lester Pigott has ridden the course, inevitably on a

**Left**, bowling green, **Nairobi Club. Above**, rugged action – Rugby Union clash under the Nairobi sun.

winner with his first ride, and has commented most favourably on the course and its facilities.

**Polo:** Polo has a small following but is played regularly at weekends on the Jamhuri Park ground, a short distance from the Nairobi city centre. Standards vary, with a few good players and a remarkable number of new players taking to the game. An international tournament is played annually. It attracts high handicap players from overseas, including the British royals. Ponies are always made available to visitors, who are warmly welcomed.

**Ball games:** Visitors will be struck by the emphasis on team games. Evenings and

It's a fact of sports life, and an acceptable one, that there are more urgent calls on development resources than games pitches. But it's also a fact that until a Kenyan hockey team can practise and compete regularly on the type of surface used in international competition, the enthusiasm and skill will never be enough to overcome that disadvantage. Nevertheless, hockey enthusiasm at a social level is widespread, and both sexes play.

**Competitive cricket:** Cricket, seen by many nations as a peculiarly British pastime, but which has been dominated by the awesomely powerful West Indian teams, has its place in Kenya's sporting calendar. It's fiercely competitive at times, with volatile

weekends see every sports ground occupied by hockey players, cricketers, soccer players and rugby men either playing a competitive match or practising. In the late 1960s Kenya held a high ranking in world hockey, but by 1984 had slumped to an Olympic 11th place.

While the world plays its international hockey on artificial "astroturf" surfaces, Kenya struggles on murram (hard-packed earth) surfaces, which are fast and true but dusty and slippery. Here is a classic example of the inherent skills and games-playing ability in the so-called Third World being wasted for want of facilities which match those in developed countries.

temperaments sometimes gaining the upper hand of reason. Watching a league match, the result of which may decide the destination of the trophy, is not for the faint hearted.

He who wrote "and umpire sits, and by decision more embroils the fray" – some ascribe this to Milton – could well have attended some of the more torrid Nairobi league or cup matches. The Kenya umpire or referee is as unfortunate as his counterparts elsewhere – seldom right, often friendless.

But Kenya cricket is not all controversy, although it is nonetheless keenly contested. Some notable cricketers have toured and coached, resulting in improved playing standards. More than a few players have gone overseas to England to make their mark in county cricket, a full-time professional occupation.

An afternoon spent watching cricket in the sylvan surroundings of Nairobi Club can be entertaining and rewarding. Should the cricket pall, a short stroll allows the watcher to view tennis, bowls or squash before returning to catch the last few overs, and before it's time to retire to the bar for social chitchat and a review of the day's events. Cricketers are social folk, and the services of any first-class player will be keenly sought to play for this or that side in an intensely competitive but sporting environment.

the blue water as the sails flutter and fill. Victims of the sudden gybe and wind shifts can be seen righting their craft before resuming the journey across the lagoon and back.

Wind-surfing acquires a new band of adherents every year. It's a sport not just for the adept, but something to be tried and enjoyed by anyone whose back can stand the strain. Tuition and board hire are available at virtually every hotel and beach resort, and a nucleus of windsurfing enthusiasts ply their hobby on the lakes and dams in up-country Kenya. The growth of the sport has been phenomenal, and Kenya with its year-round windsurfing capability is fast becoming a recognized international centre.

**Windsurfing:** The coast provides a whole range of sporting pastimes, together with sea level and sanity. Windsurfing has not bypassed the shores of the Indian Ocean. Already the venue for international windsurfing competitions, the Kenyan coast, with its constant breeze and comparatively placid and warm waters, is ideal for the sport.

Dappled waters of the sheltered lagoons and creeds are interlaced with windboards tacking, beating and running before the wind – a brilliant array of colour splashed across

**Left**, a cricket match, Nairobi Club. **Above**, Kenya archery enthusiast.

**Snorkelling and scuba diving:** The ability to swim a little, or more particularly to float, permits the less athletic to goggle. Simply by donning a glass mask, the wonders beneath the crystal-clear waters are revealed in all its brilliance. The shark-free coral gardens and inner reefs are a paradise of colour and movement – brilliant coral, fish and plant life combine in a spectacle no photograph can adequately reproduce.

The more experienced can scuba dive, spending longer periods underwater, but this is a pastime which requires practice and training. Scuba schools abound, all professionally run and offering first-rate equipment for hire. The Kenyan coast has achieved a reputation in scuba circles for the quality of its diving, and the sport competes with windsurfing for popularity and practice.

**Hotel sports:** Most coast hotels have tennis and squash courts. Mombasa and Nyali boast acceptable nine-hole golf courses, while Malindi on the north coast offers some rudimentary but enjoyable golf on its rough nine-hole course. Parasailing – an alarming activity involving elevation off the sands by means of a parachute towed behind a vehicle – is also an attractive pastime.

**Fast and furious rugby:** Tennis courts are full at weekends; squash is a rapidly growing sport and one in which Kenyan teams have

done well in international competition. An exciting brand of rugby football is played which involves a good deal of running and handling, and is a refreshing change from the over-coached and predictable stuff dished up by teams from the northern hemisphere.

An enterprising touring rugby team, the Watembezi Pacesetters, has made three trips to Dubai in the Gulf to play in the annual Dubai Sevens. Travelling under their own steam and financed by themselves, Watembezi headed a strong group of teams from outside the Gulf area, and although winning the overseas pool could not bring home the champion's trophy for a third year.

But the sheer enthusiasm and initiative of the young men who set off for foreign parts have done much for Kenya's sporting reputation beyond its borders. A popular touring destination for more and more teams of every persuasion, Kenya has enhanced its sporting prestige beyond the field of athletics. The depth of talent and ability is immense, and it can be predicted with some confidence that the international sports arenas will be all the richer for it.

So what does all this mean to those with sporting inclinations who visit Kenya? To what extent can they engage in a chosen sport or watch it?

The traditional welcome given to any visitor by Kenya is no less cordial to the sportsman. It is no less overwhelming and no less sincere. Sports people will find themselves at ease, with plenty to talk about and do.

Team games are usually played at weekends, with only a few midweek soccer and rugby matches played under floodlights. Public courts and grounds are rare but most clubs will gladly accept a visitor for temporary membership, with access to all sports facilities. Thus tennis, squash, badminton and bowls are easily available, and most clubs and hotels will boast a swimming pool. Rackets and clubs may be borrowed or hired, and unless a visitor is especially skilled or fussy about equipment, there is no need to bring it into the country.

A golf course can be found pretty well anywhere, but it's prudent to phone or visit a course to confirm there's no competition that day. Kenya caddies are a shrewd breed and, like their counterparts elsewhere, are anxious for their patrons to do well. When a caddie suggests a medium iron, listen to him even when a wood would seem to be in order. He will almost certainly be right.

There can be few countries in the world where it is possible to rise early, catch a trout in a highland stream, follow that with nine holes of golf before lunch (at which the trout caught earlier can be enjoyed), play tennis, watch cricket, soccer or rugby football and round off the day with a frame or two of snooker. Nobody with the least interest in sports could ever find Kenya boring.

<u>Left</u>, Mahmoud Abbas, one of Kenya's best known national goalkeepers – caught in the act. <u>Right</u>, soccer, the national sport.

# THE SAFARI RALLY

Every Easter, some of the world's finest rally drivers converge on Nairobi to face the multiple challenges of dust, mud, fatigue and diabolical roads in one of the world's greatest motoring events: the Safari Rally. Along with the rally crews come top mechanics, team managers, journalists, photographers and ordinary rally watchers who cannot resist the magic of the safari.

The event began simply enough. To celebrate the Coronation of Queen Elizabeth II in 1953, when Kenya, Uganda and Tanganyika had to be in standard (showroom) condition. Classification was by size or performance, so the rally quickly became a reliable indicator of which cars gave value for money.

So keen were the organisers to keep out the evils of professionalism that the first event gave class positions only and no winner was declared. No service crews were allowed; repairs had to be done by the participants themselves, although it was permitted to use a dealer's workshop en route. Route surveys were also virtually unknown in those early

were still under British rule, a competitive safari was planned on roads running throughout the three territories. Only ordinary vehicles were to be used. The instigators of the event had no idea then that the rally would be going strong three decades later, nor that it would become a classic event in the World championship calendar.

**Amateur days:** The original Coronation Safari caught the imagination of the East African public, attracting entries from farmers, garage owners, businessmen and safari specialists. No professional drivers took part in these early competitions, but the motor trade soon found the event irresistible, as the cars

days; so it was a case of "slam the door and the first one back is the winner".

The golden days of the Safari did not last long, for the event quickly became a victim of its own success. Professionalism began to creep in, and soon the Safari attracted the attention of the overseas motoring press. A few drivers from outside Kenya, Uganda and Tanganyika tackled the event on a purely amateur basis, particularly after the Safari was granted international status in 1957.

The trickle soon became a stream as major car manufacturers began to take a keen interest in the rally. By the 10th event in 1962, the East African Safari (as it was called then) attracted works participation from Sweden (Saab), England (Ford and the Rootes Group) and Australia (Ford) together with works support via a number of local dealers. Drivers included the legendary Erik Carlsson and his wife, Pat Moss. Rauno Aaltonen of Finland made the first of his many appearances that year and other visitors came from the United Kingdom, France, Australia and the United States.

Many works teams preferred to use the talent and experience of local residents, however, because knowledge of driving in East African conditions still counted for a great deal. The myth that only locals could win the Safari persisted for many years and

There is always the unpredictable factor of the weather. Depending on whether Easter falls early or late in the calendar year, the route can become downright treacherous. Local drivers have a definite edge when conditions are very bad.

**Changing face:** The character of the event has changed over the years; the problems of running the rally through Uganda and Tanzania, for example, have resulted in the Safari becoming a strictly Kenyan affair, and inclusion in the World Championship for "makes" also meant that the event had to lose some of its uniqueness in order to conform with the regulations emanating from Paris.

While some people lament this change in

it was not until 1972 that the "jinx" was broken with a victory by Hannu Mikkola and Gunnar Palm in a Ford Escort.

Nevertheless, the Safari remains one event which overseas drivers find extremely difficult to win. In its history, the rally has been won by locals on all but six occasions. Despite that, the world's top rally teams spend a small fortune to try to win the event and thereby reap international publicity.

**Preceding pages**: Safari Rally leader takes a flooded track at speed. **Left**, one of the earlier events when the Safari was just for fun. **Above**, prang in the bush.

character from the early glorious days, it would be quite impossible to turn back the clock. Most main roads around East Africa are now tarmac, so the cars inevitably have to go farther off the beaten track to find challenging conditions. And, of course, the cars themselves are faster, stronger and more highly developed for rallying.

Even then, the event has very rarely been won by a particular model of car on its first attempt. It seems that the winner at the Safari Rally also needs Lady Luck riding on his shoulder. But then, that's undoubtedly what makes the event so special for drivers and spectators alike.

Food and restaurants have changed a good deal in Kenya in just the past few years and "foodies" will not be disappointed. Before a visit to any Nairobi restaurant, try to take a quick trip to City Market. The quality and variety of vegetables and fruits in Kenya is usually a wonderful discovery for the first-time visitor. The market will prepare you for the limitless choice of foods – from asparagus to tree tomato – and is an ideal shopping place for picnics.

Your first day in Nairobi should allow you the time to select a place on your own for lunch as you explore the city. The *Norfolk Hotel* is an obvious choice. It looks like something out of Stratford-upon-Avon – clearly historic, dating back to the turn of the century and to the arrival of the first lordly settlers. The verandah features an *à la carte* menu of simple "international cuisine" with a special children's menu.

But it is the scenery and not the food that draws the crowds. Nairobi walks by as it has since 1904 when the mock-Tudor hotel was first constructed. As an historical watering hole, it has collected a fair share of tales of drunken settlers, movie stars and writers – a history surpassed only by the notorious *Muthaiga Club*. (The *Muthaiga Club* and other clubs in Nairobi and Mombasa are private, although big-name tour operators are getting clients in on the sly. Check with your tour operator for details.)

Lunchtime alternatives that will put you in the swing of Nairobi include the *Trattoria,* offering pasta favourites; *African Heritage*, a boutique and restaurant combination that serves very good local cuisine; and the *Thorn Tree* café in the New Stanley Hotel. A huge thorn tree acts as a bulletin board at this lively spot – requests are made for everything from overland ride sharing to camel stud services.

**Changing tastes:** It was the Arabs who started the cosmopolitan trend in local cuisine, sailing in with their dried fruits, rice, spices and expanding the diet of the coastal Swahilis. But it took centuries for this influence to spread inland, where people subsisted on a diet heavy in sorghum and millet, supplemented only by whatever fruits, roots and seeds they could find.

The arrival of the Portuguese in 1496 then changed all that, with the introduction of foods from newly discovered Brazil. Maize and bananas, pineapples, chillies, peppers, sweet potatoes and manioc were all brought in, most of them destined to become local staples. The Portuguese – clearly evangeli-

cal gardeners – also brought oranges, lemons and limes from China and India, as well as domestic pigs.

The British were next to influence eating and drinking habits in Kenya, importing new breeds of sheep, goats and cattle, together with the essentials of life like strawberries and asparagus. They planted high-quality coffee and taught their cooks how to make lumpy custard, as well as which way to serve the port with up-country "Njoro Stilton".

They also imported thousands of Indians to build the railway to Uganda, and with these immigrants came the curries, *chapatis* and *chutneys*, which are now as traditional a

**Preceding pages**: roasting meat in a nation of carnivores. **Left**, seafood specialities. **Above**, a traditional dish.

Sunday lunch in Kenya as roast beef is in Yorkshire.

Later, between and after the wars, the Continentals arrived with their spicy sausages and pastas. Perhaps through a recent influx of American expatriates, establishments for hamburgers, pizzas and fried chicken take-aways have also appeared in Nairobi.

Local beers have always been good value and wines are now quickly following. "White Cap" and "Tusker" are comparable to a lager and come in large and small bottles. "Premium" is the strongest of the Kenyan beers. In Nairobi at least, you can be guaranteed they will be served icy cold.

fading somewhat, but the food stays consistently superb. A visit here is more an evening out than a meal, starting in the upstairs bar with "nibbles" of maybe tiny fried prawns, coconut strips and banana crisps. For a more substantial starter, try silvered smoked trout with horseradish sauce, a mound of the minuscule Mombasa oysters, fish tartare or perhaps dried impala. For main, there are langouste (spiny lobsters), king crab claws, Malindi sole, or a mixture of the lot in a superb seafood casserole.

A restaurant which may be said to "absolutely ooze good taste" is *Alan Bobbé's Bistro* run by its namesake, for years the doyen of Kenyan restaurateurs. The bistro is "very

From Naivasha comes a good collection of wines. Although only a few years in the running, these wines are reliable and inexpensive. Lists of foreign wines are available at most restaurants and although expensive by Kenyan standards, they are still reasonable against big city prices.

In all, there are now more than 300 restaurants listed in the *Eating Out Guide to Kenya*, which is worth the investment for identifying the best of them.

**Superb seafood:** Right at the top is the *Tamarind*, in the National Bank Building off Harambee Avenue, the main street of government ministries. The sea-blue decor is

French; small and intimate" with music to match – soft Debussy and Chopin. The menu is handwritten, inscribed with Mr Bobbé's droll comments on the dishes and his moderately high prices. Much more reasonable is the lunchtime tariff for plates of seafish *meunière* or salads for well under the equivalent of $5.

More airily French, as the name indicates, is *Le Jardin de Paris* in the French Cultural Centre. It's impressionist Left Bank, with a Lautrec poster decor and a blackboard bistro-style menu of authentic food prepared under the supervision of a French chef.

At the *Red Bull*, there is less striving after

the Continental ambience in the decor, but its food is still genuinely Austrian-Swiss: crispy fried schnitzels, meats in winey sauces and a variety of *torten mitschlag.*

**Spicy hot restaurants:** Among numerous alternatives are Indian curry houses of varying quality scattered all over the city. The most distinctive of them are perhaps the *Safeer* or the three *Minar* restaurants which serve delicate Mughal cuisine. Originally created for the appetites of the rich and pampered Mughal rulers of northern India, the food here is unbelievably subtle, made from expensive ingredients like almonds, cashews, cream and exotic spices.

Even at the first try, Mughal food is highly always very popular, with the Norfolk's *Ibis Grill* as good as most of the top restaurants in the city. In cool, understated surrounding, diners (many of them locals) select from a fairly original menu of "nouvelle cuisine" dishes.

The Hilton's *Amboseli Grill* serves good food, though it is more tourist-oriented. *Le Château*, the main restaurant of Nairobi's Inter-Continental, offers elegant dining options from a varied menu of game and unusual seafood dishes, and some imaginative desserts. A resident band plays nightly.

**Nightlife:** The neon signs of the International Casino Complex light up the Nairobi sky each night. The area just beyond Mu-

acceptable to Western taste. Both the *Safeer* and the three *Minars* have similar menus and almost identical interiors, so choose the one closest to your hotel. Start with roasted *poppadoms* and move on to chicken kebabs (first marinated in spiced yogurt and grilled), followed by saucy dishes – mutton *rogongosh*, chicken *makharwallah* – and then *kulfi*, a rich, dense saffron-flavoured ice cream. It's easy to overdo it, so be careful with the sauces.

The grill rooms of the major hotels are not

**Left**, Kenya lobster arouses jaded palates. **Above**, disco at the *Carnivore* (Tamarind Group).

seum Hill offers two restaurants, the *Toona Tree* (casual with live bands) and *Galleria* (expensive), one disco (*Bubbles*), one private club (*Galileo*) and one all-night casino. The *Carnivore* is another good entertainment spot, with live bands every Wednesday, Friday and Sunday and a disco on Saturday. They pull in big names from all over Africa. The last Friday of the month features "Africa night" and once a year they host the famous "Carnival" – costumes are outrageous and the evening is not to be missed.

Other nightclubs include the *Florida* and *New Florida*. These feature disco music in smoke-filled rooms with many young girls who can give you a lot more than a good time. Men should beware.

For more subtle romance, the *Horseman* is the place where candlelight glints on the crystal and strawberries are dipped in chilled champagne. The restaurant, like a wayside Tudor inn, is about 10 miles (16 km) out in Karen, a suburb of garden estates and a centre for the horsey set. Rolf Schmidt, the polo-playing proprietor, is middle-European and so is the cuisine which is pricey but reliably excellent.

Another celebrated restaurant, entirely different in style, is on the same Langata Road to Karen but closer to town. This is the *Carnivore*, vast and immensely successful

**Up-country style:** Out of Nairobi on safari, the restaurant choices are few but, fortunately, the lodges offer bountiful food, even if the quality is variable. One of the best is the millionaires' holiday camp, the *Mount Kenya Safari Club*, which is widely known for its lunchtime buffets and for the seven-course evening extravaganzas.

Appetites sharpened in the mountain air will be honed back to normal by a free service lunch at the *Aberdare Country Club*. The *Outspan* also features a good lunchtime buffet, while dinners at the three treetop hotels – *Mountain Lodge*, the *Ark* and *Treetops* – are remarkably good, taking into consideration the difficulties of supply and

for a set menu of one great roast of meat after another – as much as you can eat of Molo lamb or skewered chickens, beef, impala or "Tommy" gazelle and *mbuzi* goat.

**Offerings from the Orient:** There are many Chinese restaurants in Nairobi and the food is good and fresh. *The Dragon Pearl* serves a good hot and sour soup. *The Bangkok* in the Rank Xerox building in Westlands offers spicy Thai food. Japanese restaurants now include the *Akasaka*, the *Shogun* and the *Japanese Club* located in Reinsurance Plaza. Korean cooking is available at the *Koreana* in Ken-India House on Loita Street and out on Thika Road at the *Safari Park Hotel*.

preparation. *Kentrout* is a bit off the beaten track but worth the effort. Their name says it all and they are very fresh.

Package tours afford travellers limited choice in dining out in such remote areas as the Maasai Mara. It's a question of whether or not the chef's "on form" the day you arrive at the tented camp. However, it's reliably "haute cuisine" at *Governor's Camp*, where the lunchtime buffet eaten *al fresco* in communication with unbeatable Nature in the Mara, is rapidly devastated by hordes of overseas visitors.

**A varied menu in Mombasa**: In striking contrast to the dry warmth of a Mara afternoon is the sticky and steamy air of Mombasa. Arriving at lunchtime at the airport is often like stepping fully clothed into a sauna. Food may be the last thing you will want until you've had a wash in the ocean or taken a nap on the beach. Then the choices for dining out in and around the Old Mombasa are legion: Chinese and Indian restaurants abound in town and some of the beach hotels offer unexpectedly ritzy grill rooms. There are even a few good restaurants, strictly for the locals, but which would interest the more adventurous tourists.

Elegant dining in town is offered at the *Capri*, a well-chilled, dimly-lit restaurant in Ambalal House, which not surprisingly specialises in fresh seafood. Downstairs, the international crowd mingles with well-heeled locals in the *Arcade Cafe*, which serves an inviting variety of Continental pastries, homemade ice cream and icy cold coffee.

The *Shehnai Restaurant* on Maungaro Street serves what could be described as "Mughal nouvelle cuisine", light northern Indian dishes eminently suited to the climate. The decor is elegantly Asiatic, with tall handcarved wooden chairs set around small tables topped with stiffly starched cloths. Ask for help in selecting from the menu as most dishes will be unfamiliar.

The standard meeting place for everyone in Mombasa is the verandah of the old *Castle Hotel*. Besides watching the busy street life, the low ramparts of the "Castle" offer light meals, and probably the best *samosas* in the country.

After a stroll around "Old Town" or Mombasa's bustling city market, you might stop into *Stephen's Bar*, a simple back-street dive which attracts just about everyone: backpackers, locals, up-market tourists and itinerant critics. They all go there for the home-cooked Goan food prepared by the manager's wife. Try the whole fish stuffed with the lady's blend of *masalas* and grilled over charcoal.

Even if dining is all "packaged" in the hotel holiday, you should try to escape for just one meal out at the *Tamarind*, a superb restaurant which can scarcely be equalled anywhere in the world. Moorish-styled, it is

set on a hill overlooking the old harbour, with the tables set out on the flower-filled terrace. It is basically a seafood restaurant, with the menu much the same as its namesake in Nairobi except, for some reason, the food always seems to taste better in Mombasa. The specialities of the house are many and varied: try lobster tamarind, fish tartare, prawns piri piri and coupe bahari, or just order oysters and Champagne and enjoy being alive.

Much less well-known, but good, is the *Seahaven* on the North Coast. Watch for its signs before Mtwapa Creek, off the main road on a mile of sandy track to a flower-covered inn. The place is run by Dolly Watts

and Roy Macharia, both of them generous with fine food garnished with flowers.

Farther down the road is *Le Pichet*, a busy outdoor seafood restaurant run by Mr and Mrs Willy Wainwiller – transplanted Belgians who oversee their domain with a certain degree of detachment. Don't expect to be courted, but do expect original food, like buttery tilapia in foil, wonderful prawns, and all sorts of lobster.

**Seafood by the seaside:** For a casual meal, visit *Au Joli Coin*, a seaside restaurant near the Severin Sea Lodge run by Rehana Bhaijee. Barely 20 feet (6 metres) from the ocean at high tide, the place offers noisy rock

<u>Left</u>, Kirinyaga restaurant, Mount Kenya Safari Club. <u>Above</u>, local exotic dish.

with simply prepared seafood. *Il Duetto* in the Nyali Golf Club offers good Italian food.

Sun-bleached Diani Beach on the South Coast has a few restaurants worth mentioning, in particular the classy *Ali Barbour's* set in a natural cave, offering a menu of interesting, if pricey dishes. Don't expect quantity but you will get quality. *Namad's* is infinitely variable – one day very good, the next day less so. But the setting is fun and the diners are usually interesting. The luxurious air-conditioned *Swahili Grill* in the Diani Reef Hotel is usually good; ask for flambé dishes here, or for the lobster and seafood fondue.

The atmosphere in the *Makaa Grill* at the

Africana Sea Lodge is much more laid-back. So is the menu which has a selection of highly original dishes mixing ideas from around the world with the best of local ingredients. The food is presented stunningly, and the experience of dining in the grill room is likely to be memorable – also, a little pricey.

At the opposite north end of the coast, just outside Malindi, is the *Umande Restaurant* for relaxed, homemade-type meals. The food is all prepared by Steve Nicholas, who manages to pour wine or liqueur into practically every dish. Try his special hot crab and the chocolate mousse.

Much more secluded is *Club Che Shale*, a quiet hideaway 12 miles (19 km) north of Malindi. Richard Burton was one of many great fans of Vanessa Anière's cooking. She makes imaginative use of ingredients such as seaweed with the freshly caught fish, which she fries, tempura-style, and serves with a variety of sauces.

**A last supper in Lamu:** Finally, Lamu, the most exotic place in Kenya, is an island where the ancient Swahili culture is mostly uncorrupted by incursions from the West or anywhere else. Unfortunately the restaurants aren't fantastic, though sometimes *Ghai's* on the waterfront can produce a really superb curry or delicious "tree" oysters, prized off half-submerged mangroves.

*Peponi's*, the one up-market hotel on the island at the village of Shela, could perhaps do better than it does, though at times it surprises clients with some really imaginative dishes. Actually, when the food supply and erratic water problems are considered, just getting a decent meal at all on Lamu is more than appreciated.

It's probably best to just wander through the streets, stopping for ice cream or yoghurt as the heat starts to shimmer on the dusty streets. Fresh juices are marvellous, notably the lip-puckering tamarind. Later in the day is the time for a thimbleful of black coffee topped with a pinch of ground ginger. Ask for a *kaimati*, a Swahili-style doughnut favoured with cardamon, or a hunk of sticky *halwa*, an Arab sweetmeat made with almonds and ghee.

**Children and food:** Kenya is a treat for children, and Kenyans in general are hospitable and welcoming to young visitors. You will find this very apparent at restaurants and never will you be turned away with kids tucked under your wings. Also, Kenyan restaurants are very reasonable by western standards and most restaurants have children's menus. A number of restaurants are semi-outdoor with either music or playgrounds to keep children entertained. In Nairobi, the two most popular are the *Toona Tree* at the International Casino and the *Carnivore*. In Mombasa, everything is very casual and it is easy to book early for children. The *Mombasa Beach Hotel* offers a water-slide near the snack bar.

**Left**, Arabian nights ambience in Mombasa. **Right**, a typical buffet repast.

# PLACES

The "state of the art" airport at Nairobi and the city itself have fairly advanced systems of living, working and taking care of visitors. But from there on, a safari in Kenya backtracks in time, following the spoor of millennia down to the origins of man around Lake Turkana.

The remains of times long past are evident all over the country. Immediately north of the capital, for instance, massive volcanoes that appeared after ancient geological upheavals have cracked and fallen in from top to bottom to form the Great Rift Valley. A sentinel Mount Kenya, with a small conceit of snow on the top, stands over the agricultural heartland of the country.

The Age of the Mammals – the "Pleistocene", as Teddy Roosevelt called it – is all over Kenya, but exemplified in over 40 national parks and game reserves, where the animals and pristine landscapes are entirely conserved.

Of these, the major spectacles are in the Maasai Mara National Reserve, seasonally inundated by the Serengeti migration of 2 million plains game; Amboseli, under Kilimanjaro; and Tsavo, immense and untrammelled wild-land almost down to the coast. In the north, high forested parkland is lit at night by the artificial moons of celebrated lodges like "Treetops", and beyond are more sanctuaries in Samburu country and along the Tana River. Again north, but in the Rift itself, is a skein of wild lakes: Naivasha; Elmenteita; Nakuru, rated the "greatest bird spectacle on earth"; Bogoria; Baringo; and ultimately the fabled "Jade Sea" of Turkana.

In the west, through Maasailand, are Lake Victoria and the subtropical homeland of the people of the Nile. And finally – although there's much more – 300 miles (480 km) of superb coastline, parts of it very little changed since Sindbad. Some isolated places – like Lamu – are still time-lapsed, appearing to exist almost entirely in the 18th century.

Mombasa, the coast pivot and main port, is more or less up-to-date, although the eastern dhow trading ambience persists. On either side, up and down the north and south coast, are fully modern, five-star beach resorts which can compete with any in the world.

**Preceding pages: Maasai Mara – hot-air balloon and impala with harem; anti-poaching patrol in Kenya's northern wilderness; Mount Kenya as seen from the lounge of the Safari Club; rafting on the waters off Tiwi. Left, rock climbing in Kenya.**

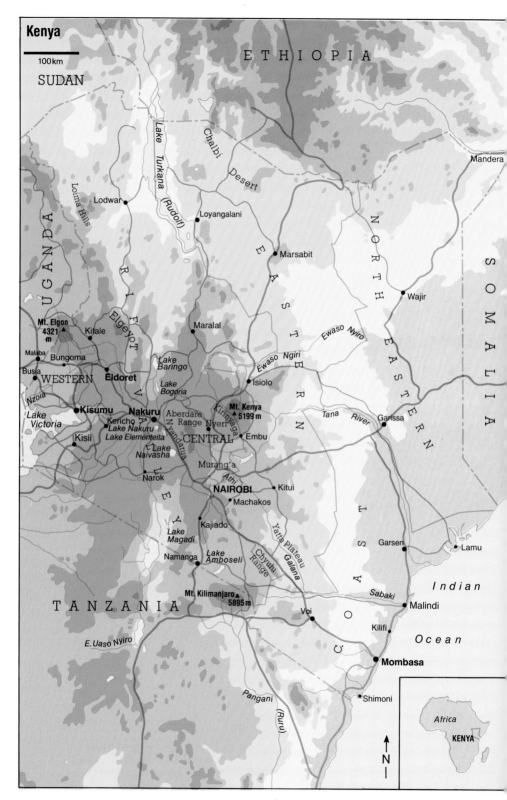

# Kenya

100km

SUDAN

ETHIOPIA

Mandera

Loima Hills

Lake Turkana (Rudolf)

Chalbi Desert

Lodwar

Loyangalani

Marsabit

NORTH EASTERN

SOMALIA

Wajir

UGANDA

RIFT

Mt. Elgon
4321 m

Kitale

Elgeyot

Maralal

Ewaso Nyiro

Malaba

Bungoma

Lake Baringo

Ewaso Ngiri

Busia

WESTERN

Eldoret

Lake Bogoria

Isiolo

EASTERN

Nzoia

Kisumu

Nakuru

Aberdare Range

Mt. Kenya
5199 m

Tana River

Garissa

Lake Victoria

Kericho

Lake Nakuru

Nyeri

Kisii

Lake Elementeita

Nyandarua

CENTRAL

Embu

Lake Naivasha

Murang'a

Narok

Athi

NAIROBI

Kitui

Machakos

VALLEY

Kajiado

Lake Magadi

Yatta Plateau

Garsen

Lamu

Namanga

Lake Amboseli

Chyulu Range

Galana

COAST

Sabaki

Indian

Mt. Kilimanjaro
5895 m

Voi

Malindi

TANZANIA

Kilifi

Ocean

E. Uaso Nyiro

Mombasa

Pangani (Ruru)

Shimoni

Africa

KENYA

N

150

# Kenya National Parks and National Reserves

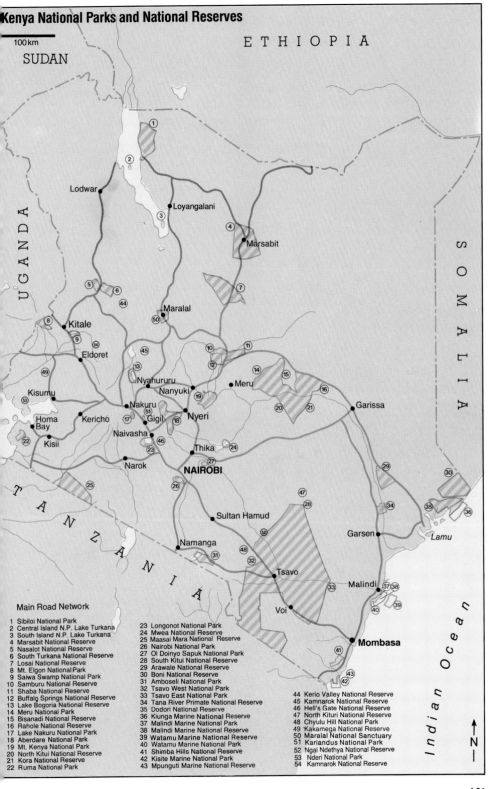

100 km

ETHIOPIA

SUDAN

UGANDA

SOMALIA

TANZANIA

Lodwar

Loyangalani

Marsabit

Maralal

Kitale

Eldoret

Nyahururu

Kisumu

Nanyuki

Meru

Homa Bay

Kericho

Gigil

Nyeri

Garissa

Kisii

Naivasha

Thika

Narok

NAIROBI

Sultan Hamud

Namanga

Tsavo

Garsen

Lamu

Voi

Malindi

Mombasa

Nakuru

Indian Ocean

N

## Main Road Network

1 Siboloi National Park
2 Central Island N.P. Lake Turkana
3 South Island N.P. Lake Turkana
4 Marsabit National Reserve
5 Nasalot National Reserve
6 South Turkana National Reserve
7 Losai National Reserve
8 Mt. Elgon National Park
9 Saiwa Swamp National Park
10 Samburu National Reserve
11 Shaba National Reserve
12 Buffalo Springs National Reserve
13 Lake Bogoria National Reserve
14 Meru National Park
15 Bisanadi National Reserve
16 Rahole National Reserve
17 Lake Nakuru National Park
18 Aberdare National Park
19 Mt. Kenya National Park
20 North Kitui National Reserve
21 Kora National Reserve
22 Ruma National Park

23 Longonot National Park
24 Mwea National Reserve
25 Maasai Mara National Reserve
26 Nairobi National Park
27 Ol Doinyo Sapuk National Park
28 South Kitui National Reserve
29 Arawale National Reserve
30 Boni National Reserve
31 Amboseli National Reserve
32 Tsavo West National Park
33 Tsavo East National Park
34 Tana River Primate National Reserve
35 Dodori National Reserve
36 Kiunga Marine National Reserve
37 Malindi Marine National Park
38 Malindi Marine National Reserve
39 Watamu Marine National Reserve
40 Watamu Marine National Park
41 Shimba Hills National Reserve
42 Kisite Marine National Park
43 Mpunguti Marine National Reserve

44 Kerio Valley National Reserve
45 Kamnarok National Reserve
46 Hell's Gate National Reserve
47 North Kituri National Reserve
48 Chyulu Hill National Park
49 Kakamega National Reserve
50 Maralal National Sanctuary
51 Kariandus National Park
52 Ngai Ndethya National Reserve
53 Nderi National Park
54 Kamnarok National Reserve

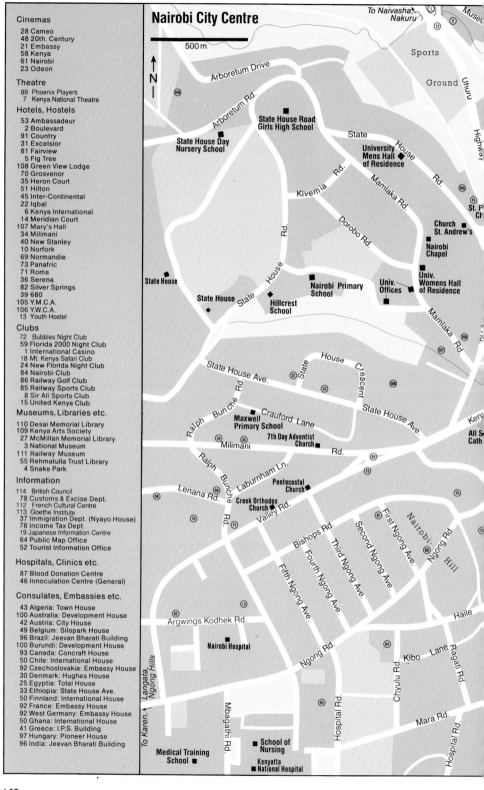

# Nairobi City Centre

500 m

N

To Naivasha, Nakuru

Museu

Sports

Ground

Uhuru

Highwa

Arboretum Drive

Arboretum Rd.

State House Road
Girls High School

State House Day
Nursery School

State

House

Rd.

University
Mens Hall
of Residence

Kivemia

Rd.

Mamlaka Rd.

St. P
Ch

Dorobo Rd.

Church
St. Andrew's

Nairobi
Chapel

State House

State

House

Rd.

State House

State

Hillcrest
School

Nairobi Primary
School

Univ.
Offices

Univ.
Womens Hall
of Residence

Mamlaka Rd.

State House Ave.

State

House

Crescent

State House Ave.

Ken

All Se
Cath

Ralph

Bunche

Rd.

Maxwell
Primary School

Crauford Lane

7th Day Adventist
Church

Milimani

Rd.

Ralph

Bunche

Rd.

Laburnham Ln.

Pentecostal
Church

Lenana Rd.

Creek Orthodox
Church

Valley Rd.

Bishops Rd.

First Ngong Ave.

Second Ngong Ave.

Third Ngong Ave.

Nairobi

Rd.

Ngong Rd.

Hill

Argwings Kodhek Rd.

Nairobi Hospital

Fifth Ngong Ave.

Fourth Ngong Ave.

Ngong Rd.

Chyulu Rd.

Kibo

Lane

Haile

Ragati Rd.

To Karen,

Langata,
Ngong Hills

Mbagathi Rd.

Medical Training
School

School of
Nursing

Kenyatta
National Hospital

Hospital Rd.

Mara Rd.

Hospital Rd.

## Cinemas
28 Cameo
48 20th. Century
21 Embassy
58 Kenya
61 Nairobi
23 Odeon

## Theatre
89 Phoenix Players
7 Kenya National Theatre

## Hotels, Hostels
53 Ambassadeur
2 Boulevard
91 Country
31 Excelsior
81 Fairview
5 Fig Tree
108 Green View Lodge
70 Grosvenor
35 Heron Court
51 Hilton
45 Inter-Continental
22 Iqbal
6 Kenya International
14 Meridian Court
107 Mary's Hall
34 Milimani
40 New Stanley
10 Norfork
69 Normandie
73 Panafric
71 Roma
36 Serena
82 Silver Springs
39 680
105 Y.M.C.A.
106 Y.W.C.A.
13 Youth Hostel

## Clubs
72 Bubbles Night Club
59 Florida 2000 Night Club
1 International Casino
18 Mt. Kenya Safari Club
24 New Florida Night Club
84 Nairobi Club
86 Railway Golf Club
85 Railway Sports Club
8 Sir Ali Sports Club
15 United Kenya Club

## Museums, Libraries etc.
110 Desai Memorial Library
109 Kenya Arts Society
27 McMillan Memorial Library
3 National Museum
111 Railway Museum
55 Rehmatulla Trust Library
4 Snake Park

## Information
114 British Council
78 Customs & Excise Dept.
112 French Cultural Centre
113 Goethe Institute
37 Immigration Dept. (Nyayo House)
78 Income Tax Dept.
19 Japanese Information Centre
64 Public Map Office
52 Tourist Information Office

## Hospitals, Clinics etc.
87 Blood Donation Centre
46 Innoculation Centre (General)

## Consulates, Embassies etc.
43 Algeria: Town House
100 Australia: Development House
42 Austria: City House
49 Belgium: Silopark House
96 Brazil: Jeevan Bharati Building
100 Burundi: Development House
93 Canada: Concraft House
50 Chile: International House
92 Czechoslovakia: Embassy House
30 Denmark: Hughes House
25 Egypta: Total House
33 Ethiopia: State House Ave.
50 Finnland: International House
92 France: Embassy House
92 West Germany: Embassy House
50 Ghana: International House
41 Greece: I.P.S. Building
97 Hungary: Pioneer House
96 India: Jeevan Bharati Building

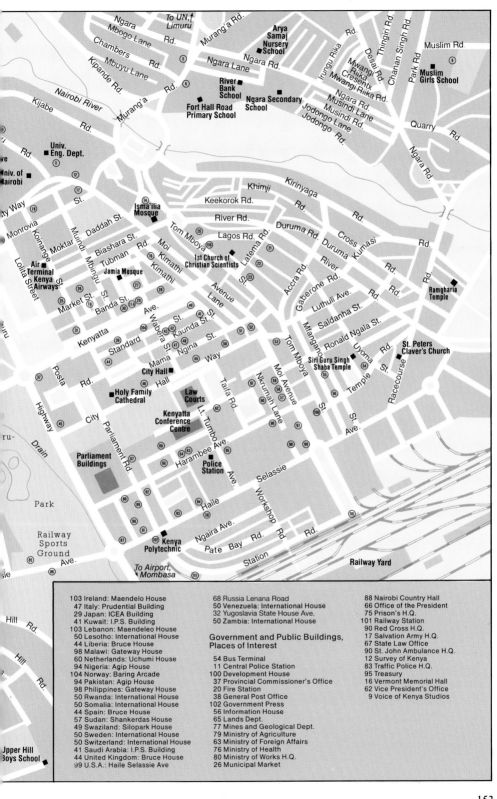

**Ngara** Mbogo Lane Rd.
To UN, Limuru
Murang'a Rd.
**Arya Samaj Nursery School**
Chambers Rd.
Ngara Lane
Ngara Rd.
Muslim Rd.
Kipande Rd.
Mbuyu Lane
Irungu Rika
Thingiri Rd.
Chanan Singh Rd.
Park Rd.
Nairobi River
Mwangi Riika Cresent
Mwangi Riika Rd.
Desai Rd.
**Muslim Girls School**
Kijabe Rd.
Murang'a Rd.
**River Bank School**
**Ngara Secondary School**
Ngara Rd.
Musindi Lane
Musindi Rd.
Jodongo Lane
Quarry Rd.
**Fort Hall Road Primary School**
Jodongo Rd.

**Univ. Eng. Dept.**
Ngara Rd.
**Univ. of Nairobi**
Khimji
Kirinyaga Rd.
ty Way St.
Keekorok Rd.
**Isma'ilia Mosque**
River Rd.
Rd.
Monrovia Moktar Daddah St.
Tom Mboya
Lagos Rd.
Duruma Rd.
Duruma Rd.
Cross
Kumasi
Rd.
Biashara St.
Rd.
Moi
**1st Church of Christian Scientists**
Latema Rd.
River
Rd.
Rd.
**Air Terminal Kenya Airways**
Tubman Rd.
Kimathi
Kimathi
Accra Rd.
Gaberone Rd.
**Ramgharia Temple**
Lolita Street
**Jamia Mosque**
Avenue Lane
St.
Luthuli Ave.
Market St.
Banda St.
Ave.
St.
Saldanha St.
Kenyatta
Wabera St.
Kaunda St.
St.
Tom Mboya
Ronald Ngala St.
**St. Peters Claver's Church**
Standard
Ngina St.
St.
**Siri Guru Singh Shaba Temple**
Uyoma Rd.
Racecourse
Posta Rd.
Mama Ngina Way
**City Hall**
City Hall
Moi Avenue
Temple St.
Highway
City
**Holy Family Cathedral**
**Law Courts**
Taifa Rd.
Nkruman Lane
Selassie Ave.
Drain
**Kenyatta Conference Centre**
Lt. Tumboa
Harambee Ave.
**Police Station**
**Parliament Buildings**
Parliament Rd.
Haile
Selassie
Workshop Rd.
Park
Ngaira Ave.
Pate Bay Rd.
Rd.
**Railway Sports Ground** Ave.
**Kenya Polytechnic**
Station
**Railway Yard**
To Airport, Mombasa

Hill Rd.

Hill

Upper Hill Boys School

# NAIROBI

In 1896, the British started work on a railway at the inception of their administration of an additional empire in East Africa. This was to run from Mombasa to Lake Victoria, eventually a distance of 620 miles (1,000 km).

For the first half of that distance, the construction was straightforward since the gradient was fairly gentle to the start of the highland massif at the centre of the country. Nor were there any particularly difficult physical barriers, apart from the intense heat of the Taru Desert and the unexpected intervention of a pair of lions, the well-known "Man-eaters of Tsavo", eating the builders.

After mile peg 327, more mundane but considerable problems presented themselves: up 30 miles (48 km) of steepish gradient to the eastern edge of the Rift Valley, and then down again 2,000 feet (600 metres) to the floor below. Across the Rift there was then the western Mau Escarpment to negotiate and afterwards a section of deeply ravined country to the lake.

With the main depot at Mombasa increasingly distant, the man in charge, Sir George Whitehouse, decided to move his headquarters as close as possible to the impending action against the Rift. This was to be on the flat-land where the Maasai grazed their cattle, close to a swamp and a small river they called *Enhare Nairobi* for its "cool" or "cold" water. A station was built there in 1899 which took up the Maasai name, ellipsed to "Nairobi".

**A shanty town grows up:** For Whitehouse and the engineers, the flats were ideal for laying out marshalling yards and there were nearby uplands which would make well-drained sites for staff housing. Probably no one was too concerned that the soil on the flats was mostly "black cotton" – thick and sludge-like, impervious to water – and thus good for dams and reservoirs. It expands when wet and contracts when

**Left**, Nairobi's urban sprawl.

dry and so is about the worst possible sub-strata for the foundations of a city.

But this was the way it would go. The government seat was moved up to the Nairobi rail centre; commercial enterprise followed and, within a short time, a shanty town had spread across the black cotton to create perennial problems of construction, drainage and sewage disposal for future developers.

Rats and plague presented several opportunities for shifting the original location but though the health authorities burned down the worst sections of the shanty town a couple of times, somehow Nairobi survived. Today, looking over the modern, green and spacious city, it's difficult to imagine its squalid and unhygienic beginnings.

The railway – the "Lunatic Line" – cost the British Government more than £5 million, an enormous sum in those days, and there was strong pressure to recover the outlay by making the enterprise profitable. The indigenous Africans were then not producing crops for cash, nor appeared likely to, so the only answer seemed to be the import of people to organise agriculture and "feed" the line with freight. To this end, the British Government solicited white farmers from elsewhere in the Empire with the promise of cheap land in Kenya.

The plan, though a good one, was advanced without sufficient forethought or preparation. Between 1903 and 1908 settlers poured in at a rate far beyond government expectations, claiming rights to the land which, though promised, was strictly not available. It wasn't the policy to "alienate" land already owned or occupied by the local tribes, but under the immigrant pressure, some of it had to be given out, including parcels in and around the northern fringes of Nairobi. This sequestration of native land was to cause the interracial resentment that lasted throughout the colonial period.

**The newcomers give a party:** The new settlers created a raffish, frontier-town atmosphere for Nairobi. The city also attracted wealthy international sportsmen from all over the western world to **Nairobi's modern skyline.**

hunt in Kenya's much vaunted game lands. They came and went, grounding Nairobi in tourism and, at the same time, spreading its reputation for wild living as characterised by some uninhibited parties, now coloured in legend. Street lights were shot out by revellers on horseback and pistols fired off at nothing in particular in the bar of the Norfolk Hotel. Wild games of improvised rugby wrecked the furniture, and anyone interfering, including the manager, was seen off the premises. On at least one occasion, a horse was ridden into the hotel dining room for a perhaps constricted but riotous steeplechase.

There were, of course, more serious goings-on in Nairobi. From the outset, the town was peopled by men of strong commercial instinct and it rapidly displaced the port of Mombasa as the country's centre of business. Indians – some of them ex-railway coolies – helped establish Nairobi's economic pre-eminence. Other immigrants, such as the "Brahmin"-style Allidina Visram family, ran an empire big enough to provide financial services to the fledgling East African governments and railway authorities.

Politically, the ground in and around Nairobi was divisive from the time the Government sought to attract white settlers. The Indians and Europeans competed with each other, but were blind or blinkered to rising African political aspirations. By 1922, under the leadership of an exceptionally wise Kikuyu, Harry Thuku, the city's African community was expressing its claims to ownership of the capital and country, with what would grow into an insistent clamour.

There was a hiatus, however, through World War II and the Mau Mau rebellion of 1952–56. These turned out, in retrospect, to be brief interludes during a phenomenally rapid process in which political power moved from immigrants to indigenous Africans.

All the same, the essential nature of Nairobi remained cosmopolitan. The city retains its disparate cultural elements and in architecture, for instance, this is readily apparent in the variety of religious buildings – mosques, temples, churches and synagogues. Perhaps less obvious are the communities themselves: Somalis, Arabs, Goans, Comoros islanders, Nubians, Indians, Pakistanis, Japanese and many European and North American nationals – all of whom live fairly easily among the majority Kenyan communities.

By far the most numerous of the city Africans are the Kikuyu, which is hardly surprising since Nairobi stands on the fringe of their traditional homelands on the mountain ridges running off the Aberdares. To a substantial degree, the city depends on them. Convoys of trucks and pick-ups stream in nightly from the rich farmlands in Kikuyu country, providing the bulk of the fresh produce that sustains the city.

Before Independence, Nairobi had already established itself as the commercial centre for all eastern Africa – Tanzania, Uganda, Rwanda, Burundi, southern Sudan and eastern Zaire. It was a dominance that caused some regional friction, but the power and influence of the Kenya capital was to double

The law courts.

and re-double after *Uhuru* (Freedom) through a monumental expansion of the national economy.

The country's business-oriented politics attracted almost a torrent of foreign assistance and investment. This and the location of Nairobi, at the point of intersection of the Great North Road (from Cape Town to Cairo) and the Trans-Africa Highway (from Mombasa to Lagos), has created a commercial, communications and diplomatic capital unequalled in Africa. Nairobi represents the first world headquarters of the United Nations in a developing country, and the UN Environment Program (UNEP) and other organisations of the world body are housed in a US$30 million complex 5 miles (8 km) north of the city centre.

**Population boom:** Nairobi's population has grown at a phenomenal rate in just 80-odd years since the tented labour lines of the founding railway. It is now crowded with more than a million people, with a projected explosion to a further 3 to 4 million by the year 2000.

This rocketing population growth is obviously a major concern to the government, with its tide of people leaving the land and pouring into the city in the hope – like Dick Whittington – of finding the streets paved with gold. For most of them, there is nothing but poverty since neither employment opportunities nor shelter could possibly be expanded fast enough.

It could conceivably turn into total chaos at some point in the future. For the present, Nairobi's centre and much of its immediate environs are still handsome but in need of a face-lift.

If anything, the city's trees and gardens are more a distinctive feature than its towering skyline. Yet when the railway arrived, the land was as bald as the proverbial coot, with no trees at all. This condition, clearly shown in the early photographs, was dealt with by Administrator John Ainsworth who immediately set about making avenues of Nairobi's dusty tracks.

He was in a hurry to bring some shade to the town and was not too particular

**Lillian Towers, Nairobi.**

158

# KIKUYU

## Central Bantu

About 40 percent of the population of Nairobi are Kikuyu, the largest of all Kenya's ethnic groups, with a total population of 4.6 million. They migrated to their present homeland in the Central Province districts of Nyeri (Gaki), Murang'a (Metumi) and Kiambu to the west and south of Mount Kenya (Kirinyaga) from Meru and Tharaka via Mbeere, Mwea and Ndia some 400 years ago. Formerly separate tribes, the Ndia and Gichugu of Kirinyaga District now count themselves as Kikuyu.

The legendary founder of the tribe was Gikuyu who was taken to the summit of Kirinyaga by the Divine Spirit *Ngei* and commanded to establish his homestead near a cluster of fig trees (*mikuyu*) in the centre of the country. There *Negi* had provided for him a beautiful wife, Mumbi. Their nine daughters originated the nine principal clans: Achera, Agachiku, Airimu, Ambui, Angare, Anjiru, Angui, Aithaga and Aitherandu. Tribal organisation is based on the family (*nyumba*). Several families live together to form a homestead (*mucii*) of a sub-group (*mbari*) and clan (*muhiriga*).

Circumcision was a prerequisite for youths to join the ranks of the warriors (*anake*) who graduated to the council of elders (*kiama*), a select few of whom composed the secret council known as *njama*. The *kiama* was responsible for the settlement of disputes. If the elders were baffled as to the guilt of those involved, the case was settled by the ordeal of the hot knife (innocence or guilt being determined by the extent of blistering on the tongue) or an oath taken on the feared seven-holed *githathi* stone.

The Kikuyu burned and cleared the dense forests of what is now known as the Central Province by purchase, blood-brotherhood and intermarriage with the original hunter-gatherer inhabitants, the now extinct Athi and Gumba and, especially in the southern Nyandarua Mountains, the Okiek.

Cattle, formerly a symbol of status and wealth, also provided hides for bedding, sandals and carrying straps. Sheep and goats (*mburi*) were, and still are, used for religious sacrifices. Permanent crops such as bananas, sugar cane, cassava (*nduma*) and yams (*gikwa*, pl. *ikwa*), together with beans, millet (*mwere*), maize, sweet potatoes, a variety of vegetables and black beans (*njahi*) form the dietary staples.

Kikuyu crafts include the making of pots for cooking, carrying and storing water, and storage of grains and other produce. Pots were also a major item of barter. Woven baskets (*kiondo*, pl. *ciondo*) are made from a variety of fibres, originally obtained from the bark of shrubs, now of sisal or synthetic thread. Flat trays (*gitaruru*, pl. *itaruru*) are woven with bark from *mugu, mugiyo* and *muthuthi* shrubs. Arrow-heads, spears, swords, cowbells, rattles and tweezers were manufactured by blacksmiths, who were believed to have magical abilities.

Livestock, agricultural produce and iron implements, tobacco, salt and ochre were bartered at regular local markets in the more populated areas of Kikuyuland. Important centres of trade were Karatina, Gacatha and Gakindu in Gaki, and Muthithi and Giitwa in Murang'a. Trading contacts were also maintained with the neighbouring Maasai, Kamba and Okiek. A caravan of women who transported goods for barter was protected by a middleman (*hinga*) related to the group with whom they traded.

A confrontation between tribal leaders, anxious to preserve their cultural heritage, and the European missionaries occurred in the late 1920s over the socio-religious rite of clitoridectomy (*irua*) of girls. Disaffection with the missionary stance led to the establishment of the Kikuyu Independent Schools Association (KISA) and the Kikuyu Karing'a (Pure) Educational Association out of which evolved the African Pentecostal Church and African Orthodox Church. These were based on the Old Testament which nowhere condemns female circumcision and indeed makes reference to polygamous marriages.

Perhaps better than any other tribe, the Kikuyu adapted to the challenge of Western culture, and displayed an early political awareness that resulted in the formation of the Kikuyu Association in 1920 which was soon drawing up a petition of grievances to present to the Chief Native commissioner. Forced labour, land expropriation, the *kipande* system and the lack of public services and educational opportunities were to remain the basic unresolved grievances until the end of the colonial era.

Today, on holdings consolidated from fragments of former tribal lands, progressive Kikuyu farmers have benefited greatly from modern agricultural practices and from the upgrading of their livestock, the accessible markets of Nairobi and a growing export trade. They have emerged as Kenya's major farming community and command much of the farmlands of the former White Highlands. They are also very active in business and commerce throughout the country. ∎

about the species. Knowledge of Kenya's indigenous trees was scant and no one was too certain if a species was quick or slow in growing.

Still, the plantings were prolific and the city today looks as if it might have been built in the middle of natural forest. The truth is that almost all the trees are immigrants; fast-growing blue gums, grevilleas and wattles from Australia. The jacaranda clouding the western suburbs in a lilac-mauve haze every October came from the Americas and the brilliant bougainvillea is also a transplant.

**Wildlife in a concrete jungle:** Even so, there is some indigenous forest within the city limits, which Ainsworth had reserved as a conservation measure. This was well outside the original township, but in due course was engulfed by the urban spread to the north. The ancient forest is now preserved as a recreational **City Park** – a distinction for Nairobi in an era of sprawling concrete jungles.

Yet the park is eclipsed in the south-eastern sector of the city, which incorporates 44 sq. miles (113 sq. km) of exclusive wildlife range. This is the unique aspect of Nairobi – a "wilderness suburb" populated exclusively by free-ranging wild animals. It happened because Nairobi was sited at the western edge of the Athi Plains which, together with the contiguous Kapiti Plains to the south and southeast, used to be inundated with fauna, not far removed from the spectacle in the Mara-Serengeti. The animals were all over the place in the early days so that night-watchmen in Nairobi's main thoroughfare, Government Road (now **Moi Avenue**), were supplied with lock-up sentry boxes. A soldier of the time, Colonel Richard Meinertzhagen, recalled at least two race meetings that were disrupted by rhinos.

The populace may not have wholly welcomed the intervention of wild animals in the centre of town but they seem to have recognised the cachet of having the wildlife around. Most of the Athi Plains were sold and settled, but a large

Giraffe towering over Nairobi National Park

area to the southwest of town was reserved as **Nairobi Commonage**. Only a few of the Somali herdsmen and their families were allowed to live there (as a reward for military service rendered to the Crown), but otherwise the land was left wild.

**Kenya's first national park:** The two world wars nearly cost the city its Commonage, which was taken over on both occasions as a weapons range. The wildlife took a hammering, and the land was gazetted a national park in 1945 – the first of what would become an extensive system of parks and reserves in Kenya, which has now grown to become an area the size of Switzerland, zoned for the protection of wild flora and fauna.

Buffaloes and rhinos were reintroduced into Nairobi Park so that the full range of the original Athi fauna was reformed. Today, a browsing rhino or sprinting cheetah is photographed against the backdrop of a modern city skyline; or, more nearly unique imagery, a lion kills a gazelle in the wild no more than a 15-minute drive from the portico of the Hilton.

This interface of the wild and the city was not without its problems, however. In 1980, a few lions left the park and took up temporary residence in the nearby suburb of Langata. They ate a cow and several horses and quickly reduced the popularity of evening jogging along the quiet suburban lanes. These incidents still happen – a leopard in the garden, a giraffe that stepped into a manhole, and so on – but, all in all, the lack of conflict between the park residents and people has been remarkable.

**Hard cash from tourism:** The National Park is now the principal attraction for visitors, who are well looked after in Nairobi. The city has had long experience of this, way back to the first station café and the Norfolk Hotel in 1904. Even before the British began formal administration of the country, it was recognised that hunting and viewing the wildlife would attract tourists and their hard currency. Money spent on safaris, together with revenue earned from ivory exports over the period immediately before and after the railway, accounted for more than half of the country's income.

It was from this early inception of tourism that Kenya – and Nairobi in particular – developed a special style in catering for visitors. First, this was presidential with professional "white" hunters providing ultimate luxury in the bush as well as the sport. The writings of Hemingway, Ruark and Karen Blixen made a legend of the safari experience. In due course, when the hunters were outnumbered by photographers and other "non-combatant" tourists, the safari system adapted to motorised game-viewing around the country's parks. With this expansion of the business came a variety of touring options from the original big-spender style to the ultra-economy of hitching a safari in the back of a truck.

This long evolution in Kenyan tourism has made Nairobi – with the possible exceptions of Cairo, Tangier and Marrakesh – the most traveller-oriented city in Africa. Served by more than 30 international airlines and providing di-

verse connections with all continents except South America, **Jomo Kenyatta International Airport**, 8 miles (13 km) from the city centre, is among the world's most modern in design.

**The pioneer Norfolk:** Visitors' accommodation in the city covers a more or less complete range of prices and standards, from do-it-yourself hostels and camping grounds to multinational (and some local) 5-star hotels. The old-timer of the industry is the **Norfolk**, scene of a 1980 bomb outrage after the Israeli rescue of hostages at Entebbe Airport in Uganda. The bomb exploded in the middle of a New Year's Eve party, with many people killed or maimed. The damaged section has since been rebuilt, preserving its Tudor-style black beams and white stucco.

The other historic hotel – built and rebuilt since its origins above a shop on the shanty town main street – is the **New Stanley**. Its **Thorn Tree** pavement café has been for years, and still is, the epicentre of safari-base Nairobi. Both the Norfolk and New Stanley are international class, as are the **Hilton, Inter-Continental, Serena, Pan-Afric** and **Six-Eighty**. The **Nairobi Safari Club** in Nairobi is one of the most recent of the prestigious hostelries in the capital, providing palatial suites for its membership of royalty, film actors and other luminaries.

**Major study centre:** Except for business, stopovers in Nairobi are normally short; it is essentially the point of departure for safaris. Nevertheless, there are a few places worth visiting in the city; the **National Museum** just outside the central grid is one of them. This houses one of the world's great zoological collections and, mainly through its connection with the Leakey family of palaeontologists, it has become a major international centre for the study of human evolution. A morning spent wandering through its halls, or in the snake park opposite, is well worthwhile.

Not far out of town, near the entrance to Nairobi National Park, is the **Bomas of Kenya**, a permanent exhibition of African dancing and culture, including a number of tribal village (or *boma*)

building styles. Troupes of professional dancers perform "traditional" dances every day in the *bomas* of this popular national park.

Other possible diversions in Nairobi include spectator sports, such as polo, show-jumping, rugby, soccer, hockey, athletics, boxing and cricket. Horse-racing at the Ngong Road track is meticulously organised by the Jockey Club of Kenya and even if you are down with the bookies, the superb garden setting of the course more than compensates. As for participant sports, there are numerous swimming pools, facilities to play tennis or squash, and nine championship-class golf courses in and around the city.

Special interests are also catered for, from skin-diving to Scottish dancing.

**Cuisine and conferences:** The main religions are well represented in Nairobi, down to innumerable splinter sects. Food is generally good and culturally varied in the city's main restaurants. Nightlife could not exactly be called Parisian, but there are cinemas (including drive-ins), a mini-theatre, two casinos, a few discotheques, and a number of fairly basic indigenous nightclubs.

In line with its evolution as an international centre in Africa, Nairobi offers some of the best major conference facilities on the continent. The **Kenyatta International Conference Centre** is the city landmark, a 27-storey round tower with a revolving restaurant on top. The building style is sober and modern, but "Africanised" with a tumbling riot of flowers and shrubs, and an amphitheatre supposedly designed in the shape of a traditional hut. The conference centre's architectural disparity somewhat reflects the city's own sharply contrasting facets and moods. The images are infinite – East and West, but essentially African.

In the centre of the high-rise glass and concrete, for instance, there may be a *moran*, a warrior of the Maasai, in an imperial red toga. He appears out of place and time, but only by the 80-odd years of the city's phenomenal growth. The speculation is: which is the anachronism – the *moran* or Nairobi?

Typical urb farm produ market.

# AMBOSELI AND TSAVO NATIONAL PARKS

Amboseli Park is everyone's picture of Kenya – a lion, elephant or cheetah; some wildlife or other against a background of Kilimanjaro. It's normally best around dawn. The animals are up and the mountain is exposed for an hour or so before pulling up a blanket of cloud. Alternatively, Amboseli at sundown tends to be as unreal as a pantomime set. In this, the mammals are down-stage, lit in strong pink and amber gels, with the mountain a gradually darkening cyclorama. Looming above that is perhaps a necklet ruff of cloud, the black hump of high moorlands and the speckled edge of the well-known snows of Kibo summit at 19,340 feet (5,895 metres).

The park is conceivably a day trip out of Nairobi, just over 300 miles (480 km) there and back on fast roads and tracks. But an overnight stay is obviously more sensible and, in any event, the intention for this safari is to keep going through Tsavo National Park down to the coast.

Out of the capital, the route is along Uhuru Highway on to the Mombasa Road, forking right at the airport turn-off and on 17 miles (27 km) or so to a landmark plume of white smoke. This is a cement works at **Athi River**, pronounced "Aathi" and named after a legendary tribe of dwarf Bushmen.

From there, a right turn heads south towards the Tanzanian border. The road is tarmac all the way through the dry heartland of the *il-Kaputiei* sub-divisions of the Maasai. Officially, the landscape is not as wild as it looks, all neatly parcelled and titled on government maps as private land in "group ranches", where wandering herdsmen are meant to settle and produce beef for the national economy. Only it hasn't happened, which is almost the entire story of the modernisation of the Maasai, and the land is still more or less open range back to the **Ngong Hills** and **Nairobi National Park**. An incidental track, rough but scenic, follows the old nomad route back towards the city.

Back on the main road, it's about 30 miles (48 km) from Athi, past **Isenya** mission and souvenir factory, to the town of **Kajiado**. This is the seat of local government of the southern half of Maasailand in Kenya, although some of the more perverse, reactionary Maasai would still give an edge of authority to the old men out in the bush, sitting as the *en-kiguena*, "Council of Elders". Other than administrate, the town trades a little and watches the trains go by, bringing up salt and soda ash from Lake Magadi to Nairobi.

Out of Kajiado, the country is hillier and bushier for 36 miles (58 km) up to the frontier township of **Namanga** at the foot of a soaring rock called *Oi-Doinyo Orok* the "Black Mountain". The word *orok* means "black" which stands for the good side of *Enkai*, the two-faced God of the Maasai. When the Almighty is displeased, the obverse is red.

**Israel's lost tribe?:** The mountain is thus a holy place and one of the tribal *laibons* – a kind of wizard-cum-Vicar-

**Preceding pages: Amboseli reserve elephant with Mount Kilimanjaro the background.**

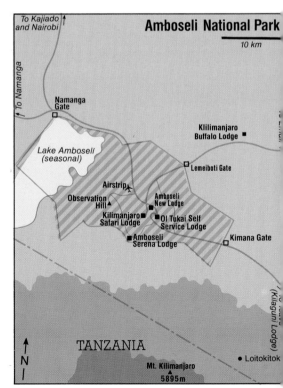

## Amboseli National Park

10 km

To Kajiado and Nairobi

To Namanga

Namanga Gate

Lake Amboseli (seasonal)

Klilimanjaro Buffalo Lodge

Lemeiboti Gate

Airstrip

Observation Hill

Amboseli New Lodge

Kilimanjaro Safari Lodge

Ol Tukai Self Service Lodge

Amboseli Serena Lodge

Kimana Gate

TANZANIA

Mt. Kilimanjaro 5895m

Loitokitok

(Kilaguni Lodge)

N

General – is buried up there somewhere. A cairn of stones at his head apparently positioned to attract a halo of the first rays of the morning sun supports the theory that the Maasai are natural aesthetes, derived from their origin as a lost tribe of Israel. (The theory is tentative, of course.)

Whatever else they are, the Maasai are in a position similar to that of the American Indians after 1862. They must either retreat to reservations that will barely support them or wash off the red paint, barber themselves of their great *shakos* of hair and join the modern, multi-tribal society. All of this may be contemplated by the Maasai, watching ex-warriors hustling beads and *simi* short-swords to tourists at **Namanga River Lodge**. Otherwise peaceful, the lodge is elderly and nostalgic like an old settler with fine gardens where you can share breakfast with weavers and starlings.

Neighbouring Tanzania is straight ahead a couple of miles, but the route into the park is a left turn just before the check-point. From there, it's about another 50 miles (80 km) to the centre at **Ol Tukai**, mostly across crumbly chalk flats devoid of vegetation apart from low tussocks of alkaline grass. Scientists rate the ecosystem as "fragile", and driving off the tracks is banned, although these are all over the place in a broad swath, like skid marks on an airport runway.

The drive skirts **Lake Amboseli**, which, except for an occasional puddle in the rainy season, is normally an empty, shallow pan of saline dust – boring too, if not for the frequent appearance of a phantom lake in a genuinely spectacular mirage. The entire horizon is liquid, with maybe a file of wildebeest reflected on itself in a shimmering mirror image.

**Green growth in a desert:** When this fades, on the approach to Ol Tukai, Kilimanjaro takes over the scenery but shows itself to be something more than mere decoration.

A run-off from the ice cap seeps through porous lava and surfaces at the

**bra and ldebeest nbling ross nboseli.**

centre of the park as springs and swamps. The desert is suddenly green, sprouting with wild palms, yellow-barked acacia and enough grass cover to attract the fauna for miles around. The Maasai until recently, were induced out of the core area by the government and the New York Zoological Society. The scheme, which was bitterly contested for a while, was to pump water from the springs to well across the park boundary. The area then excluded to the Maasai – the park proper – was reduced to a comparatively small 160 sq. miles (392 sq. km).

Other animals are resident, so that what amounts to an oasis around Ol Tukai becomes a compact, standing exhibition of wildlife. It's like a stage with a guaranteed performance by the animals, since the drama of a kill is a daily event, with a cheetah streaking after a "Tommy" gazelle or a young wildebeest, usually while it's still daylight with little or no masking cover.

Large family herds of elephant can be picked up miles away, again because of the open nature of the park. Rhino might also be sighted, perhaps in acacia woodlands bordering the springs, although there are only a few of them left after some protest spearing by the Maasai and a bout of poaching for the horn – to boost the Chinese libido and as a fever-reducing agent.

Buffaloes are permanently around the swamp areas, white cattle egrets alongside and cheeky ox-peckers riding on their shoulders or on the boss of a big bull. Other less common animals are gerenuk and fringe-eared oryx. There are two rare carnivores listed, the aardwolf and the wild dog, but the chances of coming across them are remote.

**Vultures and weavers:** The film *Where No Vultures Fly* was shot in Amboseli, which seems somewhat at odds with the location since six species of vultures – often airborne on hot up-drafts from the desert – are recorded in the park's checklist of above 420 birds. Of these, the kingfishers are perhaps the most photogenic, especially when caught making a strike, of course. The Taveta

The victor reaps his spoils.

golden weaver is the most distinctive, or emblematic, as it occurs only in this general region.

The most productive game runs are normally around the main swamps of **Enkongo Narok** ("black and benevolent") where icy water bubbles out of fissures in black lava. Another probably inevitable run is up the solitary **Observation Hill** or *Momiator*, up which one may be chased all the way – as has happened – by a mad, rogue elephant with ants up its trunk. Otherwise, the hill is for long-range lion spotting.

Accommodation is no problem at Amboseli, so long as it's pre-booked. At the last count: two first-class lodges in the Ol Tukai area, plus a self-service set of fairly basic rondavel huts, a cottage and a tented camp; another full service lodge on the eastern Kimana Gate out of the park; and one more, about 25 miles (40 km) away on the Loitokitok-Emali Road.

**Tsavo West:** For this safari, the route is out through **Kimana** village (about 80 miles/130km) on a straightish south-easterly line of dirt roads and tracks to **Tsavo West** and on to **Kilaguni**, the traditional centre of the park.

As a kind of general bearing, a high-folded range of green hills – an unusually vivid, velvety green – stays on the left but gets gradually closer. These are the **Chyulu Hills** and they may be among the world's youngest mountains, finally formed perhaps not more than a few hundred years ago. (None of the local geographers seems too precise). Anyway, it's obviously a comparatively recent happening since one of the spur ridges is still black, cauterised pumice. It's called *Shaitani* in Kiswahili, which means "devil".

Overall, the range is about 50 miles (80 km) long, 4 or 5 miles wide (7 km) and just over 7,000 feet (2,200 metres) at its highest point. A track on the crest is scenic over the expanse of Tsavo Park but is seldom used and becomes downright dangerous when the mists descend.

The Chyulus' principal contribution to tourism in the Tsavo area is to send

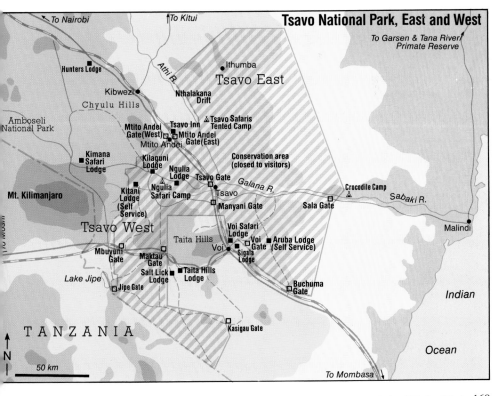

# MAASAI
### Western Nilotic

The pastoral Maasai (250,000), who share the Maa language from which their name derives, with the Samburu and Ilchamus in Kenya, and the Arusha and Baraguyu (or Wakwavi) in Tanzania, occupy the Narok and Kajiado districts of Kenya.

A fusion of Nilotic and Cushitic peoples, effected northwest of Lake Turkana a millennium ago, the Maasai ascended the escarpment out of the Kerio Valley and in the 17th century started to spread across the fertile grasslands of the Rift Valley and surrounding uplands. By the 19th century, they had established a reputation as powerful and ferocious people: their warrior bands raided deep into neighbouring territories and demanded tribute from the trade caravans. In the closing years of the 19th century, however, the Maasai herds were decimated by rinderpest and drought, and the once united people devastated by inter-sectional strife. The Government exploited the situation in treaties of 1904 and 1911 which moved the Maasai out of their northern grazing lands in Laikipia on the shoulder of Mount Kenya.

The basic economic and social unit is the *enkang*, a semi-permanent settlement of several families pasturing their stock together, perhaps 10 to 20 huts surrounded by a thorn fence. The warriors' *manyatta* (each containing 50 or more huts) are inhabited by all members of one age-set in a district.

Fresh and curdled milk, carried in long, decorated gourds, is the basic item in the Maasai diet. With it may be mixed blood tapped from the jugular vein of a bullock or cow. Sheep and goats are the principal source of meat; cattle are more only usually slaughtered for ceremonial purposes. The meat of wild animals is forbidden, except that of the eland and buffalo.

The Maasai people comprise five (some authorities claim seven) clans; *il-makesen, il-aiser, il-molelian, il-taarrosero* and *il-ikumai,* spread throughout Massailand. Each is further divided, distinguished by their cattle brands. Authority derives from the age-group and the age-set. Prior to circumcision, a natural leader or *olaiguenani* is

selected; he leads his age-group through a series of rituals until old age, sharing responsibility with a select few, of whom the ritual expert (*oloiboni*) is the ultimate authority.

Maasai youths are not circumcised until they are mature, and a new age-set is initiated together at regular intervals of 12 to 15 years. The young warriors (*ilmurran*) remain initiates for some time, using blunt arrows to hunt small birds which are stuffed and tied on to a frame to form a headdress. Taboos for warriors include prohibitions on drinking milk in their parents' huts and eating of meat in the *manyatta*. Oxen are slaughtered away from the settlements to provide meat for the warriors, who carry long-bladed stabbing spears and buffalo-hide shields with their black, red and white designs to mark their status. In their turn, the warrior age-set gives way to its juniors and graduates in a ceremony (*eunoto*) to senior status.

A warrior of repute without physical blemish and endowed with qualities of leadership is selected to "open the way" for the others of his age-set to be initiated. Once the new age-group leader (*olotuno*) is approved by the *oloiboni,* a bullock is slaughtered and the leader is the first to drink the blood from the animal's neck. The enclosure and ceremonial hut built specifically for the *eunoto* ceremony are known as *enkang o sinkira,* and it is here that the four days of rites are staged. Sitting on the same cowhide on which he was circumcised, each warrior has his head shaved by his mother. The freshly-shaved head is decorated with a mixture of ochre and fat. At the close of the ceremony the *olotuno* is invited to select a girl for a wife – signalling the next phase for the newly graduated senior warriors. After further rituals, the taboos on the handling and eating of milk and meat are lifted.

The life of the Maasai is conditioned by the constant quest for water and grazing. In more arid areas of Maasailand, livestock is moved seasonally to take advantage of undergrazed areas or new growth generated by localised rain. Cattle are culled and sold to the Meat Commission at Athi River or to buyers from Nairobi and Nakuru. Group ranching schemes in Kajiado have increased settlement of the Maasai, and in Narok, fertile wheatlands on the Mau are now being exploited by the Maasai themselves. ∎

underground rivers to a marvellous eruption at **Mzima Springs**, just south of Kilaguni. This is the park's centrepiece, a bubbling up of anything between 10 and 20 million litres of clear fresh water an hour. Part of the discharge is gravity fed to Mombasa, but most of it forms a natural jacuzzi for hippo. Prancing in the water like a fat ballet dancer on point, they can be observed from an elevated observation platform, or at snout level from the banks, or more dramatically through the windows of an underground bunker, with crocodiles, too.

Other animals water at the pools and the jungly riverine forest around them is festooned with monkeys and birds. It's a relatively small area, but Mzima is quintessential Tarzan country, bar the chimps.

More generally, Tsavo West is semi-arid, rough and wild. "More up and down than sideways", as Hemingway said about somewhere else. There are extensive plains but these are often broken up with monumental inselbergs of granite, looking like tombstones.

**Birds flock to the Ngulias:** Much of the northern sector of the park consists of a full mountain range, which is called the **Ngulias**, and many of the well-used game runs are laid out here. The range peaks at close to 6,000 feet (1,800 metres) and on the southern side drops a sheer 2,000 feet (600 metres) to the Tsavo River valley.

Apart from the permanent spectacle, the Ngulias stage a special nocturnal show towards the end of the year. Thousands of birds appear out of the nightly mountain mists. They are palearctic migrants, flying out from the European winter, and about 40 species have been recorded. More than 60,000 birds have been netted and ringed – some subsequently tracked back as far north as St Petersburg.

Most of the rest of Kenya's wildlife is resident in the park: about 60 mammals, 400 bird species and all the reptiles, including monitor lizard (similar to iguana) and crocodiles. Elephant may have built up to 8,000 animals and rhino to 100 or so after the terrible hammering

they took from poaching and drought during the 1970s.

**Animal refuge camps**: Among the rarer fauna are caracal, kudu and Hunter's hartebeest, trans-located to Tsavo East a few years ago from the Tana River area where they were in danger of extinction.

Also, somewhere in the park (west or east), is a herd of the bat-eared, pin-striped Grevy's zebra which were brought in as a refugee group from poachers in Samburu. They seem to have confounded the dismal prognosis of zoologists by surviving out of their normal desert habitat.

Generally, the game is scattered all over the park and is sometimes difficult to locate in the denser bush areas, or where the land is broken up with rocky hillocks, gullies and red sand drifts. But there are also set-piece concentrations – floodlit at night – at water holes and salt licks below the two principal lodges in Tsavo West: **Kilaguni**, the oldest animal observation post in Kenya and still exceptional, and **Ngulia**, more stylish

**eft, Maasai**
**arrior with**
**strich**
**eaddress.**
**ight,**
**rmite hill,**
**savo West**
**ational**
**ark.**

and cut out of rock. There are also two self-service lodges, one on the northern foothills of the Ngulias and the other below Mzima Springs at **Kitani**.

The safari from here on is variable. Most people have had enough of raw Africa by this time and head for the nearest access to the Mombasa Road for a sprint and a racing dive into the Indian Ocean – 150 miles (240 km) away or less, depending on the exit gate.

Tireless nature-lovers can continue their safari by crossing into Tsavo East. In any event, it has to be described as an integral part of Tsavo, despite its separate headquarters, field staffs and wardens (and entrance fees!).

On paper, the East is about two-thirds of the whole. But, sensibly, two-thirds of this tedious, flat and mostly empty bush country has been closed to humans for years. Two reasons have been advanced: that the area, being waterless, could endanger tourists and that the land needs to be left fallow for scientific study. To a non-scientist, this would seem to have about as much point as

making a national park of the Gobi Desert (strangely, a current project for the UN Environment Programme in Nairobi). In any case, there is some incursion in this "Conservation Area" by people on walking safaris out of a tented lodge near Mtito Andei.

With this exclusion, the sector ends up as a manageable 3,000-odd sq. miles (7,800 sq. km) in the form of an inverted triangle. The base line is the Galana River, with the "apex" well down towards the coast, about midway between Mombasa and Voi.

At one time, the triangle was a kind of elephant circus, a crossroads of migration routes from all directions. A story (denied by some) tells of one fabled herd, up to 1,000-strong, turning up there every other year.

**The great Tsavo controversy**: All this coming and going was fine – the park's main point of sale to tourists. But it all went wrong from the mid-1960s when the pressure of drought and poaching in the northwest had the effect of turning the elephant back into the park to mill

Cloud-covered Kilimanjaro from Tsavo West.

around and pound the vegetation into the dust. The larger thorn trees were also torn down, broken up and strewn across miles of the landscape: branches and twigs were bleached white in the sun like old bones in an unearthed graveyard. Other acacia were barked and shredded for their sap and even the monster baobabs were tusked and knocked over so that the starving elephant could get at any edible shoots on the top branches.

The "Great Tsavo Controversy" then started, mostly between David Sheldrick, warden of the park for 25 years, and a group of ecologists. Sheldrick assigned the role of Reaper to Nature, who would scythe off the right number of animals for a precise balance with the land's carrying capacity. The radicals wanted an instant cull, a scientific assassination "to prevent further irretrievable damage to the ecosystem".

As it turned out, only a few elephants were shot but drought and organised poaching affected a substantial cull. The ecologists left for Cambridge and

elsewhere, David Sheldrick died of a broken heart; ranking people in Nairobi got rich on the loot of Tsavo, and the park was left like a blitzed battlefield. It was in near total devastation in the mid-1970s and, although there has been recovery since, the park still has something of the "blasted heath" about it, especially in the southern and eastern sectors. There are also not too many elephant in these areas.

**Aruba Dam and Mudanda Rock**: There are still two or three worthwhile game runs in Tsavo East. One is in the area of the man-made **Aruba Dam**, which is in the intensely hot, waterless void of the Taru Desert. The dam which is 211 acres (85 hectares), dredged out the red dust to harvest a short, seasonal flow of the Voi River off the Taita Hills in the southwest. The run is in fact more of a saunter, except in years of exceptional rains, and usually stops altogether way ahead of its notional outlet at the ocean near Kilifi. The diversion of water to Aruba is nothing significant, but enough to last through the year as the

*Looking out from Voi Safari Lodge.*

# KAMBA
## Central Bantu

O ccupying the Machakos and Kitui districts of Eastern Province, the Akamba are a people of the plains. Numbering 1,725,600, they are the fourth largest ethnic group in Kenya. The Athi River, becoming the Sabaki in its lower reaches, is the most important drainage system in the district and there are the numerous granitic and volcanic hills, rising a thousand metres or more above the plains. The Kamba account for their presence in the region with the myth that Mulungu (God, the Supreme Being) projected the first Kamba man and woman on to Mount Nzaui. There they were joined by another couple from the centre of the earth. Mulungu sent rain, and the land was made fertile.

The Kamba probably migrated to their present homeland from Kilimanjaro in the south. Alternatively, they may have branched off from the northward drift of coastal Bantu peoples or come from an ancient dispersal centre among the Mijikenda. Hunters, who also kept some livestock and cultivated millets and sorghums, the Kamba would appear to have become established four centuries ago at Mbooni, taking advantage of the higher rainfall and fertile soils to adopt a more sedentary life as agriculturalists. From Mbooni they colonised the whole area.

Following early trade in arrow poisons and iron implements with the neighbouring Kikuyu, Embu, Tharaka and Mijikenda, a second stage in the growth of the Kamba economy began. By 1840, Kamba caravans loaded with ivory were reported almost weekly at the coast. In return they traded glass beads, copper, cotton fabrics, blue calico and salt for barter in the interior.

Masaku prophesied the coming of the railway – "the long snake" – and the Europeans who would divide the country. By this time Masaku's (corrupted to Machakos) was a thriving trading centre and it became the principal up-country administrative centre of the British. Masaku moved to Kangundo in disgust. However, with the arrival of the Europeans so soon after rinderpest had decimated their herds, and with the building of the Uganda Railway and the ban on further expansion into the vacant lands of Ulu and Yatta, the Kamba were soon in economic trouble. Their land was no longer fertile. Their refusal to reduce their herds and the erosion of the impoverished soil led to periods of famine.

Skilled craftsmen, the Kamba use iron and copper wire to make bracelets, necklets, arrowheads and spears. The same skills serve to create inlaid stools of exceptional beauty: their traditional art of woodcarving is the basis of a major handicraft industry. Clay cooking pots are made by the women, as are the finely plaited baskets (*chiondo*, pl. *vyondo*) made from fibres of the baobab and wild fig trees. Numerous kinds of animal traps are also constructed.

Smaller than the clans and sub-clans, the basic unit of Kamba life, economic, political, religious and social, is the extended family (*musyi*). Political power, as with many Bantu peoples in Kenya, used to lie in the hands of the elders (*atumia*) and in village or clan meetings (*mbai*). When this system was destroyed by the British at the end of the 19th century, appointed leaders such as Chief Kasina Ndoo were imposed.

Both sexes undergo circumcision. In some parts there are two stages: the "small" ceremony (*nzaikonini*) at four or five, and the "big" ceremony (*nzaikoneni*) at puberty with a long initiation and scarifying of chest and abdomen for purposes of ornamentation.

Traditional Kamba weapons are the bow and arrow, the long fighting sword (*simi*) and the throwing club. Kamba arrows are usually poisoned, with the iron point wrapped in a pliable piece of thin leather to keep the poison moist and to ensure optimum effectiveness as well as protection against accidental injury.

Unlike the Kikuyu, the Kamba were slow to adopt progressive agricultural methods, preferring to serve in the police and King's African Rifles. Drought and famine still plague the Kamba, especially in Kitui. Government and *Harambee* (self-help) water schemes and integrated development projects continue to be given priority. But the further desiccation of Kamba country (Ukambani) as a result of poor agricultural practices and deforestation arising from charcoal production continues to militate against successful economic development in the area. ∎

park's only permanent water hole. Occasionally it dries up, as in 1961, to the confusion of the resident wildlife.

Another safari run is around a distinctive piece of geology called **Mudanda Rock**, an isolated granite kopje north of Aruba. This is always worth checking out for game concentrations at seasonal drainage pools at the base. There could also be predators lurking in the poolside bush – and, if there are, a balcony ledge halfway up the rock provides a good overview of the action as the migrant herbivores move in.

Finally, the **Galana River** offers a scenic drive through what is left of a gallery forest, full of birds but not often a great deal of game, unless perhaps in the early morning or evening at watering time. The only certainty is the hippo and probably the crocodile. Here the rules can be bent. If you get out of the car, you're not really at much risk except in the evening when the hippo come out to graze. They tend towards lethal aggression if anyone gets between them and the water.

About midway on the run is an obvious stop at **Lugard's Falls**, named after the first British proconsul, Lord Lugard, who came up the Galana to take up governance of Uganda and to forget an unrequited love back in England. The falls are not all that grand, the main flow squeezed between a narrow crack in solid granite before cascading over a ballroom-size set of irregular steps. Below this are quieter pools at **Crocodile Point**, where the reptiles may or may not be at their appointed station.

Across the river and away in the distance is the sheer scarp of the **Yatta Plateau**, which is out of the way for most visitors and no more than a scenic statistic; one of the world's longest lava flows, squarish and straight for about 190 miles (300 km) from Sobo in south-east Tsavo almost up to Nairobi.

From the falls, it's possible to carry on down the Galana, going east to the **Sala Gate** – altogether about 65 miles (105 km) from Mtito Andei. A full service **Crocodile Camp** just outside the gate is a possible stopover, otherwise it's another 80 miles (130 km) on a sandy, sometimes boggy road to the coast at Malindi.

Other options are to stay in or around the park: a first-class lodge close to the southern gate at Voi; self-service bandas at Aruba; a wayside inn at Mtito Andei; and the Tsavo Safari Camp close to the border of the Conservation Area.

But Tsavo East was entirely a diversion from the original safari, so it's necessary to backtrack to the west and Kilaguni. From there, the selected route is 70 or 80 miles (120 km) south-east through the park to the **Maktau Gate** on the main Taveta-Voi Road. It's not a particularly interesting track, but has the advantage of leading out to the Hilton Hotel's private game sanctuary and twin lodges close to the **Taita Hills**. They are both odd to look at, but provide standard international comfort: one a village of huts on stilts overlooking a waterhole; the other a Tyrolean fortress.

Without the Hilton diversion, Maktau to Voi is about 25 miles (40km). Bypassing Voi, it's another 94 miles (151 km) on fast tarmac to Mombasa.

eft,
akamba
rrow
endor.
ight,
arabou
tork.

# MAASAI MARA NATIONAL RESERVE

In terms of statistics, Barnum & Bailey were never close. The "greatest show" has to be the Serengeti-Mara: a company of 3 million animals, a parade ring and arena 2,000 miles (3,200 km) round and a nonstop spectacle over a year, every year for the past 2 million years.

At the last count, there were 1.4 million wildebeests in the main cavalcade, 550,000 gazelles, 200,000 zebras, 64,000 impalas – and so on down the checklist of East African grazers and browsers. These are the moving herds of "The Migration".

Among the standing arena acts are territorial lions, black-maned lions, prides of 40 or more, and Jackman and Scott's "Marsh Lion". Plenty of other cats abound. Wild dogs give rare performances of relay chases and savage kills on the run, and hyenas, as they hunt, belie their image as the sneaky scavenger. In all, there are 95 separate mammals, amphibians and other reptiles, plus 485 aerial species, not counting bats, the tsetse and other insects.

**A circus and its clowns**: In this extraordinary natural circus, the wildebeest or gnu is regarded as the clown, largely because of the way it looks: a head far too big for a spindly torso and legs. An over-long snout, a pair of over-small horns and a wispy white Mandarin beard complete the assembly.

Wildebeests also play the fool much of the time. Arching their backs, they buck up and down in a straight take-off of the Maasai *ipid* dance, or then spin and fall, or generally charge about for what looks like the sheer fun of it. But there is also something of the Pagliacci about the gnu, some off-stage worry which is serious and often tragic. An animal endlessly pirouetting on itself may be a terminal casualty of a botfly crawled into its brain. A hundred may die in a crazy nose-dive into a ravine.

In Alan Root's *Year of the Wilde-*

**Preceding pages**: a topi stands sentinel in Maasai Mara. **Left**, savanna sundown.

*beest*, there is a senseless and pathetic ritual of mothers and calves separated in a lake crossing, swimming back and forth until they finally give up. It's comic, snouts sniffing out of the water, but also tragic with the babies ending up in a mewling crèche on the banks, either to starve or feed the predators.

Oddly (and incidentally), the word *mara* means "motley" and is consistent with the wildebeest in the role of Canio. It is one of 30 or more adjectives the Maasai use to describe the cow, with their skin-tones and configurations as colours and patterns. Why they applied it to the reserve is anyone's guess, although one theory is that it relates to the landscape: the "Green Hills of Africa", patched or mottled with groves of acacia and thickets of lesser whistling thorn. More likely, the Mara was named for the spotty, speckled inundation of the wildebeest and a million other herbivores any time between the end of June and the middle of September.

For anyone who hasn't seen this, read the early part of *Centennial*, say around

1750, eyes narrowed to blur out the African elements and visualise a gathering of the national buffalo herd on the Green Hills of Wyoming. Nor would the Indians be excluded from the image since, apart from the core area of about 250 sq. miles (648 sq. km), the Mara is Maasai country and the two tribal groups are similar in many aspects.

Given the option, the wildebeest would probably never come up to the Mara. They would stay down south, on the vast alluvial short-grass plains of the Serengeti which they prefer because there is virtually no cover for the predators. But they soon mow the grazing to stubble, the land dries up and they are forced to move out following the north-westerly bearing of the "long rains".

**The celebrated migration**: It's a disorderly start. None of the animals seems to know what's happening, except for some lead bull in the 1.4 million which must sniff the air, decide it's time, and amble off towards Lake Victoria. The others follow, straggling individuals and small groups, but eventually bunch-

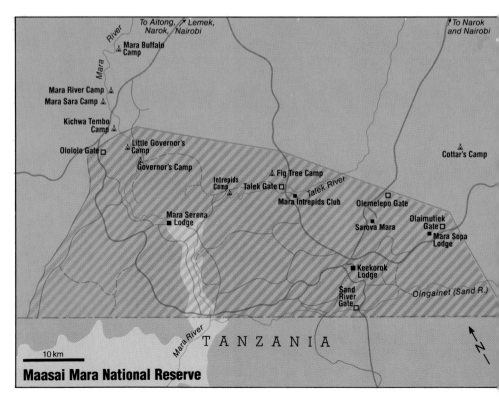

**Maasai Mara National Reserve**

ing in broad lines of march which look like columns of safari ants. They wheel before the lake, moving due north across the Mara River into Kenya, where there will be good grazing in the best-watered section of the ring from the Mara River, the Talek and a dozen other flows off the eastern wall of the Rift. (One of them has the echoing name of the *ol-oo-lolo* escarpment.)

They tend to break up and scatter across the hills, but also on valley fields of "golden grass" – actually russet red *Themeda triandra* – which contributes to the Mara motley. The bulls are highly vulnerable to predators launching out of the thickets, so whenever they smell the October "short rains" moving up from the south, the hordes reform and restart the celebrated migration. This time, for some unknown reason, the lines are narrower and more dispersed for the southeasterly arc to where it all started.

On the way, they cross **Olduvai Gorge** where Louis and Mary Leakey dug early man out of exposed banded sediments in the cliffs. They also unearthed early wildebeest, carbon-dating the bones back 2 million years. Whatever it is, the clownish gnu is clearly a survivor as a race and physically well-adapted to its peripatetic lifestyle.

A related reference in the promotion brochures, perhaps overworked, is that the Serengeti-Mara is a relic of prehistory, still in the "Age of Mammals". But ecologists argue that nothing is, or has been, constant in the area. Tomorrow there will be a monumental crash of the herds through drought or rinderpest; the day after the survivors will be squeezed out of existence by the pressure of human expansion. By the turn of the century, the fields of the Mara may be sown to barley to produce beer for the predicted 40 million people of Kenya. They may be right, but perhaps the more significant consideration is that, as of now, the Serengeti-Mara is the most extraordinary natural show on earth.

**Bloodshed at "Blood Valley":** The way to get there is out of Nairobi, either the high or the low road north towards Nakuru. "Up" is more comfortable on a new highway across the top of the Rift escarpment;

"down" is a mine field of potholes on the old road built originally by Italian prisoners of war. A church at the foot of the Rift is a memento of their Catholic presence. Either way, the route leads to the northern end of the sectoral **Kedong Valley** about 30 miles (50 km) from the city centre. In the old days, this was "Blood Valley" of the Maasai massacre of 550 caravan porters and, later, of "Trader Dick" who came after them in a reprisal raid. Close by, at **Mayer's Farm**, the *moran* dance for tourists over afternoon tea.

A left turn off the old road is signposted to Narok, about 55 miles (90 km) past Kenya's **Mount Margaret** earth-satellite station and two old volcanoes. You can hike up **Mount Longonot** and walk along the crater rim at about 9,000 feet (2,800 metres). The views from the top make the walk well worthwhile. **Suswa**, just under 1,000 feet lower, is interesting for its steam jets and caving holes, some a mile into the bowels (only for professionals or guided parties).

**Narok** town is much like its twin, Kajiado. It administers the northern half

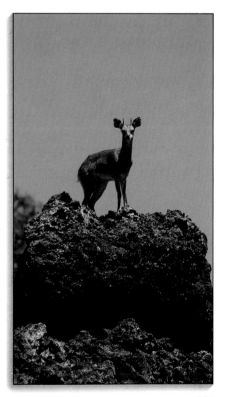

**lip-springer the chamois" of rica's crags nd cliffs.**

of Maasailand, no more effectively perhaps. It is also similarly full of strolling *moran* buying very little from shanty *duka* stores.

Ten miles (16 km) out, on corrugated murram, is a Game Department barrier at **Ewaso Nyiro** ("brown river" in Maa). At this point, there is a confusion of tracks, especially if the sign-post is missing, which it frequently is.

However, to **Keekerok**, the traditional centre of Mara Reserve, the compass bearing is southwest on the centre track for about 45 miles (72 cm) of bumpy, all-weather dirt. Altogether, the drive from Nairobi is a rough 145 miles (231 km) so that – if affordable – charter or light-aircraft scheduled services to Keekerok are worthwhile.

**African starlight dinner**: Most of the lodges and tented camps in the Mara area have their own land transport for game runs. Several of them offer hot-air balloons for an early morning sail over the migration, ending with a champagne breakfast on landing. These camps come and go, but two or three of them appear to be permanent and are romantic, with blazing campfires, African starlight, and a three-course dinner, served by liveried stewards. **Keekerok Lodge** is old-style colonial, comfortable and attractive if a scruffy industrial area behind it is discounted. **Mara Serena**, high on a ridge to the northwest, is a not too successful simulation of a Maasai *enkang* settlement – too luxurious and not enough flies! The reserve is also well infrastructured, offering good game and river runs. Periodically, one or another of the camps introduces raft safaris down the Mara River.

It's possible to complete a circuit out of the park from Keekerok up to **Ol-oo-lolo**, bearing right to the mission station at **Lemek**. (Ask for Fr. Frans Mol, an authority on the Maasai.) The road eventually ends up back at the three-pronged fork at Ewaso Nyiro.

**Narosura, a Maasai ghost town**: Another safari option – way out in the wilds and for self-contained campers only – is to head southeast across the **Loita Plains**. This area and the **Loita Hills**

Cheetah and cub.

above the Rift are the most traditional, time-lapsed section of Maasailand in Kenya, with the tribe still dressed in red 19th-century leathers as well as in shop-bought *olkila* togas. There are no formal roads, but plenty of cattle tracks, all negotiable up to the hills in a four-wheel drive vehicle, except in the rains. On bad days, use the looping all-weather track from the plains towards Ewaso Nyiro, but cutting west to **Maji Moto** ("hot water") and back down on tarmac to a sad-looking hamlet of impoverished Maasai called **Narosura**. The place is uninteresting except as a spectre of change and an indication of what could happen to the Maasai when their tribal organisation breaks up. Narosura is a dereliction: a market without cattle and a community without traditional social structures and discipline.

Out of the townships, still on tarmac, the road dips into a river and then follows an old footpath alignment meandering up the scarp of the Loita Hills. The old men of the area remember this as a kind of *via dolorosa* to a holy place

eedbuck.

just above the summit – a cathedral of seven old trees which they call *eneeni n'kujit*, "where the grass sheaves are tied". It's unmarked, unfortunately; no grass insignia of any sanctuary unless the Maasai are there in communion with their dark and authoritarian God, *Enkai*.

**Mysterious valleys, interesting people**: Just beyond is the equally mysterious, heavily forested **Valley of the Laibons** close to the village of **Entesekera**. This is the ancestral land of the dynastic *il-aiser* clan of *laibon* rulers and archbishops, whose present chief is a genial, lager-swigging old gentleman named Simel. He favours blue togas to the standard red, and is also seen wearing what looks like a smart ski-bonnet, presumably from his last wintering in Gstaad. Other interesting people in the area, if they can be found, are the *il-Konono*, a clan of blacksmiths who make the Maasai's spears and short swords.

The tracks above the summit are rough and dry-weather only. But it's extremely scenic country, much of it undeclared national park at places like **Empoopong** up to the **Nguruman Escarpment**, overlooking Lake Magadi. In the travelogue of an English writer, the scene was reminiscent of home: "We came out on to an alpine valley whose immense rolling plains, shining in the setting sun, seemed smooth as a golf course. But this was at once shattered by the sight of some russet impala that came out of a grove to stare at us.

"The grove was also something which seemed to belong to another world, for the bunched trees looked like English holly with their dark green leaves burnished in the sun.

"Then, on all the surrounding ridges, we saw great stands of deep cedar forest and like small islands in the vivid green plains, the painted herds of the witch-doctor's cattle. It was a strikingly beautiful scene."

At some stage, the area will be about midway on a new highway linking the Mara with Amboseli through the Loita, the Ngurumans, Magadi and Kajiado. It should have been built years ago to complete what would be the best safari in the country – "Through Maasailand".

# THE NORTHERN GAME COUNTRY

**Samburu National Park** is north off the shoulder of Mount Kenya, at the onset of the vast scrub desert that extends to Lake Turkana and beyond. The reserve is within the territory of the Samburu pastoralists – more decorous than their cousins the Maasai. It also has resident wildlife species rare elsewhere in the country. These include Grevy zebra, Beisa oryx, the blue-shanked Somali ostrich and the remarkable gerenuk antelope which spends most of its life on its hind legs, somehow finding moisture on top of the withered thorn bush that characterises the bleak, parched terrain in much of the reserve.

Physically dramatic, with a great table mountain called **Ololokwe** in the background, the 40-sq. mile (104-sq. km) reserve bakes red brown for most of the year. A permanent relief is in the broad green ribbon of trees along the **Ewaso Nyiro** ("Brown") **River**, which flows from the west in the Aberdares Range and vanishes beyond Samburu in the recesses of the Lorian Swamp in the east towards Somalia.

The river is at its most expansive in the reserve, wandering slowly in bends and loops, providing pools for hippos and sand spits for basking crocodiles. Large herds of elephants roam the gaunt hills of Samburu most of the day, but stop at the Ewaso Nyiro in the evenings to set themselves, photogenically, in front of often surrealistic sunsets. To add to the attraction of the river area is a wide gallery forest of acacia, doum palms and tamarind, chattering monkeys in the trees and the occasional scarlet flash of a turaco in what ornithologists consider an exceptional location for birds.

The **Buffalo Springs National Reserve** butts on to Samburu, just under 40 sq. miles (104 sq. km) of the same kind of country, but this time relief is pro-

**Preceding pages:** Kenya's northern deserts from the Lerogi Plateau, Maralal. **Left**, a white rhino in Meru National Park.

vided by an outflow of clear spring water which attracts migrant game (and often predators) from miles around.

The third and largest of the reserves lies on the south bank of the Ewaso Nyiro. Across the Isiolo-Moyale road from its sisters. **Shaba National Reserve** has a particular place in the history of Kenyan game conservation. It was there that author Joy Adamson was murdered early in 1980, leaving behind unfinished her trilogy of books on the rehabilitation of leopard to a wild environment.

The reserve takes its name from a cone of volcanic rock and evidence of the intensity of its upheaval is demonstrated by the formidable lava flow which the traveller has to cross to reach this remote and isolated wilderness. Its central attraction is again the wide, sauntering Ewaso Nyiro on its way to the Lorian Swamp, as well as the tall trees of the stark riverine forest in sharp contrast to the rugged and pitted tracts which make up much of the sanctuary. Many small hills diversify Shaba and,

with four springs, the reserve is better watered than its neighbours.

Heavy downpours often render the already rough tracks accessible only for four-wheel drive vehicles. All this only serves to enhance the traveller's sense of the reserve's isolation, which is the essence of Shaba – a place for the connoisseur, where an authentic Africa experience is the objective.

**Meru National Park** is perhaps best known outside Kenya as "Elsa country". Joy Adamson's famous lioness was rehabilitated into the wild here, as were three other lions which had previously appeared in the *Born Free* film. Her cheetah Pippa – *The Spotted Sphinx* – was also released and reared two groups of fine cubs.

**Four touring circuits:** The park is small, about 300 sq. miles (777 sq. km) in all, entirely unspoiled and scenically diverse. With a fine network of internal roads, it is exceptionally well-organised for touring. The tours are set out in four basic circuits.

**The Swamps Circuit** is a series of

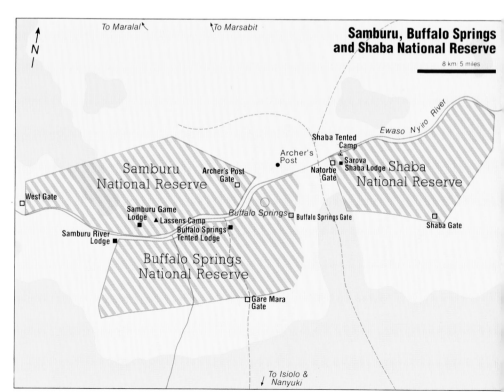

long loops in the northwest, laid out parallel to the main road leading to the park headquarters from the Murera Gate. Game abounds here, including most of the park's 5,000 head of buffalo. It's a favourite foraging ground for bull elephants, with the cows and calves concentrated farther south in bush country.

**The Plains Circuit** is a network of roads centring on the park headquarters and extending to the lone Mughwango Hill in the west; Leopard Rock in the north; Golo's Camp in the east; and the main Rojewero River crossing to the access roads of Tana River in the south. The main concentration of game is in this area, notably large herds of eland, Beisa oryx, zebra, giraffe and other plains game. It's also the best viewing area for lions.

**The Combretum (Evergreen Bush) Circuit** is a wide loop out westwards from Rhino Drift and back through the Kiolu Plains. The road to the Ura Gate also traverses the circuit and there are loops of minor tracks off this road out to Punguru Plains on the far western boundary. Rhinos are most commonly seen in this area, as well as elephants, buffaloes and plains game.

**The Commiphora Bush and Tana circuits** are long-haul roads through the dry, dusty thorn bush country to the riverine forest strips along the Ura and Tana Rivers. Included in the Tana circuit is a scenic 12-mile (19-km) riverside drive. There are cheetah, lesser kudu, gerenuk and oryx in the thick bush and, of course, hippo and crocodile in the rivers.

**A refuge regenerated**: Overall, Meru is potentially a wildlife stronghold. The game had been virtually shot out by 1959 when the local Council of the Wameru people took the initiative from the colonial government and set the area aside for conservation. Since then the herds have built up, especially buffaloes which can be seen in groups of 300 or more around the swamps and river courses of a park richly endowed with permanent water.

From fossil evidence, it is certain that there were once white rhinos in the area, but these died out and an attempt is made to reintroduce the species from an

ape Buffalo
1,200
ounds of
xplosive
emper.

# SAMBURU
## Eastern Nilotic

A nomadic Maa-speaking people, the Samburu (73,400) live mainly in Maralal and the border zones of Marsabit districts of northern Kenya between Lake Turkana and the Uasa Nyiro river. Known long ago as the *Loibor Kineji* (people of the white goats), the Samburu sometimes refer to themselves as the *Loikop*. Eight patrilineal families and 17 clans are the major groupings.

Like the Maasai, the Samburu have long resisted change. For several decades, following their move even farther south from Marsabit by the British in 1914, a policy of *laissez faire* was adopted towards them. Baragoi, Maralal and Wamba are the main centres of administration.

These cattle-owning pastoralists mainly live off the products of their herds. Milk is the principal food, augmented with blood from living cattle or sheep and goats slaughtered for meat in the dry season. Certain roots and barks are added to their soups. Semi-desert conditions preclude any form of agriculture in the lowland areas, but on the Lerogi Plateau and the uplands of the Karisia Hills, maize, sorghum and vegetables are increasingly grown and large tracts are being leased for the production of seed wheat.

The Samburu live in small settlements of between four and ten stock owners. The low huts of plastered mud, hides and grass mats stretched across a framework of poles are divided into two halves. A thorn fence encloses the huts and each family's cattle yard (*mboo*). Sheep and goats are tended by young boys, in-milk cows are herded close to the homestead, and the remaining cattle are supervised by young warriors.

Circumcision and the initiation of boys (*ilayeni*) into the warrior group (*il-murran*) and later ceremonies (*ilmugit*) are conducted during propitious phases of the moon in specially built settlements (*lorora*). Wearing charcoal-blackened aprons and earrings (*ikerno*), the initiates have their hair shaved and are provided with new sandals. Each initiate in turn is seated on an ox-hide in front of his mother's hut, supported by two ritual patrons. The operation is usually performed by a non-Samburu,

Dorobo or other circumciser, after which the initiates join together in singing *lebarta*. After a day or two, they prepare bows and arrows blunted with balls of resin with which they hunt small birds to make decorative headdresses. A month or so after circumcision these are discarded. The initiates are now *il-murran*, allowed to decorate their elaborate hair-dos and bodies with red ochre as a symbol of their new status.

Five years elapse before the *ilmugit lenkarna* naming ceremony, which signifies the progression of the junior to senior *il-murran*. The *ilmugit lolaingoni* six years later, when a bull provided by the group's ritual leader is suffocated and eaten, signals the point when the age-set may marry and achieve the standing within the community of married men (*lpayan*). Real power in Samburu society is vested in the elders, who are responsible for community decisions and ritual.

Girls are individually circumcised at about the same age as the boys and married immediately after the ceremony. The bride must provide herself with a special apron, earrings, a piece of lion's skin to be tied to her leg, beads, sandals and a stick from the *nkoita* tree. Early on the morning of the marriage, the bride is circumcised. Within an hour or two, the bridegroom arrives with his age-mates bringing a bull, a cow and a sheep. The bride's mother removes the posts blocking the settlement entrance and the bull is driven through to be slaughtered – signifying that the marriage contract is finalized. The elders divide up the meat and perform other rituals throughout the day. The next morning the bride passes between two rows of elders to receive their blessing and commences her walk to the bridegroom's home, where a new fire is kindled using fire sticks.

Unlike the war-like Maasai, whose language and cultural heritage they share, the Samburu do not adopt an aggressive and dominant cultural stance towards other tribes. Instead they place a high social value on a mature sense of respect (*nkanyit*). Today group and individual ranching schemes and improved educational facilities are bringing about long-resisted change. Many Samburu *il-murran* enlisted in the British Forces during World War II. Today, many Samburu still serve in the Kenya Armed Forces and Police. ∎

imported breeding herd. Poachers took some of them in the early 1970s, but the remainder are under guard and carefully cossetted in pens near the park headquarters. Over the years, scores of leopards have been brought in – trapped and removed from settlement areas all over Kenya – so that, probably, the park by now has a sizeable population of these elusive predators.

More than 300 species of birds have been recorded, from parakeets in the riverine forests to vast squadrons of quelea, wheeling and diving in formation among the combretum trees. The rarest bird, for determined ornithologist, is Peter's Finfoot. Apart from croc, there are catfish, tilapia and silver barbel in the rivers and these can be fished with the permission of the park warden.

The backdrops at Meru are picturesque, sometimes abstract; at **Adamson's Falls** on the Tana River, blocks of granite have been weathered and watered into weird shapes, like modern sculptures. On clear mornings, the snow peaks of Mount Kenya appear in the southwest, but perhaps the definitive skyscape for the park is with the sun directly behind the high bordering **Nyambeni Range**, the light shafting through the summits for an impression of a romanticised religious painting.

Geologically the park is extremely interesting. Most of the land surface is olivine basalt lava flows from the Nyambenis, overlaid with rich brown and gray volcanic or black cotton soils strewn with small pumice boulders. The basement rock occasionally outcrops as low inselbergs or kopjes to relieve the monotony of the dry bush country.

The park is roughly bisected by the **Rojewero River**, which marks an abrupt change of landscape. On one side, open grasslands stretch out of the Nyambeni foothills; on the other is thick *Commiphora* bush which spreads north and eastwards 300 miles (480 km) to the coast. This is arid, broken country cut by innumerable sand luggas.

There are 19 rivers and streams in the park, 15 of them permanent. In addition, numerous swamps and springs occur where the lava is spread thin on the base-

ment system and in the line of a fault running southwestwards from Kinna to Kilimakieru. The main feeder springs and swamps are the **Kithima ya Mugumu** ("Fig Tree Springs"), **Murera Springs, Bisa-nadi** and **Buguma Swamps**, and **Mulika Swamp** where the park's only fully service lodge is situated.

The eastern and southern flanks of the park are buffered by four gazetted national reserves. To the east and north of the Tana River are the **Bisanadi** and **Rahole National Reserves**; on the southern side of the river are the **North Kitui** and **Kora National Reserves**. All of them are more and less undeveloped for tourism – entirely wilderness areas, accessible only to four-wheel drive vehicles and, even then, the tracks are few and extremely rough. In 1990 a tourist lodge was being built in Kora.

**The Tana River:** Another well off-the-beaten-track safari is down the **Tana** to the coast. It's not generally on tour operators' itineraries, but can still be undertaken by more adventurous visitors equipped with four-wheel drive

vehicles, who are fully self-contained, with tented accommodation and food.

The Tana is Kenya's largest river – about 375 miles (600 km) following the main course, or 630 miles (1,014 km) counting every bend. It starts as tumbling streams on the slopes of Mount Kenya and the Aberdares, converges into a wide and powerful torrent east of these mountains, and then matures into a slow and sinuous river for the lower half of its course.

At that point, it dissects a vast and wild area of eastern Kenya where, from the air, the riverine strip makes a vivid contrast to the parched bushland stretching to the horizon on either side. And nowhere is this more apparent than in the remote **Kora National Reserve,** about 80 miles (130 km) from Garissa, where the Tana emerges from the violence of its middle section to the gentle meandering of its lower course.

Kora is one of the most desolate yet starkly beautiful places in the country, but it's rough and strictly for the connoisseur of wilderness. It is here that George Adamson, murdered by bandits in 1989, established a camp to continue his work with lions, made famous by the *Born Free* saga. Game is fairly sparse, but elephant, lion, lesser kudu and waterbuck are seen occasionally. With or without game, the river is outstandingly beautiful in this Kora section and hippos and crocodiles are plentiful.

South of Kora, the country is endless dry bush dominated by several prickly species of acacia trees and gnarled *Commiphora* bush. Arid though it is, this country is extensively used by both wildlife and domestic stock, whenever water is within reach. Some animals, such as lesser kudu, do not need to drink since they obtain sufficient moisture from their leaf diet. Most others, including cattle, have to drink regularly and as the puddles dry up after the rain, the river increasingly becomes the focus for both man and beast.

**The nomad country:** The nomadic Somali and Orma peoples have adapted to the requirements of this environment and move large distances in search of

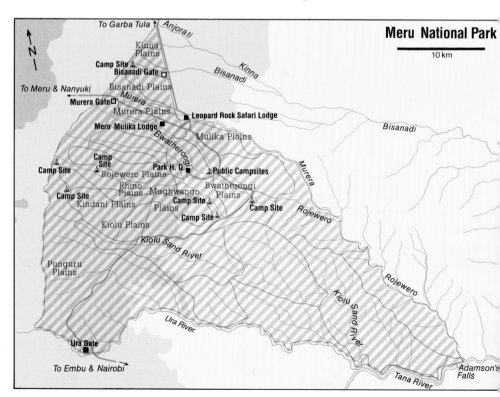

ephemeral pools and grazing. But where they are settled, there is often overgrazing and soil erosion – sadly evident around the township of Garissa.

This is the administrative headquarters of the North-Eastern Province which used to be part of the old Northern Frontier district (NFD). It still exudes something akin to a frontier spirit and is historically a base for operations against the *shifta* marauding bands.

The Somali people dominate the whole of North-Eastern Province which adjoins the Republic of Somalia. They are a proud and independent people, culturally very different from most of the other tribes of Kenya. For centuries they and the related Galla have been moving in waves towards the south and west from their original home in the Horn of Africa, forever in search of fresh pastures.

Clusters of their rough grass huts surrounded by cattle and camels are a common sight on the north and eastern side of the Tana. In contrast with these simple exteriors of their dwellings, their carved and woven artifacts are some of the finest in Kenya. Their headrest stools are particularly well made.

Around Garissa, agricultural people become increasingly evident along the river banks. They are the Korakora and below the villages of Nanigi, the various sub-tribes of the Pokomo. All of them are Bantu peoples allied to the coastal tribes and are different in every respect from their neighbours (and historic enemies), the Somali and Orma.

Their land is far too dry to grow crops on rainfall alone and they are completely dependent on the river for their livelihood. They cut dug-out canoes from the riverine forest from which to catch fish or move from one village to the next. The moisture of the river banks supports their staple crop of bananas, and the floods provide standing water for rice and maize. The river is an unpredictable life-giver; floods can easily destroy and as effortlessly produce crops. For this reason, and to expand crop production, a massive Tana River irrigation scheme has been instituted.

South of Garissa, the arid bush con-

usks locked
playful
iendship.

tinues. Below **Hola**, because of proximity to the coast and its higher rainfall, the country begins to look greener. This is also wildlife country, with several unique faunal attractions.

On the east bank of the river around Hola and stretching in a band across to the Somali border is the only home of the Hunter's antelope, a hartebeest but with lyre-shaped horns. Little is yet known about this animal but it is occasionally seen around **Ijara**. A game reserve named **Arawale National Reserve** has been gazetted for its special protection.

The Tana is also a habitat for several forest species, notably two rare animals unique to the area in Kenya – the red colobus and the crested mangabey monkeys. Both of these species have a predominantly West African distribution, and their occurrence in the gallery forests of the Tower Tana is evidence of extensive rain-forest belts across East Africa in earlier times.

The populations of both species are restricted to a strip of about 40 miles (64 km) between the villages of **Wenje** and **Garsen**. Their future has been threatened by the destruction of forest and Pokomo agriculture. The erosion was particularly acute during the *shifta* troubles when all the Pokomo on the east bank left their homes and had to start new farms on the West bank. There is, however, a **Tana River Primate Reserve** near Wenje to conserve what is left of the monkeys' remaining habitat.

The forests are as complex and variable as the rest of the flood-plain ecosystem and recent studies have shown that both of these monkeys are finely adapted to the subtleties of the river regime. The mangabey, for example, can feed on fruit in the trees or on insects on the ground and alter its social organization accordingly. The availability of these foods is as variable as the crops of the Pokomo and the species owes its survival here and nowhere else in East Africa to these adaptations.

The southern limit of the rare monkey's range is near Garsen where the flood-plain opens on to a wide grassy delta extending in a triangle down to the present mouth of the Tana at **Kipini** and the old river mouth at **Karawa**. This is the main dry season grazing land of the Galla people.

These Oromo-speaking tribes are spilt into several groups spread between the Ethiopian border and the Kenya coast. Those who live in this most southerly section are called the Orma. Linguistically and culturally, they resemble the Somalis to whom they are closely related. But their huts are taller and more carefully constructed, which accords with their more sedentary existence on the Tana delta and the more moist grasslands of that area.

Their lifestyle demonstrates yet another important principle of pastoral economy. Except at the height of the dry season the herds in the lush grasslands of the delta are nearly always composed only of calves and cows, which are milked to support most of the population. The bulls, on the other hand, are herded by the young men of the tribe and range far away to the north and west in search of scattered grazing. These are used for meat or are sold for cash to the government or Arab traders. They eventually find their way to the up-country ranches where they are fattened up for slaughter.

**Explorers' route:** The delta is also an area of historical interest, being one of the main routes into the interior prior to the construction of the Uganda Railway at the turn of the century. Explorers such as Charles New, Karl Peters, the Denhardt brothers all hoped to reach the interior via the Tana. Their accounts are full of the horrors of mosquitos, disease and floods.

One general aspect of the early years was intense missionary influence in the delta area where a section of the Pokomo tribe was converted to Christianity. They are known as the "Malachini", to distinguish them from the Pokomo upstream of Garsen who are predominantly Muslims. Islam is also apparently a conversion dating to about the same time as the first Christian influence. The Orma and Somalis have been Muslims for much longer, as have the Swahili people around Kipini.

**Right, a lion yawns – a fierce but lazy beast.**

194

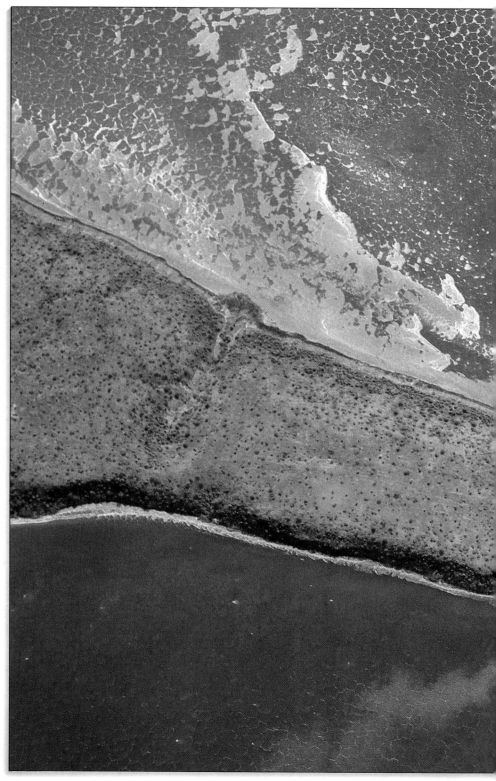

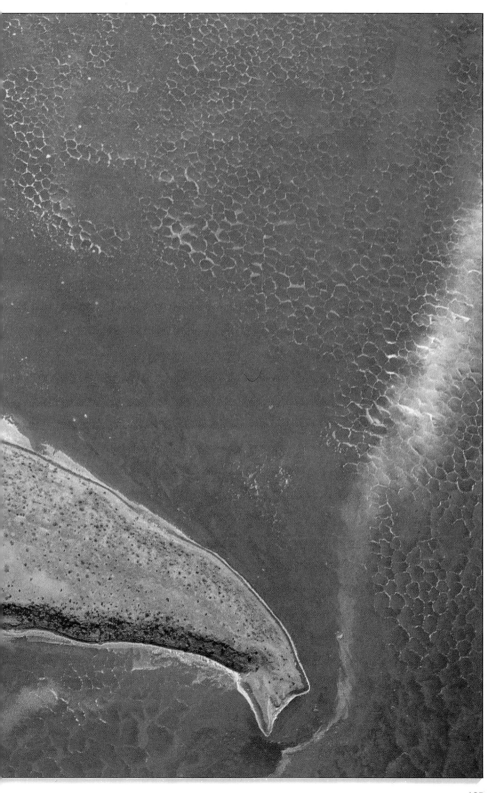

# THE GREAT RIFT VALLEY

Tectonic theory has it that the earth's crust is a set of plates floating on liquid magma deep down below. Where these plates collide, one of them rears up to form a mountain range and the other slides down to the bowels of the earth. Sometimes the plates break up and the parts drift away from one another.

Almost all these breaks are usually below the ocean surface, but one of them splits the earth. It runs from the Jordan Valley in the north, takes in the whole of the Red Sea, sheers through Ethiopia, Kenya, Tanzania and Mozambique and finally reaches the sea near the Zambesi delta.

This **Great Rift Valley** is more than 5,400 miles (8,700 km) long – a crack in the African plate that, in terms of length, exceeds one quarter of the earth's circumference.

An arm of it runs through much of the Nile Valley, scours across western Uganda and Tanzania and joins the main Rift in southern Tanzania. Another rather ill-defined offshoot runs through Zambia to the Okavango Swamp in Botswana.

The main split has already separated Arabia from Africa, which is obvious from a glance at the map. The southern outline and mountains of Arabia clearly fit into the shape of northeastern Africa and the Ethiopian massif. Almost certainly, in due course, the fault will continue to open up until the Horn of Africa and all land to the east of the Rift Valley will part further, flood with sea and become an island somewhat larger than Madagascar.

In places, the walls of the Rift rise little more than 100 feet (30 metres) above the valley floor. Elsewhere, there are steep, often sheer cliffs to above 4,000 feet (1,220 metres), but nowhere is the Rift more sharply defined than where it cuts through the highlands of Kenya. In addition to the towering walls, the whole length of valley in Kenya – known as the "Gregorian Rift"

**Preceding pages:** arid land and massive trona deposits at Lake Magadi

**Below,** Suswa volcano and inner plateau (with Mount Longonot, the Aberdares and Mount Kenya in the background)

after the geologist Gregory who first described it – is studded with volcanoes.

These start with **Shomboli** on the Kenya-Tanzania border in the extreme south and include among others **Olorgesailie, Suswa, Longonot, Eburru, Menengai, Londiani, Kakorinyo** and the **South, Central** and **North Islands** in Lake Turkana. The volcanoes vary greatly in both size and age; some, like Shomboli, are no more than plugs that had once choked the throats of volcanoes whose craters have long since been eroded.

Others – the classic is Mount Longonot – retain the textbook conical shape of the young volcano. A few are very young, with the black jagged lava flows still sterile and yet to break down into soils that support plant life.

The youngest of the lot – no more than a hole in the ground – is **Teleki's Volcano**. It seems the lava there was too hot to walk on when its namesake, Count Teleki von Szek, arrived at Lake Turkana in 1887. This volcano is only just over a century old and for geologists, the Gregorian Rift is still a volcanically active area.

**Lake country**: Also scattered along the length of the Kenya Rift is a chain of seven lakes. These lakes are unusual in that not a single one of them has an obvious outflow. Water pours in from the rainfall on the surrounding land and more or less stays there in the shallow pans. While a high rate of evaporation keeps the levels fairly constant, it also causes an accumulation of salts and minerals in the waters of the lake. As a result, all but two of the Rift Valley lakes are so saline that they are virtually undrinkable.

But a bonus for posterity also results. The high mineral content of the water and alkaline soils around the lakes constitute an ideal medium for turning bones into fossils. For this reason, Kenya's Rift Valley has been a rich source of information on the ancient past, including early human development.

The most alkaline of all these sump lakes is **Magadi**, in the extreme south of the country, but easily accessible from

amingo
ests on Lake
ogoria, Rift
alley.

Nairobi. The drive on a good road, which climbs up to the southern shoulder of the Ngong Hills before dropping precipitously into the Rift, takes little over an hour. From the high point on a clear day, the panorama takes in Kilimanjaro, more than 185 miles (300 km) to the southeast; the blue volcanic massifs of northern Tanzania; and the towering Nguruman escarpment of the Rift's western wall.

The descent to the valley close to Magadi is in stages, steep scarp following scarp in an overall harsh, stark landscape – increasingly drier and hotter as the altitude falls. Much of the rifting is clearly recent. As though laid out to illustrate geological theory, like a relief model, the valley is faulted downwards as a series of giant steps.

These flat mesas and canyons and the dry ruggedness of the area are very like Hollywood's "horse opera" country where no one would be surprised if a sheriff's posse rode over the horizon. There are only the equivalent of the Indians, however – the Maasai – who somehow eke out a living from their stock in this inhospitable terrain.

**Hot spot Magadi**: At the end of the road, at its lowest point, simmering and shimmering in temperatures above 100°F (38°C) in the shade, is **Lake Magadi** itself. At first glance, the term "lake" seems a misnomer since there is little water evident. The lake bed appears white; in fact, it's an enormous pan of trona – an agglomeration of mixed salts – over 40 sq. miles (100 sq. km) in extent.

Around the periphery is a series of hot springs, highly charged with salts and bubbling out of the ground at temperatures of about 113°F (45°C). They flow into the huge evaporation pan, where the sun and searing winds leave nothing but the thick white deposits of sludge. But in this is an almost endless source of potash, salt and related chemicals which have been exploited by the Magadi Soda Company since before the World War I.

Magadi is Kenya's oldest mining venture, with a company township built

**Dormant Mount Longonot with secondary crater in foreground.**

up on a peninsula into the lake. The residents are almost exclusively company employees and in many ways they have made themselves into a model community. The township even has a golf course although in this dry environment the greens are "browns" of carefully levelled earth. It's so hot on the course, that a round is more or less confined to soon after dawn or just before dusk.

At the far southern end of the lake, where the largest springs occur, is an area of open water. Although undrinkable, it produces a wealth of microscopic aquatic life which, in turn, attracts many water birds and bird-watchers. Many African species are permanently on show, including flamingos, and the lake also hosts waders and many others escaping the winter in Europe.

**A freshwater exception:** Going north from Magadi, the next lake along the Rift is **Naivasha**, which is also a little more than an hour's drive from Nairobi along the Trans-Africa Highway to the northwest. The view from the eastern

rim of the Rift on this route is every bit as spectacular as that from the Ngong Hills en route to Magadi. It's the same grandstand scenery over huge distances, the same immensity of scale – yet, without the harshness of the southern valley landscape.

Instead of serried scarps, the Rift above Naivasha drops down in a single sweep, leaving towering walls on either side. The lake lies on the valley floor at about 6,200 feet (1,890 metres) above sea level. Its area has fluctuated a great deal over the centuries, but currently covers about 60 sq. miles (170 sq. km). In the early 1890s it was apparently a small puddle, but by the mid-1890s had risen by some 50 feet (15 metres) and was far larger than it is now. And so it went on, up and down over the years, fluctuating in area by not less than 245 percent and in volume by 1,115 percent.

Today, fence posts stand forlornly way out from the shore as mementos of the days before 1961 when farmers and ranchers grazed their cattle far beyond the present shore.

ecretary irds live on diet of nakes and ther eptiles.

An oddity characterises Lake Naivasha; although it has no visible outlet, it is one of the two freshwater lakes (Baringo is the other) in the Rift. Many theories have been forwarded to explain the phenomenon, but none is entirely satisfactory. The most obvious is that there must be massive underground seepage through the lake flow – a diffused outflow that takes the place of a conventional discharging river.

Whatever the reason, Naivasha water is indeed fresh, potable, abundant and excellent for irrigating the surrounding fertile volcanic soils. Not surprisingly, it is also ringed by agricultural land, from which spring many tons of vegetables and flowers harvested for both Nairobi and overseas markets. Proximity to Nairobi has also turned Lake Naivasha into a recreational area for the city. A hotel and a number of lodges and camps provide reasonable overnight accommodation for a weekend of fishing, sailing and water-skiing.

Lying as it does between high walls and on the floor of the east African valley, Naivasha's location in the Rift might be likened to the centre of a venturi. Strong winds are frequent and quickly develop a heavy chop on the water, dangerous for people out in small boats. Seasoned sailors keep an eye on the gathering clouds and scuttle for home as soon as the wind builds up.

**The birds come home**: Like so many of the places in Kenya, Lake Naivasha is a dream for the ornithologist. There are few places that display so many aquatic and terrestrial species in such a pleasant environment; Naivasha is, so they say, home to more species of birds than the whole of the British Isles. It's no wonder that the lake is a focus for conservation attention. Yet few realise how much of its attraction has been contrived by man. Sport fish were introduced around 1928, with other species brought in later for commercial fishing. Aquatic plants have been transplanted from elsewhere, most notably *Salvinia* which builds up to thick carpets and can become a total menace, as in Lake Kariba. Coypu or nutria, a large South American water rat, got into the eco-

system after a few of them escaped from a fur farm. The red swamp crayfish was brought in from Louisiana in 1972 and is doing well.

But not everyone welcomes these newcomers. Ecologists deplore each introduction and any changes that may affect the ecosystem. Even so, the lake's massive fluctuations in size are likely to have far more profound influences than any of the introductions that have been made so far.

**Dry lakes, swirling dust**: One has only to drive a further 50 miles (80 km) up the Trans-Africa Highway to view two more lakes also situated in the highland part of the Rift at about the same altitude as Naivasha. The first, **Lake Elmenteita**, lies at more or less midpoint of that stretch with **Lake Nakuru** as the other; both are highly saline.

The word "Nakuru" derives from the Maasai *en-akuro* meaning "swirling dust". This may seem an odd name for a lake, but both Elmenteita and Nakuru are ephemeral. Like Naivasha, they vary enormously in size and sometimes

Pelican resting on dead tree stump at Navaisha.

disappear altogether, during which time they are reduced to white salt flats, swirling with dust-devils.

When Lake Nakuru was last dry in the mid-1950s, strong daily winds swept up the dust into a dense white soda smog which blew 40 miles (64 km) away up the Rift to the north. So dense and unpleasant was this daily dry-season event that the wisdom of any further development of the large agricultural town of Nakuru, on the border of the lake, was in some doubt. But when heavy rains fell in 1961, the lake filled to its brim and the soda smogs were soon forgotten.

The alkaline constitution of Lake Nakuru supports a vast flowering of the blue-green algae and diatoms on which flamingos live. So rich are the waters, that the birds assemble there in their millions. The roseate mass they create along the shorelines is a spectacle of immense beauty.

The lake attracted great ornithological attention and is now preserved as a permanent national park showpiece. However, the flamingos are now aware

of it and tend to come and go. Two resident species – the Greater and Lesser – migrate up and down the Rift Valley, stopping at whichever lake is producing the best food supply at the time; it might be Natron in northern Tanzania, or Magadi, Elmenteita, Bogoria or Turkana.

**Bogoria and Baringo**: To the north of Nakuru, the land falls away from the highlands. At this point, the Trans-Africa Highway veers to the west to break out of the Rift, whereas the way to the next valley lake is straight on. **Bogoria** was formerly known as Lake Hannington in Kenya's colonial era, after the missionary bishop who was murdered in Uganda. It's a slender stretch of blue water under towering cliffs, like a splinter sticking into the northern foot of the highlands. Also saline charged, this body of water has an added attraction of shoreline hot geysers spouting up from the bowels of the earth.

No one who travels a few more miles north from here misses **Baringo**, the second freshwater lake in the Rift.

Twice Naivasha's size, it poses the same question: why, with no outlet, does it stay fresh? Or perhaps the more important question is: how long will it stay as it is now? Poor agricultural and stock management in its catchment areas has produced rising silt loads which are of serious concern, particularly to many conservationists.

The fish in Baringo leave a telltale sign that the lake must have been connected at some time with the Nile system, probably in a line through Lake Turkana. The connection was cut by the eruption of Kakorinyo and subsequent faulting and tilting as the land continued to subside and settle.

**The Jade Sea:** The largest and most northerly body of freshwater in the Rift is **Lake Turkana** – the legendary "Jade Sea" (*see also North to Lake Turkana chapter, page 225*). In fact, the term "fresh" is somewhat misleading for ever since it was cut off from the Nile, the lake has become progressively more saline. In the north, where the River Omo enters with brown, silt-laden waters off the Ethiopian highlands, the salinity is not really apparent. However, at the lake's southern end, where the evaporation is greatest and there are no inflowing rivers, the water is so saline it's virtually undrinkable.

In part, the lake's location was decided by the growing Rift Valley, although in this region it appeared more like a shallow depression than a valley. The lake used to be larger; occupying large areas of northwestern Kenya for the past 3 million years or more and was previously charged by rivers flowing north from the Kenya Highlands and south from the southern uplands of Ethiopia. The lake then flowed out as a major contribution to the Nile. Its shores teemed with Pleistocene wildlife whose bones were preserved in the alkaline soils.

But after the last Ice Age, the great rivers from both the south and the north shrank, and the lake also retreated. The increasingly dry environment sucked up its waters, reducing its outflow to little more than a chain of seasonal

**Withered Suguta Valley – an African Dante's Inferno.**

swamps. And the imperceptible but inexorable lowering of the Rift Valley floor eventually trapped the lake altogether, cutting off all connections to the Nile. Eventually all that was left was a 180-mile (290-km) long and 10 to 30-mile (16 to 48-km) wide body of water in a climate so fiercely hot and dry that inflow balanced outflow, even though it was fed by one of East Africa's larger rivers, the Omo.

Still waters run deep at Turkana, an inland sea in a desert waste whose only source of bounty is fish. In a measure equal to its seductive beauty, it's a wild and dangerous lake, particularly at the southern end. Steady winds of over 40 miles per hour and gusts well above this are frequent and sudden. They tear across the surface, turning calm water into waves 9 feet (3 metres) in height within the space of an hour. This tempestuous nature of the lake makes its riches difficult to mine and many a fisherman has been blown away never to be seen again.

Despite the violence and difficulties,

Lake Turkana is still developing an extensive fishing industry and modern vessels are now replacing the lashed doum-palm logs of one local tribe – although not entirely, fortunately for Mirella Ricciardi and other photographers. "Vanishing Africa" has yet to go completely.

**A natural museum**: Even so, a more specific lake attraction is the **Sibiloi National Park** on the northeastern shores. Oryx, topi and zebra concentrate there on a narrow swath of littoral, where sufficient moisture enables short grass to flourish. On the beaches, park visitors will encounter Africa's largest surviving populations of crocodile.

Inland, in the heart of the park, several hundred square miles of fossil beds form a natural museum that covers Africa's Pleistocene period. It is in these that some of the oldest forms of man have been found, together with examples of his *Australopithecine* cousins – hence the suggestion that Lake Turkana and its surroundings form the "Cradle of Mankind".

# THE MOUNTAIN NATIONAL PARKS

The Mount Kenya and the Aberdares national parks are about 50 miles (80 km) apart and comprise the highest reaches of the country's central highlands. The Mount Kenya park covers an area of roughly 190 sq. miles (492 sq. km), above the 11,375-foot (3,470-metre) contour line, with two salients stretching down the western slopes. The Aberdares park is about the same size – high plateau, moorlands and peaks, with a forested ridge on the eastern flank known as the Treetops Salient, after the world-famous lodge.

Both parks – the country's main watersheds – are surrounded by forest reserves and stocked with a wide range of wildlife. They were set up principally as recreation areas for walking treks in the moorland-heath zones and for climbing Mount Kenya, whose highest point, the Batian summit, is 17,058 feet (5,199 metres).

**Mount Kenya National Park:** Just over 100 years ago, the mountain was barely known to the outside world. Early travellers' tales of snow on the Equator were generally disbelieved; also no one was interested in **Kirinyaga**, the sacred mountain of the Kikuyu, whose god *Ngai* was a prime target for the first Christian missionaries.

In 1887, Count Samuel Teleki von Szek and his Austrian companion, Ludwig von Höhnel, climbed to within 3,000 feet (915 metres) of the summit of Mount Kenya on their way to "discover" Embasso Narok (Lake Turkana). Twelve years later, an Englishman, Sir Halford Mackinder, finally made it to the top, but even this failed to rouse much international interest.

Thirty years elapsed before the distinguished mountaineer, Eric Shipton, made the second recorded ascent. Thereafter the climb became popular, and there are now many well established main routes to the summit and scores of minor ascents for the skilful alpine mountaineers. There are strict regulations governing a climb or an overnight stay in the park to safeguard

the visitor from the obvious hazards of cold, tricky rock-faces, wild animals and pulmonary oedema, a dangerous lung congestion, which may afflict climbers who are at 13,000 feet (4,000 metres) and above.

The two salients excepted, the park begins where the upper forest merges with the health zones of mostly *Erica arborea*, a weirdly shaped bush often as large as a tree and covered with moss and lichen. At just over 11,000 feet (3,300 metres), this giant heather is replaced by open moorland covered in tussock grass and studded with many species of giant lobelia and groundsel growing to a height of 10–15 feet (about 4 metres). The ground is a rich profusion of everlasting helichrysums and *alchemillas*, interspersed with gladioli, delphiniums and "red-hot pokers".

The many mountain ridges resemble the spokes of wheel meeting at a central hub formed by the gigantic spikes of **Batian** and **Nelion**, the second highest peak at 17,022 feet (5,188 metres). These are surrounded by many other

smaller peaks, snow fields and glaciers, tarns, lakes, waterfalls and imposing scree slopes.

The peaks are the remnants of a central core of an ancient volcanic crater, the rim of which has long since eroded away. Below these jagged summits are intersecting glacier routes up 16,300 feet (4,970 metres) to **Point Lenana**, which are suitable for visitors with little or no climbing experience.

The mountain has a wide variety of avifauna ranging from the huge eagles to the delicate multicoloured sunbirds. Among the most distinctive species are crowned eagle, mountain buzzard, Mackinder's owl, Jackson's francolin, scarlet-tufted malachite and golden-winged sunbirds, and mountain chat.

The forests below the moorlands contain a rich abundance of game animals which include elephant, rhino, buffalo, leopard, bushbuck, several species of duiker, giant forest hog, and the colobus and Sykes monkeys. The remains of an elephant and several buffaloes have been found in the peak region above 14,000 feet (4,270 metres) but as to why they ventured into these high zones, no one knows.

Lions inhabit the moorlands, although they are not common; eland are often seen on the northern and drier parts of the moors, and zebra migrate from the lower plains. Tracks of leopards and wild dogs have occasionally been recorded in the snow at around 15,000 feet (4,600 metres) above sea level. Several species of reptiles occur; among them are the Hinds montane viper, which is exclusive to the Mount Kenya and Aberdare moorlands.

The attractive features of the mountain are 32 small lakes and colourful tarns. **Hall Tarn** is superbly situated, overlooking a valley and **Lake Michaelson** which is well over 1,000 feet (310 metres) below. At the **Curling Pond**, beneath the **Lewis Glacier**, it's possible to skate and the game of curling has been played.

Dense rain forests cover the lower salients and slopes of the mountain and the main tree species are the cedar

Rare bongo, a nocturnal mountain forest antelope.

(*juniperus*), olive (*Olea*) and podo (*podocarpus*). Above this lies a bamboo zone at approximately 7,800 feet (2,380 metres), which in turn gives way to a belt of glorious rosewood (*hagenia*) trees and giant St. John's wort (*hypericum*) before dying out at the heath zone at 10,400 feet (3,170 metres).

Several vehicle tracks wind their way up the forested ridges and two of these reach the moorlands – the Sirimon route extends to 12,900 feet (3,900 metres) and the Timau track to about 13,640 feet (4,160 metres), forming the highest roadhead in Africa. The quickest access to the peaks is via the Naro Moru track which reaches just over 9,900 feet (3,020 metres) and stops immediately below the moorlands.

All visitors must sign in at the park entrance gates on the Naro Moru and Sirimon routes. Unaccompanied people are not permitted through the park gates, except when it is only for a day trip which ends at 4pm. For longer stays on the mountain, there must be at least two people, guides and porters in-cluded. Book at the **Naro Moru River Lodge.**

**Aberdares National Park:** The range in Aberdares National Park has in fact been renamed the **Nyandarua** but the old name – **Aberdares** – persists. The mountains rise in the north to the highest moorland peak of **Ol Doinyo Lasatima** at 13,120 feet (4,000 metres) and some 25 miles (40 km) to the south stands the well-known south summit of **Kinangop** at 12,816 feet (3,906 metres). Between these two peaks is a plateau of moorland – gently undulating country covered in tussock grass and large areas of mixed giant heath.

Forested patches of rosewood, St. John's wort and bamboo occur; and species of lobelia and groundsel are found in the sheltered valleys. Ice-cold streams, well-stocked with trout, thread their way across the moorlands and cascade over a series of waterfalls to form the headwaters of several of the major rivers.

To the east are superb views of Mount Kenya, and from the western rim the

of a
00-foot
s in
erdares
ional
rk.

# MOUNTAINEERING PRACTICALITIES

The prime attraction for rock climbers and mountaineers in Kenya is Mount Kenya, with its twin peaks of Batian and Nelion, both over 17,000 feet (5,182 metres). Below these, jutting upwards abruptly from fields of scree and ice, is a complex of ridges, walls and couloirs, which offers high-standard technical rock and ice routes of about 700–1,300 yards (640–1,190 metres) in length at an altitude of more than 14,500 feet (4,420 metres).

Accurate grading is impossible because of variable seasonal and meteorological conditions, but climbs here are graded. About half of the climbs are alpine Grade V, and the remainder are equally Grades VI and IV. Under prime conditions, some routes may be easier while under bad conditions, a route may be a grade or more harder.

Central Kenya is subject to two rainy seasons a year when there is also an accumulation of ice and snow. Climbing is generally attempted only during the two dry seasons: late December to early March, and July to early October. It is still possible during the off-seasons, but approach conditions are difficult and the climbs are usually at least one grade harder and take several hours longer. There have been few successful ascents during the rains.

The Equatorial location of Mount Kenya results in the seasonal variation of climbing routes. In January/February, when the sun is in the southern hemisphere, the south faces of Mount Kenya receive direct sunlight making them suitable for rock climbing, while the north faces remain iced-up and inaccessible. From July to September, the reverse happens resulting in good rock climbing conditions on the north faces. This seasonal variation is more flexible with respect to ice and snow climbing routes.

Steep rock and technical ice routes are usually climbed on two 9-mm ropes for greater security and smoother descent; easier rock and snow may be negotiated on a single 11-mm rope. Most rock routes can be climbed with a selection of nuts and slings, although a few blade and angle pitons are usually carried on unfamiliar routes for safety. Tabular screws, wart-hogs, front-point unhinged crampons and ice hammers or axes with a good drooping pick are necessary for ice routes.

A tent is not necessary as all routes can be approached from established huts, but bivouac equipment should be carried on all climbs and is especially essential for one of the longer, harder routes. Commercial establishments around the mountain provide guides, porters, cooks, pack animals, tentage, climbing and camping equipment, food provision, transport to roadheads, as well as accommodation of various standards. Altitude problems remain the most serious limitation to good performance on the mountain. Conditioning is important, technical competence essential, and acclimatisation at high altitude for a few days before the ascent is required to prevent pulmonary oedema and other altitude illnesses.

The full range of Kenyan forest animals inhabits the dense montane woodlands and bamboo thickets of the lower slopes, but are mostly invisible to casual visitors on the narrow tracks. Above this the moorland provides the transition from the tropics to the alpine zone, from about 10,500 feet (3,200 metres), where it gives way to the floors of the river valleys radiating from the central massif. Here begin the scree and talus slopes which lead to the walls of the central pyramid or to the numerous subsidiary peaks.

Several possibilities are afforded visitors according to their interests and abilities. Technical climbing on the main peaks is not for everyone. Point Lenana, the third highest summit at 16,300 feet (4,970 metres), offers spectacular ridge walks, and some of the outlying peaks are accessible to non-technical climbers.

An array of spectacular gorges and valleys, scenic glacial lakes and unique high altitude Equatorial vegetation is available to those who prefer hill walking. Day visitors can go trout fishing or motoring and picnicking on the forest tracks. A traverse of the mountain over several days can be undertaken by keen walkers or climbers wishing to acclimatise gently before attempting a summit climb.

Other mountain parks of Kenya may not have the high standard of technical climbing afforded by Mount Kenya, but they offer other attractions. **The Aberdares National Park** rises up to moorland at 13,120 feet (4,000 metres). It has a well-developed road system for scenic high-altitude motoring, excellent trout fishing, game viewing, high altitude walking, and some spectacular waterfalls. **Mount Elgon** at 14,178 feet (4,300 metres) offers trout fishing, game viewing, moorland motoring and walking. **Marsabit National Park** rises like a forested island from the arid plains. It supports a healthy population of large elephants and several scenic hidden lakes.

Other mountains include the **Matthews Range**, the **Ndotos, Kulal, Ololokwe** and the **Cherangani, Chyulu, Taita Hills**. All are more or less undeveloped for tourism, but offer interesting challenges to the more adventurous.

The Mountain Club of Kenya has opened a number of areas for technical rock climbing, including Lukenya, Hell's Gate, Ndeyia, Nzaui and Soitpus. Guide books are available from the club. Each one offers a particular type of technical climbing and all share a unique Kenya flavour which must be experienced to be appreciated. ∎

expanse of the Rift Valley is seen, dropping away to Lake Naivasha and the distant Mau range beyond.

The Aberdares are well-endowed with a great variety and quantity of wild animals despite the occurrence of periodic cold and mist. The western slopes of the range are principally part of the Rift wall, and are therefore relatively steep and generally not as attractive to game as are the more gentle slopes of the eastern side.

Elephant, buffalo, rhino, eland, bongo, waterbuck, bushbuck, reedbuck, several species of duikers, suni, bush pig, warthog, serval cat, lion, Sykes monkeys and hyena occur in varying numbers and most of them are easily seen. Rhinos are sparse here, as everywhere else in the country, but they can be seen on the moors and particularly on the **Treetops Salient**.

Herds of elephant and buffalo migrate with the rain, occupying the bamboo and rain forest zones during the dry seasons. When the rain begins, the game migrates to the plateau moorlands and the lower areas of the Treetops Salient, where the forest is not so dense and the ridges are less steep.

On early morning or evening drives, there is an excellent chance of seeing most species of game and a careful look out at the various roadside salt-licks, forest glades and open valleys is normally rewarding. If you are especially lucky, you will see the more elusive of the mountain dwellers, such as the shy bongo antelope, the black leopard, and the giant forest hog or even the crowned eagle hunting colobus monkeys, one of its favourite foods.

Black serval cat are not uncommon and are often seen on the open moors, usually hunting duiker, francolin, or rodents. Melanism is a common condition in these high altitude zones among the cats and some of the smaller predators and the Augur buzzard.

**Legendary lion:** There is a good population of lions on the Aberdares and these were once believed to belong to a different species from that of their brethren of the plains. A number of naturalists have engaged in a vain search for the legendary "spotted lion", but evidence of an exceptionally rare "Golden Cat" has been found.

The Park is criss-crossed with tracks, many of which were made by British troops during the Mau Mau rebellion in the 1950s. The most important of these is the road from **Nyeri**, which climbs the eastern slopes and across the moorlands, finally down the western slopes and across the Kinangop farmlands to Naivasha.

This road, which is partly tarred, reaches a height of 10,400 feet (3,170 metres). Before approaching the entrance gates, which may be closed during wet weather, a prior check should be made with any of the following: the AA in Nairobi; the parks' headquarters at Mweiga; the Bell Inn, Naivasha; the Outspan, Nyeri; or the Naro Moru River Lodge, close to Nanyuki.

The Parks and Police authorities maintain an efficient mountain rescue team and, if a visitor is 36 hours overdue for check-out at the Park Gate, a search operation will be launched.

Aberdare National Park
10 km

# NORTH TO LAKE TURKANA

Day, a sudden event in northern Kenya, is always spectacular. The sun breaks abruptly into an egg-shell sky, lights up mountains on the horizon, and signals an eruption of life on the plains. Women emerge from their huts to milk the cows. Bulbuls and starlings call from the bushes and camels lumber to their feet.

The tempo of the northern land is synchronised to the sun. Activity for man and beast is at its height during the early hours of the morning and in the brief cool of late afternoon. By 9am, most visitors are already bathed in sweat and, for the first day at least, preoccupied with brushing off swarms of flies. It can be an unsettling experience in this area where concrete buildings are sparse and water holes may be 30 or more miles (50 km) apart. But this removal from civilisation urges many travellers northwards.

**The north beckons**: The term "Northern Kenya" in the safari lexicon covers thousands of square miles of dusty plains, relieved by daunting volcanic formations and whimsical dry rivers known as *lagas*. Lazy avenues of sand are visible most of the time, but these are interrupted by sudden torrents of rushing water in a "flash flood". There is also the fabled Lake Turkana, spread along the Rift Valley floor in the shape of a beckoning finger. The gesture is accepted by most travellers in the north, with the lake the ultimate destination in terms of distance and spectacle.

The general area – once called the "Northern Frontier District" (NFD) – extends from Lake Baringo along the western shore of Lake Turkana to Sudan. On the eastern side, it spreads from the Lerogi Plateau in Samburu country up to Ethiopia and east to Somalia. Like much of Kenya, the approaches are delineated by the few main roads which lead to district centres: township meeting points for the nomads and the bureaucracy, such as Lodwar, Maralal, Marsabit and Isiolo. However, the writ of the law and administration does not reliably extend beyond these outposts of civilization and social welfare.

**Remnants of days gone by**: To a great extent the tribesmen who inhabit the area, all of whom are nomadic pastoralists, have been lost in the folds of time. They are hardy people born of a warrior tradition, including the Samburu, Turkana, Rendille, Boran, Gabbra and Merille. Cattle raiding among tribes is as much a sport as soccer or football elsewhere in the country. To this day, disputes are settled by gun and spear without formal law and order.

During colonial days, the British recognised this spirited independence of action and closed the area to all but civil service officials and professional hunting parties in pursuit of elephant or other game. Today, travel is unrestricted, but on the road from Isiolo to Marsabit, it's advisable to travel in convoy as a precaution against banditry by armed gangs known as *shifta*. They tend to prey on isolated manyattas but have been known to waylay solitary vehicles as well. Kenyan residents are less deterred by this, however, than by the bone-shaking miles of corrugated track.

For visitors, the safari is also an endurance test, but well worth it for the stunning scenery, colourful people and herds of wild animals. So long as you stick to the more conventional routes, you will be able to find accommodation at lodges. But if you intend to camp, you are faced with the dilemma of what food and equipment to pack into a limited space, bearing in mind the need to carry plenty of fuel and water. Local advice on tactical problems of the northern safaris is essential.

Other essentials include cold patches to fix punctures and an adequate range of spare parts in case of a breakdown. Garages are rare in the desert but, even if you are not endowed with a mechanical bent, you can normally press the problem and the tools on a passing trader who is almost certain to oblige.

**The traveller's challenge**: The roads – beyond the realm of comparison with standard thoroughfares – pose a challenge to both man and machine. In the dry season, it's a bit like driving on an old-fashioned washing board and, after rain, on a river of mud. Also take a high-rise "Tanganyika" jack with you, plus a shovel, and two planks for getting out of a bog or soft sand drifts.

Disregard distances on maps when it comes to planning schedules and seek local advice instead. Depending on weather and road conditions, it may take a whole day to drive 50 miles (80 km). In fact, schedules should be discarded entirely, so far as this can be reconciled with pre-arranged bookings at lodges. Part of the allure of the north is to succumb to its gentle pace.

By way of irreverent comment on western preoccupation with time-keeping, the Samburu tend to wear beaded bracelets in the shape of a watch. In fact they can tell the time of day to within half an hour by the position of the sun, which is as close as you need to get with no appointments to keep.

As you travel, it is often worthwhile to make the acquaintance of the locals, many of whom speak English. These exceptionally friendly people come from a tradition of oral communication and delight in explaining the history, customs and geography of their homeland. Seen through their eyes, a superficially stark countryside unfolds into a rich tapestry of intricate social customs and intriguing natural history.

**A no-transport land**: Because there is virtually no public transport, men, women and children think nothing of embarking on a 50-mile (80-km) trip on foot. There are no exceptions; even the blind walk alongside a friend, guided by the sound of footsteps. When asked the objective of a journey, the customary reply is simply, "to visit my brother", or something similar. These hikers, when encountered on the road, are incidentally delighted to be given a lift.

Most people travel without food or water, which can be acquired on the way. But Samburu and Rendille men arm themselves with a spear, a short sword called a *simi* and the ubiquitous and lethal *rungu*, a stick which might be topped with a nut from a 7-ton truck. Turkana and Borana men also carry

**South Horr, gateway to Suguta.**

spears and the odd Merille and Gabbra may have an old gun and leather bullet pouches slung from their waists.

Weapons are obviously a precautionary measure against human belligerency and wildlife, like lions, which are widespread in the north. These are rarely seen, although many communities can still produce a lean, sinewy man whose scars bear out his tale of stabbing or spearing a rogue lion.

Should destinations differ on an encounter on the road, a drink of water is a welcome gesture of friendship. It can also lead to a photographic session which might otherwise not be possible for these camera-shy people. It goes without saying that if they're reticent, don't press the point of taking pictures.

Similarly, village teashops provide entertaining insights into community life just as boulevard cafés do in Europe. Even though they may be somewhat fly-blown and dirty, don't be deterred. They can be good stopovers for a tin mug of sweet, milky tea and a plate of *maandazis*, triangular cakes that taste like unsweetened doughnuts.

**Maralal, the "glittering" town:** Perched on the edge of forested hills, is **Maralal**, the administrative centre for Samburu District. The town's name – Samburu for "glittering" – was inspired by the first building, erected in 1934: a shack with a corrugated iron roof that gleamed in the sun. Since then the town has grown, but still has all the aspects of a frontier dorp. Pepper trees line, but do not shade, the dusty main street. So do a colourful cross-section of people: indolent warriors leaning on the walls of flaky *duka* stores are a preview of what is ahead on the route. Maralal's most precious amenity is a fuel station, almost the last between there and the Ethiopian border farther north.

Just out of town, left at the main roundabout and a mile or so down the road, is the **Maralal Safari Lodge**, the only comfortable accommodation in the area. Overlooking a water hole where zebra, impala and buffalo gather, the spacious rooms have high-pitched cedar ceilings and fireplaces. (Evenings are always chilly.) The lodge arranges

trips to a hide on a nearby hill from where you can silently watch a leopard approach goat bait hung in a tree. (Take advantage of this: these shy cats are difficult to view close at hand.)

Also ask at the lodge for a guide to take you to a look-out point farther north along the road where the Lerogi Plateau drops steeply to the rugged country below. The best time is during the hazy hours of early morning when layer upon layer of volcanic ranges can be seen stretching northwards to the southern shore of Lake Turkana.

Other Maralal attractions include a featureless bungalow, which has been turned into a national monument, where Mzee Jomo Kenyatta was detained by the British in 1961. A current resident of note is the British explorer, Wilfred Thesiger, although he is not easily engaged in conversation.

**Tribesmen's lifestyle:** From Maralal, the Samburu tribe spreads over an area of about 11,000 sq. miles (28,490 sq. km). This includes the higher **Lerogi Plateau** rimmed with cedar forests, as well as the arid scrubland to the north where thorn trees mark the course of river beds and people dig in the sand for water. The tribe, considered to be related to the better-known Maasai, is a splinter group which broke away from the other East Nilotic tribes and migrated south down the Nile in the 16th century. They refer to themselves not as Samburu but *il-oikop*.

As with other pastoralists of the north, their lifestyle has changed little over the last hundred years. They live in low huts carefully crafted with interwoven sticks and plastered with mud and cattle dung. In some areas, wild sisal is also strung into roof mats for extra protection. Traditionally, each hut has two spacious beds, again woven from branches, covered with goat and cow hides. The larger bed is for the mother, the smaller for her children. Samburu men, who are polygamous, rotate among their wives.

Incidentally the beds are virtually wall to wall, with only a small space in the centre for a cooking fire and small stools for visitors. Samburu →*page 222*

# TURKANA
**Eastern Nilotic**

The Turkana (207,250) inhabit the whole north-west of Kenya between Lake Turkana to the east and the escarpment marking the Uganda boundary on the west. The administrative centre is Lodwar. The Muruaolon massif in west-central Turkanaland dwarfs the other hill ranges, with the exception of Lorionetom in the northeast.

The Turkana originated from the area further west. Legend has it that young Jie men in search of a stray ox wandered into the Tarash Valley and there met an old woman of their tribe gathering wild fruit. Impressed, they persuaded other young men and women to join them and returned with their stock to settle. The Jie and Turkana have been traditional allies ever since.

Turkana are either of the forest people (Nimonia) or the people of the plains (Nocuro) into which all territorial districts are irrationally divided. There are 20 or so clans (*ategerin*) but the effective Turkana community is a neighbourhood (*adakar*). All Turkana men belong to one of two generation-sets: the Stones (Nimur) or Leopards (Nerisai).

Milk and blood are the main diet, and cattle provide the hides for sleeping mats, to cover the huts against rain, and to make sandals. The horns are used for snuff containers. Camels are also important in the Turkana economy. Goats and sheep, herded by small girls or boys, are killed for guests, minor rituals or meat. Donkeys are used solely as pack animals; the hides are cut into strips for panniers.

Dried milk (*edodo*) is made by boiling large quantities of fresh milk and drying it on skins. Camel milk cannot be churned for butter but is good for babies as it has a low fat content and is easily digested. Wild berries are crushed and made into cakes with blood or ground into a dried meal. Women cultivate their homelands (*akwap*) near watercourses in the rainy season (*agiporo*) where they grow millet and gourds. Fishing in Lake Turkana is especially practised in the dry season (*akumo*) or famines.

A Turkana homestead (*awi*) comprises a man and his wife and children. Sons remain within the family group, but daughters leave their fathers' home-steads on marriage. A family *awi* is rarely a single enclosure and *awi napolon* and *awi abor* are the names given to the principal enclosure where the head of the family lives and to the secondary enclosure of additional wives and their children and married sons. Turkana homesteads are built in association with *awi* of other families. The main entrance faces east, and the day hut (*ekal*) and night hut (*akai*) of the chief wife are on the right of the entrance.

For the Turkana, marriage is a three-year ceremonial process is designed to ensure the ritual, spiritual and social well-being of those involved. Not until the first child has been weaned and has reached walking age can the marriage process be completed. Considerable numbers of large stock (cattle or camels) are required to meet the bride price, and these the suitor obtains from his own herds and those of his father, his father's and his mother's brothers, stock associates and bond-friends. The important position of the wife in the *awi* is reflected in the close ties that will be perpetuated between her husband on one hand and her father and brothers on the other.

The Turkana have evolved a material culture peculiar to themselves. Water troughs and containers are carved from wood and decorated with poker work; fat, butter and milk containers are made from hides (particularly camel) decorated with beadwork and cowries. Traditional weapons are an 8-foot (2.4-metre), leaf-shaped spear, knobkerrie, fighting stick, wrist knife, finger hook and for defence a buffalo, giraffe or hippo hide shield. The women wear enormous quantities of beads around the neck and a neck-ring (*alagam*) of brass or aluminium.

The Turkana have a reputation as skilled herdsmen and fearless watchmen. Improved communications are slowly eroding their traditional insularity, brought about by the inaccessibility of their desert homeland. Settlement schemes based on irrigated plots along the Turkwel and Kerio rivers and fishing cooperatives along the western shore of Lake Turkana are being encouraged by the government and Christian missions. The ambitious Turkwel Gorge hydroelectric and irrigation scheme will provide thousands of hectares of irrigated land for agricultural settlement. ∎

**Above**, Turkana girl with elaborate necklace.

# BORAN
## Eastern Cushitic

A section of the Oromo-speaking peoples of southern Ethiopia, the Boran (69,000) moved south at the turn of the century into the arid areas of northeast Kenya to settle around Moyale, Marsabit, along Uaso Nyiro River and in Isiolo District. The Oromo erupted into the Christian kingdom of Ethiopia in the 16th century, conquering and settling in large parts of the country. But between 1890 and 1900, their vast territories were subdued by Emperor Menelik II, and his policy of ruthless extermination and demands for tribute forced the Boran and other Ethiopian peoples (notably the Burji) to migrate into Kenya.

Predominantly cattle holders, the Boran believe in a supreme deity, Wak, with whom they communicate through a priest, the Qallu, and with sacrifices and prayer (*wadaja*). (Southernmost Boran, however, have been converted to Islam.) Living Qallu are regarded as the embodiment of the first: he was discovered as a full-grown man herding three black cows and a ram by a hunter-gatherers, the Wata. Despised though they are, for no Boran would take a Wata for his wife or give his daughter to one, the Wata play an important role in Boran rituals. The Qallu continue to maintain herds of black cows, descendants of those found with the first Qallu.

The Gona group, divided into the Ful'leli (Oditu, Dacitu, Gallantu, Konitu, Macitu, Bacitu and Sirraiyu) and Haroresa (Arussi, Hawartu, Qarcabdu, Jilitu, Nonitu and Dambitu) sub-sections, together with the Sabho (Digalu, Matari and Karaiyu) make up the Boran people.

A series of complex rituals and festivals marks the birth and naming of a Boran child. The first ceremony is more usually confined to relatives and close friends, whereas the whole community participates in the *jilla* ceremony – to name a child, to thank and seek the blessing of Wak. A large *galma*, modelled on that of the *Qallu*, is built in which a Wata, using firesticks, kindles the first fire. If the child is a boy, his head-tuft (*gutu*) is shaved off by

<u>Above</u>, a young Borana girl.

his father who, after further feasting and singing, names the child. The following dawn a bullock is blessed and sacrificed. Kin bracelets are cut from its hide for the child and relatives; a diviner reads the boy's fortune and the meat is divided – the Wata, in gratitude for discovering the first Qallu, receive a share, together with gifts of milk. A girl child goes through a simpler *jilla* ceremony.

Before a young man is again allowed to grow a *gutu*, he has to establish his manhood by killing a man of another tribe, a lion or an elephant, or prove his virility as a father of a homestead (*aba worra*) by marrying and begetting a child. In the final year of the *gadamoji* cycle this *gutu* is plaited into the halo-like *guduru* to which is added the metal or ivory *kalacha*. There is a *gadamoji* ceremony every eight years. Each candidate makes a series of sacrifices – a bull on *barati* day at the start of the ceremony, a sheep on *elejesa* day and another bull on *buffat* day, when his elaborate *guduru* hair-do is ritually shaved by his wife and buried in the cattle-dung *dobu*. After a Boran has completed decorating his head and undergone the *gadamoji* ceremony and shaved off his *guduru*, he should never again carry a spear, swear or become involved in an affray (unless extremely provoked). He is respected and honoured.

The Boran are divided into five generation-sets (*luba*), each of which has its father (*aba gada*) nominated by the elders, and takes the name of the appointed *aba gada* as its own. Four eight-year initiation cycles separate the generations; 40 years thus elapse between the initiation of father and son.

Payment of the bride price for a Boran girl, who may be circumcised any time and without ceremony, is made in cattle, tobacco or dried coffee berries (*buni*). A Boran woman is confined to the *galma* for three weeks following childbirth, and fed a diet of meat, soup and blood.

International and district boundaries and tribal grazing restrictions increasingly curtail the movement of the Boran, who congregate around the limited water points in the dry seasons and disperse to grazing areas after the rains. They dislike wage labour and few migrate to towns. Skilled stockmen, they are found on many farms. Despite educational advances and irrigation schemes along the Uaso Nyiro, their traditional lifestyle has so far been little disrupted. ∎

homes are windowless and dark so as to keep out flies. They also keep in smoke, which probably accounts for the existence of chronic chest infections and trachoma, which can eventually result in blindness.

An extended family of brothers, wives and parents live in a circular formation of huts surrounded by a high thorn branch fence called a *boma*. Livestock is herded inside at night where the thorn forms an effective barrier against marauding predators. The smallest animals are brought into the huts.

The Samburu live on the livestock, of course – mostly on a thick curdled milk which tastes like smoke-flavoured yoghurt. Sometimes this is mixed with cattle blood and – on special occasions only – they eat meat. Their entire lifestyle is centred on cows, camels and goats, which they refer to as their wealth and only sometimes slaughter for ritual events. Money doesn't mean much to them and the little they have is carried by the warriors in socks, knotted and hung from their belts.

**"White cows" and "black cows"**: To an outsider, the Samburu may appear to lead a random, capricious existence, with little direction. But, in fact, their society is disciplined by ritual and is also rigidly compartmentalised according to age-groups and age-sets. A man's life cycle from birth to death is phased every 14 years or so by ceremonies marking transition from one age-set to the next. Each child is born in a particular age-group and its male members enjoy a special bond for the rest of their lives. In addition, the tribe is divided into eight clans: four belong to the "white cows" and four to the "black cows", with these further divided into series of sub-clans. Greetings between strangers always include a who's who breakdown of clan, sub-clan, and age-group, which usually results in the satisfying discovery of a distant relationship of some sort.

As a child, a boy tends his father's herds. Then, when he reaches puberty, he is circumcised and becomes a warrior, also known as a *murrani* or a

**A heavily decorated Borana woman.**

*moran.* From there, he moves on to become a junior elder and finally a senior elder. Circumcision is considered essential to most polygamous societies. The old men need a regular supply of young girls from which to pick their second and third wives, so they jealously exclude the handsome warriors by forbidding them to marry. Only when the younger men become junior elders can they look for their first wives. At this point, the bridal economy shifts to a seller's market and for the first few years the competition for young girls of 12 to 15 is intense.

**"Beaded" Samburu girls**: These ochre-smeared, bare-breasted *en-toyie* girls are as pert and provocative as any teenager at a disco. They are cheeky, chattering starlings, their hands covering their laughter as they lean on their herding sticks. They delight in teasing warriors with their alternating moods of welcome and feigned arrogance. In truth, each girl hopes to become "beaded" by a warrior which means that he will delve into his sock to buy layer

after layer of necklaces for her as a form of commitment. This does not indicate marriage, however; a girl may still be married to an elder. She will be circumcised the morning or the day before the ceremony and, once a wife, will become pregnant as soon as she can.

The warrior years are halcyon for the young men, whose role is comparable to the knights of the Middle Ages. But they also undertake tough and sometimes dangerous assignments to ensure the safety and well-being of their community. As the traveller leaves Maralal and drops over the lip of the plateau on to the ochre plains of **El Barta**, he may encounter caravans of cattle herded by these warriors carrying twin spears. During droughts, they may drive their herds hundreds of miles from one patch of sparse grazing to another.

For those who have not travelled the area on foot, this dusty landscape, speckled with cattle, ostrich and zebra may seem monotonous. But it has its tales to tell. The road passes through the town of **Baragoi** and winds on, flanked

desiccated
len – fossil
rest, Alia
ay, Turkana.

by Koitokol Mountain on the right and the saw-toothed Kowop Range on the left. Here the Turkana trespassed and clashed with the Samburu as recently as 1980. Only one man was wounded in the skirmish, a warrior who was speared in the back. But it seems that a friend gripped the spear shaft and pulled it out from the front. The wound was packed with herbs and the injured man survived. Deeds such as this accord these young men their heroic reputations.

From there, it's on to **South Horr**, sandwiched between Ol Doinyo Mara mountains to the right and Mount Nyiru on the left. This lush valley grows bananas and paw-paws which are brought in to the towns. The Catholic mission also sells lemons to thirsty travellers. **Home of the God Enkai**: Towering above the village, on Nyiru's flank is **Kosikosi**, a brown and fissured outcrop of rock gleaming in the sun. This is the home of the Samburu god, Enkai or Ngei. A sacrificial bull is slaughtered on this natural altar to mark the start of tribal circumcision ceremonies.

On the far side of South Horr is **Kurungu Camp**, a welcome stopover with double cabins and cold beer. Kurungu puts on spectacular dances where warriors and young girls move in a snorting, yelling throng, as spears twirl in the air. Men and women each have their special songs that must be sung separately. Once, when a priest asked his congregation to raise its voice in unison in a hymn of thanks for the onset of the rains, the request also gave rise to much anxiety. The churchgoers feared this social violation would induce yet another drought.

Before reaching South Horr, there is a road to the left that leads to **Tum**, a seldom visited village nestling against Nyiru's western slopes. This is the home of Lesepen, the aged astrologer and oracle of the tribe, who foretells the future by gazing at Mars and Venus – the morning and evening star.

Tum is also the gateway to the **Suguta Valley**, an alien moonscape originally moulded by erupting volcanoes on the approach to the southern end of Lake Turkana. A track from the village leads down to the tiny settlement of **Parkati**, "the place of no water", on the valley's edge and halfway down that is a roadside cross, fashioned from orange pipes. Its inscription in Turkana says: "Rest in peace. We will see you again." The simple monument commemorates a Catholic priest who was murdered nearby in 1981 by Turkana bandits known as *N'goroko*.

They have since been subdued by the army and no longer present a menace to travellers. Even so, the Suguta's jagged scarps of black lava (the height of office blocks) impede a vehicle's progress and inspire visions of ambush. The Turkana live here, tending their goats and camels, alongside silver-backed jackals and Grant's gazelle.

**Site of a broken dream**: Some years ago, another indomitable Catholic priest persuaded a wealthy foreigner to spend a million shillings on the construction of a tourist lodge close to Parkati. When he eventually saw the wasteland in which he had ploughed his money, he scrapped the deal. The priest

**Rendille women in Kaisut Desert.**

sold the truck he had bought and returned the money, but the airstrip he built still remains.

On the floor of the valley is **Lake Logipi**, framed by an amphitheatre of rust-red hills. **Logipi Hill**, ringed by silver, rises from its centre like a shining Excalibur. This shallow soda pan is visited seasonally by thousands of flamingos that form a shimmering cerise carpet as they sift the waters with upside-down beaks. It is the canthaxanthin in the soda, a substance similar to vitamin A, that imbues the birds with their pink colouring.

**Lake Turkana, "Jade Sea":** Logipi's northern neighbour, **Lake Turkana**, is the final destination for every safari in this area, a journey of at least two days from Nairobi. It is a place of spellbinding beauty. The algae that abound in the lake change their colour from charcoal grey to Delft blue as clouds scud overhead. But most often its surface dances deep green in the sunlight, giving it the nickname "Jade Sea".

But be prepared for beguilement

from the siren lake. With temperatures touching 145°F (63°C), Turkana's cool depths are tempting, but the bitter alkaline waters can never quench your thirst, and swimming is a pastime to be treated cautiously. There are plenty of crocodiles, seen basking along the shore, seldom going far off the beaches. For the most part they are fish-eaters, hence the belief that the saurians in Turkana *never* eat humans. But when a scientist, Alistair Graham, conducted a study of crocodile behaviour at the lake in 1965–67, and in the process lost his colleague who was seized by the reptile, it was determined that the Lake crocodiles do eat large mammals, albeit infrequently. And perhaps it is this infrequency that makes Turkana relatively safe to swim in.

Sportsmen appreciate Turkana for its fishing possibilities and have this in mind when they head for either the lodge at **Ferguson's Gulf** on the western side, or Oasis Lodge at **Loyangalani** on the eastern shore.

Anglers in search of sport try for the great Nile perch (*Lates niloticus*), a melancholy but enormous fish that can tip the scales at 400 lb (180 kilos). As an angling challenge, however, it is a disappointment, providing about as much fight as an outsized goldfish. Less spectacular but more exciting are the tigerfish which can be reeled in from the shore. Commercial fishermen go for the more abundant and palatable Nile tilapia. Their catches are marketed, dried or frozen, in Kenya's urban centres away to the south. One of the lake's more unusual denizens is a small puffer fish that inflates itself to a prodigious size with air or water when threatened. Their occurrence here is a reminder of the times when Turkana was connected to the Mediterranean in the north via the Nile, since such fish are more usually associated with coral reefs.

**A tribe that time forgot:** The El-molo are a marketed tourist attraction. The inhabitants of settlements here are paraded as the last survivors of a dying tribe. But the fact is, that until a few decades ago the El-modo spoke their own East Cushitic language, but then ➤*page 228*

# RENDILLE
## Eastern Cushitic

The northeastern neighbours of the Samburu with whom, despite linguistic and cultural divisions, they have age-old ties of kinship and economic co-operation, are the 22,000 camel-owning Rendille of Marsabit District.

The Rendille, known to the Samburu, also have a close affinity with the Somali probably extending back several centuries. The composite character of the Rendille people is reflected in their folklore, which stresses the inter-tribal links and migrations of the past. The Ariaal (or southern Rendille) have a cattle economy and strong links with Samburu.

Long ago, say the Rendille, nine Somali warriors herding camels from a remote camp became lost. After many days of wandering, they eventually reached the outskirts of Samburu country. Before they were permitted by the Samburu elders to marry women from that tribe, the strangers were instructed to discard their customs and throw away the Qur'an, the Holy Book of Islam. The Somalis agreed, and from these fist unions grew the Rendille tribe. There are two Rendille groups, one of five and the other of four clans, the Belisi Bahai (the Dibshai or Dubsahel, the Uiyam, Nahagan, Matarpa and Rongumo) and the Belisi Beri (the Saale, Urwen, Tubsha or Turcha and Galdeelan or Galthile).

The camel economy of the Rendille is centred around large semi-permanent settlements of married men, women and children, and the mobile camps where the older boys and young men look after the balance of the herds, moving frequently to ensure adequate browse. The male pack camels may carry up to 1,800lb (80 kg) over 40 miles (60 km) a day. The large flocks of sheep and goats are shepherded by the young girls. The Rendille mix the camel's milk with blood: a small knife or blunt arrow is used to open a vein in the throat which, after sufficient blood has been drawn off, is closed with a mixture of hair and camel dung.

The Rendille hut (afaf) is covered with woven fibre mats (eima) and hides; the fire stones (kindase) are on the left of the entrance, and a leather water container (haan, pl. haanan) is placed ready in the right-hand corner. Pots (thiri, pl. thiryo), gourds and sleeping mats of camel hide (nim, pl. niiboi) are the main household items. Water buckets are made from giraffe hide and plaited fibre containers hold milk and water. Fetching water is a woman's task.

Members of a Rendille age-set are circumcised at the same time; each clan has one circumcision settlement inside which a large initiates' hut (mingidakhan) is built. Circumcision is by seniority. If the youth bears the pain without flinching, his kinsmen reward him with a present of a heifer-camel. Initiation (khandi) ceremonies usually follow two or three years after those of the neighbouring Samburu. A year or so after circumcision, an age-set receives its name. The ceremony (galgulumi) is performed in one vast specially built settlement on the eastern shore of Lake Turkana.

The Rendille annually celebrate two major festivals, soriu, involving the whole family, in January/February and in June/July after the rains when there is good grazing close to the settlements so that the youths in the cattle camps can be present; and almhato at the onset of the long rains. Each family provides an animal for slaughter during soriu. The elders witness the killing of each beast and mark their bodies with its blood. The remaining camels and small stock are daubed with blood by the father or eldest married son. Almhato is a festival of milk to ward off misfortune. The ceremony is performed age-set by age-set and vast quantities of fresh milk are drunk before the final ritual and removal of the settlement to a fresh site.

For a Rendille girl to become pregnant before circumcision is a matter of great dishonour. In former days, it is said the girl and her lover were tied together on a camel to be driven over a high cliff. Rendille girls are married immediately after circumcision, following payment of a bride price made in camels. On the birth of the first male child, the women plait their hair into a cock's comb (doko) embellished with fat and ochre.

The Rendille still herd their stock across the harsh semi-desert and scrub, but the schools and hospitals of the Consolata Mission are preparing these nomadic people for the confrontation with the realities of the 20th century. ∎

Above, yoke necklace worn by a Rendille woman.

# EL-MOLO

**Eastern Cushitic**

---

The El-molo (less than 500 in number) live on two small islands and at Loyangalani in the southeastern corner of Lake Turkana (formerly Rudolf) in northern Kenya, an inhospitable region of wind-lashed lava and sun-scorched desert scrub. Only a few stunted acacias along the dried-up watercourses and clusters of doum palms relieve the desolation. The El-molo subsist by fishing.

The history of the El-molo is obscure. The name derives from the word *molo* meaning "man", to which the Maasai-Samburu plural prefix *il* was added and anglicised as El-molo. The El-molo, who call themselves Ldes, are divided into four clans: Lmarle, Orikara (Amkara), Origijijo and Ndes. They are neither, as often depicted, "Africa's smallest tribe" nor a "dying race". Even in Kenya the Yaaku and other hunter-gatherer peoples may be numerically smaller than the El-molo who, by intermarrying with neighbouring Samburu and Turkana, have avoided extinction.

The El-molo travelled to their present home in el-Molo Bay from the northern tip of Lake Turkana, perhaps from the Omo delta. The oral traditions of the El-molo detail not only how they came to start their 155-mile (250-km) journey south, but also catalogue the promontories and sand-spits at which they stopped, perhaps for decades at a time, en route. Legend has it that long ago the El-molo lived far to the north. One day the men left to go fishing some distance from their village. While they were away, raiders from the interior attacked the defenceless village, spearing to death the unprotected women and children left behind and looting their belongings and livestock. Saddened by the killing and fearful that the raiders might return, the men, with a few survivors, decided to set out south, eventually reaching El-molo Bay.

Most of the El-molo now speak Samburu. Only a few elders still speak the tribe's indigenous language. Shared cultural traits such as the burying of the dead in stone cairns and belief in a deity called

**Above**, el-Molo fishermen of the Jade Sea.

Wak suggest that the El-molo may derive from earlier neighbouring Rendille pastoralists turned permanent fishermen.

Fresh or dried fish form the staple food of the El-molo, augmented by crocodile, turtle and hippo meat. Wild game and birds are also eaten. The El-molo account for their former lack of husbandry with the tale that, long ago, they too owned stock. Their animals, however, were not camels, cattle, sheep and goats but hippos, crocodiles, and turtles. Each morning these would be driven to feed on the grass and aquatic weeds along the lake shore. Just like camels and cattle, they were milked and bled for food.

The El-molo construct doum palm rafts with which to fish and communicate with el-Molo Island. Part of the bride price payment traditionally consisted of two such fishing rafts. When dry, these El-molo rafts are capable of transporting three to four adults (larger rafts incorporating perhaps a dozen logs are used to move whole families and their belongings) but the fibrous wood of the doum palm quickly becomes waterlogged, limiting the use of the rafts to no more than a few hours.

The El-molo employ three traditional methods of fishing: harpooning, netting and hook and line. In recent years, the Turkana basket fish-trap has also been adopted. Harpoons are made by inserting a barbed metal head, to which a long fibre rope is secured, into one end of a wooden shaft so that it can be jabbed or thrown to catch the giant Nile perch.

Ornaments are not as elaborate as in neighbouring Samburu and Turkana. Women wear strings of ostrich-egg shells or glass beads. Metal wrist and elbow bracelets are worn by men and women. Bowl-shaped clay pottery vessels have been replaced by cheap aluminium cooking pots (*sufuria*). The dome-shaped, circular huts are built of interlaced acacia branches and covered with doum palm leaves, reeds, grass or other vegetation held down by stones. Woven palm-leaf mats are used for sleeping.

The El-molo are changing rapidly. New fishing techniques are being introduced and at Loyangalani, they are turning to cattle-keeping and wage-employment at the nearby lodge, or fishing commercially to supplement their traditional form of subsistence in larger and better housed settlements. ∎

adopted not just the East Nilotic language of their neighbours, the Samburu, but also their customs and traditions.

The myth of a disappearing race that was advanced by the media in the 1960s has no basis in truth as the population continues to grow. About 300 El-molo live in close contact with the Catholic mission in Loyangalani that was established in 1967.

It is ironic that Lake Turkana, where men and animals struggle for survival, may actually have been the birthplace of mankind itself. Kenyan palaeontologist Richard Leakey and a team of international scientists have spent many years carefully brushing away sand and dust from a treasure trove of hominid bones and stone tools. These finds prove that man-like creatures with a relatively high level of intelligence inhabited the lake shores as far back as 2 million years ago.

**The first human?**: **Koobi Fora**, the name given to this palaeontological site that fans out over 1,000 sq. miles (2,600 sq. km), burst into the public arena in 1972. This was when Bernard Ng'eneo, a Kenyan field worker, was passing through a gully he had often walked before when a tiny fragment of skull caught his eye. Eventually more than 300 segments were sifted from the sand.

When reconstructed, the skull simply known by its index number of "1470" had a large braincase of 46½ cubic inches (775 cubic cm) compared with that of the *Australopithecines* (500 cubic cm), who are believed to be cousins of *Homo Sapiens* (1,800 cubic cm). Anyway, the landmark "1470" skull is the earliest firm evidence of human's evolution from apes.

This *Homo habilis* or "handy man" has replanted our ancestral roots by half a million years. Visitors can reach the site by a chartered plane or on a track from Loyangalani, although this is rough even by northern standards. There are self-help cabins, which can be booked through the National Museums of Kenya in Nairobi.

Koobi Fora is a part of **Sibiloi National Park**, a little used wildlife sanctuary where visitors can watch lion, cheetah, oryx, zebra and topi in almost guaranteed solitude. Just before the park's entrance, on the right, is **Sibiloi Mountain** where giant petrified trees 4 feet (1.25 metres) in girth are strewn, like building blocks of the gods. Seven million years ago, these junipers stood at 49 feet (15 metres) and could have flourished because of high rainfall.

**Mirages in the Chalbi**: To vary the return journey, turn right on the way southwards to **North Horr** and thereafter drive across the **Chalbi Desert**. Here, in this stretch of true desert, mirages play tricks on the traveller. Dark triangular blobs drifting effortlessly through ribbons of water evaporate as you approach. In their place are a string of several hundred dusky camels in the care of Gabbra tribesmen who will raise their rifles in friendly salute.

On the far side of the Chalbi is **Marsabit**, perhaps the most fascinating of the myriad volcanic mountains in the north. Long extinct, it is capped with mist forests where elephant and greater kudu live. Just 2½ miles (4 km) from the town, in **Marsabit National Park**, is **Marsabit Lodge** overlooking a crater lake. Farther up the mountain is an enchanting water-filled crater, known as **Lake Paradise**. This tranquil setting, which provides a breathtaking view over several hundred miles, is a place that travel writers of less generous spirit are tempted to keep to themselves.

Another point of interest is the **Singing Wells** on the track to **Ulanula**. This watering spot for the Rendille cattle consists of hand-dug wells many feet deep, and it derives its name from songs chanted by the chain of men who pass the water up to the troughs above in leather calabashes. It is a rich photographic opportunity, but one that cannot be explored until a mutual price has been agreed upon.

The road south from Marsabit to Isiolo, at the foot of the Mount Kenya massif, is best driven in convoy. This may not allow the traveller to linger by the Matthews Range on the right. But, at this stage, it won't matter too much. The rest of the northern safari will have been more than enough.

**Right, giant Golde Nile perch.**

# WESTERN KENYA: A SCENIC CIRCUIT

The Trans-Africa Highway climbs the western wall of the Rift Valley by a less spectacular route than its descent on the eastern side. It is a steep climb nonetheless since Nakuru, lying on the valley floor, is around 6,000 feet (1,830 metres) above sea level, and the highest point the road reaches above the western wall is well over 9,000 feet (2,700 metres).

At that point, 5 miles (8 km) off the main trunk route, is the small farming town of **Molo**. The town is set in high altitude open downs which are more reminiscent of Scotland than Africa: more so with the chill and mists of the morning. It's not surprising that the Molo area attracted the early white settlers who saw it as prime sheep country. It wasn't quite like that, however, since the pests and blights were distinctly African. But the settlers won out in the end and the result is the superb "Molo" lamb as a staple on many dinner tables in Kenya.

The white settlers have all gone, with their large farms subdivided and given out to the local African community. But the echoes are still there, across the wheat fields, in a faint "gone away" from the extinct "Molo Hunt". It was there until just recently – "full fig", with the pinks and the baying hounds.

Close by Molo, at **Mau Summit**, the trunk route splits. One arm continues as the Trans-Africa Highway, which heads northwest across the northern half of the highland plateau west of the Rift, eventually reaching the Uganda border at Malaba. The other heads away southwest as the main road route to Lake Victoria.

**Eldoret and Elgon:** Not far from the fork, the highway crosses the wide level plain of the Uasin Gishu Plateau to the town of **Eldoret**, or "64" as it's sometimes called. (It was set up on mile-post 64 from Londiani on the ox-wagon route of the local "voertrekker" South Africans.)

When they arrived before World War

I, the plateau was teeming with wildlife. It was something like the Athi Plains around Nairobi or the Mara-Serengeti. The game soon disappeared as the settlers turned the Uasin Gishu into Kenya's main granary. Maize and wheat fields stretched from horizon to horizon and still do in parts.

Beyond Eldoret, filling much of the western horizon, is the massive extinct volcano of **Mount Elgon**. It is around 3,000 feet (880 metres) short of Mount Kenya, but the circumference of its base makes it a bigger massif. At its foot stands **Kitale**, the northernmost of the agricultural towns built by the settlers in the colonial era. With Elgon's slopes to the west and the high range of the Cheranganis to the east, the agriculture about Kitale is as diverse as it can get in Kenya. Beef and dairy farms, coffee estates, wheat and maize fields surround the town and on the higher slopes are orchards of temperate European fruits, like apples.

In its upper, forested reaches, Mount Elgon is a national park, but one of the least developed. Dense, tall forest and a lack of roads inhibit game viewing, but it is possible to hike up to the summit, across moorlands of giant heather beyond the distinctive **Kitum Cave**.

While the volcanic soils of Kenya's mountain ranges are fertile, they don't seem to yield the minerals the elephant crave – except at rare salt licks, one of which is in the Kitum Cave which has attracted the big mammals for centuries. Quite literally, the elephant mine the cave – gouging out the walls and extending the shafts hundreds of feet into the mountain.

From Elgon, the country falls away fairly gently towards Lake Victoria and the Nile Valley. The highway passes **Webuye**, where Kenya's fledgling paper industry is located in an area of dense settlement, principally of the Luhya peoples. Their headquarters are in the township of **Kakamega** which is 26 miles (42 km) to the south of the highway.

Not far from the town is the **Kakamega Forest** and a neighbour, the **Kaimosi Forest**. Both are centres of conservationist attention since they are relics of the Equatorial rain forest which once spread from West Africa to the East African coast. Zaire is not easy to get to for tourists, so the Kakamega and Kaimosi fragments of "jungle" are increasingly popular for specialists looking for West African kinds of animals, birds and plants. The trouble is that the future of these rare habitats is insecure through massive population increase in the area.

About 30 miles (48 km) south of Kakamega is the town of **Kisumu**, on the shores of Lake Victoria. Ranked third in size after Nairobi and Mombasa, Kisumu was once "Port Florence" and the original terminus for the Uganda Railway. The town has since developed not only as the major administrative centre for most of western Kenya, but also as a port with shipbuilding and repair facilities. Its atmosphere is still distinctly "nautical", which is not surprising given the vast size of Lake Victoria – its area of 26,500 sq. miles (63,000 sq. km) makes it the largest lake

in Africa and the world's second largest freshwater lake.

Kisumu's fortunes were reversed in 1977 after the disruption of the East African Community, a political and economic arrangement whereby three countries – Kenya, Uganda and Tanzania – shared inter-territorial steamer and general communications services. The town is now recovering through diversification into light industry and is once more a regional centre of economic activity for 2 million Luo people of the Lake and Kavirondo Gulf region. Many of them are still fishermen, still generally known as "fish eaters". In any event, the Luo are found around many fish-bearing lakes, rivers and dams in Kenya and outside – in Uganda and down to south Tanzania.

**Arab sails on Lake Victoria**: The fishing fleets of Lake Victoria – white lateen sails against a deep blue background – appear to be out of the romantic myths of the Sindbad coast, and there is in fact a connection. This goes back to the time when the Arab slavers were marauding **Kericho tea plantation – a prime export.**

234

around Victoria, building boats for the lake in the same style as the dhows on the ocean. The lateen sail was thereafter adopted by the Luo shipwrights.

Giant Nile Perch were recently introduced into the lake, at first unsuccessfully. By themselves, of course, they couldn't get farther up than the blockade of Murchison Falls between Lake Albert and Kioga in Uganda. So a transplant was tried in the 1950s, only nothing happened.

A decade later, scientists of the East African Freshwater Fisheries Organization at Jinja gave the matter more thought and repeated the introduction. This time it worked and there was an explosion of Nile perch throughout the lake and particularly in the Kavirondo Gulf. As usual, man's intervention in the natural environment had unforeseen results. The two indigenous species of tilapia have since disappeared, much to the Luo's dismay since they don't much like the taste of the now dominant perch.

Kenya's main sugar-growing area lies close to Kisumu, in the **Nyando Valley** at the head of the Kavirondo Gulf. Production is from both large estates as well as from smallholders in a policy unusual in Africa for its tolerant flexibility.

On the far side of the Gulf from Kisumu, in the lee of Homa Bay town lies the **Ruma National Park**. This is mostly uninhabited because of tsetse fly and the sleeping sickness it carries, which is no worry to in-and-out tourists. At some stage, this refuge for the roan antelope left in Kenya will be integrated into the country's wildlife circuits. For the moment, however, it's something of a back-water for the specialist.

**Tea plantations at Kericho:** Back to the fork at Mau Summit, the southern highway runs some 30 miles (48 km) through forest reserve and plantations before reaching the "tea capital" of **Kericho**. High ground, temperate climate and high rainfall off Lake Victoria make the district ideal for the production of tea.

When the Europeans first arrived,

**Weighing tea pluckers are paid by the basket.**

# LUO
## Western Nilotic

The second-largest of the non-Bantu ethnic groups in Kenya after the Kikuyu (2.2 million), the Luo of Central and South Nyanza districts, around the Kavirondo Gulf of Lake Victoria, represent the most vigorous of southward drives of Nilotes from the Sudan.

The first wave of Luo immigrants probably arrived in Nyanza about five centuries ago. The arrival of the last of the Luo groups in the 18th century coincided with the thrust into South Nyanza, causing the Gusii, Kuria and Suba to retreat and bringing the Luo into contact with the Maasai and the Kipsigis. Four major groups, Joka-Jok, Joka-Owiny, Joka-Omolo and Joka-Suba, make up these Dholuo-speaking peoples, who claim common descent from the mythological patriarch Ramogi, supposedly the founder of the first Luo settlement on a hill in Kadimu.

Cattle and constant migrations in search of pastures for their herds dominated the life of the first Luo immigrants. The Luo adjusted to growing population pressures by adopting a sedentary way of life in relatively isolated homesteads. Although cattle continued to dominate ritual and economic activities, agriculture and fishing became increasingly important for subsistence. Sorghum, sim-sim and finger millet were the traditional crops grown, and now vegetables, groundnuts, coffee and sugarcane

are valuable additions in a cash economy. These people still maintain their migratory instincts – tens of thousands seeking employment have flooded the major towns, especially Nairobi and Mombasa.

Foremost among Kenya's people in their fishing skills, the Luo today mainly use gill nets and long-line fishing to catch tilapia (*rigege*) and other fish. Extensive use is still made of basket traps, either on their own or in conjunction with the *osageru* fish maze and the *kek* river fence and its modification the *obalala* at the mouths of rivers. The Luo formerly used crude log and bundle rafts of papyrus or saplings on Lake Victoria. In deeper water, hollowed-out log canoes or plank-built craft of considerable complexity and size are employed. The dhow-type fishing boats used in offshore fishing seem to

have been first constructed on the Winam Gulf by Asians and later adapted and built by the Luo themselves, leading to more intensive exploitation of the fisheries in the Winam Gulf and along the shores of the open lake. The more advanced Ssesse canoe of the Baganda has also been adopted and many are now moulded in glass fibre. Powered by outboard motors, the canoes are used not only by the Luo fishermen of Lake Victoria but on most of Kenya's inland waters.

The head of a homestead has his own hut (*duol*) built near the cattle enclosure. Here, important matters relating to the household and community are discussed among the clan elders. Wives have their individual huts and may not sleep in the *duol*. Traditionally, a young woman whose suitor had paid sufficient bride price to the parents would be carried off by force by the bridegroom and his friends. A number of ceremonies followed on this abduction (*meko*), culminating in the feast (*riso*) given by the husband for his relatives. Today, bride prices are often met by a cash payment in lieu of cattle and marriages are formalised by Christian rite.

Expectant mothers observe certain customs and dietary taboos. A new-born child may have cold water poured over it to make it cry, or tobacco smoke blown up its nose. The Luo practise neither circumcision nor clitoridectomy, but more young boys now undergo circumcision for religious reasons or to conform to the accepted belief that this operation is the mark of manhood.

The ancestors play a vital role in the community, and the spirits of the truly great – Gor Mahia, Ramogi, and Lwanda Magere – are revered. Good spirits (*nyasaye*, pl. *nyiseche*), however, must contend with a host of hostile spirits (*jochiende*) and wizards (*jajuok*). Witchcraft flourished on the finges of this "shadow" world.

The Luo, an articulate, community-conscious people, were prominent in the struggle for independence, providing many leading trade unionists and politicians, of whom the late Tom Mboya and the former Vice-President of Kenya, Oginga Odinga, fanned the flame of *Uhuru* ("freedom"). Luo folklore has been imaginatively captured in the modern fiction of Grace Ogot and Tom Okoya. ∎

**Above**, drying fishes in the sun at Mbita Point, Lake Victoria.

much of it was under tall montane forest. With a massive import of capital, the land was cleared and planted so that ridge after ridge is now patterned a bright, almost apple-green as one of the most productive tea areas on earth. As a consolation for the conservation purists, who regret the loss of natural forest, there is no erosion. The tea plants retain the soil and anyway have an attraction of their own in a distinctive greening of the hills.

At Kericho a major road descends to Kisumu while another holds to the high ground through **Sotik, Kisii** and eventually to the Tanzanian border at **Isebania** which is some 113 miles (182 km) beyond.

**Rich highlands:** The Kisii highlands, which is the home of the Gusii people, are exceptionally rich, although very little of their land is now left fallow. As in other areas of the western highlands, the population growth is exceptionally high and causes a constant migration of people to other parts of the country in search of employment or new land to cultivate.

Hidden away in southwest Kenya, the agricultural contribution that the Gusii people make to the country's economy is often overlooked. Yet they produce tea, coffee and pyrethrum – major foreign exchange earners – in considerable quantity.

In contrast to Kericho, where the tea plantations are owned and run by large commercial concerns backed by international capital, production by the Gusii and their neighbours is mainly from smallholdings. For a century or more, conventional wisdom held that tea could only be efficiently grown on large plantations. This was challenged by Leslie Brown, famous as an authority on birds of prey, but also Kenya's senior agriculturalist at the close of the colonial era.

He was right; Kenya is now the world's third largest tea producer after India and Sri Lanka, and more than half the output is being collected from thousands of individual African planters on small plots of tea-growing land. As a result, the local tea economy is particu-

larly robust and the same policy is now being applied to the country's sugar production.

Because Kisii and the southwest of Kenya generally are so densely populated, it's not wildlife country and thus off the main tourist circuits. The visitor is unlikely to have any contact with the Gusii or their culture, except through soapstone carving in curio shops all over the country. These are attractive if somewhat stereotyped artifacts, mostly animal figurines dyed black or left in the natural pinks, whites and greys of the soft stone.

From Kisii, it is possible to travel southward to the Tanzanian border, which is 61 miles (98 km) away at Isebania. From there, one can continue down to the lakeside town of Musoma. However, most visitors turn off east on the way – at **Suna**, 48 miles (77 km) from Kisii – and then head through **Lolgorien** (the scene of a minor gold rush in the inter-war years), down the Siria escarpment and into the Maasai Mara National Reserve.

*Irrigation schemes bring green revolution to Kenya's arid lands.*

# MOMBASA ISLAND

In the days before Christ, Mombasa was apparently called "Tonika", which is a fit description for Kenya's main seaside town and the major centre for rest and relaxation.

Just the sight of it, from an escarpment above the island, is instant relief for the weekender from Nairobi and the up-country interior. It was just as attractive to earlier arrivals from further afield. Winston Churchill, for instance, was typically eloquent in 1908: "The aspect of Mombasa as she rises from the sea and clothes herself with foam and colour at the swift approach of the ship is alluring, even delicious."

The main access is of course by air these days, but the view from the plane has the same impact. Churchill's dictum holds true, though: "To appreciate all these charms, the traveller should come from the north."

Most travellers do – a quarter of a million of them a year from Germany, Britain and Scandinavia.

Incidentally, the sea route to Mombasa today is almost impossible. Cargo ships sail out of a dozen North Sea and Mediterranean ports, but the chances of a passenger berth are slim to non-existent. The only possibility is aboard a world cruise liner, or on a dhow down from the Gulf.

Mombasa is seen as a "melting pot" for all the coastal cultures – indigenous, colonial and transient – and increasingly for migrants from mainland Africa. They all steam together in Mombasa like the classic curry of the region which, as it happens, is not a bad simile, appropriate down to the condiments on the side: mangoes, pineapples, pawpaw (papaya), coconut – all of which are locally grown.

It is pungent, tangy, spicy – essentially a sailor's town. It's also hot, at least when the sun assumes the perpendicular from mid-morning to mid-afternoon, when Mombasa dozes off. It's also impossible to determine the sepa-

**Preceding pages:** Nyali Bridge (on the left) with Mombasa Island and Makup causeway (in right foreground).

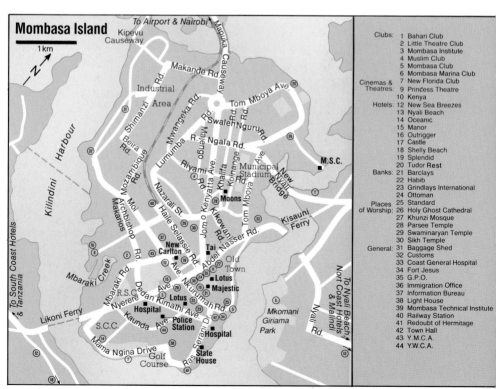

**Mombasa Island**

1km

To Airport & Nairobi
Kipevu Causeway
Makande Rd.
Makupa Causeway
Industrial Area
Shimanzi Rd.
Tom Mboya Ave.
Swaleh Nguru Rd.
Mwangeka Rd.
Harbour
Kilindini
Beira Rd.
Lumumba Rd.
Mvuleje R.
Ngala Rd.
Mombasa
Mozambique Rd.
Nazarali St.
Riyami
Khalifa
Kilindini Rd.
Municipal Stadium
New Nyali Bridge
M.S.C.
Moons
Haile Selassie Rd.
Jomo Kenyatta Ave.
Kikowani Rd.
Tom Mboya
Kisauni Ferry
New Carlton
Tai
Abdel Nasser Rd.
Old Town
Archbishop Makarios Rd.
Moi Ave.
Mbaraki Creek
Mbaraki Rd.
Dedan Kimathi Ave.
Nkurumah Rd.
Lotus
Majestic
Lotus
Mkomani Giriama Park
To South Coast Hotels & Tanzania
Likoni Ferry
R.S.C.
Nyerere Ave.
Police Station
Hospital
S.C.C.
Kaunda Ave.
Serani Rd.
Hospital
Mama Ngina Drive
Golf Course
State House
To Nyali Beach & North Coast Hotels & Malindi
Nort Coast Hotels

| | |
|---|---|
| Clubs: | 1 Bahari Club |
| | 2 Little Theatre Club |
| | 3 Mombasa Institute |
| | 4 Muslim Club |
| | 5 Mombasa Club |
| | 6 Mombasa Marina Club |
| Cinemas & | 7 New Florida Club |
| Theatres: | 9 Princess Theatre |
| | 10 Kenya |
| Hotels: | 12 New Sea Breezes |
| | 13 Nyali Beach |
| | 14 Oceanic |
| | 15 Manor |
| | 16 Outrigger |
| | 17 Castle |
| | 18 Shelly Beach |
| | 19 Splendid |
| | 20 Tudor Rest |
| Banks: | 21 Barclays |
| | 22 Habib |
| | 23 Grindlays International |
| | 24 Ottoman |
| Places | 25 Standard |
| of Worship: | 26 Holy Ghost Cathedral |
| | 27 Khunzi Mosque |
| | 28 Parsee Temple |
| | 29 Swaminaryan Temple |
| | 30 Sikh Temple |
| General: | 31 Baggage Shed |
| | 32 Customs |
| | 33 Coast General Hospital |
| | 34 Fort Jesus |
| | 35 Immigration Office |
| | 36 Immigration Office |
| | 37 Information Bureau |
| | 38 Light House |
| | 39 Mombasa Technical Institute |
| | 40 Railway Station |
| | 41 Redoubt of Hermitage |
| | 42 Town Hall |
| | 43 Y.M.C.A. |
| | 44 Y.W.C.A. |

rate ingredients or how much of what went into the stew.

**How it all began**: Most of it, as might be expected, is history – distinctly separate generations of it since geographer Ptolemy marked the town on his map in AD 150. All the seaborne trading nations of the Middle and Far East came and went until 1528, when Mombasa fell to the Portuguese. Ali Bey the Turk threw them out half a century later, but they came back and retook the town with a mercenary army of people-eating Simba. They built the massive Fort Jesus and stayed for a century before being starved out by a siege force of Omani Arabs.

For the next three generations, until towards the end of the 19th century, Mombasa was occupied as an outpost of Islam under the Mazrui family and eventually the sultans of Oman and Zanzibar. Christianity was reintroduced in 1845 by two Protestant pastors from Germany, Johann Ludwig Krapf and Johannes Rebmann.

About the same time, a Captain Owen sat in Mombasa as a one-man, pre-emptive British presence. He was ordered off after a few months, but the British were back in force in 1873 after Sir Bartle Frere put down the slave trade through a treaty with Zanzibar. Freretown, a settlement for freed slaves, was set up just across from the old harbour in Mombasa.

After a few rounds of gun-boat diplomacy, aimed accurately at Fort Jesus, Britain began wheeling and dealing with the Zanzibar Sultan who was eventually persuaded, in 1888, to cede the Kenya Coast to the Protectorate of Her Britannic Majesty (at an annual rent of £17,000).

Thereafter the British stayed and, to their credit, put far more into the development of the area than any of the previous foreign administrations. They built a gentlemen's club, of course; a cathedral; the railway; the great deepwater harbour of Kilindini; and generally turned the place into a superior resort with holiday villas along the coast from Malindi to Shimoni.

Nyali, the best littoral and beach close to Mombasa town, became an English garden plantation and an "officer's R and R area", complete with golf course and eventually five first-class hotels. In the process they also set up what they saw as an "Other Ranks" mess in Mombasa, made up of Indians mostly, who brought along with them their temples, mosques, bazaars and, of course, their curries.

The world wars came and went without incident at Mombasa, except for one fool gunner firing a shot over the bows of *HMS Ark Royal* in Kilindini. The official municipal guide records that "at the sight of the carrier's massive armament swinging round to retaliate, the Commandant of the Coast battery jumped on his bicycle and rode into town to change his library book."

Kenya's national independence arrived in 1963 and, for Mombasa, it was something of a cultural shock. Actually it was more economic, with the simultaneous arrival of the up-country African communities and their more vigorous commerce and industry. Finally, tourism renders the more subtle change of flavour, with a swelling tide from continental Europe. They find it all in Mombasa, and increasingly in their own language. Over the two millennia, Mombasa has learned to be hospitable to visitors.

**The Old Town**: Joined to the mainland by a wide causeway, Mombasa town is mostly spread over a small coral island, flanked by two creeks, Tudor and Kilindini ("deep water"), which provide its natural harbours. The **Old Town** grew up beside the northern Tudor inlet, but as trade grew in the early part of this century and when the harbour capacity became overstretched, a new port was built at Kilindini on the southern side of the island.

Thus the traditional and interesting waterfront of the Old Town was spared demolition and redevelopment; today it remains as a "period piece" attraction.

Characteristically it has an Arab-Indian mix and is a maze of narrow streets and passages (many impassable to motor traffic), with overhanging "Juliet"

balconies and carved doorways. Goldsmiths and silversmiths are traditional craftsmen in the Old Town, but other traders conduct a substantial import-export business despite the quaint and unpretentious appearance of their storefronts.

At the old harbour is an open square containing the Customs House, a fish market, and several shops specializing in carpets, chests and brassware brought by dhows from the Persian Gulf. A short distance away is a shop selling "non-alcohol-based perfumes", presumably for the teetotal Muslim ladies of the town.

Usually in the harbour are small coastal dhows from Lamu and Somalia at anchor, trading in fruit, dried fish and similar commodities. It's only during the December to April season of the *kusi* monsoon that the large ocean-going booms and sambuks from farther afield can be seen. Nowadays, these amount to little more than a picturesque remnant of the dhow fleets of the heyday of slaves and ivory. Even these – or most

**Graceful sailing on a dhow off Lamu.**

of them – have diesel engines to supplement the traditional lateen sailing power.

Still, there is plenty to see and absorb at the old harbour during the relatively quieter months – fishermen, stevedores and sailors unconsciously photogenic, and perhaps the *Nakhoda* (a dhow captain) offering cups of sweet black coffee during a drawn-out discussion over the purchase of a Persian carpet or a Zanzibar sea-chest.

Nearby is the bulk of **Fort Jesus**, constructed in 1593 as the ultimate in indestructible fortresses. Now a museum of coastal antiquities, it has fine exhibits of ceramics and carved doors. The fort is administered by the National Museums of Kenya which charges a small entrance fee.

**A colourful sprawl**: Mombasa expanded rapidly this century beyond the Old Town, and after 1930, it spilled beyond the confines of the island on to the mainland. Along **Digo Road** are religious buildings of many sects – churches, mosques and Hindu temples.

There are administrative buildings dating from early colonial days; street markets for souvenirs, fruits and colourful cloth; and a jostle of pavement vendors of coffee, coconut milk, roasted maize and cassava. In sharp contrast are the new office blocks, the smart Post Office and modern shops stocking goods from all over the world.

**Moi Avenue** links the old and new port areas and supports most of the travel and shipping agencies, local tour operators, curio shops, and the better hotels, bars and restaurants. The dual carriageway is spanned by the city landmark – four crossed (steel) elephant tusks constructed to commemorate Queen Elizabeth's visit in 1952. They locate Mombasa's efficient **Visitor Information Bureau**, and nearby is a park in which resides the national *Uhuru* (Freedom) monument.

Enthusiasts may continue on to visit **Kilindini Docks**, which are modern, efficient and still expanding. A distant view will surface for most visitors, however, and this is particularly attrac-

tive in the night as the ship and shore lights reflect on the waters of Kilindini Greek. A walk at dusk along **Mama Mgina Drive** also provides a chance to breathe the cool sea air and join the colourful promenade of the city's diverse populace.

Mombasa is essentially casual and visitors will soon be as relaxed as the residents. The right clothes are cool cotton prints, such as the *kikoi* sarong, the strikingly patterned *kanga* or white full-length *khanzu*, bought perhaps after a happy haggle with the laconic (and experienced) shopkeepers of **Biashara (Bazaar) Street.**

**Delightful diversions**: At night the city shakes off its languorous daytime air and offers its visitors a lively nightlife, ranging from sophisticated dining and dancing at smart beach hotels to the uninhibited atmosphere of strip clubs and sailors' bars. A casino is a fairly recent innovation, and there are cinemas and a theatre for those who prefer vicarious to live excitement.

A wide variety of good food is available in Arab, Chinese, Indian, Pakistani and European styles. In addition, seafood is inexpensive as well as plentiful. The city hotels are generally nowhere near as stylish as the best of the beach palaces, since traditionally they have catered for a business clientele. Nonetheless, they are generally comfortable and not costly.

The island itself has no extensive leisure beaches, but the fabulous "Coral Coast" north and south of the island is only a short trip away. Excursions farther afield, to **Tsavo National Park** and the **Shimba Hills National Reserve**, are easily arranged through local tour operators or car-hire firms.

A number of sightseeing trips in the immediate vicinity of Mombasa may also interest some visitors. For instance, just over Nyali Bridge, towards the north coast, is **Freretown**, the site of one of the oldest churches in East Africa. The settlement for freed slaves was founded in the 1870s by Sir Bartle Frere and many of their descendants still live there. A right turn off Nyali Bridge leads to a memorial to **Dr Johann L.**

**Krapf**, the first Christian missionary (after the Portuguese), and the graves of his young family who died "of the fever" there in 1844.

Nearby is **Princes Park** extending round to **Mackenzie Point**. This was land donated to Mombasa for the recreation of its people by the British Dukes of Gloucester and Windsor. Today it is the venue for the annual Mombasa Agricultural Show. Straight ahead from the bridge is the **Nyali Estate**, the town's best garden suburb, offering a fine beach, a sports club, a 12-hole golf course, and three of the finest hotels on the coast.

Another excursion is to the workshop of the Wakamba carvers situated 100 yards or so (about 90 metres) along the airport road where it branches from the main Nairobi road at Changamwe. Many of the stereotyped wooden wildlife on sale in the middle of the town are produced at this workshop, whose showroom also displays some unusual pieces.

At **Mazeras**, about 12 miles (19 km) along the Nairobi road, are the small municipal botanical gardens which contain a wide range of tropical shrubs, flowers and trees – many of which are used eventually to beautify the city streets, parks and public places.

The mission stations of **Rabai** and **Ribe**, established by Lutheran pastors in the mid-19th century, are situated a few miles inland and near Mariakani, 10 miles (16 km) farther on, is a traditional *kaya* or stockaded settlement of the Giriama tribe.

Mombasa is inevitably the communications centre of the coast region. The airport, named after President Moi, is fully international, having been expanded to take 747s and DC 10s. Kenya Airways and a number of private air charter companies operate services from the airport to Kenya's main tourist destinations, including the coastal resorts up to Lamu. For the old-fashioned up-country safari, the railway terminus is located in the centre of the town, as are bus and taxi stops for departures to the beaches and beyond, north and south of Mombasa Island.

Portuguese cannon and shot – reminders of the first European presence in Mombasa.

# THE COAST: LIVING AT LEISURE

A Swahili proverb sums up the pervasive atmosphere of the Kenya coast: *Haraka haraka haina baraka* – "haste, haste brings no blessing".

Here the gentle philosophy of the Swahili people spawns a leisurely pace of life, as might be expected at zero altitude on the Equator. It's hot, humid and yet tempered all the time by the northeast or southeast monsoon, the trade winds of the Indian Ocean determining the seasons. The northeasterly *kaskazi* blows from October until March, with its rainfall peak in November. It's the warmer of the two monsoon seasons with the hottest months occurring on the coast in January and February. The dhows sail south on this wind from the Middle East and Gulf ports, down to East Africa and across to India.

The southeasterly *kusi* blows from April until September, and its rainfall peak is from May until July. It's the stronger of the two winds, the colder and the less comfortable, but this is relative since the climate stays mostly benign. Ancient dhows returned north on the *kusi*, carrying ivory, frankincense, gum arabic and slaves. Cargo nowadays is mostly mangrove poles from Kenya's tidal flats which are used for building throughout the Arabian Gulf.

Facing winds that have blown across several thousand miles of ocean, it might be expected that Kenya's beaches are constantly battered by surf – wild, dangerous playgrounds. But they are not; for almost the entire length of the coast, the shallows and sands are protected by a coral reef, which is set about a mile off shore and stretches from Vanga in the south to Lamu in the north. The only breaks found are facing the creeks of Mombasa, Mtwapa and Kilifi – the outlets of now extinct rivers; and at the Sabaki and Tana rivers (north of Malindi), which also cut through the reef with their outpouring of fresh water and millions of tons of silt.

**Preceding pages:** Lamu fishing vessel heads home. **Below,** a touch of creativity on the prow.

Between the fringing coral reefs and the shoreline are shallow, safe waters. There are few or no sharks, only scores of species of spectacular coral fish easily observed in the clear, warm ocean. As for the beaches, they're often miles on end of fine white sand, edged in dunes and serried ranks of coconut palms and wispy casuarina trees. All this – the patterned sheen of the ocean, the sun-beaches and the palm shading – combines into a setting which is less Africa than a Gauguin seascape of the South Pacific. But it's that much closer to Europe, hence it lures an increasing tide of Palearctic tourists from the winter in Frankfurt, London and other cities of the gray and frozen north.

This exceptional coastline effectively runs out north and south from Mombasa, the largest port on the eastern littoral of the continent with the exception of Durban in South Africa. The town-port is the commercial gateway to a vast "interior", stretching out into Zaire, northwest into Sudan, and southwest into Zambia. Countries without a

seaport, such as Rwanda and Uganda, depend to a large extent on Mombasa for imports and exports of their cash crop commodities.

Originally the town was contained wholly on Mombasa Island, but mostly this century, it has spilled on to the mainland in all directions. To the south, the link between suburbs is the Likoni ferry which plies across the mouth of the deep-water Kilindini Port. To the west, Makupa causeway carries road, rail and fuel arteries to Nairobi and up-country Kenya. To the north, the connection is via the new Nyali toll bridge which spans the upper reaches of Tudor Creek.

**Sindbad, spice and sin**: Mombasa's old town is interesting for its eastern ambience of Scheherazade spice and sin. The streets are narrow like a casbah and bedaggered Arab sailors still come ashore, dressed in period costume for a Sindbad epic. The brooding bulk of Fort Jesus is a symbol of the old conflict between East and West, now relatively peaceful in a counterpoint of cathedral

break
efore the
aul.

bells and the call of the faithful to prayer. Not that the town is all saintly and devout. Like all big ports, Mombasa has its bawdy side to accommodate curious tourists and liberty sailors.

Trade is essential to life in Mombasa, as it has been for at least two millennia. Exports of tea, coffee, pyrethrum, potash and many other commodities pour out of the interior, through acres of warehouses and on to the quays. The cross-flow of imports is anything from heavy industrial plant to basic foodstuffs. Tankers discharge crude oil into Kenya's refinery, almost the sole source of processed fuel for the East African region. Bulk cement carriers load cargo from the Bamburi silos on the mainland north of Mombasa, where the continent's largest cement works are located. Apart from the vast array of export and import operations, Mombasa has its own industrial complex which manufactures anything from pins to hull plates for ocean-going ships.

An indicator of the importance of Mombasa to the Kenya economy is **Moi International Airport**, a few miles to the west of the island. Fully equipped and big enough for the intercontinental jets, the airport brings tourists directly to the coast from Europe.

**The price of expansion**: The town is not without its problems, of course. The most evident is the infamous "urban drift". Mombasa's thriving commerce draws in the poor, the displaced and the ambitious from all over the countryside; and the price it pays is the strain in attempting to match the pace of population growth with the provision of accommodation, services and facilities. It's a losing battle. Water supply – another major problem – is inadequate to meet needs and is fractured occasionally along the pipelines from Mzima Springs, 150 miles (240 km) away in Tsavo West, or from sources on the Sabaki River, 80 miles (130 km) to the north above Malindi. Overwhelmed by the problems of essential maintenance and development, the Town Council was temporarily replaced by an administrative Governing Commission, appointed by the central government. Yet,

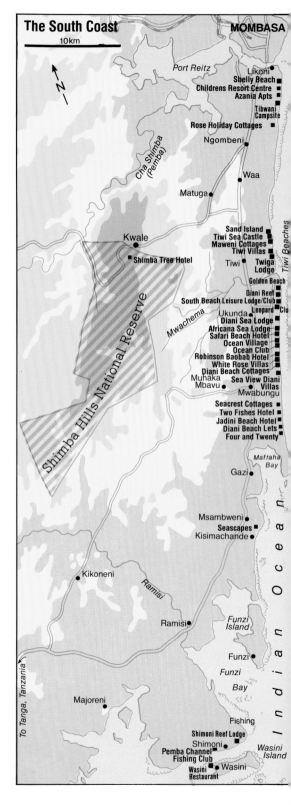

for all this, the town's attraction – especially for short-stay visitors – is undiminished.

Tourist accommodation in Mombasa starts at the luxury level at the **Oceanic**, a modern, handsome building looking out over the entrance to Kilindini harbour. It's comfortable, fully air-conditioned and offers a casino for evening diversion. An older establishment is the **Manor Hotel**, which has stood its grounds virtually unmoved by developments all around it over the past 80 years. The ambience is somewhat jaded English, but it's still a comfortable base from which to explore the island.

Away from Mombasa, the pace of coastal life has always been hardly more than subsistence. Agriculture feeds the locals, but where it's expanded to copra production from coconuts, cashew nuts, sisal or sugar, it's normally fuelled with imported labour. There are signs of an awakening from traditional, local inertia – but it's slow.

**A population fed by tourism:** The main business all along the coast is tourism.

The industry is rooted in the colonial era, from the time of solar topees, spine pads and conviction that too long in the highlands would make a fellow decidedly odd. There was something in this, of course; at least it was taken seriously enough for most families to have at least a fortnight's holiday at the coast every year. Some built beach chalets and, in due course, retired to them.

The first tourist development started in the 1940 – nothing more than roofs of palm thatch, called *makuti*. It became smarter through people resting up at the coast after dusty, buffeting safaris around the interior. The word got around, and the beach, as a destination in itself, began to develop in the 1950s with arrivals from South Africa and what was then Southern Rhodesia (Zimbabwe).

In 1963, this colonial flow stopped but the new African government soon substituted it with tourists from Europe. This became a flood by the 1970s when the beach eclipsed the safari in terms of volume and frequency of package tours.

amu women
:iled
iscreetly in
ccordance
ith Islamic
iles.

The north and the south "coasts" are highly competitive for the trade. There are endless debates about which has more to offer; each has its solid block of local supporters. But, in fact, it's all subjective and there's not a great deal of difference between the two sectors.

**The South Coast**: The South Coast has a longer unbroken stretch of reef and, debatably, a larger and more varied lagoon area between the reef and beaches. Across the Likoni ferry, the major road south to Tanzania runs parallel to the shore, about a mile inland. The best beaches are located between the townships of **Tiwi** and **Diani** – a 13-mile (21-km) stretch starting about 12 miles (20 km) south of Mombasa. In this sector, hotels, campsites and private properties line the entire length of the beach.

**Diani Beach** in particular has been dubbed the prime site for the complete holiday destination in Kenya. It is a ribbon of flawless tropical beach: unspoiled – straight for over 8 miles (13 km) and probably 80 yards (73 metres) wide at low tide. The sand is white, fine-grained, gently cambered to the ocean and shaded on the spectator side with palms and casuarina.

Overall, the impression is of an immense, immaculate procession to nowhere in particular – in fact to a coral cliff and outcrop island, both of them uninhabited sanctuaries for seabirds. In recent years Diani Beach has developed into an important tourist centre with numerous hotels, restaurants and watersports facilities.

The ocean at Diani, or rather the inshore shallows, are entirely protected by the fringing reef – massive and solid like a sea-wall. Nothing gets in – no sharks, no other large marine life, no pollution and not even seaweed, for when the southern monsoon veers off its normal parallel course, sweeping in and out, it leaves the beach in its usual pristine state. The ocean scenery also seems on a larger scale than anywhere else on the Kenya coast, subtle and infinitely varied.

When the tide goes out, a half-mile stretch of coral and sand between the

**Unspoilt Diani Beach, south coast.**

reef and shore is exposed as a mosaic of rock pools full of stranded small fry. A narrow lagoon at the outlet of the **Mwachema River**, at the northern end of the beach, is a decorative pattern of islands. At high tide, it's all covered but to no great depth. The coral formations show on the mirror flat surface as a burnished colour wash and as a vast abstract, with changing warmer tints around dawn and in the early evening.

A sense of space and personal detachment is tangible and even more so at night when Diani is less visual than atmospheric. Everything is black void, apart from the beach strip itself which is softly luminous.

At the same time, development on the Diani Strip has been fairly intense, not only in tourist accommodation, but in a whole range of ancillary services. Included are a shopping centre, restaurants, hairdressing salons, vehicle hire, training facilities and equipment for scuba diving, windsurfing, glass-bottomed boating and deep-sea fishing. Hotel types available here range from air-conditioned concrete and glass to vintage, open villa style fanned by breezes off the ocean. All offer reasonable services and the majority cater for package tours from Europe.

The land immediately behind the beach is scenic, although it is only partially developed, mostly with coconut, banana and citrus cultivation. Elsewhere there are patches of original forest, the most extensive of which is **Jadini**, a morning's trek from the beach hotels for a sight of mammals – colobus monkeys and baboons – but mostly birds and butterflies.

Some of the lesser forest tracts, called *keyas*, are said to have some ancient Polynesian connection and are revered by the local Wadigo people as sanctuaries. One of them, the **Kaya Tiwi** above a 3-mile (5-km) extension beach north of the Mwachema, has the status of an indigenous cathedral.

Another recent religious site is marked by a grove of flat baobabs, the "upside-down tree with its roots in the air". This is the 16th-century pilgrims'

are roan
ntelope,
himba Hills
eserve.

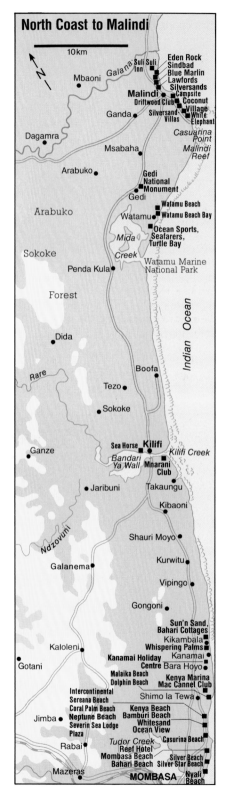

## North Coast to Malindi

10 km

Mbaoni
Galana
Suli Suli
Inn
Eden Rock
Sindbad
Blue Marlin
Lawfords
Silversands
Malindi
Campsite
Driftwood Club
Coconut
Ganda
Silversand
Village
Villas
White
Elephant
Casuarina
Point
Dagamra
Msabaha
Malindi
Reef
Arabuko
Gedi
National
Monument
Gedi
Watamu Beach
Arabuko
Watamu
Watamu Beach Bay
Ocean Sports,
Mida
Seafarers,
Turtle Bay
Sokoke
Creek
Watamu Marine
Penda Kula
National Park
Forest
Indian Ocean
Dida
Boofa
Rare
Tezo
Sokoke
Ganze
Sea Horse
Kilifi
Kilifi Creek
Bandari
Ya Wall
Mnarani
Club
Jaribuni
Takaungu
Kibaoni
Ndzovuni
Shauri Moyo
Kurwitu
Galanema
Vipingo
Gongoni
Sun'n Sand,
Bahari Cottages
Kikambala
Kaloleni
Whispering Palms
Kanamai Holiday
Kanamai
Gotani
Centre
Bara Hoyo
Malaika Beach
Kenya Marina
Dolphin Beach
Mac Cannel Club
Intercontinental
Sereana Beach
Shimo la Tewa
Coral Palm Beach
Kenya Beach
Jimba
Neptune Beach
Bamburi Beach
Severin Sea Lodge
Whitesand
Plaza
Ocean View
Tudor Creek
Casurina Beach
Rabai
Reef Hotel
Mombasa Beach
Silver Beach
Bahari Beach
Silver Star Beach
Mazeras
Nyali
MOMBASA
Beach

mosque at **Kongo** which stands on one of several coral cliffs behind Diani and Tiwi beaches.

Occasionally the coral is scoured out into deep caves, some with black felt ceilings of countless bats. They peel off and erupt in the evenings, great clouds of them against the sunset.

A few miles inland, running parallel to the Tiwi-Daini beaches, are the **Shimba Hills** – a set of gentle rolling downs, rising up to 1,500 feet (450 metres) from the coastal plain. Covered with short grass and patches of forest, the upper reaches are a National Reserve established to protect relic species of fauna and flora. Seventy-four sq. miles (192 sq. km) of parkland, this is a set of near-English downs reserved for Kenya's last breeding herds of roan and sable antelope.

The park also offers buffaloes, a shy resident herd of elephant, and a few cats namely lions and leopards. Birdlife is profuse and sometimes rare, like the Fishcher's turaco and the palm nut vulture. The spur fowl – *kwale* in Kiswahili – is the local emblem and the name of the Administrative District which includes Diani.

An easy car drive from any of the beach resorts, the Shimba Hills not only give the visitor a chance to see distinctive wildlife but also offer a cool change from the humid coastal strip. In addition, there are long-range views from the hills over the ocean or, to the south, the Usambara and Pare mountains of Tanzania.

Officially, the immediate ambit of the Tiwi-Diani holiday ends at **Chale Island**. This is a speck of coral and a stopover for boat trips at the south extreme of the beach. Beyond that, down to the Tanzanian border at **Vanga**, is what the Diani planners describe as a "remote area" for longer excursions out of the beach hotels.

**Kinondo** and **Gazi** are time-lapsed fishing villages. **Msambweni** has a superb, empty beach and a large hole in the ground, reputed to be an old slave pen. At the far end of the South Coast, about 45 miles (72 km) from the ferry is the **Pemba Channel Fishing Club** at

Shimoni. The deep trench of this channel between the Kenya coast and the Tanzanian island of Pemba is the main run for the big marlin. It's therefore also a main base for the dedicated serious deep-sea fishermen in Kenya. It is said – in the bar of the fishing club – that world record marlin are out there somewhere. One of them, well over a thousand pounds, was once hooked but slipped the line.

**Shimoni**, now a village, was once headquarters of the Imperial British East Africa Company. Across a narrow sound, on **Wasini Island**, is an Arab settlement almost as ancient as Lamu.

There is also the ocean itself, or more precisely its submarine landscapes. Inshore are acres of coral parks around atolls called **Kisite, Mpunguti Juu** ("up") and **Mpunguti Chini** ("down") and "the rock of small dhow" (**Jiwe la Jahazi**).

All this – the sport, beach, ocean, forests, wildlife and historic sites – is brought together as the "corporate" attraction of the South Coast. It is a formidable package, competitive with any other beach destination in the world.

**The North Coast**: The North Coast can be divided into several sections. The first of these extends from **Nyali Bridge** about 12 miles (19 km) to **Mtwapa Creek**, an old river course cut deeply into the coral limestone. The beach is dense with private properties and hotels, of which the doyen is the **Nyali Beach Hotel** and, for many years, the trend-setter for standards of excellence. Again, the hotels are backed by a wide set of ancillary services which, through proximity to Mombasa, are probably more varied than those available on the South Coast.

The main road up the North Coast also runs a mile or so back from the sea front. Halfway between Mombasa and Mtwapa, passes the Bamburi cement factory. This is the largest of its kind in Africa, producing upwards of a million tons of cement a year, and it has been the main supplier of the Arabian peninsula countries during the recent boom years.

The base material is the coral lime-

Swimming
pool at a
five-star
coast hotel.

Malindi – Lamu – Kiunga

G A R I S S A

Dodori Nat. Res.

Mundane Range

Kiunga
Mararani
Mambore
Rubu
Mangai
Simambaya
Ashuwei
Oseni
Mokokoni
Kiwaiyo Lodge
Milimani
Faza
Bajumwali
Kilweni
Ankish
Siyu
Bodhei
Pate Island
Majengo
Magumba
Pate
Bargoni
Manda Island
L A M U
Mwana
Mariyamu
Takwa
Hindi
Mokowe
Milinga
Lamu
Shela
Mahrus Hotel
Hidio
Matondoni
Petleys Hotel
Peponi Hotel
Koreni
Mkunumbi
Kiongwe
Pananguo
Msuakini
Pangani
Wema
Hewani
Nyangore
Witu
Matapani
Dida
Waredi
Kau
Kipini
Garsen
Idsowe
Ozi
Kibusu
Ngao
Tana River
Minjila
Anasa
Golbanti
Laini
Oda
T A N A
R I V E R
Karawa
Indian
Ocean
Waressa
Holiday Centre
Hadu
Fundisa
Ngomeni
Ramada
K I L I F I
Shauri Moyo
Mizijini
Mambrui
Marafa
Sabaki River
40 km
Malindi
N

stone underlying much of Kenya' coastal plain up to 4 miles (7 km) from the sea and the vast amount quarrie over the past three decades left an enor mous unsightly depression. The expert said nothing could be done, that th ground was too saline to support trees o even grass. It would have to be left as a unavoidable wound inflicted on the en vironment in the interest of profit. Th factory owners then turned to a agronomist, René Haller, a Swiss c considerable optimism, who said tha he might be able to do something wit the quarry.

**Environmental wonder:** The result o René Haller work is the **Bambur Quarry Nature Trail**, which ranks a one of the most remarkable environ mental rehabilitation projects any where in the world. He planted trees i what they said was sterile lime and within two decade, has built up a fores producing commercial timber. Wher the experts said grass wouldn't grow there are now the green meadows of small wildlife park. The quarry are also features fish and crocodile farms an experimental banana plantation and even a vineyard. All this is open t visitors.

Beyond Bamburi, a single-span sus pension bridge crosses Mtwapa Cree leading to the next sector of the nort coast, 25 miles (40 km) up to **Kilif Creek**, an even bigger extinct rive course. In this area, only relatively shor lengths of beach are developed for tour ism, but some of them – especially a **Shanzu** – have exceptionally fine ho tels. However, for the most part, th road runs through the vast **Vipingo Si sal Estate**, one of the largest and bes run in Africa. Lines of the sharp-pointe plants stretch to the horizon, their leave eventually cut and the fibre extracte for manufacture into coarse string.

A new bridge across Kilifi Creek ha replaced the rather unreliable ferrie and has removed the necessity of takin the long dirt road detour many mile inland.

On the creek's north shore stands th township of **Kilifi**, administrative cen tre of a district that stretches into th interior to the borders of the great Tsavo National Parks. Of all the coastal centres, Kilifi has held out more strongly against the mammon of tourism than the others. Most of the sea-front land is privately owned, much of it in the hands of retired farmers from the highlands. The presence of sleek, ocean-going yachts and powerful fishing cruisers, however, attests the attractions of Kilifi to up-market visitors – notably deep-sea fishing.

Farther north, the land around **Arabuko-Sokoke**, a preserved patch of indigenous coastal forest, is heavily farmed. The name derives from the Watta hunters who were once the only inhabitants of this region, with *Arabuko* referring to a point at the north end of the forest which they knew as *Arrba Huko*, or "Huko's elephant".

No one knows who this Huko fellow was, but clearly he killed or had an adventure with an elephant which created a lasting impression on the local Watta of the time. *Sokoke*, incidentally, is a corruption of their word *Soke*, for

"red soil". Although the extremely dense vegetation of the Arabuko-Sokoke forest does not permit ready game viewing, it is nonetheless an interesting place for the specialist to watch birds, in particular, the endemic Sokoke-Scops Owl.

**Disco dancing till dawn**: Some 25 miles (40 km) north of Kilifi is another popular beach resort called **Watamu**. Again the strip is lined with beach bungalows and hotels, most of them providing facilities and equipment for deep-sea fishing and water sports. Watamu is a favourite watering place for locals, and provides perhaps the most frantic New Year's Eve in the country, drawing up to as many as 2,000 young people who disco till sun-up at **Ocean Sports**. This is on **Turtle Bay**, the best beach section of Watamu, which takes its name from a turtle-shaped coral outcrop just offshore.

Inland, not far away, is the lost city of **Gedi**. This was clearly an Islamic port several centuries ago which was suddenly and inexplicably abandoned,

elow,
windsurfers
nd relaxed
ourists.
ight, a
emote,
ncrowded
dian Ocean
each.

# BAJUN, SWAHILI AND SHIRAZI
## Eastern Bantu

The Swahili-speaking people of the Kenya coast share a common language, religion (Islam) and culture. Of Bantu origin, Swahili has become the national language of Kenya and is widely spoken throughout East and Central Africa and Zaire.

The Bajun (37,000) of the Lamu archipelago and coastal strip to the north, and those islands parallel to it, speak a dialect of their own known as Kitikuu, with Kiamu and Kivita, one of more than a dozen forms of Swahili still spoken. Like the Pokomo and the Mijikenda, the Bajun are thought to have originated from a homeland in Shungwaya at an undetermined location to the north. Arabian settlement from the Hijaz, the Persian Gulf and south Arabia brought about a further evolution of the Bajun people, as did the later incursions of the Oromo-speaking people. Centuries of immigration and conquest, transmigration and miscegenation, resulted in the Bantu-speaking Swahili absorbing immigrants of Arab and Persian descent. Loosely applied, the term Swahili has come to mean almost any Muslim from the coast.

The Shirazi (numbering, together with the Swahili, 5,500) are a scattered maritime and agricultural people who claim to have originated from a homeland in Persia in the 10th to 12th centuries and once made up the aristocratic families and dynasties of Ozi kingdoms of Shaka, Mwana and Ungwana, Malindi and Mombasa. The modern view places no credence in the legend of their origins and today little remains to set them apart from the Swahili other than pride in a shady past.

Fishing and agriculture feature prominently in the economy of the Bajun, Swahili and Shirazi. Fish spears, handlines (*mishipi*) on which *chungu, danfu, kile kole* and *nguru* are caught, several different types of basket traps made of palm rib or split bamboo and weirs are all common methods of catching fish. The fine-meshed cast nets (*kidifu*) used for catching *dagaa*, the drift nets (*majerifa*) employed in surface fishing from boats and the long seine nets (*majuya*) positioned from boats and then hand-hauled up on the beach are employed in communal fishing.

From recorded time, the peoples of the Kenya coast have engaged in shifting agriculture. The bush fires on the mainland, to clear land for planting before the rains, are mentioned in the 2nd-century *Periplus of the Erythraean Sea*. Of considerable importance in the economy is the ubiquitous coconut, which provides the raw material for building and thatching, rope-making and plaited basket work, food, drink and oil. The coastal people cultivate numerous root crops, including cassava (*muhogo*), sweet potato (*kiasi*), yam (*kiasi kikuu*) and taro (*majungwa*); cereals such as millet (*mtama*), rice (*mpunga*) and maize (*mahindi*) and a wide variety of fruit trees including banana (*mgomba* – the fruit is called *ndizi*), mango (*mwembe*), orange (*mchungwa*), lime (*mlimao*) and pawpaw. Cashews, cotton, and mangrove cutting in the Lamu area provide important cash incomes.

Ocean-going dhows (*madau*) used for trade down the East Coast from Arabia, the Persian Gulf and even India still arrive in Lamu, Malindi and Mombasa at the start of the southwest monsoon. The dhow fleet once numbered several hundred; today a few individual, motorised dhows maintain these trading links. In creeks and harbours a dug-out canoe (*mtumbwi*) is often used; occasionally a double-outrigger canoe (*ngalawa*) may be seen. The graceful *jahazi* with a billowing triangular sail and coconut-matting splash "boards" is common in the Lamu archipelago, along with the all-purpose, keel-less *dau la mwao*.

Many coast people are skilled craftsmen. Lime burning from coral is still an important industry; ship-building and wood-working, plaiting of baskets, mats and other items, rope-making from coir and metal and leather work remain traditional occupations of the villagers.

Formerly the coastal strip was a possession of the Sultan of Zanzibar (leased as a protectorate to Great Britain in 1895) and many of the Kiswahili-speaking community placed higher regard on their affiliations with the Arabs than those with the peoples of the hinterland. Today this stance has been abandoned, and the Bajun, Swahili and Shirazi have integrated as an African people and united with other Kenyans. ∎

**Above**, Swahili men: theirs is the national tongue.

probably in the 17th or 18th century. Although an invasion of trees and bush home has reduced the town to a ruin, there are many well-preserved relics of a mosque and some houses in the traditional Swahili style.

For anyone interested in archaeology and the past, Gedi is well-worth a visit. It is all something of a mystery how, presumably, the sea front receded to leave the port high and dry. It is curious, too, why there is barely a mention of Gedi in any of the ancient maritime literature, whereas there are full Arab and Portuguese logs on all the other coastal ports down from Lamu to Vanga.

Above Gedi, about 12 miles (19 km) north, is the last of the coastal region's main tourist resorts: the town and flanking beaches of **Malindi**. It's entirely developed for local and immigrant tourism from Europe, especially Italy and Germany, and well set up for the hedonist on holiday with its lively hotels, nightclubs and bars. It's also Kenya's principal ocean sports centre after Mombasa, or perhaps may even eclipse the coastal capital.

There is one critical flaw – the seasonal dumping of brown silt from the **Sabaki River** which outlets at the north end of the bay. The peasants cultivate too close to the banks all the way up river towards Nairobi, with the erosion in the rains turning the Sabaki into a flood of silt. This in turn kills the coral heads in the bay, as well as muddies the bathing shallows. All manner of corrective actions, including the erection of a vast retaining sea-wall, are in the planning files. Something will have to be done eventually to clean up the bay and secure Malindi's potential as Africa's Costa de Sol.

**The remote north**: From Malindi, the 140-mile (225-km) road to Lamu first crosses the Sabaki River over a suspension bridge. This was constructed after the previous more flimsy structure was swept away by a massive flood of the river in 1961–62. Three miles (5 km) on is the turning to **Mambrui** which, unlike Malindi, is strongly Muslim in

character. It has a fine mosque and pillar tomb and an access to a vast expanse of beach stretching up a spit of sand dunes.

An alternative access to this beach is a turning two or three miles beyond Mambrui which leads to **Ngomeni** facing the Italians' San Marco satellite launching pad half a mile or so out of sea. A worthwhile deviation in the area is to **Marafa**, or "Hell's Kitchen", which is about 20 miles (32 km) on a rough road left out of Mambrui. Once at Marafu, a track runs down to a spectacular gorge of eroded rock pinnacles and cliffs in striking colours.

Back on the main route, the road continues through the village of **Gongoni** where there is an extensive salt works and finally begins to move inland opposite an atoll called **Robinson Island**. As the name suggest, this a Crusoe-style castaway island where a local family entertains with an exclusive and upmarket style of hospitality – notably superb seafood meals. A variety of water sports are also possible.

Beyond this, cultivated areas are gradually left behind and the road passes through a belt of coastal thicket for about 25 miles (40 km) or so to a possible detour to **Karawa**, a government holding ground for cattle. The only reason for a visit – strictly for the adventurous – would probably be to see the sand dunes of **Formosa Bay**, the largest beach on the whole East Africa coast, entirely waterless, undeveloped and deserted.

Another possible deviation is on a track sign-posted to **Tarasaa**, which is perhaps only worth a visit by someone with a particular interest in the Tana delta region, although it used to be an important area during the early European exploration of Kenya. Tarasaa is in fact a relatively new settlement, serving the older but less accessible villages of **Golbanti** and **Ngao**. Golbanti was the site of a Methodist mission station set up in 1885 by the Rev. Thomas Wakefield. One year later it was raided by Maasai tribesmen and the incumbent missionary, the Rev. Houghton, his wife and 11 others were killed. The fact

**Women selling** *khangas* **on Mombasa beach.**

that the Maasai could raid as far east as this is an indication of their power over a huge area at the time.

The rival German Lutheran missionaries established themselves at nearby Ngao and built an impressive and defensible house on top of a hill in 1893. A hospital was also started by the Lutherans, but taken over and extended by the Methodists after a German missionary was found transmitting radio messages to the Italians during World War II. This change of patrons was never fully accepted by the local Pokomo people. A religious "debate" between the village and hospital remains to this day as a sad tribute to competitive missionary zeal.

Back on the main road, a couple of miles before Garsen, is a small hill affording the only view in the entire lower Tana basin – a hazy vista of endless dry bush country, broken only by the green ribbon of the riverine strip. To the right, over the hill, is an old pill-box built during the war as a defence against an expected Italian invasion from Somalia. Down below, on a 3-mile (5-km)

track towards the river is **Idsowe**, a typical village of the lower Pokomo, or "Malachini", who are all Christian converts. It's otherwise unremarkable except for a famous heron breeding ground on a nearby lake. If the river floods in May, the whole delta supports a huge number of water birds and many species of heron breed on this lake in June-July. **Garsen** itself is an important local trading centre and Waldei Gabbra (Somalis), Orma and Pokomo people crowd the street on any morning. It's halfway to Lamu and a good place to buy a soda and sit and watch the scene.

**The Lower Tana**: Just before Garsen, the road to Lamu divides with the left, northerly fork going off eventually to Nairobi. It's a major detour off the route to Lamu, but perhaps worth it for self-contained travellers who would like to take in a game reserve or get a feel of the vastness of the bushland in eastern Kenya. Ten miles (16 km) up the road is an unmarked turning to a village called **Maziwa** on an old course of the Tana. The defunct river spills out on to a

omad's
each Bar
staurant.

shallow pan called **Lake Billisa** between Maziwa and Garsen, which contains uncounted thousands of duck and other water birds. Elephants and other game are often seen crossing the road in this area and a little farther on is the **Tana River Primate Reserve**, for a possible glimpse of red colobus or mangabey monkeys.

This is perhaps about as much of a detour off the Malindi-Lamu road as anyone would make. So it's back on the main route which, out of Garsen, crosses the Tana on a bridge. From there a 5-mile (8-km) hazard runs across a flood-plain on a raised road. This is treacherous black-cotton soil which can be impassable after rain.

The road then crosses a larger area of grassland maintained by the river floods and extensively used as a dry season grazing area by the Somali and Orma pastoralists. Depending on the season, water birds and topi antelope are also common. Much of the grassland, however, is derived from burned out forest. Leaving the flood-plain at a

bridge called **Lango la Simba** (Lion's Gate), the road enters another woodland thicket zone before **Witu**, the next place of interest. The now deserted and overgrown mango plantations of the area give a hint of its prosperous past, but few would guess that this sleepy village was once the centre of an important sultanate and, briefly, the capital of the short-lived state of "Swahililand"?

The Sultan of Witu in fact came from Paté in 1862 to escape the troops of the Sultan of Zanzibar, with whom he had unwisely quarrelled. Simba, as the sultan was known, was visited by the German Denhardt brothers who declared Witu a German Protectorate in 1888. But this was not to last for long because two years later the Treaty of Berlin brought the whole of Kenya under British jurisdiction.

Nine Germans stayed on and persisted with a plan to set up a sawmill operation near Witu to which Simba's son, the new Sultan, strongly objected. After an argument, the leader of this group, a man named Kuntzel, shot one

**A tourist admires woodcarver crafts.**

of the Sultan's guards and was promptly shot himself. After this, a number of other Germans were killed and the Sultan refused to discuss his actions with the new British administration. Accordingly a reprisal force of 950 men was dispatch from Lamu under Admiral Freemantle to destroy the original town and surrounding plantations. Some rebellion continued, but peace was eventually restored and two new estates were set up by British colonists just before World War I. One of these, known as **Coconut Charlie**, was run by Charles Winton, and the other by Percy Petley who went on to run a famous pub – **Petley's Inn** – in Lamu.

Just beyond Witu is a possible turnoff to the beach, about 12 miles (19 km) away at the village of **Kipini**. This is at the present mouth of the Tana and was the district headquarters until this was subsequently moved to **Hola** well up river. Like Witu, the village is Swahili in character with stone-walled houses and *makuti* roofs.

The river outlet to the sea has been there only since the 1860s when the Sultan of Witu had a canal dug between the old course of the river and a small stream called the Ozi, which flowed into the sea at Kipini. During a big flood in 1892 the river adopted the canal as its main course and the old flow has largely silted up. The canal was also the site of another enterprise, the Belazoni Estate, which was founded in 1906. Percy Petley was one of the managers and the estate produced a wide variety of crops, including rubber, until it went bust in 1931 during the Depression.

**Haunted house:** As a district headquarters, Kipini acquired notoriety through the suicides of three administrators, and the old DC's house is supposedly haunted. The village still has a sultry, jaded and a very romantic atmosphere. The DC's launch, *The Pelican*, which used to patrol upstream as far as Garissa, is still there though in a sad state of disrepair. A track leads along the coasts to the east and there are several old Swahili ruins, the best being at **Ras ya Mwana**, 7 miles (11 km) from Kipini. This is a fine coastline and a good place to camp.

Beyond Witu the road passes through the edge of **Witu Forest**, once much more extensive than it is now. The surrounding area is largely a parkland of doum palm and bush interspersed with grassy *ziwas* – shallow depressions which flood during the rains. Baboons, topi and elephants are numerous in this area which is now gazetted the **Pandanguo Game Reserve**.

At the village of **Mkunumbi**, the road turns inland for some distance to go around the creeks and mangrove swamps that lace the area. Eventually the sea is reached again at **Mokowe**. At this point, travellers must take a boat across to the island of **Lamu**. Cars may be left at the jetty where a night watchman guards them (a service for which he should be tipped). Alternatively they can be left at a park behind the garage in the village of Mokowe or sometimes at the police station. Both of these car parks are more than a mile from the jetty so you'll have to hitch a ride if you have too much baggage to carry.

Ruined mosque at "lost city" of Gedi, north coast.

# MARINE PARKS AND RESERVES

Kenya took the lead in Africa by establishing national parks and reserves in the richest sections of its Indian Ocean reef. In these areas, it's forbidden to spear-fish, or remove shells or coral, or disturb the occupants of a balanced but highly sensitive ecosystem. For a small fee, though, it's possible to goggle or scuba dive among gardens of coral which, for attraction and diversity, challenge the fêted reef of the Red Sea.

Not that the protected areas are the only places for underwater safaris; there are many others, some of which may also become sanctuaries in due course. These are all along the fringing reef which parallels the entire coastline, apart from breaks at *mlangos* (Kiswahili for "doors") at the outlets of extinct or extant rivers.

The shallows and lagoons between the reef and the beach vary in width and depth. In places, it's possible to wade out in ankle-deep water half a mile to the reef and open ocean; in others, you have to swim or take a boat.

Incidentally, it's perfectly safe in these inshore waters, since in the small minds of the sharks there's an awareness that, inside the reef, they would be trapped and possibly beached by the receding tide. They have to be constantly on the move in order to filter sufficient oxygen from the water through their gills. So they stay out, except occasionally to follow the garbage trail of a big ship into the harbours. So far, Kenya has never had a "jaws" incident, although the Great Whites may be out there somewhere.

Parks and reserves were set up essentially as a conservation measure; one of the main concerns is to combat the serious threat of over-exploitation of shells on the reef by thoughtless souvenir hunters. Efforts have been made to control the number of shell dealers, who must obtain a costly licence, but sadly it's still common to see illegal collectors approaching the beach with sack-

**Preceding pages:** scuba diver. **Below, coral trout.**

fuls of cowrie shells, conches, wing shells, helmets and tritons.

Corals and starfish obviously belong underwater and, once removed, lose their brilliant colours, become brittle and give off an unattractive stench. Neither are the reef fish of much use – most of them are bony and unpalatable – and yet they were once taken out indiscriminately. The same goes for the small crabs and other shellfish which should be allowed to grow to a respectable size before they are removed.

**First reserve**: The first reserve to be established was the **Malindi-Watamu Marine Reserve**, stretching from just south of Malindi town to below Watamu at Mida Creek at the southern end of Turtle Bay. The reserve extends out to sea for 3 nautical miles (5.5 km) and the landward boundary is 100 feet (30 metres) from the high-water mark.

Inside the reserve are two national parks; the first, **Malindi**, extends about a mile out from the shore between Chanoni Point and Leopard Point, with the park base between the two at Cas-

uarina Point. In this, the main area of interest is known as **North Reef**, which lies roughly parallel to the shore. Low tide exposes much of this reef, leaving numerous shallow pools.

The southern part comprises the coral gardens, which slope off on the seaward side into **Stork Passage**, some 50 feet (15 metres) deep. On the shore side, the coral is flanked by the slightly shallower **Barracuda Channel**. Fish in these gardens are marvellously colourful, perhaps the most common being the blue surgeon fish with its built-in "scalpel" at the base of the tail. This is a defence mechanism, with the very sharp spine drawn and extended when the fish feels threatened. Although not poisonous, the scalpel can inflict a severe wound, and the fish is generally treated with caution by fishermen emptying their nets.

Many varieties of butterfly fish (*Chaetodontidae*) occur, including the Coachman (*Heniochus acuminatus*) with its long trailing dorsal fin. This fish is often mistaken for the similar Moor-

ish Idol (*Zanclus cornutus*), which is also very common. Angel fish (*Pomacanthops*) abound, their immature coloration being so different from the adult that identification is not easy for the beginner.

Holes and crevices in the coral are hiding places for the shy reef residents, including moray eels, soldier fish, barbel eels and octopus. Turtles are frequently seen and may allow the occasional lightweight snorkeller to hold on to their shells for a short but extremely exhilarating ride. Needless to say, it is an offence to collect turtles' eggs, of which many hundreds at a time are laid and buried in the sand above the high-water mark.

**Coral gardens:** The **Watamu Marine National Park**, some 15 miles (24 km) south of Malindi, is the second park in the Reserve waters, wit h the outside of the reef wall forming its eastern boundary. A channel runs inside the lagoon for the length of the bay, on the eastern edge of which are the scattered coral heads of much visited coral gardens. Buoys mark the boundaries, so that the boats moor outside without damaging the coral.

A horde of black and white damsel fish, commonly called Sergeant Major, now associate the arrival of glass-bottomed boats with the possibility of a free meal. These fishes are almost tame and they will jostle in a shoal for titbits of food.

The most exciting area of the Watamu Park is the **Big Three Caves**, at the entrance to Mida Creek on the southern boundary. This is named after a trio of resident giant grouper, or rock cod, or *tewa* in Kiswahili. They are as big as a hammerhead shark and arguably just as ugly, for which reason one of them was called "Edward G". Few people, apart from experienced divers, get to see these 450-pound (200-kg) giants. The caves are all about 13 or 14 feet (about 4 metres) below the level of high tide and stay covered when the tide is out. Park wardens protect the area possessively and they tend to limit the number of visitors to the caves. In fact access is not easy – only by boat and only during a very short period of slack tide which moderates a current that can run at up to 5 knots (9 km/h).

There's a soft and colourful carpet of corals around and inside the caves. The fish are somewhat confused by it all and swim upside down on the roof of the caves, picking up particles of food, entirely unconcerned by the disorientating effect they obviously have on watching divers.

Inland of the creek, the tidal flats have their own claim for attention, particularly for ornithologists. Surrounded by mangroves, this estuarine area is home to half a dozen species of heron and egret. During November to March, migrant waders such as curlews, whimbrels, sanderlings, turnstones, sandpipers and plovers appear in large numbers, many roosting at the northern end of the creek at low tide. The hotels will arrange boat trips to the creek but it's also possible to approach on foot.

**Whale Island and Blue Lagoon:** Another location for birds is **Whale Island**, particularly terns which breed there in Au-

Dragonfish, a deadly denizen of the coral gardens.

gust and September. This is just outside Mida Creek at the southern end of the Marine Park. It appears inhospitable but in fact can be explored on foot at low tide. The rock pools are alive with crabs and other nautical small fry.

To the north of Turtle Bay is the shallow, sheltered **Blue Lagoon**, sandy bottomed and free of currents. At low tide, woolly-necked storks can often be seen foraging for food, and the cliffs at the southern end are heavily populated with multicoloured crabs, skittering over the sharp terrain.

Most of the hotels have facilities for visitors to explore the marine parks and glass-bottomed boats are available for hire at reasonable rates. Masks and snorkels can usually be hired by those who feel restricted by the confines of a square viewing window in the bottom of the boat. For those who have their own equipment, it's often possible to persuade the local fishermen to transport passengers to the reef in their *nga-lawas*. These simple dug-out craft are fashioned from a single tree trunk, but with outriggers which make them surprisingly stable.

There are also commercial operators in the Malindi-Watamu areas who will hire diving equipment – tanks, weightbelts, regulators, life jackets and even underwater cameras – so long as divers can produce the required certificates of competence and proof of fitness. In Malindi, the **Driftwood Club's** resident instructor takes divers to accessible sites in the Park. In Watamu, **Ocean Sports, Seafarers, Turtle Bay**, and **Watamu Beach** hotels have boats and equipment for hire, and a diving centre operated by Lorenz Riedl offers self-catering accommodation as well.

It's always worth seeking out these operators, whose knowledge saves the visitor valuable time in locating the prime dive sites. These are often named after their "discoverers" – "Hancock's Hole" or "Ed's Caves" – known by the local diving fraternity, but not marked on any maps.

About 75 miles (120 km) south of Mombasa is the town of **Shimoni**, "the place of the caves", where slaves were kept while awaiting shipment. The **Kisite-Mpunguti Marine National Park** was established near this small township in 1978, as Kenya's second marine reserve. The reserve boundary encompasses the Inner and Outer Mpunguti Islands and the sand bar of Kisite. Kisite itself has been designated a national park, understandably since it's unrivalled on the Kenya coast for clarity of water. One first-time snorkeller is reported to have popped up exuberantly and exclaimed: "It's like being in a gin and tonic."

The Kisite-Mpunguti Park can only be reached by boat, and low spring tides provide the ideal condition. The boat trip from Shimoni takes approximately 1½ hours. Bottle-nosed dolphins can frequently be seen during the ride out, but they rarely stay close when people enter the water. The journey is along the edge of one of the finest deep-sea fishing areas on the East African coast, the **Pemba Channel**, which drops away to a depth of more than 1,000 feet (300 metres). Not infrequently, schools of

oral reef off himoni.

yellow-fin tunny can be seen in the area. Boats – but not equipment – can be hired from the Parks' base near the jetty to the west of Shimoni village, or from the **Shimoni Reef Lodge**. This lodge arranges daily dhow trips to the reserve, calling on the way back for a leisurely and gargantuan seafood meal at their restaurant on **Wasini Island**.

Accommodation at Shimoni itself is limited. The **Pemba Channel Fishing Club** is small, homely and comfortable, catering for deep-sea fishing trips rather than snorkelling or diving forays into the reserve. The nearest commercial operators with diving equipment and compressors are at **Diani Beach**, some 30 miles (48 km) to the north. These may be persuaded to take large groups to Shimoni, but will not hire out their diving equipment to people who do not also utilise their boats.

In addition to basic precautions against sunburn, great care must be taken when walking in rock pools and while swimming. Stout shoes should be worn and care taken to avoid sea urchins

in shallow water. The spines are mildly toxic and tend to break off in a hand or foot, resulting in discomfort for days.

Stone fish may be encountered, particularly in areas of dead coral, and a sharp eye must be kept open for these very poisonous masters of camouflage. Their dorsal fins inject a dose of venom into anything that touches them, and the excruciating pain that follows will cause severe symptoms of shock, even unconsciousness and sometimes death. After a sting, it's essential to immerse the wound in *very* hot water and to seek medical help immediately.

Minor discomfort can be caused by stinging coral, which in Kenya is a fern-like hydroid, growing abundantly on hard corals. The pain is sharp but soon disappears. Jellyfish and other small organisms, known as standing plankton, cause blisters on the skin and if possible alcohol should be applied. This counteracts the action of the stinging cells, whereas water aggravates it.

Several fish have poisonous defence mechanisms and it is best to avoid touching any of them and though few are aggressive, it is unwise to poke into holes or under coral rocks. Shells should also be handled with caution, if at all, particularly the cone shell which has a poisonous barb at the sharp end. Generally, though, Kenya's underwater world is non-aggressive and welcoming, with water temperatures seldom falling below 24°C (75°F).

When snorkelling or diving, it's imperative to consult the tide tables available for reference at most hotels, or in bookshops for a few shillings. Conditions are best at low tide and if this occurs in the early morning, the water surface will not be too disturbed by wind. In between tides, the water tends to be murky and currents can be strong.

Exploration of the marine world is somewhat seasonal, with ideal conditions prevailing when the northeast (*kaskazi*) monsoon is blowing from approximately October to March. From April to September, the southeast monsoon (*kusi*) brings somewhat cooler conditions, rougher waters and also high winds.

**Left,** a scuba diver heads for the surface. **Right,** shoals of small fry proliferate in the tropic waters.

# THE LAMU ARCHIPELAGO

Lamu and neighbouring islands on the far north of Kenya's coastline have become a fashionable destination for discerning tourists. The port of Lamu is the only substantial survivor of an urban civilization which has existed for at least 1,000 years on this part of the coast. It retains an almost entirely unspoiled 19th century appearance and lifestyle and, since access is now fully developed, has become one of Kenya's premier visitor attractions.

Settlements in the archipelago were first noted in the 2nd century although no evidence of habitation earlier than 9th century has yet been excavated. The settlements of **Weyuni** and **Hedabu** date back by tradition to the 7th century but are, according to recent archaeological research, no older than 13th century. Hedabu, once a principal township, was finally engulfed by sand dunes probably 500 years ago and these shifting sands are now threatening **Shela**, a picturesque village and fabulous tourist beach at the southern tip of the island.

**Mosques galore:** In Lamu town itself, the oldest of 29 island mosques is the **Pwani**. Its qibla dates back to 1370. The **Friday Mosque** was started in 1511, but almost all other buildings are late 18th century. Very little architectural development has taken place since this time and the narrow cloistered town plan and arabesque structures are intact.

Lamu was a thriving port by 1505, when it surrendered meekly to Portuguese invaders. It managed to avoid involvement in the ensuing wars between the colonists and neighbouring island and city states, but there were frequent troubles between Lamu and the sultanates of Mombasa, Zanzibar and Paté (pronounced as the French liver paste), the dominant island port to the north. The town was then surrounded by a defensive wall and, according to a Portuguese historian, Duarte Barbosa, its Arab inhabitants were constantly skirmishing with their Afri-

can neighbours. At this time, the Lamu economy was slave-based. Like most other states in the archipelago, its production was mainly grains and fruits, and its exports included ambergris, mangrove poles, turtle shells, rhino horn and ivory. These highly profitable commodities were sent out on dhows to Yemen, Arabia, the Persian Gulf and on the reverse trade winds to India.

During the 17th century, the nomadic Oromo tribes invaded from the north and sacked most of the coast settlements, except on the islands. The effect was migration to Lamu, Paté, Siyu and Faza, all of which developed rapidly with Paté becoming pre-eminent by the 18th century. Culture flourished at this time; a great tradition of poetry was developed and architecturally ambitious houses were built, some with hot-and-cold plumbing systems which made European ablutions primitive by comparison. Clothing was elegant and jewellery ornate, with gold and silver cloth woven in Lamu and furniture inlaid with silver and ivory.

But paradise was not complete. For two generations the island states warred with each other until 1813, when the people of Lamu trounced an army of the Nabhani of Paté at the battle of Shela. From then on, Lamu began its golden age lasting more or less until 1873 when Britain forced Zanzibar to sign an anti-slaving pact. The Royal Navy patrolled the coast and prevented the Sultan's attempt at slipping slave dhows past the blockade from Kilwa to Lamu. By 1897, there were fewer than 10,000 slaves on the island and 10 years later, slavery was abolished once and for all.

**The first tourists**: The cheap labour on which Lamu's prosperity depended was gone and the island plunged into decline. An American visitor at the time wrote: "The freeing of the slaves has reduced most of the free-born inhabitants to a state of poverty and, moreover, those with property and coconut shambas find it difficult or impossible nowadays to find sufficient labour. I fear there is, then, little hope of their ancient prosperity returning to them, for they have no arts, large industries or resources on which to fall back."

He was among the island's first "tourists", which included Henry Morton Stanley who, according to legend, distributed small gold American dollars which still circulate in the area. A few years later, the Germans moved in to establish the short-lived "Protectorate" around Witu on the mainland and opened the Lamu Post Office, the first established outside Germany.

For 70 years, Lamu merely jogged along, half comatose – isolated from developments within the new British East African Protectorate and later the Kenya Colony. The technology from Europe's industrial revolution was not imported, nor was the competitive ambition and materialism of the 20th century. The island is still largely untouched by "civilization" which accounts for its unique charm. Then, in 1962, shortly before Kenya's Independence, Lamu's economy began to rally, principally from a new role as shipper of Somali cattle to Mombasa.

Houses along the waters of the Indian Ocean.

276

Tourism arrived in 1967 with an initial eight beds at the Peponi ("breezy") Hotel in Shela and since then two more first-class hotels have been built, with scores of lodging houses opened by the local people offering unbelievably low tariffs to itinerant young visitors.

The government has set up an administration on the island to oversee the archipelago and adjoining Lamu District of the hinterland. This has stimulated agricultural and fisheries development and, hopefully, it will attract visitors to the Pandanguo and other new reserves on the mainland. Communication with the island is also being improved, with the upgrading of the Malindi-Mokowe road and of airstrips on Manda Island and mainland Mokowe.

**Old world intact**: But, for the moment, the old-world ambience remains a major visitor attraction. The approach to the town is still exclusively by sea – usually by creaking diesel-powered launches from the road-head at Mokowe or a jetty close to the light aircraft strip on Manda Island.

A strong sea wall runs the length of the town, decorated in places with black, defunct cannon. Many buildings facing the sea are pillared, or castellated, or verandahed in Arab/Swahili style and behind them is a maze of narrow streets no wider than the span of a donkey cart (which is the only haulage vehicle in Lamu apart from boats).

Inset in the unbroken lines of tall buildings are heavy, ornately carved timbered doors and shuttered windows precluding a glimpse of often attractive courtyard gardens inside. There are tiny shops in alleyways, always thronged with strollers – the men in white full-length *khanzu* and *kofia* caps, and the woman almost all in black cover-all dresses, called *bui buis* in Swahili.

Close to the *Boma* (District Commissioner's Office) is an excellent **Lamu Museum**. Just behind is the main town square and market, dominated by a Fort, built in 1821, which is now a museum and public library. Behind this, on rising ground, are some of the larger houses of the town, many of which span

and dunes
◀ Shela
each,
amu.

the streets and create mysterious cloisters of light and dark. These give way to a mosaic of Swahili mud-and-wattle houses, which are roofed with *makuti* thatch, leading to the viewpoint summit of the hill. On the high ground is the old town hospital.

The beach tourism sector of Lamu is at Shela village with **Peponi Hotel** situated at the beginning of an 8-mile (13-km) beach of uninterrupted, empty sand flanked by high dunes. Across the channel on Manda Island is exclusive Manda Island Village, the most recent tourist development. Both hotels offer facilities for fishing, water-skiing, goggling, or expeditions to Paté, Siyu and Faza. At the end of Shela Beach is the village of **Kipungani**, noted for its mango orchards and two old mosques. On the west side of the island, the nearest settlement to the mainland is **Matondoni**, whose people are friendly and addicted to music and dance festivals.

These celebrations or *ziaras* give special eminence to Lamu in the Muslim world. The most important of them is the *Maulidi al Nebi* (birthday of the Prophet) which occurs shortly after Easter. Thousands of pilgrims from East and North Africa, Arabia and the Arabian Gulf inundate the town for the event. They sing and dance in the square before the principal **Riyadha Mosque** and there is an impressive evening worship in the open air under the stars.

Among many visitor attractions of Lamu are the typical souvenirs available of Arab silver jewellery, brassbound and carved chests, model dhows, and Swahili furniture, sometimes of ebony inlaid with ivory.

Crossing the narrow channel to Lamu is an impressive introduction to the area with a profusion of sailing craft, the palm-fringed shore and the attractive waterfront. For the first few months of the year there are often ocean-going dhows moored in the channel.

**Excursions from Lamu**: About 20 miles (32 km) northeast of Lamu is **Paté Island**. The ruined towns of **Faza** and **Siyu** (which also has a well-preserved fort) can both be visited at any tide. The town of Paté itself is more difficult to reach. However, on the right tide it is possible to land there, but otherwise it means a long but fascinating hike from a landing stage on the southern end of the island.

On **Manda** are the ruins of a village of the 16th and 17th centuries called **Takwa**, which compares in interest and state of preservation to Gedi. The Manda town ruins at the island's north end are completely overgrown and buried, but recent archaeological work has determined this to be the oldest (9th century) settlement on the Kenyan coast. There is game on Manda Island and elephants have been known to swim across from the mainland.

A road safari is possible from **Mokowe** farther north to the border with Somalia. This is only for entirely self-contained travellers, and then only in the dry season. For this, the route backtracks southwards, then heads north in the direction of **Kiunga**, about 80 miles (130 km) away.

**Boni Game Reserve** has been established, but only on the map; it's otherwise entirely undeveloped. However, it lies in the heart of primeval forest, rich in wildlife, though often screened by thick vegetation. One day, it will be opened up as an attractive parkland.

In the meantime, travellers normally stick to the main road which eventually climbs over the Mundane Range, a low ridge of ancient sand dunes, and on down to the ocean at Kiunga. The village itself is attractively set, with a beautiful old district officer's house perched on a coral headland.

**Kiunga** harbour is protected by a string of raised coral islands half a mile off the present road coastline. These are important breeding grounds for seabirds which nest there between July and October. It's also the site of **Kiunga Marine National Reserve**.

North of the village, a track goes up to the international boundary with Somalia, just beyond **Shakani**. To the south, the track follows the coast, past ruins at **Omwe** and **Ashuwel**, ending at the bay of **Mkokoni** opposite **Kiwaiyu Island** – a marvellous spot for reef goggling or castaway beachcombing.

**Right, ivory Siwa are traditionally used for wedding fanfares.**

# INSIGHT GUIDES
# TRAVEL TIPS

# Let your message travel with Insight Guides

With 200 titles covering the world, Insight Guides can convey your advertisement to sophisticated international travellers.

## HÖFER MEDIA PTE LTD

Singapore : 38, Joo Koon Road, Singapore 628990
Tel: (65)-865-1629/30  Fax: (65)-862-0694

London : PO Box 7910, London SE11 8LL, United Kingdom
Tel: (44 171)-620-0008, Fax: (44 171)-620-1074
e-mail: insight@apaguide.demon.co.uk

# INSIGHT GUIDES

# TRAVEL TIPS

# Getting Acquainted

## The Place

**Area**: 582,644 sq. km (224,959 sq. miles) and 13,600 sq. km (5,250 sq. miles) of inland water.

**Population**: 26 million. Nairobi: 1.5 million.

**Language**: Kiswahili and English.

**Religion**: 30 percent traditional religions; 60 percent Christian; 10 percent Muslim.

**Capital**: Nairobi

**Currency**: Kenya Shilling (Ksh), divided into 100 cents. The exchange rate tends to fluctuate. Money must be bought locally.

**Electricity**: 240 volts, three-pin plug.

**Weights and measures**: metric

**Dialling Code**: 254 + 2 (Nairobi), + 11 (Mombasa).

**Time zone**: 3 hours ahead of GMT. Daylight is almost a constant 12 hours with fast sunups and sundowns around 6.30am and 6.30pm.

---

### Situation

Kenya bounded in the north by the deserts of Somalia, Ethiopia and the Sudan; to the east by Somalia and the Indian Ocean; and to the south and west by Tanzania and Uganda. Broadly, the country may be divided into four main physiographic regions:

**Rift Valley and Central Highlands**: Fertile, mountainous, lake-studded, and the most developed region economically and in human settlement.

**Western Kenya**: Low plateau farmland to the east of Lake Victoria.

**Northern and Eastern Kenya**: A vast T-shaped swath of country from west of Lake Turkana (Rudolf) across the north to the Somalia border and to the Tanzania border in the south. This is mainly semi-arid rangeland for nomadic pastoralists and wildlife.

**The Coastal Belt**: 300 miles (480 km) of Indian Ocean littoral, including coral reefs and beaches and a narrow fertile strip for sub-tropical agriculture, giving way to bush and semi-desert.

**Principal Mountains**:
Mt Kenya (Batian) – 5,199 metres (17,057 ft)
Mt Elgon (Sudek) – 4,510 metres (14,796 ft)
Aberdares (Ol Doinyo Lasatima) – 3,964 metres (13,005 ft)
Cheranganis (Chepkotet) – 3,370 metres (11,056 ft)
Sekerr Range (Mtelo) – 3,325 metres (10,908 ft)
Mau Range (Melili) – 3,097 metres (10,160 ft)

**Principal Rivers**:
Tana – 700 km (435 miles)
Athi-Galana-Sabaki – 390 km (242 miles)
Suam-Turkwel – 380 km (236 miles)
Mara – 290 km (180 miles)
Nzoia – 260 km (161 miles)
Voi – 210 km (130 miles)
Uaso Nyiro – 140 km (87 miles)

**Principal Lakes**:
Victoria (Kenya section) – 3,785 sq km (1,461 sq miles)
Turkana (formerly Rudolf) – 6,405 sq km (2,473 sq miles)
Baringo – 130 sq km (50 sq miles)
Naivasha – 115 sq km (44 sq miles)
Amboseli (seasonal) – 0–115 sq km (0–44 sq miles)
Magadi – 100 sq km (39 sq miles)
Jipe – 40 sq km (15 sq miles)
Bogoria (formerly Hannington) – 34 sq km (13 sq miles)
Nakuru (seasonal) – 5–30 sq km (2–11½ sq miles)
Elementeita – 18 sq km (7 sq miles)

**Principal Waterfalls**:
Gura – 273 metres (896 ft)
Kindaruma (Seven Forks) – 135 metres (443 ft)
Nyahururu (Thomson's Falls) – 73 metres (240 ft)

## Climate

With an altitude that ranges from sea level to 17,056 ft (5,200 metres), the temperature, rainfall, and humidity variations in Kenya are extreme.

In relation to the four physiographic zones, the climate and land-types can be generalised as follows:

**Rift Valley and Central Highlands**: This highland region of Kenya is generally fresh and invigorating overall, rather like a Swiss summer. The climate ranges from temperate in the Central Rift Valley to arctic on the Mount Kenya peaks. Statistics for Nairobi at the centre of the region are:

• Altitude: 1,661 metres (5,450 ft).
Rainfall: Minimum 20 mm/0.8 inch (July); maximum 200 mm/8 inches (April); average annual 750–1,000 mm (30–40 inches), mainly in two seasons March–May and October–December.

• Sunshine: Averaging from maximum 9½ hours daily in February to minimum 5 hours (April).

• Temperature: Minimum 50°F–58°F (10°C–14°C); maximum 72°F–79°F (22°C–26°C).

The land here is the most productive in Kenya. In the uplands, between 1,500–2,000 metres (4,900–6,600 ft), the greater part of Kenya's agricultural output is produced. In the Rift itself, production is mixed – arable, dairy and livestock.

The central massif of Mount Kenya and the high Aberdares form the country's main water catchment area, with rainfall of up to 3,000 mm (120 inches) a year on the mountains, producing run-offs to the main Rift lakes.

**Western Kenya**: Hot, wettish, with the rain spread fairly evenly throughout the year. Most of the rain falls in early evening. Climate at Kisumu, centre of the region, may be taken as indicative of the region:

• Altitude: 1,157 metres (3,795 ft)

• Rainfall: Minimum 60 mm/2½ inches (June); maximum 200 mm/8 inches (April); annually between 1,000 and 1,300 mm (40–50 inches).

• Sunshine: Between 7 and 9 hours daily throughout the year.

• Temperature: Minimum 57–64°F (14°C–18°C); maximum 86°F–93°F (30°C–34°C).

**Northern and Eastern Kenya**: The land ranges from bleak lava desert around Lake Turkana (Rudolf), where west of the lake rainfall averages below 255 mm (10 inches) a year and temperatures rise to 104°F (39°C), to sand desert at the Chalbi in the north, arid pastoralist bush, vast dryish grass and acacia rangeland down to the baking soda lake of Magadi in the south, where again temperatures will be as high as 100°F (38°C). It is difficult to set an average climate for this vast T-section of the country, but one indicative example may be Garissa, at the eastern edge of the dry savannah belt.

- Altitude: 128 metres (420 ft).
- Rainfall: Minimum zero (July); maximum 80 mm/3 inches (November); average annual, 255–510 mm (10–20 inches).
- Sunshine: Averaging 9 hours a day over the year.
- Temperature: Mean annual minimum, 72°F (22°C); mean annual maximum 93°F (34°C).

**Coastal Belt:** The coral beaches are hot with about 70 percent humidity but tempered by sea breezes. Then comes a thin plain, suitable for agriculture (fruits, nuts, dairy, cotton) but this soon gives way to thorn scrub and semi-desert. An indicative climate is that of Mombasa:

- Altitude: 17 metres (57 ft)
- Rainfall: Average minimum 20 mm/ 0.8 inch (February) to 240 mm/9 inches (May); average annual 1,000– 1,250 mm (40–50 inches).
- Sunshine: Average maximum of 9 hours a day in March, 7 hours in May.
- Temperature: Mean annual minimum 72°F (22°C); mean annual maximum 87°F (30°C).

## Etiquette

Visitors should show respect to the local people, basically by exercising tact, tolerance, and applied common sense. A few **"don'ts"** might be helpful:

**Don't** show disrespect for authority, starting with the president. Don't try to take his picture – nor that of any of the other leaders, and don't tear up his portrait on a banknote. It has been done before by people getting rid of the last of their Kenyan cash at the airport before they leave – and they've been in trouble for it.

**Don't** photograph anyone without their consent, not even the tribesmen way out in the bush. Smile, wave your camera around, offer a few shillings and that ought to do it. The Maasai have got wise, by the way. They're looking for up to $10 a shot of their handsome profiles. But tell them to forget it – in English, they'll understand – and offer them 10 to 50 shillings. Otherwise, look for someone with a less opportunistic eye.

**Don't** make a show of your wealth anywhere. The obvious temptation is to relieve you of some of it in some way or other.

**Don't** break the law, of course. For tourists, the main hazards are the Exchange Control Act (illegal deals with money), the traffic regulations, and the ordinances against prostitution, sexual offences and drug taking.

The law is in fact fairly benign in Kenya, especially in application to tourists. Where there is a problem, it's dealt with through the due process of law modelled on the British system. No arrest without a warrant; no holding without a charge; no detention without trial. What happens when a visitor is in trouble is that he's usually handed over to the care and admonishment of his embassy; then, in an exceptional case, he may be escorted to the airport and requested not to come back. Very few are actually jailed, except for murder and mayhem. For criminal and some civil offences, there would probably be an appearance in court, a fine and an order to depart the country.

Prostitution is a risk for tourists, not so much for life and limb as for the local strains of infection and HIV. There's no regular health check on the women who crowd the hotel bars and dance halls, so the advice is **don't**. Male prostitution is on the increase, especially on the beaches, but there's usually trouble attached, including prosecution and severe retribution.

### FORMS OF ADDRESS

A waiter is addressed as steward or maybe "b*wana*" which means "mister".

The hoi-polloi in Kenya are called the *"wananchi"* – the people – and the word carries a connotation of respect. Do not use "blacks" or "coloureds"; the term is "Africans" or "Asians".

In addressing an old man – anyone over 35 – call him *"mzee"* pronounced mim-zay. It's a term of respect, meaning "old man" or "elder" and you can use it anywhere, in restaurants, hotels, or wherever. Call a mature woman (over 21) *"mama"* and a child *"toto"*. A word you will hear constantly is *"wazungu"*, meaning white people; *"mzungu"* in the singular.

### TIPPING

The rules you use at home when tipping should apply here. For instance, add 10 percent to a restaurant bill unless it's there already. The biggest tip will probably go to your tour driver if he has been helpful and responsive on the trip. Around £3/US$5 per person per day is expected on safari, more if the guide was exceptional.

### OTHER LARGESSE

Use your judgment, but as a rule don't give to beggars on the streets in towns. The authorities are trying to eliminate this practice and the best deterrent is the sure knowledge that pan-handling doesn't pay.

### DRUGS

The soft smoke is called *bhang* locally and, like most horticulture in Kenya, it grows wild and phenomenally. People may get away with the occasional pot party, but it's still against the law. More serious trouble for tourists is when they try to export it, stashed in a hollowed-out "souvenir". The Customs are wise to it all. Hard drugs are virtually ignored by the youngsters in Kenya, and the only stuff in common use is a mild narcotic grass called *miraa*. It's grown extensively in the wet hills above Meru and Embu and chewed for mild stimulation, mostly by the northern nomads. It's supposed to keep them awake through the long night looking after the camels.

## Economy

On its own account, Kenya is among the world's leading exporters of quality coffee, teas, and pineapples. Other primary exports are horticultural produce, pyrethrum, sisal and other cash crops. Tourism is an important source of foreign exchange, with further substantial receipts from Kenya's position as the regional centre for communications, banking, insurance and general commerce.

## Government

President Daniel arap Moi holds executive power assisted by a Vice-President and Cabinet chosen from the legislature, the National Assembly. This body consists of 158 members elected by universal suffrage, 12 Presidential nominees, the Speaker and the Attorney-General. The Assembly's term is for five years unless dissolved by the President or its own majority "no confidence" vote.

The process of Government in Kenya is democratic and the first multi-party elections in 26 years took place in December 1992. There are now 11 registered political parties in Kenya.

Kenya is an independent republic, a member of the Organisation for African Unity (OAU), the Commonwealth and the United Nations.

The country's record of stability, as well as its development performance since independence in 1963, has slipped in recent years, with an increase in the incidence of poverty. Kenya is a major recipient in Africa of international development aid.

# Planning The Trip

## What to Bring

Besides a **camera** and **binoculars** for game-viewing, other equipment is not necessary, unless you intend to engage in some particular activity like golf or fishing.

**Film** in Kenya is readily available but very expensive, so the best advice is to bring your own. Kodak, Agfa and Fuji have laboratory services, so there should be no problems in having developing done as fast as you need it. There are no facilities for developing Kodachrome slide film in Kenya.

**Toiletries** and make-up are available locally but mostly imported and comparatively expensive, especially high factor sunblock – it is best to bring your own. Also bring enough personal prescription medicines to last through the stay in Kenya.

US visitors should bring a small step-down **voltage converter**. Sockets in Kenya are 3-pin square so adaptors for other type of sockets will be needed.

If you want to hire a vehicle, an **international driving licence**, or a valid national licence is needed, provided it is endorsed at the Road Transport Office, Nyayo House, Kenyatta Avenue, Nairobi.

## What to Wear

For much of the year, Nairobi is like a summer city in Europe. Smart, comfortable jackets off in the heat of the day, and back on again for dinner in a good restaurant. Ladies should wear skirts below the knee or pants, and shorts only at tourist resorts, not in town.

Some months, like August, can be overcast: cool in the daytime and chilly at night. So, at this time of year, the wardrobe should include some warm cardigans and sweaters. Again, maybe smartish, medium-weight clothes for the evenings.

If you are planning to spend most of the time on safari, you should bring a small, select wardrobe for all seasons – depending, of course, on where you intend to go. Light and casual for the coast and game park safaris, and not necessarily the full professional hunter rig-out – muted colours, shirts, jeans and the like will do, plus, of course, the hat. For the forest lodges, dress (almost) as for evening in a European ski lodge, or at least well wrapped up.

Women will probably find cotton dresses cooler and more comfortable than trousers, particularly for daytime. If trousers are preferred, the "baggy" rather than the skin tight are obviously better ventilated. For footwear, comfort should take precedence over style, as many pavements are uneven in the cities and towns and non-existent, of course, in the bush.

Specialised sports clothes, including swimwear, should be packed. It's all available in Nairobi and Mombasa, but in a limited range and often at over-extended prices.

Drip-dry clothing is recommended and plenty of it. In places of red dusty soil – which is just about everywhere – clothes get grubby and two or three changes a day are possible for the more fastidious. Don't bother bringing rainwear, even if the safari is timed for the rainy season. If necessary, something light and disposable can be picked up locally.

Safari clothes and boots for both men and women are available throughout Nairobi, and are very reasonably priced. Tailor-made safari suits can be run up in a few days and men particularly find them a valuable addition to their holiday wardrobe, since they look smart, feel cool, and cost only a fraction of a regular suit, with the added bonus of being washable.

For women, the local *kanga* dresses or loose blouses are the most versatile and popular wardrobe addition, available in an infinite variety of designs and for little outlay. The *kikoi* (simple wrap-around sarong) is also useful.

At the coast, shorts are marginally all right for visitors in Mombasa during the day – but the rule is to keep in mind the Muslim ethic for "decency" in dress. This, incidentally, precludes nude or topless bathing on the beach.

## Entry Regulations
### Visas & Passports

All visitors must be in possession of a valid passport. Visas are required by all but citizens of most Commonwealth and certain other countries with which Kenya has reciprocal waiver arrangements. The Commonwealth exceptions are Australia, Nigeria, and Sri Lanka.

Citizens of the United Kingdom of Indian, Bangladeshi or Pakistani origin also require visas, as do all arrivals from the Republic of South Africa.

At present, visas are not required from nationals of Denmark, Eire, Ethiopia, Finland, Germany, Holland, Italy, Norway, Spain, Sweden, Turkey and Uruguay.

Since these arrangements may change, it is essential to double-check on visa requirements with airlines, tour operators, or Kenya Government offices abroad well ahead of the trip. Normally it takes up to six weeks to process a visa application. Visas are usually issued to cover a period of three months.

Arrivals holding onward or return tickets may obtain a "Visitor's Pass" on arrival at any Kenya port of entry for a fee of about US$30 or the equivalent in convertible currency. Its validity is normally for three months.

No visitor is permitted to take up work or residence in Kenya without the authority of the Principal Immigration Officer.

These are the normal entry requirements, but prior to travel, intending visitors are advised to consult Kenyan embassies or representatives abroad in case of changes in immigration regulations.

## Customs

Unused personal effects, unexposed film, cameras and accessories (except cine and slide projectors) may be temporarily imported duty-free.

Among items which must be declared, but will be admitted duty-free, are: 250 gm of tobacco, or the equivalent in cigarettes (200) or cigars (50); one litre of alcohol; and one litre of perfume.

Refundable deposits may be required for the import of radios, tape-recorders and similar equipment, musical instruments, etc.

Firearms may only be imported if accompanied by a permit issued by the Central Firearms Bureau, P.O. Box 30263, Nairobi.

The import of agricultural or horticultural produce, or animal pets, is not permitted.

## Health

### Malaria

Malaria is endemic in Kenya below altitudes of 1,830 metres (6,000 ft) so prophylactics are essential. Take pills as prescribed two weeks before arrival, during the stay and for two weeks after departure. Unless the intention is to stay for the duration in Nairobi, where malaria is rare, there is a risk of being bitten by a carrier mosquito outside the capital – especially at the coast or up at Lake Victoria.

### Yellow Fever and Cholera

Protection against Yellow Fever and cholera is recommended but not mandatory to enter Kenya if arriving directly from Europe, North America or Australia. However if you will be travelling from Yellow Fever areas (such as West or Central Africa) proof of vaccination is required. Please consult your doctor at home for advice.

### Swimming

Swimming is not recommended in slow-moving rivers or at the edge of lakes with reeds, no matter how inviting the water appears. The risk is bilharzia, from a parasite that moves from host water snails to man, attacking vital organs like the liver.

## Ocean Swimming

Ocean swimming is almost entirely safe, mainly because there is no fear of sharks in the Indian Ocean since these and other predators rarely get past the fringing reef. On this, however, there are a few pests which warrant caution in the form of protective footwear (light canvas shoes will do). The worst of them is the stone fish, which is well adapted to look like a lump of coral. But if anyone steps on it, he can receive a painful and highly venomous injection which requires immediate medical attention. Other barbed poison – but nothing as dangerous – is delivered by a number of creatures of the coral, notably a pretty, feathery fish with a variety of names, including the dragon fish.

## The Equatorial Sun

Tourists often feel that the sun in Kenya is no stronger than, say, on the west coast of America or on the European continent in the summer. But, being directly overhead in Kenya, the sun is unexpectedly powerful and light skins, in fact any non-Kenyan, must be exposed very gradually. At the coast, the drill is to always use a strong sunblock and if you must, start the sun-bathing in the early morning and late afternoon, extending the exposure time each day as the skin begins to tan. High factor lotions are strongly recommended because they provide protection for the skin and sensitive areas like eyes, head, the nape of the neck and back (use waterproof cream when snorkelling and swimming).

Apply a powerful, waterproof sunblock to children's delicate skins. Also insist that children wear a hat to protect them from the sun's strong rays and swim in T-shirts for peace of mind and peaceful nights.

Early in the exposure process, Vitamin A supplements are sometimes recommended.

## Altitude

It generally takes a couple of days to acclimatise to high altitude locations like Nairobi. The effect of the thinnish oxygen on new arrivals is a tendency to tire around the middle of the day, or to cause a passing light-headedness. Up on the mountains, above 4,000 metres (13,000 ft), there is a risk of *pulmonary*

*oedema*, a capricious suffusion of the lungs which might bring down an athlete and yet leave a habitual smoker to go on blithely to the summit. The only antidote is a swift retreat back down the mountains, otherwise the consequences may be serious.

## Tap Water

In Nairobi, the water is drinkable, but the chances are that new arrivals are going to get "the runs" anyway from a change of diet as well as water. Anywhere outside the city, the water should be boiled unless it's been drawn from ice-cold mountain streams. Bottled mineral water is widely available.

## Public Holidays

**January 1** – New Year's Day
**April** – Good Friday
**April** – Easter Monday
**May 1** – Labour Day
**June 1** – Madaraka Day (anniversary of self-government)
**October 10** – Moi Day (anniversary of President Moi's inauguration)
**October 20** – Kenyatta Day
**December 12** – Jamhuri Day (Independence Day)
**December 25** – Christmas Day
**Dec 26** – Boxing Day
**variable** – Idd ul Fitr (Muslim holiday, timed for the first sighting of the new moon)

## Getting There

### By Air

While Kenya runs its own national airline, Kenya Airways, it also has the benefit of 35 international airlines currently providing regular air services to and from the country.

Kenya has two main points of entry by air: Jomo Kenyatta International Airport, Nairobi, and Moi International Airport, Mombasa. The capital's airport is one of the most modern in Africa. Mombasa's is not so prestigious, but big enough for the wide-bodied jets with full passenger facilities.

#### FROM LONDON

Flights leave regularly from London (British Airways now runs to Kenya via Gatwick) to Nairobi; some direct, others with European stopovers. Passengers from Ireland must connect in London.

From Nairobi, there are Kenya Airways flights from the capital to Mombasa and other internal destinations.

Available fares are: first, business and economy class; an excursion fare can be booked any time for stays from 19 to 45 days; and an APEX (Advance Purchase Excursion) fare can be reserved one calendar month in advance, allowing stays of 19 to 90 days. The price of APEX fares – obviously low compared with other fares – varies according to season, with June to September and December to January considered "high" seasons. You can make stopovers en route with all fares except APEX. Reductions are available for children.

It is also possible to fly to Nairobi by Aeroflot, via Moscow, and on a number of African national airlines. Reconfirmation of return flights is essential.

TRANSIT/TRANSFER

The normal facilities exist at Nairobi airport for passengers transferring to other flights, with no need to formally enter the country through Customs and Immigration. The only exceptions are for transfers to Kenya Airways internal flights.

**Kenya Airways**
**Kenya**: Barclays Plaza, Loita Street, P.O. Box 41010, Nairobi. Tel: 229291/210771; Airways Terminal P.O. Box 99302, Mombasa, tel: 221251; P.O. Box 634, Malindi, tel: 20237.
**United Kingdom**: 16 Conduit Street, London W118, tel: 0171-409 0185.
**United States**: 424 Madison Avenue, New York, NY, tel: 212-832 8810. 9150 Wilshire Boulevard, Beverly Hills, Ca, tel: 310-2780850.

## By Sea

Long gone are the days when a leisurely cruise to Mombasa was possible – not now, apart from one or two really outside chances. It's conceivable that a passenger berth can be found and negotiated on a cargo ship out of London or one of the European ports. The odds – negligible – are about the same as a sail down in a dhow from Abu Dhabi or elsewhere in the Gulf. The only real prospect, for those who can afford it, is a short stopover in Mombasa as part of a

luxury liner trip (Cunard/Ellerman). These usually include short safaris around the country if desired.

It is also possible to take a dhow or catamaran from Zanzibar or Dar-es-Salaam in Tanzania to Mombasa, but this is not recommended as the journey can take many days and can be quite dangerous.

## By Rail

No access to Kenya is possible by rail – except by an unlikely roundabout route from Dar es Salaam in Tanzania, up to Mwanza on Lake Victoria, then by lake steamer operated by the Kenya Railways Authority to Kisumu, and from there down the old *Lunatic Line* to Nairobi and Mombasa. It's difficult to imagine anyone doing this trip, except possibly a historian researching the relics of the old imperial lines.

## By Road

From the north it is difficult – because of problems of uncertain transit through northeast Africa. But it has been done, and outfits in London seem to be the market leaders for group overland safaris to Kenya – really for the young and adventurous. Advertisements can be found in Britain's national press.

Again it's conceivable, but improbable, that private overland expeditions can be organised. In this case, thorough advance planning would be necessary, especially in consultation with the embassies of countries on the selected route. People have come down from the north solo on motorbikes and so on, but more sensibly with two or more four-wheel drive trucks, fully rigged for long desert crossings. Ambitious highways are being built to Juba in southern Sudan and up north through Ethiopia. The overland trip will obviously be more viable when these are completed. If anyone does want to attempt the road access, the required documents for entry into Kenya are:
• International Touring documents: Carnet de passage and Triptique
• International Certificate of Insurance
• International Driving Licence (visitors may use their domestic licenses for up to 90 days providing that they have been endorsed at the Road Transport Office in Nairobi).

Overland entry into Kenya from Tanzania and Uganda is less problematic.

Buses run from Dar-es-Salaam to Mombasa , or train to Tanga and bus over the border. A well used and popular route is from Arusha or Moshi to Nairobi which takes about five hours by bus or minibus and the border crossing is straightforward.

**Note**: Advice might be obtained by writing ahead to the Automobile Association ("AA") of Kenya, P.O. Box 40087, Nairobi.

## Useful Addresses

### Kenyan Diplomatic Missions Overseas
**Australia**, 6th Floor, QBE Building, 33 35 Ainsli Avenue, Box 1990, Canberra ACT 2601. Tel: 474788, P.O. Box 1990, Canberra, ACT 2600.
**Canada**, Gillin Building, Suite 600 141 Laurier Avenue, West Ottawa, Ontario KIP 5J3. Tel: 5631773-6.
**United Kingdom**, 45 Portland Place London, WIN 4AS. Tel: 0171-630 2371.
**United States**, 2249, R Street, NW Washington DC 20008. Tel: 202-387 6101/4; 866 United Nations Plaza New York 10017. Tel: 4214740

### Kenya Tourist Office Overseas
**United Kingdom**, 25/25 New Bond Street, London W14 9HD. Tel: 0171 3553144.
**United States**, 424 Madison Avenue New York, NY 10017. Tel: 4861300 111 Doheny Plaza, 9100 Wilshire Boulevard, Beverly Hills, California 90121. Tel: 2746635.

### Special Information
East Africa has a number of non-governmental organisations (NGOs) which complement official conservation efforts.

**African Fund for Endangered Wildlife (AFEW)**, P.O. Box 15004, Nairobi. Tel: 891658.
**African Wildlife Foundation (AWF)** P.O. Box 48177, Nairobi. Tel: 710367 71.
**The David Sheldrick Memorial Appeal** P.O. Box 15555, Nairobi. Tel: 891996
**The East African Wildlife Society**, P.O. Box 20110, Nairobi. Tel: 748170-3.
**Elsa Wild Animal Appeal (Elsa)**, P.O. Box 30092, Nairobi. Tel: 742121
**Friends of Conservation**, P.O. Box 59749, Nairobi. Tel: 339537/243976

Gallmann Memorial Foundation (GMF), P.O. Box 45593, Nairobi. Tel: 521220.

Wildlife Clubs of Kenya, P.O. Box 40658, Nairobi. Tel: 891903/4.

Wildlife Conservation International (WCI), P.O. Nox 48177, Nairobi. Tel: 332963/223235.

Worldwide Fund for Nature (WWF), P.O. Box 62440, Nairobi. Tel: 332963/223235.

## International Organisations

Most of the United Nations Organisations represented in Kenya are located in the UN complex at Gigiri, about 11 km (7 miles) from the centre of the city close to the suburb of Muthaiga. These include UNESCO and UNICEF.

## Other Organisations

Food and Agriculture Organisation of the United Nations (FAO), Utumishi Co-operative House, Mamlaka Road, P.O. Box 30470, Nairobi. Tel: 725128/725069.

Organisation of African Unity (OAU), 5th and 6th floor, Mandeleo House, Monrovia Street. Tel: 338042/338519.

United Nations Children's Fund (UNICEF), Gigiri. Tel: 621234.

United Nations Development Programme (UNDP), KICC Building, Harambee Avenue, P.O. Box 30218, Nairobi. Tel: 228776-8/223548.

United Nations Educational Scientific and Cultural Organisation (UNESCO). Tel: 621234.

United Nations High Commission for Refugees (UBHCR), Chiromo Road, Westlands, P.O. Box 43801, Nairobi. Tel: 443028/-34.

World Bank and Affiliates (IBRD), View Park Towers, Monrovia Street, P.O. Box 30577, Nairobi. Tel: 228477.

World Health Organisation (WHO), 6th Floor, Afya House (Ministry of Health), Cathedral Rd (off Ngong Road), PO Box 45335. Tel: 723069/71/72/74.

## Lions Clubs

### MOMBASA

Central: P.O. Box 82569, Mombasa. Tel: Sec 25061;

Pwani: P.O. Box 81871, Mombasa. Tel: Sec 20731.

### NAIROBI

Host: P.O. Box 47447, Nairobi. Tel: Sec 742266;

Central: P.O. Box 44867, Nairobi. Tel: 338901;

City: P.O. Box 30693, Nairobi. Tel: Sec 27354;

North: P.O. Box 42093, Nairobi. Tel: Sec 21251;

Westlands: P.O. Box 42539, Nairobi. Tel: Sec 556020;

Kikuyu: P.O. Box 47301, Nairobi. Tel: Sec 24023.

Lions International (District 411), P.O. Box 45652, Nairobi. Tel: Sec 331709.

## Rotary Clubs

### UPCOUNTRY

Eldoret, P.O. Box 220, Eldoret. Tel: Sec (Eldoret) 2936.

### MOMBASA

Kilindini, P.O. Box 99067, Mombasa. Tel: Sec 25157.

Mombasa, P.O. Box 90570, Mombasa. Tel: Sec 226330 (Jitesh Shah).

### NAIROBI

North: c/o P.O. Box 30751, Nairobi. Tel: 719800 (Harry Mugo).

South: c/o P.O. Box 46611. Tel: Sec 540300 (Simon Glover).

Rotary International (District 920), PO Box 564, Kampala, Uganda. Tel: (041) 259604.

## Other Clubs

### NAIROBI

African Cultural Society, P.O. Box 69484, Nairobi. Tel: 335581. (Cultural Festivals Lectures and Theatre).

American Women's Association, P.O. Box 47806. Nairobi. Tel: 574124 or go through the US Embassy tel: 334141. (Membership Chairman).

The Caledonian Society of Kenya, P.O. Box 40755, Nairobi. Tel: Sec 520400 (evenings).

Geological Club of Kenya, P.O. Box 44749, Nairobi.

Geographical Society of Kenya, P.O. Box 41887, Nairobi.

Nairobi Branch of the Royal Society of St George, P.O. Box 48360, Nairobi. Tel: 891262.

Nairobi Photographic Society, P.O. Box 49879, Nairobi. Tel: 337129. Meetings are held at the St John Ambulance Headquarters (behind Donovan Manle Theatre) at 8.30pm on the first and third Thursday of each month.

# Practical Tips

## Emergencies

### Security & Crime

Kenya is among the more secure countries in Africa, though there have been unprecedented attacks on visitors recently, including hijacking and armed robbery, which has led to the establishment of a Tourist Police Force.

Crime is not insignificant in the towns, and tourists should take care, especially in Nairobi and when arriving in the country. The commonsense rules are to keep out of the dark back streets at night and out of the sleazier bars and dance dives. Some of the African dance halls are the liveliest places in town, and there is no reason why the visitor can't partake of the fuggy, sweaty, exotic experience. But go in a group, and leave the commercial ladies alone.

Don't carry too much money or valuables around. Muggings and bag-snatching happen, and there's a rather savage deterrent for it. Someone shouts "thief" and suddenly it's a Roman holiday, with the mob giving chase and meting out summary justice when they catch up. Only shout if you really think the situation warrants the severe beating the accused will receive.

Rape and sexual assault are uncommon in a society which has fairly liberal access to sex. Should you be accosted, it's more likely that the villain is after your property, not your body.

Problem areas of violent crime are deserted beaches and drunken, mixed-company parties. Probably the commonest urban crime in Kenya is car theft, followed by house-breaking. For tourists, it's the "con" and the lifting of valuables left lying around. In any threatening situation, the rule is not to panic nor make any sudden moves in attack or retreat. Keep quiet and do what you're told (within reason) – basically, apply common sense.

Instant crowds with expert pickpockets and confidence tricksters are the most common problem for tourists. Elaborate and convincing stories involving money catch even the most experienced traveller.

Up-country, theft is about the only real problem from the Somali *shifta* gangs and tourists have been warned to stay out of the area. It has also happened in Maasai country, but there has usually been some serious provocation. In general, the vast bush areas in Kenya amount to one great camp site and are entirely safe providing people stick to the few fundamental rules.

There have been problems recently for travellers on the Mombasa to Lamu road with *shifta* gangs holding up the buses. Armed convoy buses accompany the regular services as a precaution when deemed necessary.

---

## Medical Services

Overall, medical services are better in Kenya than in most other African countries. There are one or two first-rate hospitals in Nairobi and at the coast; a surprising number of specialist physicians and surgeons, a few with international reputation, and some fine dentists and opticians.

For emergency services, including ambulance, dial **999**, or St John's Ambulance, Nairobi. Tel: 224066/ 222396; Police Hotline, Nairobi. Tel: 728888/717777/240000.

### MEDICAL INSURANCE

Medical insurance can be bought locally at reasonable cost from indigenous and locally based multinational insurance firms. Another option and a supportive gesture is to buy inexpensive insurance from the famous Flying Doctor Service in Kenya. One-month membership costs US$25. To arrange this call Nairobi. Tel: 502699 or their emergency line, Nairobi. Tel: 501280. In the event of serious illness or accident on safari, the doctors will fly out from their headquarters at Wilson Airport and either treat the casualties themselves or fly them to a hospital back in Nairobi.

### CHEMISTS/PHARMACIES

There is no shortage of chemists or pharmacies in Kenya, all of them staffed with qualified pharmacists. Most drugs are available, although sometimes with what may be unfamiliar brand names. If a visitor's specific prescription is not available, the pharmacist will often be able to prescribe a suitable alternative without the need of a visit to the doctor. Advice and treatment for minor ailments is always generously available.

Most chemists close on Saturday afternoons, Sundays, and public holidays. When closed, the name and location of the duty chemist is usually posted on the shop door, or may be obtained at the nearest hospital. Weekend chemist opening times are advertised in the local newspapers. Two late-night pharmacies in Nairobi are Shield Pharmaceuticals. Tel: 743710/750876, and Laureace Pharmacy. Tel: 335093.

### HOSPITALS

**The Aga Khan Hospital**, 3rd Parklands Avenue, P.O. Box 30270, Nairobi. Tel: 742541/740015/740729.
**Coast General Hospital**, P.O. Box 90231, Mombasa. Tel: 314201.
**Gertrude's Garden Children's Hospital**, Muthaiga Road, P.O. Box 42325, Nairobi. Tel: 763474/763475.
**Mater Misericordiae Hospital**, Dunga Road, South B, P.O. Box 30325, Nairobi. Tel: 556666/556298.
**Mombasa Hospital Association**, P.O. Box 90294, Mombasa. Tel: 312191/ 312099.
**Nairobi Hospital**, Argwings Kodhek Road, P.O. Box 30026, Nairobi. Tel: 722160.

---

## Business Hours

Any time from 8am to 5.30pm with some general stores or Indian *dukas* staying open well into the evenings and most of the weekend. In Mombasa, trade may start as early as 7am with a long siesta break any time from 12.30pm to 4pm, and then re-opening until after dark. Buying in the retail trade has a touch of the Persian market about it, with haggling possible in Nairobi and mandatory in Mombasa.

Almost all city and principal town banks have a Bureau de Change. Sometimes these are open for longer than the normal banking hours of 9am to 2pm, Monday to Friday. Some banks open between 9am and 11am on the first and last Saturday of each month. Branches of banks at Jomo Kenyatta International Airport run a 24-hour service. Now many private Bureaux de Change have sprung up in major cities.

---

## Religious Services

Cathedrals, churches of many denominations, chapels, synagogues, mosques and temples are located all over the country – in the cities, towns and rural areas. Locations and times of services etc, are published in the national newspapers.

---

## Media

The English speaking radio station and one television station is operated by the government. There is one other privately owned television station, Kenya Television Network, which offers a good variety of programmes together with CNN.

There are three English-language daily newspapers: the *Standard*, the *Nation* and the *Kenya Times*. There is one weekly newspaper, the *East African*, which contains news from all around East Africa. Foreign newspapers and magazines can be bought in Nairobi.

There is a private music radio station, *Capital FM*, and one can subscribe to a wide variety of satellite TV.

---

## Postal Services

There is a post office in most major shopping centres in Nairobi, and the system is efficient. Mail can also be sent from major hotels. International and local speed post and parcel services are offered by several independent operators.

Poste Restante is free; the main pick-up point is the Central Post Office, Haile Selassie Avenue. Telegrams can be sent by phone; call the operator (900) and ask for assistance, although it may be better to make the trip to Extelcom House on Haile Selassie Avenue and send the telegram in person.

---

## Telephone

Kenya has a communications system for both domestic and international services, which often breaks down or suffers delays. If you have trouble getting connected, ask for assistance from the International Operator, dial 0196 (there will be a charge for this all). Microwave relays provide direct dialling between most centres in the country and a full international STD system has recently been introduced. There are also internal and external telex facilities, providing direct dialling to most major capitals and many nations on a 24-hour basis. This service operates through the Mount Longonot earth satellite station.

## Tourist Information

There are two official bureaus for tourist information: one in front of the Hilton in Nairobi centre; the other close to the street-spanning tusks on Moi Avenue in Mombasa.

Most private tour companies scattered around the urban centres are fairly liberal with information and there are plenty of publications – maps, guides of varying quality, brochures, pamphlets. The newspapers also provide information on any available "special offer" tour packages or cut-rate accommodation.

A message-board in the Nairobi New Stanley's **Thorn Tree Cafe** offers lifts or shared-cost safaris for younger travellers and others on tight budgets.

## Photography

Don't forget to always ask permission before attempting to photograph people. Tread carefully and don't be insensitive.

**Technical Tips:** As a choice of film to bring – Kodachrome 64 is fine for quality transparencies. Black and white medium speed (125 ASA), and for those tricky lighting conditions where no flash can be used, i.e. artificially lit waterholes, faster films up to 1000 ASA can be used, though obviously quality will suffer. Lenses for 35 mm cameras should include telephoto and zoom up to 300 mm. Keep colour films in a cool box when in very hot temperatures.

The best light in Africa for photography is in the early morning and late afternoon. Midday vertical shadows tend to have disastrous effects. A compact camera, one of the new "foolproof" varieties is a good addition to your equipment, even for the most professional photographer. After all, there are times when a good shot will be missed if you're not "at the ready" fast.

**Australia**, Riverside Drive, P.O. Box 39341, Nairobi. Tel: 445034-39.
**Canada**, Comcraft House, Haile Selassie Avenue, P.O. Box 30481, Nairobi. Tel: 214804.
**Ireland**, Maendeleo House, Monrovia Street, P.O. Box 30659, Nairobi. Tel: 226771-4.
**United Kingdom**, Bruce House, Standard Street, P.O. Box 30465, Nairobi. Tel: 335944-60.
**United States of America**, Moi Avenue/Haile Selassie Avenue, P.O. Box 30137, Nairobi. Tel: 334141-50.

# Getting Around

## Public Transport

### By Air

Kenya Airways, the only national airline, operates scheduled services to Mombasa, Malindi and Kisumu. In addition, private air charter companies based at Wilson Airport, also just outside town, run regular, scheduled services in five-to-ten seater light aircraft to destinations like Lamu and the Maasai Mara. Half a dozen companies at Wilson charter aircraft, from small monoplanes to Lear jets. Some of them have branch operations out of Mombasa and Malindi, where there are also coast-based air charter companies. Another possibility for qualified pilots is to rent a plane at the Nairobi Aero Club.

Nairobi airport offers all usual passenger services, including a 24-hour currency exchange facility, post office, shops, restaurants, coffee stations, duty-free shop and bars. A porter service is available both inside and outside the customs area. Tips, about Kshs 20 a bag, would be generous.

For visitors without health certificates, a vaccination service is available in the arrivals building.

The Kenya Airways bus usually travels from the airport to the centre of Nairobi frequently, though the service was recently shut down. Taxis cost about Kshs 900 to the centre of town, and are of course cheaper if shared.

### By Rail & Lake Steamer

The train is exceptionally good value, and comfortable in both first and second class (sexes are separate unless a whole compartment is reserved). It's roughly a 12-hour overnight between Mombasa and Nairobi – a night trip in both directions – with 2- or 4-bunk sleeping compartments and a fully serviced bar and restaurant car. The service extends up-country from Nairobi to Kisumu and Lake Victoria, where Kenya Railways run a lake steamer service to Mwanza and other Tanzanian ports.

### Buses

It may be difficult for visitors to find their way about the urban routes on the local buses and they also tend to be jam-packed at rush hours 7–9am and 4.30–6.30pm. They're the cheapest form of travel in Kenya with a nationwide network wherever there are reasonable roads. The long-haul buses out of Nairobi and Mombasa are by no means excluded to visitors, but they're rough and ready. Beware! The buses travel at break-neck speed and have many accidents.

### Taxis

The only properly organised taxi service is a fleet of Mercedes, operated by the state Kenatco Transport Company from the international airports and main urban hotels. You can take the driver's word (usually) for the set per-kilometre rate.

Other than this, taxis are something of a free-for-all in Kenya – all marked with yellow stripes but otherwise a motley collection of vehicles, in various stages of dilapidation, and none with meters. The fares are always negotiable, which presumes foreknowledge of reasonable rates. At the airport, ask advice at one of the hotels or tour operator booths, in town from your hotel or the Tourist Information Bureau.

### Other Vehicles

*Matatus* are cheap private enterprise vehicles, running around the urban centres and between towns. They're crowded, sometimes dangerous and generally not recommended to visitors. A long-distance Peugeot taxi service is more of a prospect out of Nairobi to towns in the Rift Valley and elsewhere. A number of luxury coaches, also privately operated, run between Nairobi and Mombasa. One enterprising local runs a 4- or 5-day safari aboard his "Turkana Bus" to the northern desert and lake.

*Over-night bus rides should be avoided at all costs due to the high road-accident rate.*

## Private Transport

### Car Hire

Hertz and Avis operate in Nairobi and Mombasa, together with numerous other local entrepreneurs offering everything from Range Rovers to small saloons. In many cases, the option is chauffeur-driven or self-drive. It's perfectly possible for even first-time visitors, who do not want to be "packaged" by a tour firm, to merely hire a car and set off for a safari or to the coast. There is nothing particularly hazardous about driving round the country, after all, several hundred thousand locals do it. What you need to do is keep the distances fairly short from point to point, pre-book the accommodation, and take a few necessities like a map, a few tools, and something to eat and drink.

This isn't standard advice, by the way. Most locals might warn newcomers of all sorts of problems – the state of Kenya's bush roads, a nation of *kami-kazi* drivers, the chances of getting lost and so on. But this is probably overdone. Any sensible driver can make his way round the country's main tourist circuits, like Amboseli, Tsavo and so on, and certainly down the 483 km (300 miles) of uneventful, even boring road to Mombasa.

Driving in the more remote areas – up north to Turkana, for instance – is a different story. On these out-of-the-way safaris, you need four-wheel drive and a good deal more supplies, equipment, and local experience, plus someone else driving in convoy. However, all is possible for the enterprising.

At the coast, vehicles for hire include breezy Mini-mokes which are ideal for running up and down the beach strip.

A departure tax of US$20 (or the equivalent in Kenyan Shillings) cash per person is charged on departure. The receipt is a stamp fixed to the air ticket which is inspected at the entrance to the departure area. On domestic flights, Kshs 100 must be paid before boarding.

# Where to Stay

## Accommodation

Hotels and lodges are officially graded in Kenya, each given star rating from 1 to 5 and corresponding classification, E to A. Only Classes A, B or C are recommended to the average visitor, although people on budgets can, of course, go right down the D and E establishments and below that for a bed (and bugs) for a few shillings.

Accommodation rates change with the seasons, inflation, group deals, duration of stay, and whether or not meals are included. The advice is either check prices with main tour or travel agents or write ahead to the selected hotels.

Generally, expect to pay upper-middle level European or American prices for the 5-star accommodation in Kenya; a little less for the best of the beach hotels and lodges.

## Hotels

### Nairobi

#### 5-STAR (CLASS A)

**The Grand Regency**, P.O. Box 40511, Nairobi. Tel: 211199. Fax: 21720. City Centre. Formal atmosphere.

**Hilton International Hotel**, P.O. Box 30364, Nairobi. Tel: 334000. Fax: 226477. City Centre – all you would expect from this multinational chain. Mostly businessmen use it.

**Hotel Inter-Continental**, P.O. Box 30353, Nairobi. Tel: 335550. Fax: 210675. Within the central city grid. Similar to the Hilton in that it is a businessman's hotel.

**Nairobi Safari Club**, P.O. Box 43564, Nairobi. Tel: 330621. Fax: 331201. Up-market, suites only hotel in the centre of town.

**Nairobi Serena Hotel**, P.O. Box 46302, Nairobi. Tel: 725111. Fax: 725184. Stylish enterprise of the Aga Khan; set in a park of the edge of the city grid. Excellent food and service.

**Norfolk Hotel**, P.O. Box 40064, Nairobi. Tel: 250900. Fax: 336742. Historic favourite of visitors; fully modernised; just a short walk to the city centre.

**Safari Park Hotel & Casino**, P.O. Box 45038, Nairobi. Tel: 802493-6. Fax: 802477. Out of town on the Thika Road. Large hotel with all the facilities. Very well-appointed.

**Windsor Golf & Country Club**, P.O. Box 45887, Nairobi. Tel: 802259/219784. Fax: 802322. Fifteen minutes drive from the centre of Nairobi. Very attractive hotel with the main feature being the 18-hole championship golf course.

#### 4-STAR (CLASS B)

**Holiday Inn Mayfair Court Hotel**, P.O. Box 74957, Nairobi. Tel: 748288/748278. Fax: 746826. Newly refurbished hotel in the suburb of Westlands.

**New Stanley Hotel**, P.O. Box 30680, Nairobi. Tel: 333233. Fax: 229388. City Centre; safari epicentre is the hotel's pavement cafe.

**Panafric Hotel**, P.O. Box 30486, Nairobi. Tel: 720822-8. Fax: 726356. On a hill overlooking the central grid; full amenities and services.

#### 3-STAR (CLASS C)

**Boulevard Hotel**, P.O. Box 42831, Nairobi. Tel: 227567/8/9. Fax: 334071. Just beyond the Norfolk; smallish garden hotel; excellent value for money.

**Fairview Hotel**, P.O. Box 40842, Nairobi. Tel: 723211. Fax: 721320. Long-established, set in lawns; reasonable accommodation for families.

**Landmark Hotel**, P.O. Box 14287, Nairobi. Tel: 448713/7. Fax: 448977. Family style in the suburb of Westlands. Recently taken over by a major local hotel chain.

**Six-Eighty Hotel**, P.O. Box 43436, Nairobi. Tel: 332680. Fax: 332908. Modern town hotel. Reasonably priced.

## Hostels

MCA Hostel, P.O. Box 30330, Nairobi. el: 724116/7. Fax: 728875.
outh Hostel, Ralph Bunche Road, Nairobi. Tel: 723012.
WCA Hostel, P.O. Box 40710, Nairobi. el: 724699

## The Coast

### 5-STAR (CLASS A)

South Coast
Diani Reef Grand Hotel, P.O. Box 35, Ukunda. Tel: Diani 2175/2723. Fax: 196.
Golden Beach Hotel, P.O. Box 31 Ukunda. Tel: Diani 2625/2054. Fax: 321.
ndian Ocean Beach Club, P.O. Box 0075, Nairobi. Tel: Diani 3730. Fax: 557. Nairobi. Tel: 540780. Fax: 45954.
Kaskazi Beach Hotel, P.O. Box 135, Ukunda. Tel: Diani 3170.
Leisure Lodge Club, P.O. Box 84383, Mombasa. Tel: Diani 2011/2. Fax: 2159.

North Coast
Mombasa Inter-Continental Hotel, P.O. Box 83492, Mombasa. Tel: 485811. Fax: 485431.
Mombasa Beach Hotel, P.O. Box 90414, Mombasa. Tel: 471861.
Nyali Beach Hotel, P.O. Box 90581, Mombasa. Tel: 471551.
Reef Hotel, P.O. Box 82234, Mombasa. Tel: 471771/2. Fax: 471349.
Serena Beach Hotel, P.O. Box 90352, Mombasa. Tel: 485721. Fax: 485453.
Whitesands Hotel, P.O. Box 90173, Mombasa. Tel: 485763. Fax: 485652

### 4-STAR (CLASS B)

South Coast
Africana Sea Lodge, P.O. Box 84616, Mombasa. Tel: Diani 2624. Fax: 2145.
Ladini Beach Hotel, P.O. Box 84616, Mombasa. Tel: Diani 2622. Fax: 2269.
Safari Beach Hotel, P.O. Box 84616, Mombasa. Tel: Diani 2726. Fax: 2357.
North Coast
Bamburi Beach Hotel, P.O. Box 33966, Mombasa. Tel: 485611. Fax: 485900.
Plaza Hotel, P.O. Box 88299, Mombasa. Tel: 485321.
Severin Sea Lodge, P.O. Box 82169, Mombasa. Tel: 485001.
Traveller's Beach Hotel, P.O. Box 37649, Mombasa. Tel: 485121.

### 3-STAR (CLASS C)

South Coast
Beachcomber Club, P.O. Box 54, Msambweni. Tel: Diani 52033. Fax: 3112.
Trade Winds Hotel, P.O. Box 8 Ukunda. Tel: Diani 2016.
Two Fishes Hotel, P.O. Box 23, Ukunda. Tel: Diani 2101-4. Fax: 2106.

North Coast
Kenya Beach Hotel, P.O. Box 95748, Mombasa. Tel: 485821.
Neptune Beach Hotel, P.O. Box 83125, Mombasa. Tel: 485701.
Sun 'N' Sand Beach Hotel, P.O. Box 2, Kikambala. Tel: 32621/32008. Fax: 32133.
Whispering Palms Hotel, P.O. Box 5, Kikambala. Tel: 320045.

## Mombasa Town

### WATAMU, MALINDI & LAMU (NORTH COAST)

Oceanic Hotel, P.O. Box 90371, Mombasa. Tel: 311191/312838.
The Outrigger Hotel, P.O. Box 82345, Mombasa. Tel: 220822/3.

### 5-STAR (CLASS A)

Hemingways, P.O. Box 267, Watamu. Tel: 32624. Fax: 32256.

### 4-STAR (CLASS B)

Peponi Hotel, P.O. Box 24, Lamu. Tel: 33421/2/3. Fax: 33029
Turtle Bay Beach Hotel, P.O. Box 457, Malindi. Tel: 32226/32080. Fax: 32268.

### 3-STAR (CLASS C)

Ocean Sports, P.O. Box 100, Watamu. Tel: 32008. Fax: 32266.
The Driftwood Beach Club, P.O. Box 63, Malindi. Tel: 20155.
Lawfords Hotel, P.O. Box 20, Malindi. Tel: 20440.
Watamu Beach Hotel, P.O. Box 300, Malindi. Tel: 32001/32010.

## Up-Country Hotels

### 5-STAR (CLASS A)

Mt Kenya Safari Club, P.O. Box 35, Nanyuki. Tel: 22960/1. Nairobi. Tel: 216940.

### 4-STAR (CLASS B)

Aberdare Country Club, P.O. Box 58181, Nairobi. Tel: 216920/40. Fax: 216796.
The Outspan Hotel, P.O. Box 47557, Nairobi. Tel: 540780. Fax: 545954.
Lake Baringo Club, P.O. Box 47557, Nairobi. Tel: 540780. Fax: 545954.
Lake Naivasha Country Club, P.O. Box 47557, Nairobi. Tel: 540780. Fax: 545954.
Naro Moru River Lodge, P.O. Box 18, Naro Moru. Tel: 0176-62622/62212. Fax: 0176-62211.

### 3-STAR (CLASS C)

Golf Hotel, P.O. Box 42013, Nairobi. Tel: 229751; Kagamega. Tel: 0331-30150.
Safariland Lodge, P.O. Box 72, Naivasha. Tel: 0311-21034/47. Fax: 0311-21216.
Sirikwa Hotel, P.O. Box 3361, Eldoret. Tel: 31655.
Sunset Hotel, P.O. Box 215, Kisumu. Tel: (035) 22324. Fax: 22745..
Tea Hotel, P.O. Box 75, Kericho. Tel: 20280.

## Game Lodges

### 5-STAR (CLASS A)

Amboseli Serena Lodge – Amboseli National Park, P.O. Box 48690, Nairobi. Tel: 711077. Fax: 718103.
Borana Lodge – Timau, P.O. Box 24397, Nairobi. Tel: 568804. Fax: 564945.
Keekorok Lodge – Maasai Mara National Reserve, P.O. Box 47557, Nairobi. Tel: 540780. Fax: 545954.
Mara Serena Lodge – Maasai Mara National Reserve, P.O. Box 48690, Nairobi. Tel: 711077. Fax: 718103.
Rusinga Island Fishing Lodge – Lake Victoria, PO Box 24513, Nairobi. Tel: 447224/447228. Fax: 447268.
Taita Hills Lodge, P.O. Box 30624, Nairobi. Tel: (0147) 30250/30270. Fax: (0147) 30007/30235.
Salt Lick Lodge, P.O. Box 30624, Nairobi. Tel: (0147) 30250/30270. Fax: (0147) 30007/30235.

**Sarova Shaba Lodge** – Shaba National Reserve, P.O. Box 30680, Nairobi. Tel: 333233. Fax: 211472.
**Samburu Lodge** – Samburu National Reserve, P.O. Box 47557, Nairobi. Tel: 540780. Fax: 545954.
**Samburu Serena Lodge** – Samburu National Reserve, P.O. Box 48690, Nairobi. Tel: 711077. Fax: 718103.

### 4-STAR (CLASS B)

**Amboseli Lodge & Kilimanjaro Safari Lodge** – Amboseli National Park, P.O. Box 30139, Nairobi. Tel: 227136/337510. Fax: 219982.
**The Ark** – Aberdare National Park, P.O. Box 58581, Nairobi. Tel: 216920/40. Fax: 216796.
**Kilimanjaro Buffalo Lodge** – Amboseli National Park, P.O. Box 30139, Nairobi. Tel: 227136/337510. Fax: 219982.
**Kilaguni Lodge** – Tsavo West National Park, P.O. Box 30471, Nairobi. Tel: 336858. Fax: 218109.
**Lion Hill Lodge**, P.O. Box 30680, Nairobi. Tel: 333233. Fax: 211472.
**Mara Sopa Lodge** – Maasai Mara National Reserve, P.O. Box 72630, Nairobi. Tel: 220182/336088. Fax: 331876.
**Ngulia Lodge** – Tsavo West National Park, P.O. Box 30471, Nairobi. Tel: 336858. Fax: 218109.
**Treetops Lodge** – Aberdare National Park, P.O. Box 47557, Nairobi. Tel: 335807. Fax: 340541.
**Voi Safari Lodge** – Tsavo East National Park, P.O. Box 30471, Nairobi. Tel: 540780. Fax: 545954.

### 3-STAR (CLASS C)

**Buffalo Springs Lodge**, P.O. Box 30471, Nairobi. Tel: 336858. Fax: 218109.
**Mountain Lodge**, P.O. Box 30471, Nairobi. Tel: 336858. Fax: 218109.
**Lake Nakuru Lodge**, P.O. Box 70559, Nairobi. Tel: 212405/226778. Fax: 230962.
**Maralal Safari Lodge**, P.O. Box 45155, Nairobi. Tel: 211124. Fax: 2142.
**Olkurruk Mara Lodge**, P.O. Box 30471, Nairobi. Tel: 336858. Fax: 218109.

## Tented Camps

### 5-STAR (CLASS A)

**Africa Expeditions Private Tented Camp** – Loita Hills, P.O. Box 24598, Nairobi. Tel: 561882/561959. Fax: 561457/561054.
**Africa Expeditions Private Tented Camp** – Maasai Mara National Reserve, P.O. Box 24598, Nairobi. Tel: 561882/561959. Fax: 561457/561054.
**Finch Hattons** – Tsavo West National Park, P.O. Box 24423, Nairobi. Tel: 604321/2. Fax: 604323.
**Governor's and Little Governor's Camps** – Maasai Mara National Reserve, P.O. Box 48217, Nairobi. Tel: 331871/2. Fax: 726427.
**Kichwa Tembo Camp** – Maasai Mara National Reserve, P.O. Box 74957, Nairobi. Tel: 746707/750780. Fax: 746826.
**Larsens Camp** – Samburu National Reserve, P.O. Box 47557, Nairobi. Tel: 540780. Fax: 545954.
**Mara Intrepids Club** – Maasai Mara National Reserve, P.O. Box 74888, Nairobi. Tel: 338084/335208. Fax: 217278.
**Mara Safari Club** – Maasai Mara National Reserve, P.O. Box 58581, Nairobi. Tel: 216920/40. Fax: 216796.
**Samburu Intrepids Club** – Samburu National Reserve, P.O. Box 74888, Nairobi. Tel: 338084/335208. Fax: 217278.
**Siana Springs Camp** – Maasai Mara National Reserve, P.O. Box 74957, Nairobi. Tel: 746707/750780. Fax: 746826.

### FOUR STAR (CLASS B)

**Delamere Camp** – Lake Elmenteita, P.O. Box 48019, Nairobi. Tel: 335935/331191. Fax: 216528.
**Fig Tree Camp** – Maasai Mara, P.O. Box 40683, Nairobi. Tel: 221439/218321. Fax: 332170.
**Island Camp**, Lake Baringo – Lake Baringo, P.O. Box 60342, Nairobi. Tel: 340331/213033. Fax: 336890.
**Kindani Camp** – Meru National Park, P.O. Box 56118, Nairobi. Tel: 445795/444494. Fax: 440749.
**Mara River Camp** – Maasai Mara National Reserve, P.O. Box 48019, Nairobi. Tel: 335935/331191. Fax: 216528.
**Tsavo Safari Camp** – Tsavo East National Park, P.O. Box 30139, Nairobi. Tel: 227136/337510. Fax: 219982.
**Ziwani Tented Camp** – Tsavo West National Park, P.O. Box 74888, Nairobi. Tel: 338084/335208. Fax: 217278.

## Central Booking Offices

Some out-of-Nairobi hotels and lodges have a central booking system based in Nairobi. The management groups and appropriate numbers are listed below:

**Alliance Hotels**, P.O. Box 49839, Nairobi. Tel: 330357/337508/220149. Fax: 219212.
Africana Sea Lodge – Diani Beach
Jadini Beach Hotel – Diani Beach
Naro Moru River Lodge – Naro Moru
Safari Beach Hotel – Diani Beach

**African Tours & Hotels**, P.O. Box 30471, Nairobi. Tel: 336858. Fax: 218109.
Buffalo Springs Lodge – Buffalo Springs National Reserve
Kabarnet Hotel – Kabarnet
Kilaguni Lodge – Tsavo West National Park
Milimani Hotel – Nairobi
Mombasa Beach Hotel – North Coast
Mountain Lodge – Mount Kenya
Ngulia Safari Lodge – Tsavo West National Park
Olkurruk Mara Lodge – Maasai Mara National Reserve
Trade Winds Hotel – Diani Beach
Voi Safari Lodge – Tsavo East National Park

**Block Hotels**, P.O. Box 47557, Nairobi. Tel: 540780. Fax: 545954.
Keekorok Lodge – Maasai Mara National Reserve
Indian Ocean Beach Club – Diani Beach
Lake Baringo Club – Lake Baringo
Lake Naivasha Country Club – Lake Naivasha
Larsens Camp – Samburu National Reserve
Nyali Beach Hotel – North Coast
Outspan Hotel – Nyeri
Samburu Lodge – Samburu National Reserve
Shimba Lodge – Shimba Hills National Park
Treetops – Aberdare National Park
Ol-Tukai Lodge – Amboseli National Park

Hilton Lodges & Hotels, P.O. Box 30624, Nairobi. Tel: 334000. Fax: 339462.
Hilton Tents – Taita Hills. Tel: (0147) 30270. Fax: (0147) 30007.
Nairobi Hilton Hotel – Nairobi
Taita Hills Lodge – Taita Hills
Salt Lick Lodge – Taita Hills

Lonrho Hotels, P.O. Box 58581, Nairobi. Tel: 216920/40. Fax: 216796.
The Ark – Aberdare National Park
Aberdare Country Club – Mweiga
Mara Safari Club – Maasai Mara National Reserve
Mount Kenya Safari Club – Nanyuki
Norfolk Hotel – Nairobi
Sweetwaters Tented Camp – Nanyuki

Serena Lodges & Hotels, P.O. Box 48690, Nairobi. Tel: 711077. Fax: 718103.
Nairobi Serena Hotel – Nairobi
Mara Serena Lodge – Maasai Mara National Reserve
Samburu Serena – Samburu National Reserve
Serena Beach Hotel – North Coast

Sarova Hotels, P.O. Box 30680, Nairobi. Tel: 333233. Fax: 211472.
New Stanley Hotel – Nairobi
Ambassadeur Hotel – Nairobi
Panafric Hotel – Nairobi
Lion Hill Lodge – Lake Nakuru National Park
Sarova Shaba Lodge – Shaba National Reserve
Whitesands Hotel – North Coast
Mara Sarova Lodge – Maasai Mara National Reserve

The Conservation Corporation, P.O. Box 74957, Nairobi. Tel: 746707/ 750298/750780. Fax: 746826/ 750512.
Holiday Inn Mayfair Court – Nairobi
The Windsor Golf & Country Club – Nairobi
Kichwa Tembo Camp – Maasai Mara National Reserve
Siana Springs Tented Camp – Maasai Mara National Reserve

Let's Go Travel, PO Box 60342, Nairobi. Tel: 340331/213033. Fax: 336890.
Island Camp – Lake Baringo
Ol Pejeta, PO Box 47665, Nairobi. Tel: 332301. Fax: 214752.

# Eating Out

## What to Eat

Restaurants serving the cuisine of all nationalities can be found throughout Kenya. In general, the food is of excellent quality and is reasonably priced.

Wines and spirits are imported and, therefore, cost their European equivalent in Kenyan shillings.

## Restaurants

### Nairobi

African Heritage Cafe, Banda Street. Tel: 337507/222010. Local specialities.
Akasaka Restaurant, Muindi Mbingu Street. Tel: 220299. Japanese cuisine.
Alan Bobbe's Bistro, Koinange Street. Tel: 226027. French and expensive.
Carnivore Restaurant, Langata Rd. Tel: 501775. Barbecued meats and great atmosphere.
Daas Ethiopian Restaurant, Lenana Road. Tel: 712106.
Dawat Restaurant, Shimmers Plaza, Westlands. Tel: 749337. Indian.
Haandi Restaurant, The Mall, Westlands. Tel: 448294. Excellent Indian but not cheap.
Horseman Restaurant, Ngong Road. Tel: 882033/882133. International cuisine and karaoke bar.
Minar Restaurant, Sarit Centre, Westlands. Tel: 748340. Indian.
Pagoda, Shankardass House, Moi Avenue. Tel: 227036/230230. Chinese.
Siam Thai Restaurant, Unga House, Westlands. Tel: 751727/751728.
Tamarind Restaurant, Harambee Avenue. Tel: 338959/217990. Seafood specialities.
Toona Tree, International Casino. Tel: 744477. Italian/International.
Tusks Restaurant, Limuru Road. Tel: 521231/2. Continental.

# Attractions

## Culture

### Museums

Before you go on any safari, it's a good idea to visit the National Museum of Kenya in Nairobi. The Museum houses exhibits on the geology of Kenya, the Leakeys' excavations in the "Cradle of Mankind", African tribal jewellery and clothing, Joy Adamson's paintings of Kenyan people and plants, as well as exhibitions of modern African Art. The Snake Park is in the same grounds, but displays there are "live". An aquarium also provides a preview of what may be seen when snorkelling at the coast. Books and information leaflets on just about everything in nature that might interest you are also available at the museum.

### Art Galleries

African art, to those foreign to the continent, is often an acquired taste. On first exposure it can appear utterly alien and sometimes incomprehensible, perhaps also crude and rough. There is some reasonably good work, particularly from the younger artists, but it has to be hunted down. The fact is that East Africa has nothing like the tradition of West Africa for any of the arts, including music. That will obviously be disputed locally, but the vast majority of paintings, batiks, carvings and sculptures offered to tourists look as though they came off some elementary assembly line.

The best of the indigenous art is usually found in small galleries, most of them in Nairobi – notably a store called African Heritage. This establishment seems to bring in materials from all over the continent, including the Makonde carvings from Tanzania.

Local artists, including Europeans, occasionally exhibit paintings in places like the New Stanley Hotel or the cosmopolitan French Cultural Centre.

Recommended places for up-market art and artifacts in Nairobi are:

**Gallery Watatu**, Standard Street; **Paaya-Paa Gallery and Workshop**, Ridgeways Road (just out of town); and **African Heritage Ltd.**, Banda Street.

## Music

Check the entertainment page of daily newspapers for listings of live bands. Most hotels generally provide traditional dancing and, occasionally, live music. Otherwise, the Carnivore (Langata Road) offers live band entertainment with Wednesday and Friday nights being the most active. The International Casino complex offers a disco, three restaurants and a casino. A good place to meet anyone is the Holiday Inn in Westlands which has a lively pub called Mischiefs. If you feel like a bit of a Karaoke, then try the Zanze-Bar located in the Kenya Cinema building.

## Concerts

The Nairobi Music Society promotes musical activity by local amateurs and occasionally by foreign professionals. The Nairobi Orchestra is renowned in Africa and holds concerts three times a year and combines with the Music Society several times a year for choral events.

## Theatres

**The National Theatre, Phoenix Players, Braeburn Theatre and French Cultural Centre** all offer classical, traditional and contemporary stage productions of a high standard. Check the entertainment page of daily newspapers for listings.

## Movies

There are 13 cinemas in Nairobi including one drive-in and four cinemas in Mombasa. In Nairobi, the Nairobi, Kenya and 20th Century offer the best facilities and latest films. Check newspapers for listings.

## Cultural Centres

Several foreign countries maintain Cultural Centres in Nairobi featuring book, record and video libraries. Many offer local theatrical productions and musical entertainment open to the public. Check with the individual centres or the entertainment section of daily newspapers for activities.

**American Cultural Centre**, Barclays Plaza, Loita Street, 3rd Floor, P.O. Box 30143, Nairobi. Tel: 240290/240502/240533.

**British Council Library**, ICEA Building, Kenyatta Avenue, P.O. Box 40751, Nairobi. Tel: 334855/7; Biashara Bank Building, Nyerere Avenue, Mombasa. Tel: 223076.

## Travel Packages

Tour operators "charter" blocks of seats on scheduled flights for their clients, and in this way greatly reduce the per-head ticket price through available "Group Inclusive Tour" (GIT) fares. The flights are normally part of an all-in holiday "package" offered by tour wholesalers and big retailers all over Europe and North America. (The "High Street" travel agency will either use or recommend the specialist Africa operators.)

The packages cover a wide variety of options: Kenya coast or safaris, or a combination of both – with the price varying according to factors. For example, length of stay, distances covered, type and style of accommodation and transport, etc. The big expense outlays are included in the tour cost, leaving the traveller to include in his expenses only beer money, tips, a budget for shopping and so on.

"Packaged" safaris are often organised for groups with special interests, like historians, anthropologists, geologists and zoologists.

At the top end of the package tour market are tour operators offering deluxe, hand-tailored safaris for individuals or small groups. These can run up to $1,000 a day – but they're marvellously pampered, including private safari vehicles and light aircraft transport, fully serviced camps or lodge accommodation, superb food, a retinue of staff, and the freedom to go when and wherever the clients decide. These operators are generally not into mass-marketing their safaris; so to identify them, enquire with the larger Africa tour retailers or the overseas tourist offices of the Kenya Government.

At the other end of the expenditure scale, it's possible to find operators chartering aircraft to Kenya, full of "travel club" members. The flight is included in a "package" tour, normally a couple of weeks at the coast. This option is surprisingly cheap, but are available only from places that have to be hunted down, like Basel, Switzerland.

Tourists come all year round. There are normally two seasons of rainy weather – the "long rains" (about end-March to mid-June) and the "short rains" (end-October to early December). Safari travel is restricted during these periods due to soggy roads; on the other hand, these are low seasons for the hotel and lodge operators and many offer correspondingly low rates.

The high seasons, when coast and safari accommodation may be difficult without pre-booking, are December through March and the school holiday period from July to September.

## Safaris

There are literally scores of tour operators in Nairobi, and more in Mombasa, offering minibus safaris on various permutations of itineraries round the country. The tour cost normally includes full board at lodges or tented camps in the parks and reserves. The duration of the tours can be anything from two to 14 days.

### Sample Safari Tours

#### TWO-DAY TOURS

**The Forest Lodges**: Around 161 km (100 miles) north of Nairobi on the slopes of the Aberdares Range and Mount Kenya. These are **Treetops, The Ark and Mountain Lodge**, all offering a nightly parade of wildlife at floodlit waterholes and saltlicks. A typical tour is: Nairobi to the Outspan Hotel, Nyeri, for lunch, on to Treetops for the night, back to the Outspan for breakfast, then return to the capital – about 24 hours in all.

**Amboseli**: As for the day trip (above), but extended with an overnight at one of the park lodges.

**Maasai Mara Game Reserve**: Hemingway's "Green Hills of Africa" – the most spectacular of Kenya's game areas, especially in the season of the migration of a million or more plains animals out of the contiguous Serengeti. "The Mara" is 274 km (170 miles) from Nairobi and tight for a weekend road safari. A more comfortable alternative is by light aircraft, for which the tour is: hotel to Wilson Airport; breakfast, check in at a lodge or luxury tented camp; game drives in 4-wheel drive safari vehicles until the return to Nairobi after lunch on the second day.

## LONGER SAFARIS

These can be pre-booked with travel or tour operators in the States or Europe, or alternatively book after arrival in Kenya. Basically, you decide where you want to go, then shop around for preferred itinerary, duration of the tour and price. Decide also on what you can afford so as to determine how you will go on your safari – minibus, light aircraft or combined air and road.

As a rough planning guide, the following are Kenya's principal tourist destinations:

**North of Nairobi:** The forest lodges on Mount Kenya and the Aberdares; Mount Kenya Safari Club; Samburu National Reserves; Marsabit, Maralal and Meru National Park. The Rift Valley Lakes – Naivasha, Nakuru, Bogoria, Baringo and Turkana – are also spectacular.

**West of Nairobi:** The Maasai Mara Game Reserve, Lake Victoria.

**Generally southward** (S, SW and SE): Amboseli and Tsavo National Parks; the Hilton's Taita Hills and Salt-Lick lodges to the coast.

**Principal Beach Attractions** (from south to north): The Pemba Channel/ Shimoni for deep-sea fishing; Diani (superb 19-km/12-mile, palm-fringed beach); Mombasa Island (cosmopolitan town and fine beach at Nyali); Bamburi, Shanzu and Kikambala beaches immediately north of Mombasa; Kilifi Creek, Watamu and Malindi (good facilities for fishing) and fabulous Lamu well to the north.

## "SAFARITRAIL"

Most of Kenya's tour operators run a system of regular minibus safaris in and around Nairobi. The way it works is that individuals or couples buy seats on these set departures, joining up with whoever else goes along. Samples of "Safaritrail" tours are as follows:

**Nairobi City Tour:** Two hours' orientation – main shopping area; main buildings; the Railways and National Museums, and Snake Park.

**"Bomas of Kenya":** Traditional dancing, building styles, artifacts and so on at a special complex 14 km (9 miles) from the city centre.

**Nairobi National Park:** Just 13 km (8 miles) out of the city, but authentic Africa – in no way a plastic safari park. Resident wildlife includes lion, cheetah, rhino and hippo, with various antelope species migrating in and out from the open Kitengela-Athi plains to the south.

**The Giraffe Centre:** About 20 minutes' drive from the centre of Nairobi in the suburb of Langata. An education centre for children and also a sanctuary for the endangered Rothschilds Giraffe. Feeding the giraffe is one of the main attractions here.

**Amboseli National Park:** A 485-km (300-mile) round trip in a day, but worth it for a few hours in Kenya's most photogenic wildlife sanctuary under Kilimanjaro. Lunch at one of the park's safari lodges is included. Further information about safaris throughout Kenya can be found at the following specialist tour companies:

**Abercrombie & Kent Ltd**, P.O. Box 59749, Nairobi. Tel: 334955. Fax: 215752.

**Africa Expeditions Ltd**, P.O. Box 24598, Nairobi. Tel: & Fax: 561882/ 561959/561054.

**Ker & Downey Safaris Ltd**, P.O. Box 41822, Nairobi. Tel: 553212/ 556466. Fax: 552378.

**Let's Go Travel Ltd**, P.O. Box 60342, Nairobi. Tel: 340331. Fax: 336890.

---

## Safari Notes

Caution and common sense must be exercised in both national parks and reserves. The Ministry of Tourism and Wildlife has improved some rules and regulations and these are for the protection of the animals as well as the people. Many tourists from time to time forget that a reserve or park is not an open zoo with invisible bars. The rule is to stay in the car and if animals approach, close roofs, doors and windows.

Touring the parks and reserves is restricted to daylight hours – from 6am to 6pm. Before dusk is the time the carnivores begin their hunt for dinner and more timid animals come out of hiding.

Driving speeds are limited to 48 km/h (30 mph) – but slower is better as you'll be able to see more.

Rangers are available as guides on game runs, and it's often a good idea to employ one since they know the area and the animals like the back of their hands.

In the florally rich rain forest west of Kenya to the Atlantic, in particular the Congo, there are elephants, rhinos, gorillas, chimps, and lots of species inbetween. However, poaching has taken its toll – Burundi and Rwanda have virtually no big animals left. On the other hand, the open plains and mountain areas of East Africa – Kenya especially – support a greater diversity of mammal species than any other continent. For example, there are 90 species of ungulates (grazing animals) in the region compared with 70 in the whole of Asia, 16 in South and Central America, 13 in Europe, and 11 in North America. Add to this, the cavalcade of predators and scavengers that go along with the grazers – around 1,500 resident species of birds, plus riverine and reptilian species – and about all that's left out (of note) in the range of African fauna are the big primates, the chimpanzee and the gorilla.

A common, but by no means exhaustive list, is as follows (Kiswahili names, where existing, in brackets):

**Elephant**, _Loxodonta africana_ (Tembo/Ndovu): Widely distributed. Rain, secondary and highland forests, open woodlands, savannas, dry bush, swamps. Tsavo, Mt Kenya, Aberdares and Meru National Parks, Amboseli, Samburu, Maasai Mara.

**Rock hyrax**, _Heterohyrax brucei_ (Pimbi): Widely distributed, cliffs, rocky hills, stony mountain slopes, usually seen on Hyrax Rock, Nairobi National Park. Many at Hell's Gate National Park.

**Tree hyrax**, _Dendrohyrax arboreus_ (Perere): Widely distributed. Forest. Nocturnal, more often heard than seen.

**Black rhinoceros**, _Diceros bicornis_ (Kifaru): Widely distributed but few. Bush, savannas, light forest, highland forest, high altitude moorlands. Tsavo National Park, Nairobi National Park, Amboseli, Samburu, Maasai Mara, Mt Kenya and the Aberdares.

**White rhinoceros**, _Ceratotherium simum_ (Kifaru): Introduced. Meru National Park. Nakuru National Park.

**Burchell's zebra**, Equus burchelli (Punda milia): Widely distributed in grasslands, open savannas, grassy flats surrounded by bush. Large numbers seen at Amboseli and Maasai Mara, Nairobi National Park.

**Grevy's zebra,** Equus grevyi (Punda Milia): Northern Kenya, east of Lake Turkana, north of Tana River. Dry grassy bush country. Seen in Samburu, Marsabit, also in Meru National Park.

**Buffalo,** Syncerus caffer (Nyati or mbogo): Widely distributed. Rain forests, secondary forests, highland forests, open woodlands, savannas, bush, swamps. Large numbers in Tsavo, Meru and Mountain National Parks, Samburu, Amboseli, Maasai Mara.

**Wildebeest,** Connochaetes taurinus (Nyumbu): Widely distributed southern Kenya, north to Mau Forest and Thika River. Grasslands, savannas, open woodlands. The mass migrations in Maasai Mara are a very impressive spectacle.

**Coke's hartebeest,** Alcelaphus buselaphus cokii (Kongoni): Widely distributed in southern Kenya, north to Lake Naivasha, upper Tana, Galana. Grasslands, open grassy savanna. Nairobi National Park; Amboseli, Maasai Mara.

**Lelwel hartebeest,** Alcelaphus buselaphus lelwel (Kongoni): Northwestern Kenya. Savannas. A hartebeest resembling the Lelwel (Jackson's) is found in Lambwe Valley of western Kenya, another (Kenya hartebeest) on Laikipia and north of Mount Kenya.

**Hunter's hartebeest,** Damaliscus hunteri (Kongoni): Also known as the Hirola Antelope, it is an endangered species. Restricted to an area of sanseviera bush with grassy clearings from the Tana River to southern Somalia. Some specimens have been transferred to Tsavo Park.

**Topi,** Damaliscus korrigum jimela (Nyamera): Western Kenya, along Kenya coast from the Sabaki River to the Somalia border. Grasslands, open savannas. Numerous in Maasai Mara.

**Harvey's duiker,** Cephalophus harveyi (Funo): Widely distributed in forests, bush, high grass jungles. Being secretive in their habits, duikers are only encountered accidentally.

**Blue duiker,** Cephalophus monticola (Paa): Widely distributed in forests, gallery forest, bush.

**Yellow-backed duiker,** Cephalophus sylvicutor (Paa): Mau Forest of Kenya. Forests with plenty of undergrowth, gallery forest, dense savannas.

**Grey duiker,** Sylvicapra grimmia (Nusa): Widely distributed. Bush, forest edges, cultivations, high grass.

**Suni,** Nesotragus moschatus (Paa): Locally in highland forests, coastal forests, dense bush.

**Steinbok,** Raphicerus campestris (Dondoro): Widely distributed. In Kenya as far north as Laikipia, foot of Mt Elgon. Grasslands, with a certain amount to scattered bush.

**Klipspringer,** oreotragus oreotragus (Mbusi mawe): Widely distributed but confined to rocky hills and mountain ranges. In Tsavo National Park on old lava streams.

**Oribi,** Ourebia ourebia (Yaya): Widely distributed. Grasslands, open savanna woodlands, hilly country, scrubby bush.

**Kirk's dikdik,** Rhycchotragus Kirki (Dikidiki or suguya): Widely distributed in dry bush country. Often seen in Tsavo National Park, Amboseli and Mara.

**Guenther's dikdik,** Rhynchotragus guentheri (Dikidiki or suguya): Northern Kenya. Common in Samburu Reserve.

**Waterbuck,** Kobus ellipsiprymnus (Kuro): Widely distributed in eastern Kenya. Savannas, bush, gallery forests. Tsavo National Park, Amboseli. Nairobi National Park has a mixed population of common and Defassa Waterbuck.

**Defassa waterbuck,** Kobus defassa (Kuro): Widely distributed in western Kenya, east to Nairobi National Park and Maasai Mara. Laikipia Plateau, Nakuru National Park and Maasai Mara.

**Uganda kob,** Adenota kob thomasi. Western Kenya, where it is now rare. Grasslands, savannas, never far from water.

**Bohor reedbuck,** Redunca redunca (Tohe): Widely distributed in grassy areas with patches of bush, reedbeds, never far from water. Can be seen especially well in Nairobi and Nakuru National Parks.

**Chandler's mountain reedbuck,** Redunca fulvorufula chandleri (Tohe): Central and western Kenya. Rocky slopes, escarpments, stony ridges. Seen in Nairobi National Park.

**Impala,** Aepyceros melampus (swala or swara pala): Widely distributed in Kenya north to Wamba and northern Ewaso Nyiro (Samburu). Can be seen in large numbers in Tsavo and

Nairobi National Parks, in Amboseli, Maasai Mara.

**Thomson's Gazelle,** Gazella thomsoni (Swala tomi): Laikipia Plateau, southeastern Kenya, west to Lake Victoria, east to Tsavo West. Grasslands, savannas. Common Nairobi National Park. Amboseli, Maasai Mara.

**Grant's gazelle,** Gazella granti (Swala granti): Widely distributed throughout Kenya, east almost to Indian Ocean, west to Lake Victoria. Grasslands, open savannas, dry bush. Can be seen in Tsavo and Nairobi National Parks. Amboseli, Maasai Mara, Samburu. The Grant's gazelle of northwestern Kenya is known as Bright's gazelle.

**Gerenuk,** Litocranius walleri (Swala twiga): Northern and eastern Kenya. Mostly in dry bush country. Tsavo, Meru, and Samburu are good places to see this species.

**Beisa oryx,** oryx beisa beisa (Choroa): Northern Kenya, south to Laikipis Plateau and Tana River. Desert scrub, dry bush, grasslands with scattered trees. Can be seen in Samburu, Marsabit, Meru National Park.

**Fringe-eared oryx,** oryx beisa callotis (Choroa): From Tana River south to Kilimanjaro area and Lake Magadi. Dry bush country, tree grasslands. Can be seen in Tsavo National Park and Amboseli. West of Lake Magadi.

**Sable antelope,** Hippotragus niger (Palahala, mbarapi): Rare in Kenya, coastal areas north to Bamba, inland from Kilifi, Savannas with patches of bush and open meadows, especially of the miombo forest type. Shimba Hills National Reserve near Mombasa.

**Roan antelope,** Hippotragus equinus (Korongo): Fairly rare in Kenya. Savannas interspersed with grassy patches, rolling uplands with bush and open forest. Small herds, Maasai Mara, Lambwe Valley; Introduced into the Shimba Hills.

**Eland,** Taurotragus oryx (Pofu or mbunja): Widely distributed though much reduced in densely settled areas. Grasslands, savannas, mountain moorlands. Nairobi, Tsavo, Maasai Mara.

**Bushbuck,** Tragelaphus scriptus (Mbawala or pongo): Widely distributed. Occurs wherever bush and undergrowth offer good cover. Nairobi and Mountain National Parks are good places to see this species.

**Greater Kudu**, *Strepsiceros strepsiceros* (Tabdkak mkubwa): Rare and local in southern Kenya, more common on the mountains of the northern regions. Dense savannas, especially of the miombo forest type, rocky hills covered with forests and thorn thicket belts of dense bush along rivers. Can be seen in Marsabit and Lake Bogoria.

**Lesser kudu**, *Strepsiceros imberbis* (Tandala ndogo): Northern Kenya, south through eastern part of country to Kilimanjaro region and southern Ewaso Nyiro. Tsavo, Amboseli, Meru.

**Bongo**, *Boocercus euryceros*, Highland forests of Kenya, usually between 2,100 and 3,300 metres (6,890 and 10,830 ft): Mt Kenya, Aberdares, Mau Forest, Cherangani Hills. Rarely seen.

**Sitatunga**, *Limnotragus spekei*, (Nzohe): Western Kenya. Swamps. Can be observed in the Saiwa Swamp near Kitale.

**Maasai giraffe**, *Giraffa camelopardalis* (Twiga): Widely distributed in southern Kenya, north to the Tana River. Dry thorn country, acacia grasslands, savanna, bush, forest, highland forest. Tsavo and Nairboi National Park. Maasai Mara, Amboseli and many other places.

**Reticulated giraffe**, *Griaffa camelopardalis reticulata* (Twiga): Northern Kenya. Meru National Park, Samburu, Marsabit. The giraffes seen near Eldoret belong to the sub-species known as Rothschild's Giraffe, *Giraffa camelopardalis rothschildi*.

**Bushpig**, *Potamochoerus porcus* (Nguruwemwitu): Widely distributed. Forests, gallery forests, bushy savannas. Crepuscular and nocturnal. Rarely seen.

**Giant forest hog**, *Hylochoerus meinertzhageni* (no authentic Kiswahili name known!): Mt Elgon, Cherangani Hills, Mau Forest, Mara River, Aberdares, Mt Kenya. Rain forests, gallery forests, highland forest.

**Warthog**, *Phacochoerus aethiopicus* (Ngiri): Widely distributed. Savannas, bush grasslands, common in Nairobi National Park and many other reserves.

**Hippopotamus**, *Hippopotamus amphibius* (Kiboko): Widely distributed. Rivers, lakes, swamps. Good places to see this species are the Mzima springs (Tsavo West), the Hippo Pools of Nairobi National Park, the Mara River.

---

## Carnivores

**Lion**, *Panthera leo* (Simba): Still widely distributed. Grasslands, savannas, open woodlands, bush, semi-deserts. Nairobi National Park, Maasai Mara. Tsavo West, Amboseli, and Samburu are good places to see and study lions.

**Leopard**, *Panthera pardus* (Chui): Widely distributed. Forests of every type, savannas, bush, grasslands, semi-deserts, rocky mountain areas. Usually very secretive and rarely seen.

**African wild cat**, *Felis sylvestris lybica* (Paka pori): Widely distributed. Nocturnal.

**Cheetah**, *Acinonyx jubatus* (Duma): Fairly widely distributed in grasslands and open savannas. Can usually be seen in Nairobi National Park. Amboseli, Samburu, Maasai Mara.

**Serval cat**, *Leptailurus serval* (Mondo): Widely distributed. Bush, savanna, grasslands, cultivations. Mainly nocturnal.

**Caracal**, *Caracal caracal* (Simba mangu): Widely distributed, but rarely seen. Shy, solitary, mainly nocturnal. Dry bush country, savannas.

**Spotted hyena**, *Crocuta crocuta* (Fisi): Widely distributed throughout the country. Mainly nocturnal, but also encountered in the daytime.

**Striped hyena**, *Hyaena hyaena* (Fisi): Nocturnal and rarely seen.

**Aardwolf**, *Proteles cristatus* (Fisi maji): Widely distributed around rivers, lake shores, papyrus marshes, reed beds, quiet backwaters. Especially common around Lake Victoria. The clawless otter, *Aonyx capensis* (Fisi maji) can be found in rivers, streams, and swamps up to 3,000 metres (9,840 ft).

**Honey badger**, *Mellivora ratel* (Nyegere): Nocturnal. Can be seen regularly near several lodges and do-it-yourself camps. Can be aggressive.

**Grey or Golden jackal**, *Canis aureus* (Mbweha): Grasslands, savannas. Can be seen in Amboseli.

**Black-backed jackal**, *Canis mesomelas* (Mbweha): Widely distributed. Savannas, grasslands. The jackal most commonly seen in Nairobi National Park, Amboseli, Maasai Mara, and many other places.

**Side-striped jackal**, *Canis adustus* (Mbweha): Widely distributed, though much reduced in numbers. Bush, light forest, savannas, grasslands. Can be

seen in Tsavo. Maasai Mara, Samburu and occasionally Nairobi National Park.

**Bat-eared fox**, *Otocyan megalotis* (Mbweha masikia): Widely distributed. Grasslands, open woodlands. Can often be seen in Amboseli, occasionally in Nairobi National Park.

**White-tailed mongoose**, *Ichneumia albicauda* (Nguchiro): Widely distributed. Nocturnal. Often seen in car headlights.

**Black-tipped mongoose**, *Herpestes sanguineus* (Nguchiro): Widely distributed. Diurnal. Often seen crossing the road.

**Dwarf mongoose**, *Helogale parvula* (Nguchiro): Widely distributed. Diurnal and gregarious. Often on termite hills.

**Banded mongoose**, *Mungos mungo* (Nguchiro): Grasslands. Often seen in Maasai Mara. Diurnal and gregarious.

**Genet**, *Genetta* spp. (Kanu): Widely distributed. Nocturnal. Have become very tame at several lodges.

**Civet cat**, *Civettictis civetta* (Fungo): Nocturnal, Treetops Lodge in Aberdares.

---

## Primates

**Bushbaby, Greater galago**, *Galago crassicaudatus* (Komba): Widely distributed. Gallery forests, highland forests, bamboo thickets. Nocturnal. Can often be heard wailing and screaming.

**The Senegal galago**, *Galago senegalensis*, is found in savannas and woodlands.

**Pott**, *Perodicticus potto*: Western Kenya (Kakamega, Kaimosi, Mau Forest). Nocturnal and rarely seen.

**Olive baboon**. *Papio anubis* (Nyani): Most of Kenya (Nairobi National Park, Aberdares) Savannas, gallery forests, bush, rocky mountains.

**Yellow baboon**, *Papio cynocephalus* (Nyani): Southeastern Kenya – Amboseli, Tsavo West.

**Crested mangabey**, *Cercocebus galeritus*: Lower Tana, Witu, hinterland of Lamu.

**Red colobus**, *Colobus badius*: Tana River, Sokoke-Arabuko Forest near Malindo.

**Guereza, Black-and-white colobus**, *Colobus abyssinicus* (Mbega): Forests, especially highland forest of Mt Kenya, the Aberdares, Elgon. Nakuru National Parks.

**Vervet, Grivet, Green guenon**, *Ceropithecus aethiops* (Tumbiri or tumbili): Widely distributed. Savannas, woodlands, mountain, forests, gallery forest.

**Blue monkey,** *Cercopithecus mitis* (Kima): larger and very variable in colour, favours denser and more extensive forests.

**Red-tailed guenon,** *Cercopithecus nictitans:* Western Kenya. Evergreen forests, gallery forest.

**Brazza monkey,** *Cercopithecus neglectus:* Western Kenya (Mt Elgon, Kitale) forests, especially along rivers and swamps.

**Patas monkey,** *Erythrocebus patas:* Northwestern Kenya (Uasin Gishu, Laikipia), Savannas, acacia scrub.

## Birds

Due to its position astride the Equator – halfway between north and south Africa –and to the fact that the country ranges from tropical coast to glaciers, contains a large number of lakes, both freshwater and saline, and a great variety of plant associations extending from semi-desert to close-canopy forest and from mangrove swamp to alpine zone, Kenya supports most of the 1,500 or so species listed for the eastern half of tropical Africa, from Mozambique to the northern border of the Sudan. In the forests of western Kenya, in the Kenya highlands and in the coastal area are many birds which belong to the fauna of the Equatorial forest belt.

A safari devoted to Kenya's birdlife is highly rewarding both for ornithologists and amateur bird-watchers. Visits to Lakes Naivasha, Nakuru and other Rift Valley lakes are a must, but the itinerary of a bird safari should also include the coast, the savannas and bushlands of the Tsavo and Meru National Parks, the forests of Mt Kenya, the Aberdares and Mt Elgon and the dry country of Lake Baringo and Samburu. Up to 300 species can be identified in the course of a fortnight's trip.

The following list contains a few of the more common or more spectacular species. No mention is made of the numerous migrants which visit the country during northern winter.

**Ostrich:** 2 subspecies: **Maasai Ostrich,** *Struthio camelus massaicus:* widely distributed in grasslands and open savannas, north to Tana River. **Somali** or **Blue-shanked Ostrich,** *Struthio camelus molybdophanes:* Dry bush country in northeastern Kenya (Samburu).

**Pelicans: Gray Pelican,** *Pelecanus rufescens:* White, grayish on wings, head and belly, tinged pinkish on back and rump. Inland lakes. **White Pelican,** *Pelecanus onocrotalus:* Somewhat larger, white, tinged with pink during breeding season. Common on Lakes Naivasha and Nakuru.

**Cormorants: White-necked Cormorant,** *Phalacrocorax carbo,* and **Pigmy Cormorant,** *Phalacrocorax africanus:* common Lakes Naivasha and Nakuru. **Darter,** *Anhinga rufa,* related to Cormorants. Long, thin neck. Widespread in lakes, rivers.

**Herons: Blackheaded Heron,** *Ardea melanocephala:* Common and widely distributed; lake shores, river banks, swamps; often quite far from water. **Goliath Heron,** *Ardea goliath:* Largest African heron. Never far from water. Can be seen in Lake Naivasha. **Night Heron,** *Nycticorax nycticoraxy:* Lakes, rivers, marshes; can be seen in Lakes Nakuru and Naivasha.

**Egrets:** Yellow-billed Egret, *Mesophoyx intermedius:* Swamps, rivers, lakes; locally numerous. **Little Egret,** *Egretta garzetta:* Smaller, Bill black. **Cattle Egret,** *Bubulcus ibis:* Widely distributed, usually in flocks, accompanying game/domestic stock to feed on insects disturbed by grazing animals.

**Storks: Saddle-billed Stork,** *Ephippiorhynchus senegalenis:* Swamps, marshes, reedy lake shores. Singly or in couples. Seen fairly regularly in Buffalo Springs, also Amboseli, Maasai Mara. **Yellow-billed Stork,** *Ibis ibis:* Widely distributed. Flat shores and sandbanks of shallow lakes and rivers. Often in small parties. **Open-billed Stork,** *Anastomus lamelligrua:* Lakes, marshes, large lagoons. Sometimes in large flocks. Often seen Galana River and Aruba Dam (Tsavo East). **Marabou,** *Leptoptilus cruminiferus:* Widely distributed. Open savannas, often in big flocks. A stork with the habits of a vulture. **Hammerkop,** *Scopus umbretta:* Rivers, pools, shallow lake shores. Big spherical nest can be seen in riverine forests. **Abdim's Stork,** *Sphenorynchus abdimi:* Visits East Africa from Sudan, often in large flocks.

**African Spoonbill,** *Platalea alba:* Shallow lakes, lagoons, dams. Can be seen in Rift Valley lakes.

**Ibises: Sacred Ibis,** *Threskiornis aethiopicus:* Widely distributed; lakes,

rivers, marshes; often in flocks. **Hadada,** *Hagedashia hagedash:* Well watered and well wooded areas; can be seen in Nairobi National Park, Lake Naivasha. Usually singly or in pairs.

**Flamingos: Lesser Flamingo,** *Phoeniconaias minor:* Bill dark red, tipped black. Common Lakes Magadi, Elementeita, Nakuru, Bogoria. **Greater Flamingo,** *Phoenicopterus ruber:* Bill pink and black. Recorded breeding Magadi, Elementeita, Nakuru; often in close association with smaller species.

**Geese: Egyptian Goose,** *Alopochen aeghptiaca.* Common and widely distributed. Lakes, ponds, dams rivers, marshes; in pairs and family parties.

**Spurwing Goose,** *Plectropterus gambiense:* Lakes and rivers, often in big flocks. **Knob-billed Goose,** *Sarjuduirbus melanotos:* In small flocks on lakes, pools, wooded swamps. Can be seen in Lake Naivasha.

**Ducks: African Pochard,** *Aythia erythrophthalmus:* Common on lakes, often in flocks of 50 or more. **Yellow-billed Duck,** *Anas undulata:* Open waters, reedy ponds, rivers; gregarious. **Redbilled Duck,** *Anas erythrorhyncha:* Common in swamps, reedy pools, inlets of lakes. **Hottentot Teal,** *Anas punctata:* Shallow saline and freshwater pools with mud banks; shallow grassy coves. Can be seen in Lake Nakuru. **Cape Wigeon,** *Anas capensis:* Large and small sheets of saline water; marshes. **White-faced Tree-duck,** *dendrocygna viduata:* River flats, swamps, saltwater lagoons, estuaries, pools, rivers. Often in large flocks. **Fulvous Tree-duck,** *Dendrocygna bicolour:* Inland lakes, marshes.

**Secretary Bird,** *Sagittarius serpentarius:* Often seen in grasslands, savannas, light bush. Forages on ground.

**Vultures:** Animal carcasses very quickly attract vultures of several species, especially **Hooded Vultures,** *Necrosyrtes monachus,* **White-backed Vultures,** *Pseudogyps africanus,* and **Rueppell's Griffon Vultures,** *Gyps rueppellii.* They all give way to the large **Lappet-faced Vulture,** *Torgos tracheliotus.* The **Egyptian Vulture,** *Neophron percnopterus,* uses stones to break ostrich eggs. **Laemmergeyer** or **Bearded Vulture,** *Gypaetus barbatus:* Rather scarce, but can be seen around Mt Elgon, Rift Valley (Hell's Gate), Mt Kenya.

**Kites and Buzzards: Black-shoul-dered Kite,** *Elanus caeruleus*: Savannas, dry grasslands, cultivated areas; often seen Nairobi National Park. **Yellow-billed Kite,** *Milvus migrans*: A subspecies of the European Black Kits. Common in savannas, along lakes, rivers; also in towns. **Augur Buzzard,** *Buteo rufofuscus*: Very common; mountains, open savannas, cultivated areas.

**Eagles: Verreauzx's Eagle,** *Aquila verreauxii*: Rocky hills, mountains, gorges; has bred in Nairobi National Park. **Tawny Eagle,** *Aquila rapax*: Widely distributed. Common in open savannas, cultivated areas, bush, semi-deserts. **Martial Eagle,** *Polemaetus bellicosus*: Widely distributed; woodlands, savannas, thornbush: can be seen Nairobi National Park. **Long-crested Hawk Eagle,** *Lophaetus occipitalis*: Riverine forests, well wooded and cultivated areas, bush; fairly common; can often be seen perched on telegraph poles. **Bateleur Eagle,** *Terathopius ecaudatus*: Fairly common in open savannas and thornbush country; flight swift and rocking. **African Fish Eagle,** *Cuncuma vocifer*: Common along rivers, lakes, estuaries, seashore; loud, ringing call.

**Falcons:** Many different species can be seen. **Peregrine,** *Falco peregrinus*, is a small race of the well-known cosmopolitan species. The **African Hobby,** *Falco cuvieri*, is a distinct species; it occurs in savannas and thorn-bush country. **Lanner,** *Falco biarmicus*. Seen fairly often in savannas and in dry country, usually near rocks. The shrike-sized **Pigmy Falcon,** *Poliohierax semitorquatus*, is the smallest of African raptors. It occurs in thornbush and semi-desert areas. Especially common in northern Kenya (Samburu).

**Hawks:** There are several species of goshawks and sparrowhawks. The **Pale Chanting Goshawk,** *Melierax metabates,* is often seen in acacia and bush country.

**Guineafowl: Helmeted Guineafowl,** *Numida mitrata*: Widely distributed and often seen in big flocks. **Vulturine Guineafowl,** *Acryllum vulturinum*: Dry bush. Northern and eastern Kenya; especially common in Samburu.

**Francolins: Yellow-necked spurfowl,** *Francolinus leucoscepus*: Widespread and common in dry open bush,

grasslands, in the vicinity of cultivated areas. **Jackson's Francolin,** *Francolinus jacksoni*: Mountain forests; can be seen in the Aberdares and Mt Kenya National Parks.

**Rails: Black Crake,** *Limnocorax flavirostra*: Marshes, swamps, river banks, lake shores; common and often seen; will walk around on a hippo's back. **Red-crested Coot,** *Fulica cristata*: Lakes, dams, swamps. Very common Lake Naivasha. **Purple Gallinule,** *Porphyrio porphyrip*: Swamps, papyrus marshes; can often be seen in Lake Naivasha.

**Crowned Crane,** *Balearica regulorum*: Widely distributed; swamps, lake shores, grasslands; in pairs, small parties or flocks.

**Bustards: Kori Bustard,** *Ardeotis kori*: Open savannas, thornbush, grasslands. Nairobi National Park, Amboseli, Samburu. Maasai Mara. **Black-bellied Bustard,** *Lissotis melanogaster*: Fairly common in open grasslands and cultivated areas. Maasai Mara, Tsavo National Park. **White-bellied Bustard.** *Eupodotis senegalensis*.

**Stone Curlews:** *Burhinus* spp.: Of the three species of Stone Curlews, two are mostly found near water, one in dry scrub, bush and open woodlands.

**Jacana or Lily Trotter,** *Actophilornis africanus*: Walks on floating vegetation; common in Lake Naivasha, Amboseli.

**Plovers** and related species: **Crowned Plover,** *Stephanibyx coronatus*: Not bound to the vicinity of water; very common on grasslands, especially in short grass areas. **Blacksmith Plover,** *Haplopterus armatus*: Common near rivers, swamps, lakes. **Spurwinged Plover,** *Haplopterus spinosus*: Along rivers and lakes; can be seen in Rift Valley lakes, Samburu. **Wattled Plover,** *Afribyx senegallus*: Locally in western Kenya (Maasai Mara); swamps, damp areas with short grass. Of the smaller species, **Kittlitz's Plover,** *Charadrius tricollaris*, are widely distributed on sand banks and mud flat along lakes, rivers and dams. The **Chestnut-banded Plover,** *Charadrius pallidus venustus*, is found on Lake Magadi only. **Black-winged Stilt,** *Himantopus himantopus*: marshes, salt lakes; very common Lakes Magadi and Nakuru. **Avocet,** *Recurvirostra avocetta*: mud flats, es-

tuaries, lagoons; seen in Lakes Nakuru and Magadi.

**Coursers:** Several species on grasslands and dry bush country. **Temminck's Courser,** *Cursorius temmincki*, can often be seen on recently burnt ground. **Heuglin's Courser,** *Hemerodromus cinctus*, occurs in Tsavo National Park.

**Gulls:** The **grey-headed Gull,** *Larus cirrhocephalus*, is the most common gull on East African inland waters. The **Sooty Gull,** *Larus hemprichii*, occurs on the Coast.

**Sandgrouse:** Several species, of which the **Yellow-throated Sandgrouse,** *Eremialector gutturalis*, is one of the most common and widely distributed. At Amboseli and in many other places, it can be seen coming to water holes in large flocks.

**Pigeons and Doves:** Numerous in respect both to species and individuals. One of the most handsome is the **Speckled Pigeon,** *Columba guinea*. The widely distributed **Ring-necked Dove,** *Streptopelia capicola*, is very common in savannas, bush and cultivated areas. The pretty little **Namaqua Dovem,** *Oena capensis*, occurs in dry bush and semi-desert areas.

**Cuckoos:** Well represented in East Africa. The widely distributed **Red-chested Cuckoo,** *Cuculuc solitarius*, calls "tit-tit-whoo". The **White-browed Coucal,** or **Waterbottle-bird,** *Centropus superciliosus*, skulks in dense bush, especially near rivers, and in reed beds; it has a bubbling call, like water being poured out of a bottle. The **Emerald Cuckoo,** *Chrysococcyx cupreus*; **Didric Cuckoo,** *Chrysococcyx Klaas*; are distinguished by the metallic coloration of their upper parts.

**Parrots: The Gray Parrot,** *Psittacus erithacus*, the largest African parrot, and a renowned "talker", is found locally in western Kenya. The **Red-headed Parrot,** *Polocephalus guilelmi*, inhabits mountain forests; it is seen quite regularly along the Naro Moru River.

**Turacos:** Several species of Green Red-winged Turacos (*Touraco* spp) inhabit coastal, highland and mountain forests. The gray touracos or "go-away" birds are partial to savannas and dry bush. The **White-bellied Goaway Bird,** *Corythaixoides leucogaster*, is common at Samburu.

**Rollers:** The Rollers are represented by several species, of which the **Lilac-breasted Roller**, *Coracias caudata*, is commonly seen in savannas and bush country. The **Broad-billed Roller**, *Eurystomus glaucurus*, inhabits forests, savannas, riverine forests, mountain areas, going up into the bamboo zone.

**Bee-eater**, *Melittophagus* eaters are represented by a number of species. The **Little Bee-eater**, *Melittophagus pusillus*, is widely distributed, while the **White-fronted Bee-eater**, *Merops bullockoides*, can often be seen in the Lake Naivasha region, including Hell's Gate. The Naro Moru River is a good place to observe the **Cinnamon-chested Bee-eater**, *Melittophagus oreobatus*. The **Carmien Bee-eater**, *Merops nubicus*, is common in coastal areas from November to April.

**Kingfishers**: Of the kingfishers, some are always found close to water; the **Giant Kingfisher**, *Megaceryle maxima*, along well wooded rivers and streams; the **Pied Kingfisher**, *Ceryle rudis*, on large rivers and lakes; the pretty little **Malachite Kingfisher**, *Corythornis cristata*, along steams, rivers and lake shores fringed with reeds, papyrus and other dense vegetation. The **Gray-headed Kingfisher**, *Halcyon leucocephala*, can be seen far away from water, while the **Brown-hooded Kingfisher**, *Halcyon albiventris*, and the **Striped Kingfisher**, *Halcyon chelicuti*, are mainly birds of savannas and woodlands.

**Hornbills**: The **Tokos** (*Tockus erythrorhynchus* and others) are widely distributed in savannas and bush country, while the large forest hornbills, such as the **Trumpeter Hornbills**, *Bycanistes bucinator*, and the **Silvery-cheeked Hornbill**, *Bycanistes brevis*, can be found in coastal, riverine and mountain forests. The turkey-sized **Ground Hornbill**, *Bucorvus leadbeateri*, which forages on the ground, occurs in grasslands and savannas.

**Hoepoes and Wood Hoepoes**: The African Hoepoes (*Upupa* spp) closely resemble the European species. The Wood Hoepoes are long-tailed birds, iridescent green, black or blue in colour. The **Green Wood Hoepoe** or **Kakelaar**, *Phoeniculus purpureus*, which inhabits woodlands and riverine forests, is usually met with in small, noisy flocks.

**Nightjars**: Some nightjars have dis-tinctive calls, but seen flitting at night or sitting on a road in the car lights, the many different species are not easy to distinguish from each other.

**Owls**: The **African Marsh Owl**, *Asio capensis*, is quite frequently flushed out of high grass. **Verreaux's Eagle Owl**, *Bubo lacteus*, can often be discovered sitting on an acacia tree in riverine forest or savanna country.

**Mousebirds: Speckled Mousebird**, *Colius striatus*: Common and wide-spread along forest edges, bushy savannas, thick scrub and cultivated areas. **Bluenecked Mousebird**, *Colias macrourus*: dry bush.

**Trogons: Narina's Trogon**, *Apoloderma narina*, is one of the most beautiful of East African birds. It can be found in highland and mountain forests.

**Barbets**: Among the many species of Barbets, the **Red-and-yellows Barbet**, *Trachyphonus erythrocephalus*, is one of the most striking; it can often be seen perched on termite hills in dry bush country (Samburu, Tsavo National Park). **D'Arnaud's Barbet**, *Trachyphonus darnaudii*, is less colourful, but is worth watching for its interesting mating behaviour. Male and female sing and posture together, bobbing, bowing and wagging their tails.

**Honey Guides**: The **Greater** or **Black-throated Honey Guide**, *Indicator indicator*, will guide humans or honey badgers to bees' nest.

**Woodpeckers**: Of the many woodpeckers, one of the most common and widely distributed is the **Nubian Woodpecker**, *Campethera nubica*, found in all types of savanna country.

**Swifts**: of various species are to be seen practically everywhere, from the streets of Nairobi (**Little Swift**, *Apus affinis*) to the crags of Mt Kenya (**Alpine Swift**, *Apus melba*).

**Passerines**: Of passerine birds there are so many that only very few can be mentioned. Among the more colourful are the glossy starlings; the **Superb Glossy Starling**, *Spreo superbus*, has become very tame around lodges and picnic sites. At Kilaguni Lodge, the magnificent **Golden-breasted Starling**, *Cosmopsarius regius*, can be observed and photographed at close range. The small, often colourful birds which dip their beaks into flowers, must not be mistaken for humming birds; they are Sunbirds, not at all related to the American humming birds. The **Scarlet-chested Sunbird**, *Nectarinia senegalensis*, is a very striking and often seen species. The beautifully woven nests of the weaver birds, often arranged in large colonies, cannot possibly be overlooked. Many weavers are yellow, or sport a combination of yellow and black. One of the most common and wide-spread species, the **Sparrow Weaver**, *Plocepasser mahali*, has a brown and white plumage. **Dine-melli's Buffalo Weaver**, *Dinemellia dinemelli*, a common and very characteristic bird of the dry bush country, is black, white and red. The male of the **Common Buffalo Weaver**, *Bubalornis albirostris*, is black. The enormously long-tailed wydahs and widow birds are related to the weavers. The widely distributed **Pintailed Wydah**, *Vidua macroura*, is black and white. The **Long-tailed Widow Bird**, *Coliuspasser progne*, for which a lookout should be kept between Nanyuki and Nyeri, is black with some red and white on the wings. At mating time, the widow birds can be seen performing interesting courtship dances. Among the finches, there are many small and colourful species, such as the **Cordon Bleu**, *Uraeginthus bengalus*; the **Purple Grenadier**, *Uraeginthus ianthinogaster*; and the **Fire-finch**, *Logonosticta rubricata*.

A bird that must surely come to the notice of every East African traveller is the black and white **Fiscal Shrike**, *Lanius collurio*, of which in some places there seems to be a couple to practically every bush. The Shrike family, as a whole, is very well represented, but many species are of skulking habits, less easily seen than the Fiscal and its close relations.

The game watcher will certainly become aware of the two Oxpeckers (**Red-billed Oxpecker**, *Buphagus erythrorhynchus*, and **Yellow-billed Oxpecker**, *Buphagus africanus*), which climb around on rhinos, buffaloes, giraffes and other animals in search for ticks.

---

## Reptiles & Amphibians

**Nile Crocodile**, *Crocodylus niloticus*. Widely distributed in rivers, lakes and swamps, but much reduced through uncontrolled shooting and trapping. There is often a spectacular concentration at Crocodile Point, below the Lugard Falls of the Galana River (Tsavo East). During the last few years crocodiles have been on the increase in the Ewaso Nyiro (Samburu); a few can usually be seen at Mzima Springs, at the Hippo Pools of Nairobi National Park and on the Mara and Tana Rivers. One of the last great sanctuaries of crocodiles is Lake Turkana.

**Lizards:** Monitor lizards can attain a length of 2 metres (6 ft) or even more. The **Nile Monitor**, *Varanuns nulioticus*, mainly found along rivers, is known to dig up crocodile's nests and to eat the eggs. The **Spotted Monitor**, *Varanus niloticus*, can be found in dry bush and savanna country, at a considerable distance from any water. The little **Geckos** have established themselves in human habitations, the adhesive pads on their toes allowing them to run up and down walls and even to walk on the ceilings. The beautiful **Rock Agama**, or **Rainbow Lizard**, *Agama agama*, can be seen around many of the lodges and do-it-yourself camps. The males are blue, with red heads, and it is fascinating to watch their colours become more intense or fade away, according to their state of emotional agitation.

**Chameleons** are represented by a number of species, some of which are armed with horns.

**Turtles** are common in streams, rivers and the sea.

**Tortoises** – especially the **Leopard Tortoise**, *Testudo pardalis* – can often be found in grasslands and savannas.

**Snakes:** Visitors to Kenya are usually surprised at the apparent scarcity of snakes. These reptiles are, however, shy and secretive, and some have predominantly nocturnal habits. On rare occasions only will the tourist travelling around the country by car catch a short glimpse of one slithering across the road. A person living in the country and often moving about on foot soon comes to realise that snakes are by no means uncommon. Most of the venomous species have a marked tendency to get out of the way of any human being, warned of his approach by the vibration of the ground. The **Black Mamba**, *Dendroaspis polylepis*, has a sinister reputation of occasionally attacking without provocation, but this probably happens most often when it finds itself accidentally cut off from its hiding place. In Kenya this species is not at all common. The **Puff Adder**, *Bitis arietans*,

widespread and fairly numerous, must be considered as the most dangerous of Kenya's snakes. Relying on its wonderful camouflage, it usually does not take evasive action but remains motionless, and a person walking through scrub or high grass can easily put his foot close enough to make it strike with lightning speed. The **Black-necked (Spitting) Cobra**, *Naja nigricollis*, when cornered accidentally, ejaculates its venom, aiming, if possible, at the face of its presumed enemy. The **Green Tree Snake** or **Boomslang**, *Dis-pholidus typus*, may be seen slithering along a branch. It carries its poison fangs so far back in its jaws that a human being, in order to be bitten, would have it put a finger into its mouth. **The Rock Python**, *Python sebae*, is a truly magnificent snake that often attains length of up to 5 metres (16 ft). There are records of pythons over 11 metres (37 ft) long. Although widely distributed and not uncommon in some places, this impressive creature is not often seen.

**Amphibians:** are presented in East Africa by Caecilians, toads and frogs. There are no newts or salamanders. Frogs are especially numerous, ranging from tiny **Tree Frogs** with adhesive pads on their toes to the huge **Bull-frog**, *Pyxicephalus adspersus*, up to 10 inches in length and able to dig itself into the earth, vanishing from sight within about 20 minutes. The **Clawed Frog**, *Xenopus laevus*, only rarely leaves the water. It has a flattened body, small forelimbs, large hind-limbs and carries sharp, black claws on the first, second and third toes. The males have a rattling call note which can be heard a considerable distance away. The legless, worm-shaped **Caecilians** spend most of their time underground or under stones, fallen leaves, in rotten tree trunks or termite hills, and are rarely seen.

---

### Insects & Arachnids

Most tourists who come to Kenya to collect insects are looking for butterflies, moths, or beetles. These groups occur all over Kenya, with some species found only in confined areas.

Of the butterflies, around 600 species are found in the republic, with closely defined limits for the coastal, dry-country and upland species and those which occur in western Kenya.

Only a very few common species are found over the entire country.

Along the coastal belt, from the Tanzania border northwards to Malindi, there are several interesting species. One, *Euphaedra neophron*, a purplish-brown butterfly is to be found in the forests and under the cashew-nut and coconut plantations. A browner form of the same butterfly is found also at Taveta Forest and around Meru, near Mount Kenya. It seems strange, at first, to find the same butterfly as far inland as Meru, but quite a number of the coastal butterflies can be found there, having made their way across the dry semi-desert plains along the Tana river. Also rarely found in this area is the magnificent *Papilio ophidicephalus*, a large black and yellow butterfly with long tail and a brilliant blue and red patch at the base of the tail. It is sometimes quite common in the forest at Kibwezi, between the town and where the railway line crosses the road.

Between the coastal belt and just short of Nairobi are the great grassy plains of Kenya, this area also covering the Rift Valley. Here, for the most part, not enough rain falls to allow trees to grow, and so a special group of butterflies has evolved to cover this niche. The *Colotis* (white butterflies with brilliant red or orange tips) are common, as are the Blue and the Yellow Pansies (*Precis*, spp) which can be seen settled on their territories of dry earth amongst the grass. Where the forest has been cut down, for example for housing in the Nairobi area, these butterflies are also to be found. The northern deserts of Kenya are a major extension of this area, which is poor in species even during the infrequent rains.

The small mountains and hills are much more interesting. These include the Taita Hills with a blue and black swallowtail (*Pailio taita*) and *Cymothoe taita*, a creamy-white and black butterfly. Both these are to be found in Mbololo forest on the top of the hills close to Voi on the Mombasa-Nairobi Road.

Western Kenya also has a fauna of its own, but only in one area, the Kakamega forest, is this shown in all its richness. It is here, on an outlier of the great rain forests of the Congo Basin, that the largest number of species can be seen and caught in any one day.

The best butterfly areas are also good for moths, but reference to the rains is important. The first night of the rains is always the most productive. It is advisable to use either a black-white or an ordinary pressure lamp and a white sheet for collecting, or the moths will be badly damaged by large beetles in some areas; no one in Kenya uses the ordinary moth-trap.

If it starts raining in a normally dry area, any light will produce magical results, with great clouds of moths appearing along with millions of termites which always come in the wet weather, even in the centre of Nairobi.

Again the best areas for beetles have been defined as for butterflies, except that for the first one or two nights of the rains, the area around Voi is very good for Coprinid Dung-beetles.

A spectacular manifestation of insect life which no one can possibly overlook is the termite hills dotted all over the countryside, up to 3 metres (10 ft) in height, often crowned by a series of turrets containing air-shafts, or running straight up in one single hollow tower that looks like a miniature factory chimney.

Termites are often referred to as "White Ants", but they are, in fact, insects of a very ancient lineage related to the cockroaches, and may have been the first creatures on earth to establish a social organisation. Deep in the centre of the termite castle, there is the strongly cemented royal cell, in which the gigantic queen, tended by an army of workers and guarded by well-armed soldiers, spends her life producing eggs at a rate of about one every two seconds.

During the wet weather, there is a good chance of coming across columns of the famous Soldier ants, Safari Ants or "Siafu" – black bands meandering for hundreds of yards through bush and forest formed by a two-way stream of bush ants and guarded on both flanks by aggressive, large-pincered "soldiers".

At some place or other, the column fans out and if a few painful nips are acceptable, close observation will show a wholesale massacre of spiders, cockroaches, crickets, caterpillars, even of frogs, lizards and small snakes.

An arthropod not classified among the insects is the Giant Millipede, popularly known as "Tanganyika Railway" a glossy black creature with reddish-brown legs, up to a foot in length. It is perfectly harmless, but this cannot be said of the big centipedes which lurk under tree trunks and fallen leaves, for they have a venomous bite.

There are a number of species of scorpions in Kenya; most are small, and their sting, while disagreeable at the time, need not cause any worry.

In hot, dry bush country, however, there are scorpions up to eight inches (20 cm) long, which are as dangerous as they look.

Scorpions are related to the spiders, among which are some striking and beautiful species – especially the huge, yellow and black *Nephilia* spiders, which construct amazingly tough, golden yellow webs. They are harmless, as are practically all other East African spiders. The one known exception is an uncommon species related to the Black Widow (*Latrodectes*) of red markings and a globular body. Its bite is quite definitely venomous, though not necessarily fatal.

# Shopping

## Shopping Areas

The City Market in Nairobi has a good broad selection of curios and basketwork for sale, but be prepared to be hassled and harassed. It's very much bazaar-style buying, starting with an offer of about half the asking price, then walking out a couple of times. At that point, you'll think you have a bargain when you pay a shade more.

For tribal artifacts – spears, shields, masks, gourds, cow bells, jewellery and so on, the range of souvenir and curio shops is wide. However, a select list is as follows: African Arts & Crafts, University Way; African Heritage Ltd., Banda Street or Libra House on the Airport Road; The Craft Market, ABC Centre, Waiyaki Way; Rowland Wards, Standard Street; The Spinner's Web, Viking House, Wayaki Way; The East African Wildlife Society Shop, Museum Hill Centre.

For a wide selection of ceramic beads, a trip out to Kazuri Beads in Karen is well worth the effort.

## Export

Trade in ivory, rhino horn, skins and all other anatomical relics of wildlife is prohibited. It happens occasionally that some local "entrepreneur" will offer this type of "curio" for covert sale to the tourist, but if either one is caught it would almost certainly mean prosecution. The export of live animals, birds and reptiles is also banned, except where the dealer is a professional and licensed. The same goes for diamonds, gold and gemstones.

## What to Buy

Visitors will have collections of curios thrust upon them at every street corner by casual street traders. The form is to establish prices in the shops before haggling with the hawkers and getting genuine bargains. They're up to all sorts of "cons", of course, like elephant or giraffe hair bracelets which turn out to be plastic. Test them with a match at one end before buying.

A popular item with tourists is the *kiondo* basket, handwoven in sisal. They're often made by old Kikuyu women, sometimes seen walking along, weaving as they go without breaking their stride. Some of them produce small masterpieces in basketwork which find their way into stores in London and New York. Locally, they're first-class value.

Soapstone carvings from Kisii District are popular with visitors. Some are polished black, but they are better left in their natural greys and pinks.

There are a few good local buys at the coast – like intricately carved, brass-bound and studded Zanzibar chests, varying in size from a small jewellery box to a steamer trunk. Coastal jewellery, in sterling silver, corals and so on, is very attractive.

302

Ethiopian rugs in brown-sandy tones are worth buying except they have been known to carry unhatched insect eggs. It may be apocryphal, but check anyway since the unlicensed export of wildlife from Kenya is prohibited.

# Sports

## Outdoor Pursuits

Check sports clubs (see following listing) for most field and court activities. Deep sea fishing and other water sports can all be arranged through hotels at the coast.

### CALENDAR OF EVENTS

**January** – International Bill fishing competition, Malindi.

**February** – Mombasa Fishing Festival

**March** – Kenya Open Golf Championship

**Easter** – Safari Rally

**November** – Malindi Fishing Festival

## Participant Sports

### Sports Clubs

Temporary memberships are offered to visitors in most sports clubs around Kenya. Listed below are some of these clubs and the sporting activities you may find there.

**Impala Club**, Ngong Road, P.O. Box 41516, Nairobi. Tel: 568573/565684. (Tennis, Squash, Rugby, Football, Hockey, Cricket)

**Nairobi Club**, Ngong Road, P.O. Box 30171, Nairobi. Tel: 336996. (Squash, Tennis, Cricket, Hockey, Bowls, Basketball)

**Parklands Sports Club**, Ojijo Road, P.O. Box 40116, Nairobi. Tel: 742829. (Tennis, Squash, Rugby, Hockey, Cricket, Snooker)

### Golf Clubs

The following have 18-hole courses.

**Karen Country Club**. Tel: 882801/2.

**Muthaiga Golf Club**. Tel: 762414/761713.

**Royal Nairobi Golf Club**. Tel: 724215.

**Sigona Club**. Tel: (0154) 32431.

**Windsor Golf & Country Club**. Tel: 219784.

### Mountaineering/Caving

**Mountain Club of Kenya**, P.O. Box 45741, Nairobi. Tel: 501747.

**Cave Exploration Group of East Africa**, P.O. Box 47583, Nairobi. Members of both the above clubs meet every Tuesday after 7.30pm at the Mountain Club of Kenya Club House, Wilson Airport. Tel: 501747.

### Water Activities

**Kenya Divers Association**, P.O. Box 95705, Mombasa. Tel: 471347.

**Mombasa Sea Angling Club**, P.O. Box 82345, Mombasa. Tel: 220823.

**Mombasa Yacht Club**, P.O. Box 90391, Mombasa. Tel: 313350.

**Nairobi Sailing Club**, Nairobi Dam, P.O. Box 49973. Tel: 501250.

## Fishing

### Ocean Fishing

While Kenya was famed for its big game hunting from the start of this century, it was not until the 1950s that serious attention was turned to the big fish in the waters off its coast.

It was customary for "up-country" white farmers and businessmen to take an annual beach holiday. This was necessary – so it was said – because being too long in the highlands was "bad for the brain". Some acquired beach cottages and boats in which they pottered about the fringing coral reefs, snorkelling and fishing for the small species of the shallows. But eventually they went out beyond the reef, lured by the larger fish the Bajuni and Swahili coastal fishermen occasionally brought in on their hand-lines.

Today, sports fishermen are active all along the coast from Shimoni in the south to Mambrui in the north. They go out in all manner of boats, from small outboard dories and canoes to luxury cruisers with every conceivable convenience and the most modern fighting chairs, harness, rods, lures, lines and equipment.

Whatever the size of the conveyance, the ambition is the same. All of them venture out 40 km (25 miles) or so in the hope of bringing back a world record marlin of above 454 kg (1,000 lbs), which is out there somewhere. It

has yet to be caught, but it's been seen many times! It will be towed home one day, probably by some ridiculously small boat, at least by Acapulco standards. However, lesser marlin have been gaffed and brought in.

The visiting angler can organise a big game fishing safari at many centres along the coast, but principally at Shimoni, Mombasa, Kilifi and Malindi. Charter boats, for anything up to $550 a day, can be hired out with an experienced crew and all the necessary equipment.

The usual procedure is to go aboard before dawn and set out alongside the local commercial fishermen in their outrigger canoes. They take advantage of the *umande*, the gentle offshore breeze that develops every night, filling their triangular lateen sails and getting them to the reefs where they will anchor and fish for most of the day.

Out in the deeper water, the sports fishermen's hopes are always highest in the first few hours of daylight. It's normally cool and calm then, but later on in the day the onshore monsoon wind will overpower the *umande* and kick up a chop – and for some people, perhaps, a touch of Neptune's colic.

Every fisherman has his own favourite speed for trolling; some prefer a fast pace, others move slowly. It doesn't seem to matter, they all catch fish. The event is signalled by the whine of the ratchet on a rod, at which point everyone else reels in to get their lines out of the way. The skipper throttles back and watches.

After the initial flurry, all eyes are on the angler's line for a first glimpse of what's on the end of it. If it's one of the coveted marlins, or a sailfish, no one is left in doubt for long. The sea erupts as one or other of the great billfish goes into a tail-stand on the surface and shakes violently.

If it is tunny or a shark, this will also be immediately evident since they sound as soon as they have taken the bait. The fishermen are then kept guessing on size and precise species until the catch is reeled in from under the boat.

There may be an argument against fishing for sport, but there are few experiences to rival the surge of excitement as a large marlin breaks out of the sea and tail-walks on the surface.

Then, the tension and anguish increases as the fish bores into the depths, stripping away metre after metre of the line despite all the skipper does to recover it. It could end – maddeningly – with the sound of a dull "snick" as the line breaks from the reel. But more often, the race of the line finally slows and peters out. The retrieval starts, sometimes reversed in another flurried rush of the fish. But gradually the line is drawn back on the reel until, deep below, the dark form of the marlin appears.

**"The Moment of Truth":** The guesses start; each estimate of weight reveals the observer to be a natural optimist or pessimist. Finally the fish is alongside for the angler's "moment of truth". A badly set gaff or a loose tie on the tail can mean yet another one that got away.

The tension can be extreme at this point for people in small boats. As the gaff is set, the shock often triggers one final burst of energy in the fish which thrashes about and deluges the boat with water. But if all goes well, the quarry is secured and the fisherman relaxes – maybe with the exhilaration muted with a shade of remorse at the killing. A sudden display of defiant colour when a sailfish dies, for instance, might well trigger regret in a fisherman. Silver, violet and translucent blues shimmer for a moment across the body and base of the fins, before fading to the leaden tones of death. Alternatively, you can arrange through hotels or fishing guides to tag the fish and let it go.

Sailfish (*Istiophorus gladius*) are still the most highly prized of the game fish along with three species of marlin – black, blue, and striped (*Istiopax indicus, Makaira nigricans* and *Makaira audax* respectively). In addition, the Indian Ocean off Kenya is as well endowed with a range of pelagic species as any other tropical water – including Hemingway's "Gulf Stream".

Tunny or tuna are represented by yellowfins (*Thunnus albacares*), two species of skipjack bonito (*Euthynnus affinis* and *Euthynnus pelamis*), and the much smaller frigate mackerel (*Auxis thazard*).

Wahoo (*Acanthocybium solandri*), kingfish (*Scomberomorus commerson*) and barega (*Scomberomorus lineolatus*) are common. So is the

adept catcher of flying fish, "the dorado" (*Coryphaena hippurus*), which is frequently caught when a lure is dragged past its ambush lair of a raft of seaweed.

There are also plenty of sharks around – hammerheads, greys and tigers – all of which grow to great sizes. Only the *mako* is considered a game fish.

**On and Off Seasons:** The season lasts while the northeast monsoon blows between November and March. This is a relatively gentle wind, with an accompanying Somali current touching the Kenya coastline before heading eastward as the counter-equatorial current. This stream of water is charged with nutrients by a great upwelling from the ocean floor off the blunt end of Arabia and is thus rich in fish.

Between April and October, the reverse southeast monsoon batters the East African coast after having picked up speed across thousands of miles of empty ocean. The monsoon creates heavy swells so that only fishing fanatics with strong stomachs and large boats tend to go out. This is done more for the cruise than anything else since a largely uncharged current across the ocean from India carries few fish with it.

However, there could be compensation in incidental sightseeing – perhaps a ballet of flying fish, or a school of dolphin, or a mammoth whale shark (the largest fish which could measure up to 15 metres/50 ft long). As ugly as they are amiable, they will allow a snorkelled human to swim along with them. They are fazed by nothing and certainly not by a man holding onto a barn door of a dorsal-fin. The man himself might be a shade perturbed by a flotilla of lesser shark – less tolerant – swimming alongside. But that adds something to the Indian Ocean adventure for a more offbeat story back in the fishermen's bar.

**The Giant Perch:** However, the ultimate fishing adventure in Kenya is arguably the search for the giant perch at Turkana in northern Kenya. A preferred safari starts at Nairobi's Wilson Airport soon after dawn when two aircraft take off – one for the anglers, the other carrying supplies.

These include the minimum of camping gear, no more than a sleeping bag and groundsheet for each person,

cooking utensils, vegetables, lots of drinking water and a chest of dry ice for preserving the catch. Other equipment includes a 25 HP inflatable dinghy with a back-up trolling motor; plus of course, the fishing tackle with up to 3 rods per angler, a light casting rod medium heavy spinning gear, and a short trolling rod with big-game reel containing 500 metres (1,640 ft) of 20 kg (44 lbs) test nylon.

For the first hour, the plane overflies the lush farmlands and lakes of the southern Rift Valley, past Naivasha, Elementeita and Nakuru fringed by a pink strand of a million flamingos. Then it wings past Baringo, a freshwater lake, and Bogoria, with its spouting geysers and ghostly beauty.

Soon the land changes to scrub bush and twisted flows of black lava, a barren place of no water and 104°F (40°C) temperature. The caldera of Nyambuatom finally marks the southern extremity of Lake Turkana, at which point the pilot scans the surface water to estimate the strength and direction of the wind which could make landing on South Island, a few miles ahead, impossible.

The strip is short, almost too short. Steep rising ground at its far end and a fierce down-draft makes an over-shoot a dangerous manoeuvre. But the Kenya bush pilots are well-inured to such local hazards; the landing is accomplished without mishap and any passenger tension is soon dissipated in setting up camp and preparing the inflatable.

South Island is black, more a moonscape and a kind of virgin desolation where you imagine you're making the first footfalls. There have been others of course, back to the Creation when some nameless Adam stood on two feet for the first time, cried defiance at the sun, and took the first few steps on Darwin's long road of evolution.

Only two anglers fish from the boat. The others wait their turn, perched like sea birds on a guano-covered "White Rock", a small conical atoll close to South Island. With light spinning rods the fishing among the shoals of native fish is diverting enough to deflect the often fierce onslaught of sun and wind.

**For the Bouillabaisse:** Large tilapia (3kg/7 lbs) are put aside for lunch with a smaller fry rigged as live bait on the sturdier gear. Tiger fish are care-ully returned after – even more care-ully – removing the hooks from their ormidable jaws. A catfish may be re-ained for the evening bouillabaisse, ut definitely thrown back are the *parbus, labio* and *sahani*, which have nore bones than they could ever need.

Of these, the most endearing to the angler is the hump-backed, dish-shaped, inedible *sahani* – Kiswahili for "plate". For some reason it's only nooked in the dorsal fin. Then, on be-ng tagged and quite unrestrained by a nook in the jaw, it immediately sets off at a great speed for the distant shore. t's a skilled but exhausted angler who inally beaches one of these creatures, astonished that one so small, usually no more than 4 kg (9 lbs), could test numan strength and skills for 20 min-utes or more.

Fun though all this is, the real ac-tion is aboard the dinghy. Perhaps every 15 minutes or so, the wooden plug, feather jig or plastic squid is ac-cepted in a series of line-screaming runs by monster Nile-perch anything from 22 to 204 kg (50 to 450 lbs). The flight of these great beasts occasion-ally erupts through the surface, with some serious head shaking from the fish at the cruel angler and his bait. They're underrated as fighters by the heavy tackle brigade, but these crea-tures – pewter coloured and with strange bulbous, luminous yellow eyes – will fight a rare battle on a light line.

The perch are not returned, except for the 13½-kg (30-lb) infants, since these largest of the freshwater fish are excellent eating. Choicest cuts like the cheeks are grilled and taste like rock-lobster. Part of the catch may be salted and sun dried and the larger fil-lets packed in ice for eventual trans-port home. The debris is abandoned to the multitude of crocodiles which in-habit the lake.

Then it is back to camp for perhaps a cautious swim before dinner, one eye cocked for the 10-foot crocs which cruise across the entrance to the bay. Inshore, it's generally safe, the water is cool and clear while elsewhere it's milky with alkaline salts. Beyond the bay is the green vastness of the lake, well dubbed the "Jade Sea", although it frequently shows a darker shade in a sudden, violent squall. Angry waves, large enough to destroy craft far stur-dier than the dinghy, are whipped by

gale-force winds tearing in from Kulal mountain on the mainland to fill the low pressure area in the superheated lake basin.

A few days of total isolation is prob-ably enough for first-time visitors; the planes return and camp is struck. But without the assistance of a head wind, a phased evacuation of anglers and equipment is necessary – first to the mainland, then a high-lift take-off from savage Turkana after what, without question, will have been a fisherman's trip of a lifetime.

## Freshwater Fishing

The world's freshwater angler may not give Kenya a passing thought in his search for productive waters. Yet the country offers the expert ample and varied reward for his skills. Even a be-ginner has a sporting chance of land-ing a fish he needn't lie about.

In the Central Highlands, above 2,286 metres (7,500 ft) are innumer-able trout streams of a quality that – were they in Europe – would command formidable fees. But in Kenya, they're available for locals and visitors for no more than the nominal cost of a sports fishing licence. An equally inex-pensive alternative is fishing the fresh-water lakes for exotic largemouth bass, native sweet-tasting tilapia, and gigantic Nile perch up north in Lake Turkana.

**Streams of Trout:** Fly-fishing came to Kenya just before World War I, when the European settlers became nostal-gic for their native lochs and moorland streams back home. They imported rainbow trout fingerlings from South Africa where they had been success-fully introduced from Europe some years earlier. These imported trout, in turn, are doing exceptionally well in the parasite- and predator-free streams of Mount Kenya and the Aberdares.

Later, when refrigerated air cargo became common, ova of brown trout were imported from the trout farms of Scotland and England. So there are trout now in all the myriad streams that rise from the springs and snowmelt of the high mountains.

In the moorland brooks, long and lean trout offer the wet-fly fisherman a hard challenge in a landscape devoid of cover to conceal him either from the fish or from the short-tempered buf-falo and elephant sneaking up behind.

It's always surprising how silently these animals approach and more than one angler has been obliged to make a forward, discretionary dive to the opposite bank of an icy stream.

Below the moorland, the streams dart through thick tropical woodland. Trout are more numerous here in these forested areas, and are fatter and more cooperative than their high-land kin. With them, common Euro-pean and American patterns work well; *Coachman, Invicta, Dunkeld* or *Watson's-Fancy*, tied to a size 10 hook is fully competitive with local favourites such as the *Kenya Bug* and the *Oliver Black*.

Incidentally, located close to Nairobi is a thriving local fly-tying industry, with a growing international market. It's manned by handicapped people, as part of the training scheme of a chari-table trust. At a fraction of the cost of flies tied elsewhere, a lure to order is created.

Up in the forests, it's an unlucky angler who fails to capture his bag limit of six fish per day per river, either of the vermillion-flanked rainbows or of "brownies", appearing freshly enam-elled in Chinese lacquer as they leap to throw the deceiving fly.

Below the forests, the rivers are larger, deeper and no longer crystal clear. They're milky with sediment, but still offer an occasional heavyweight trout. By that time, the fish are wise in the ways of the world and choosy in what they will eat. They're not easily lured, but when they are, they may make a mark in the specimen book or otherwise a fine metal – surprisingly fine fleshed for their size.

**Storms after the Morning Calm:** Below the highlands in the Central Rift is the superb fisherman's lake of Naivasha, Massai for "still water". It's roundish, but with a Crescent Island indent on the eastern side, which is part of an otherwise collapsed and submerged volcano. It's also a wildlife sanctuary for a number of mammals and birds.

The lake is to some extent well-named. Mornings are usually calm with the glassy surface disturbed only by the hunting fish eagle, cormorant, or pelican garnering breakfast among the unwary tilapia venturing too near the surface. Hippo also occasionally break the mirrored surface to snort and recharge their lungs before sinking again to continue their breathless snooze on the lake floor.

But Naivasha can also get fairly violent, mostly in the afternoons, when the calm is sometimes severely interrupted by electric storms generated over the Aberdares. These tend to spill over into the Rift with blustering winds, heavy showers and at times even hail.

An earthworm, fished under a small bob float, will attract plenty of small tilapia for a good day's sport but the angler's favourite quarry is the largemouth, or black bass, as it's known locally. This native of the southern United States, introduced to Naivasha in 1930, owes its popularity to a voracious appetite, a catholic diet and a hair-trigger temper which leads it to attack anything within range of its saw-toothed bucket of a mouth. Sizes range from a modest ½-kg (1 lb) or so to 3 kg (6 lbs) or more and the possibility of a world record has been mooted following the capture of a 9-kg (20-lb) in an African fisherman's net.

Opinions as to the best bass lure vary in direct proportion to the number of anglers polled. The vast range of patterns available are seemingly designed more to attract money from the angler's pocket than fish into his landing net. However, common preferences are for the floating hula-skirted popper, the shallow running *shiner minnow*, and the bottom fished plastic worms and feather jigs. A current favourite is the *Bayoo Boogie* which wiggles seductively at mid-level in the lake. Colour preferences range from silver to black and have included an orange monstrosity with blue spots, representing nothing on earth or in water; yet, for a time, it was singularly successful.

Meanwhile, the bass, with stoic indifference to lure size, shape or colour, accept almost every offering thrown at them. Few anglers have a blank day, and bags of 20 or more of good-size bass would be considered average. While not as spectacular a fighter as the trout, the largemouth will nevertheless give good account of itself when hooked, particularly in its ability to tail-walk the surface, seemingly in defiance of all natural laws. There is an after-bonus as well. Deep-fried English-style, or smoked, or included in an oriental curry, or just baked over the camp fire, the firm white flesh of the bass will defy the worst cook at the end of the day.

## Spectator Sports

Horse racing takes place most Sundays at the Ngong Road racecourse. **Safari Rally Ltd.**, PO Box 59483, Nairobi. Tel: 723147. Fax: 728575. The Safari Rally takes place every Easter, and is internationally acknowledged as the most gruelling race of its kind. **Jockey Club of Kenya**, P.O. Box 40373, Nairobi, tel: 560000/ 569060. Racing most Sundays (check the newspapers). First race at 2.15pm. Admission: Adults Kshs 100, Children Kshs 20. Silver Ring free.

# Language

## General

English is understood by many people in up-country Kenya, but not so much at the coast which is predominantly Muslim, speaking the Afro-Arab-Indian mix *Kiswahili*. It's not a difficult language and it's worth learning a few words.

English is taught in schools all over the country, so there is always someone who will understand what you're talking about, even in the remote bush. At the coast, more locals are responding to the European continental tourist invasion and speak German, French and Italian.

A few useful *Kiswahili* words and phrases are as follows.

### Useful Phrases

Hello/*Jambo*
How are you?/*Habari?*
I am well (good, fine, etc.)/*Mzuri*
Thank you (very much)/*Asante (sana)*
Goodbye/*Kwaheri*
Where is the hotel?/*Hoteli iko wapi?*
Where does this road lead to?/ *Nija hii ina-enda wapi?*
Please help me push this car/

*Tafadhali nisaidie kusukuma gari*
Please change this wheel/ *Tafadhali badilisha gurudumu hili.*
Good morning/*Habari ya asubuhi*
Good afternoon/*Habari ya mehana*
Good evening/*Habari ya jioni*
Please come in/ *Karibu ndani tafadhali*
Please sit down/*Keti tafadhali*
You're welcome/*Una karibishwa*
Where do you come from?/ *Ume kuja kutoka wapi?*
I come from..../*Nime toka....*
What is your name?/*Jina lako nani?*
My name is..../*Jina langu ni....*
Can you speak Swahili?/ *Waweza kuongea kiswahili?*
Yes/*Ndiyo*
No/*Hapana*
Only a little/*Kidogo tu*
I want to learn more/ *Nataka kujifunza zaidi*
How do you find Kenya?/ *Waonaje Kenya?*
I like it here/*Hapa napenda*
The weather is hot, isn't it?/ *Hewa hapa in joto sivyo?*
Yes, a little/*Ndiyo kidogo*
Where are you going?/ *Una kwenda wapi?*
I am going to..../*Nakwenda....*
Turn right/*Geuka kulia*
Turn left/*Geuka kushoto*
Go straight/*Enda moja kwa moja*
Please stop here/ *Simama hapa tafadhali*
How much?/*Ngapi?*
Wait a minute/*Ngoja kidogo*
I have to get change/ *Ni badilishe pesa kwanza*
Excuse me/*Samahani*
Where is the toilet?/*Wapi choo?*
In the back/*Upande wa nyuma*
Where may I get something to drink?/ *Naweza kupata wapi kinywaji?*
One cup of coffee/ *Kikombe kimoja cha kahawa*
How much does this cost?/ *Hii pesa ngapi?*
Can you reduce the price?/ *Waweza kupunguza?*
Fine/*Sawa*
I will buy it/*Nita nunua*

### Useful Words

Mr/*Bwana*
Mrs/*Bibi*
Miss/*Bi*
I/*Mimi*
You/*Wewe*
He, She/*Yeye*

We/*Sisi*
They/*Wao*
What?/*Nini?*
Who?/*Nani?*
Where? (Place)/*Mahali gani?*
Where? (Direction)/
*Wapi (Upande gani)*
When?/*Hini?*
How?/*Vipi?*
Why?/*Kwanini?*
Which?/*Ipi? (gani)*
To eat/*Kukula*
To drink/*Kukunywa*
To sleep/*Kulala*
To bathe/*Kuoga*
To come/*Ijayo*
To go/*Ku-enda*
To stop/*Kusimama*
To buy/*Kununua*
To sell/*Kuuza*
Quickly/*Haraka*
Slowly/*Pole-pole* (Pronounced poH poH)
Street/Road/*Barabara*
Airport/*Uwanja wa Ndege*
Shop/*Duka*
Money/*Fedha*
Cent/*Senti*
Hotel/*Hoteli*
Room/*Chumba*
Bed/*Kitanda*
Hospital/*Hospitali*
Police/*Polici*
Food/*Chakula*
Coffee/*Kahawa*
Beer/*Tembo* (or *Pombe*)
Cold/*Baridi*
Hot/*Moto*
Tea/*Chai*
Meat/*Nyama*
Fish/*Samaki*
Bread/*Mkate*
Butter/*Siagi*
Sugar/*Sukari*
Salt/*Chumvi*
Bad/*Mbaya*
Today/*Leo*
Tomorrow/*Kesho*
Now/*Sasa*

### Numbers

One/*Moja*
Two/*Mbili*
Three/*Tatu*
Four/*Ine*
Five/*Tano*
Six/*Sita*
Seven/*Saba*
Eight/*Nane*
Nine/*Tisa*
Ten/*Kumi*
Eleven/*Kumi na moja*

Twelve/*Kumi na mbili*
Thirteen/*Kumi na tatu*
Twenty/*Ishirini*
Twenty-one/*Ishirini na moja*
Twenty-two/*Ishirini na mbili*
Twenty-three/*Ishirini na tatu*
Thirty/*Thelathini*
Forty/*Arobaini*
Fifty/*Hamsini*
One hundred/*Mia moja*
One thousand/*Elfu moja*

# Further Reading

## General

Adamson, Joy. *Peoples of Kenya*. London, 1967.
Amin, Moll. *Portraits of Africa*. London, 1983.
Amin, Willetts and Tetley. *Journey through Kenya*. London, 1982.
Baker, Sir Samuel. *Albert Nyanza, Great Basin of the Nile*.
Bartlett, Jen and Des. *Nature's Paradise*. London, 1967.
Boxer, C.R. and Carlos de Azevado. *Fort Jesus and the Portuguese in Mombasa*. London, 1960.
Brown, Leslie. *Eagles*. London, 1955.
*East African Coast and Reefs*. Nairobi, 1975.
Burton, Jane. *Animals of the African Year: The Ecology of East Africa*. London, 1972.
Burton, Sir Richard. *The Lake Regions of Central Africa*.
Carr, Archie. *The Land and Wildlife of Africa*. Time-Life Nature Library, 1965.
Clark, J. Desmond. *The Prehistory of Africa*. London, 1970.
Coe, Malcolm J. *The Ecology of the Alpine Zone of Mount Kenya*. The Hague, 1967.
Cole, Sonia. *The Prehistory of East Africa*. London, 1964.
*Leakey's Luck: The Life of Louis Seymour Bazett Leakey 1903–72*. London, 1975.
Cott, Hugh. *Looking at Animals: A Zoologist in Africa*. London, 1975.
Cullen, Anthony. *Downey's Africa*. London, 1959.
Dorst, Jean and Pierre Dandelot. *A Field Guide to the Large Mammals of Africa*. London, 1970.
Douglas-Hamilton, Ian and Oria. *Among the Elephants*. London, 1975.

(Available in a paperback edition.)
Dugmore, A. Radclyffe. *Camera Adventures in the African Wilds*. London, 1925.
Edey, Maitland A. and John Dominis. *The Cats of Africa*. New York, 1968.
Gallmann, Kuki. *I Dreamed of Africa*. Penguin, 1992. *African Nights*. Penguin 1995.
Gregory, J.W. *The Great Rift Valley, being a Narrative of a Journey to Mount Kenya and Lake Baringo*.
Grzimek, B. *Serengeti Shall Not Die*. (Available in a paperback edition.)
Guggisberg, C.A.W. *Simba, the Life of the SOS Rhino*. London & Nairobi, 1966.
Guggisberg, Rosanne. *Cooking with an African Flavour*. Nairobi, 1976.
Hamilton, G. *In the Wake of da Gama*. London, 1951.
Hill, M.F. *Permanent Way: The Story of the Kenya and Uganda Railway*. Nairobi.
Huntingford, G.W.B. *The Nandi of Kenya*. London, 1953.
Ionides, C.J.P. *A Hunter's Story*. London, 1965.
Isenmonger, R.M. *Snakes of Africa, Southern, Central and East*. Edinburgh, 1962.
Jewell, John H.A. *Dhows at Mombasa*. London, 1976.
Johnson, Martin. *On Safari*. New York, 1928.
Johnson, Osa. *Four Years in Paradise*. New York, 1941.
Ker, Donald I. *Through Forest and Veldt*. London, 1957.
Kinloch, Bruce. *The Shamba Raiders: Memories of a Game Warden*. London, 1972.
Kirkman, S. *Men and Monuments of the East African Coast*. London, 1964.
Krapf, J. L. *Travels, Researchers and Missionary Labours During Eighteen Years' Residence in Eastern Africa*.
Kruuk, Hans. *The Spotted Hyena: A Study of Predation and Social Behaviour*. Chicago and London, 1972.
Leakey, L.S.B. *The Wild Realm: Animals of East Africa*. Washington, 1969.
Leakey, L.S.B and Goodall W.M. *Unveiling Man's Origin*. London, 1969.
Lind, E.M. and Morrison M.E.S. *East African Vegetation*. 1974.
Macdonald, M. *Treasures of Kenya*. London, 1965.

Martin, C. Mc C.P. and E.B. *Quest for the Past: A Historical Guide to Lama.* Nairobi, 1970.

Martin, E.B. *Malindi, the Historic Town on the Kenya Coast.* Nairobi, 1975.

Martin, E. and C.B. *Run, Rhino, Run,* London. 1983.

Meinertzhagen, R. *Kenya Diary, 1902–06.* Edinburgh, 1951. *Army Diary, 1899–1926.* Edinburgh, 1960.

Miller, Charles. *The Lunatic Express.* London, 1971. (Available in a paperback edition.)

Mitchell, John (Editor). *Guide Book to Mount Kenya and Kilimanjaro.* Nairboi, 1971.

Mollison, Simon. *Kenya's Coast.* Nairobi, 1971.

Moorhead, Alan. *The White Nile.* London, 1960. (Available in a paperback edition.)

Mosley, I. *Duel for Kilimanjaro: The East African Campaign, 1914–18.* London, 1963. (Available in a paperback edition.)

Moss, Cynthia. *Portraits in the Wilds: Animal Behavioru in East Africa.* London, 1975.

Murdock, G.P. *Africa, Its People and History.* New York, 1959.

Mwangi, Meja. *Going Down River Road.* Heinemann, 1976; *Striving for the Wind.* Heinemann, 1992; *The Cockroach Dance.* Addison-Wesley, 1990; *The Return of Shaka.* African Book College, 1991.

Myers, Norman. *The Long African Day.* New York, London, 1972.

Owen, D.F. *Tropical Butterflies: The Ecology and Behaviour of Butterflies in the Tropics with Special Reference to African Species.* Oxford, 1971.

Patterson, P.H. *The Man-eaters of Tsavo.* (Available in a paperback edition.)

Percival, A.B. *A Game Ranger on Safari.* London, 1928.

Pratt, D.J. and M.D. Gwynne (Editors). *Rangeland Management and Ecology in East Africa.* London, 1977.

Prickett, R.J. *The African Ark.* Newton Abbot.*A Guide to Night Photography in African Game Lodges.* Nyeri, 1975.

Riccardi, Mirella. *Vanishing Africa.* London, 1977.

Roosevelt, Theodore. *African Game Trails.* London, 1910.

Schaller, George B. *The Serengeti Lions.* Chicago & London, 1972.

Sheldrick, Daphne. *The Tsavo Story.* London, 1973.

Shipton, Eric. *Upon That Mountain.* London, 1947.

Sibley, J.R. *Tanganyika Guerilla: East African Campaign 1914–18.* London, 1973.

Sikes, Sylvia K. *The Natural History of the African Elephant.* London, 1971.

Simon, Noel. *Between the Sunlight and the Thunder: The Wild Life of Kenya.* London, 1962.

Speke, John Hanning. *What Led to the Discovery of the Source of the Nile.*

Stanley, H.M. *How I Found Livingstone in Central Africa.*

Stigand, C.H. *The Land of Zinji.*

Strandes, Justus. *The Portuguese in East Africa.* Nairobi, 1961.

Sweeney, Charles. *The Scurrying Bush.* London, 1966.

Thomas, E.M. *Warrior Herdsmen.* London, 1965.

Thomson, Joseph. *To the Central African Lakes and Back. Through Masailand.*

Tilman, H. *Snow on the Equator.* London, 1937.

Van Someren, V.D. *A Bird Watcher in Kenya.* Edinburgh, 1958.

Van Someren, V.G.L. *Days with Birds: Studies of Habits of Some East African Species.* Chicago, 1956.

Vaucher, Charles A. *East African Wildlife.* Lausanne, 1967. *Nakuru, the Lake of a Million Flamingos.* Nakuru.

von Lawick, Hugo. *Solo: The Story of an African Wild Dog Puppy and Her Pack.* London, 1973. (Available in a paperback edition.)

von Lawick, Hugo and Jane von Lawick-Goodall. *Innocent Killers.* London, 1970.

*In the Shadow of Man.* London. (Available in a paperback edition.)

von Lettow-Vorbeck, P. *My Reminiscences of East Africa.* London, 1920.

Wa Thiong'o, Ngugi. *Grain of Wheat.* Heinmann, 1993; *Devil on the Cross.* Heinmann, 1992; *Petals of Blood.* Heinmann, 1986; *The River Between.* Heinmann, 1990; *Weep Not Child.* Heinmann, 1990.

Williams, J.A. *A Field Guide to the Birds of East Africa.* London, 1967; *A Field Guide to the National Parks of East Africa.* London, 1967; *A Field Guide to the Butterflies of Africa.* London, 1969.

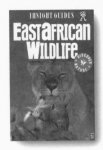

# Index

A
B
C
D
E
F
G

I
J
a
b
c
d
e
f
g
h
i
j

I

# The Insight Approach

The book you are holding is part of the world's largest range of guidebooks. Its purpose is to help you have the most valuable travel experience possible, and we try to achieve this by providing not only information about countries, regions and cities but also genuine insight into their history, culture, institutions and people.

Since the first Insight Guide – to Bali – was published in 1970, the series has been dedicated to the proposition that, with insight into a country's people and culture, visitors can both enhance their own experience and be accepted more easily by their hosts. Now, in a world where ethnic hostilities and nationalist conflicts are all too common, such attempts to increase understanding between peoples are more important than ever.

### Insight Guides:
### Essentials for understanding

Because a nation's past holds the key to its present, each Insight Guide kicks off with lively history chapters. These are followed by magazine-style essays on culture and daily life. This essential background information gives readers the necessary context for using the main Places section, with its comprehensive run-down on things worth seeing and doing. Finally, a listings section contains all the information you'll need on travel, hotels, restaurants and opening times.

As far as possible, we rely on local writers and specialists to ensure that the information is authoritative. The pictures, for which Insight Guides have become so celebrated, are just as important. Our photojournalistic approach aims not only to illustrate a destination but also to communicate visually and directly to readers life as it is lived by the locals.

### Compact Guides
### The "great little guides"

As invaluable as such background information is, it isn't always fun to carry an Insight Guide through a crowded souk or up a church tower. Could we, readers asked, distil the key reference material into a slim volume for on-the-spot use?

Our response was to design Compact Guides as an entirely new series, with original text carefully cross-referenced to detailed maps and more than 200 photographs. In essence, they're miniature encyclopedias, concise and comprehensive, displaying reliable and up-to-date information in an accessible way.

### Pocket Guides:
### A local host in book form

However wide-ranging the information in a book, human beings still value the personal touch. Our editors are often asked the same questions. Where do *you* go to eat? What do *you* think is the best beach? What would you recommend if I have only three days? We invited our local correspondents to act as "substitute hosts" by revealing their preferred walks and trips, listing the restaurants they go to and structuring a vis-it into a series of timed itineraries.

The result is our Pocket Guides, complete with full-size fold-out maps. These 100-plus titles help readers plan a trip precisely, particularly if their time is short.

### Exploring with Insight:
### A valuable travel experience

In conjunction with co-publishers all over the world, we print in up to 10 languages, from German to Chinese, from Danish to Russian. But our aim remains simple: to enhance your travel experience by combining our expertise in guidebook publishing with the on-the-spot knowledge of our correspondents.